CROSSING HITLER

CROSSING HITLER

The Man Who Put the Nazis on the Witness Stand

BENJAMIN CARTER HETT

OXFORD
UNIVERSITY PRESS

2008

OXFORD
UNIVERSITY PRESS

Oxford University Press, Inc., publishes works that further
Oxford University's objective of excellence
in research, scholarship, and education.

Oxford   New York
Auckland   Cape Town   Dar es Salaam   Hong Kong   Karachi
Kuala Lumpur   Madrid   Melbourne   Mexico City   Nairobi
New Delhi   Shanghai   Taipei   Toronto

With offices in
Argentina   Austria   Brazil   Chile   Czech Republic   France   Greece
Guatemala   Hungary   Italy   Japan   Poland   Portugal   Singapore
South Korea   Switzerland   Thailand   Turkey   Ukraine   Vietnam

Published by Oxford University Press, Inc.
198 Madison Avenue, New York, New York 10016

www.oup.com

Oxford is a registered trademark of Oxford University Press

Library of Congress Cataloging-in-Publication Data
Hett, Benjamin Carter.
Crossing Hitler : the man who put the Nazis
on the witness stand / Benjamin Carter Hett.
p.   cm.
Includes bibliographical references and index.
ISBN 978-0-19-536988-5
1. Litten, Hans, 1903–1938.   2. Lawyers—Germany—Biography.
3. Anti-Nazi movement—Biography.
4. Criminal justice, Administration of—Germany—History—20th century.
5. Political participation—Moral and ethical aspects—Germany.   I. Title.
DD247.L58H47 2008
943.086092—dc22   2008004964

1 3 5 7 9 8 6 4 2

Printed in the United States of America
on acid-free paper

*For Corinna, another brave
idealist, with love*

The more we know, the more we think we have learned, the more hopeless it becomes to live and not to be responsible for everything. For everything, and especially for what goes on in the small circle around oneself. That is why it is so difficult to write about Hans Litten.... I must tell the Hans Litten story very briefly.... But I will tell it, because "he was a part of myself."

—Max Fürst, *Gefilte Fisch: Eine Jugend in Königsberg*, 1973

Contents

CROSSING HITLER

Prologue: Summoning Hitler

"In the name of the private prosecutors I request the summoning of the following witnesses," began the document, a plain sheet of vellum paper, handwritten, the letters looping and even schoolboyish. The first of three witnesses named was "the party employee Adolf Hitler, Munich, 45 Briener Street ('The Brown House')." Calling Hitler a "party employee" was deliberately demeaning. Hitler himself preferred to be called a "writer," to enhance his independence and to distance himself from gritty partisan politics. Hitler was to supply evidence that "there is no serious ban on weapons" in the National Socialist Party; more important, that the Party had formed "roll commandos," essentially paramilitary units whose function was to seek out and attack or even kill political opponents. Finally, Hitler was to confirm that Berlin's "Storm 33," a unit of the Nazis' "Storm Sections" (*Sturmabteilungen*, or SA), was such a roll commando. The four defendants in this trial, the case against Konrad Hermann Stief et al., better known as the Eden Dance Palace trial, were members of Storm 33. At the bottom of the document was a signature: "Litten. Advocate." The letters of the last name looped much larger than the rest of the text, conveying determination, pride, and perhaps even arrogance. The request was dated April 17, 1931.[1]

That same tone breathes through a letter that this advocate wrote to his parents on May 7, 1931. "I am lying in bed at the moment with the grippe," he informed them, "which must without fail be cured within 24 hours, as tomorrow I will have the pleasure of cross-examining Herr Hitler personally in Moabit."[2]

In May 1931 Hitler was forty-two years old, the leader of the National Socialist German Workers' Party (NSDAP), which, in national elections held the previous September, had surged from a previous high of 2.6 percent to 18.3 percent of the popular vote and hence of the seats in Germany's Parliament. This was the largest gain any German political party had ever made from one election to the next. Hitler had gotten himself into this position largely through his rhetoric, his ability to move crowds with words. By 1931 millions were looking to Hitler, some with terror, some with eager anticipation, as the man who might soon cast aside Germany's shaky democracy and usher in a new kind of state, a "Third Reich."[3]

In May 1931 Hans Joachim Albert Litten had not yet reached his twenty-eighth birthday. Friends knew him to be shy, scholarly, and reserved. He had been practicing law in Berlin for all of two and a half years. Beyond a handful of youth movement activists and the small circle of lawyers and judges who frequented the criminal courts of Berlin's Moabit district, he was unknown. Yet he had summoned the most formidable public speaker of his age and was preparing to take him on in rhetorical battle.

Who was Hans Litten? Years later his closest friend, Max Fürst, remembered him as "more than a brother . . . 'a part of myself,'" but also as a fanatical warrior who fought with the desperation of "one who fights the last battle." Countess Marion Dönhoff, editor in chief of the weekly *Die Zeit* (*Time*), believed that Litten was "one of those righteous men for whose sake the Lord did not allow the city—the country, the nation—to be entirely ruined." Kurt Hiller, a friend from Berlin political circles and later a cellmate in a concentration camp, called him "a true Christian by nature, and also by conviction." Another fellow prisoner was more sardonic: "A definite genius, but not easy to live with."[4]

Photographs show a serious, bespectacled young man, already growing portly and inclined to a double chin, with thinning hair combed back from a widow's peak and worn unusually long for the time ("Only soldiers and slaves get their hair shorn," he liked to say). He was tall: his closest friends' small daughter remembered him as "the big man with glasses," and a youth movement friend described him as a "tall, pale young man." Beyond his height, the photos do not suggest a man who would be striking or memorable. Yet people meeting Litten for the first time invariably gained a strong impression. Rudolf Olden, a distinguished lawyer and journalist, remembered the first time he saw Litten. It was in 1928 at a meeting of the League for Human Rights (*Liga für Menschenrechte*), a very modern kind of political lobby group that had grown out of a left-leaning association called New Fatherland founded during the First World War by Albert Einstein and the future mayor of West Berlin, Ernst Reuter. Litten asked a question during the discussion. "The speaker had a striking head, a smooth face, rimless glasses over round bright eyes. He wore his shirt open at the throat, and short pants, below which the knees were bare." Olden took the young man for a schoolboy. After the debate, one of Olden's friends, smiling, told him that the "boy" was in fact the *Assessor*, or newly qualified lawyer, Hans Litten. The next time Olden saw Litten was in a courtroom. Olden was struck by the contrast between the "childlike face" with the eyes that "gazed pure and clear through the glasses," and the calm expertise of the lawyer who refused to let anyone intimidate him.[5]

Max Fürst had a similar recollection of meeting Litten, then seventeen, at a party in their hometown of Königsberg, East Prussia: "Hans, wearing a blue, very bourgeois suit, was leaning on the piano, a circle had formed around him . . . the conversation was cultivated. I had the suspicion that it was something involving Nietzsche. In any case, I didn't understand a word." "A big boy with yet bigger glasses" was his description. But like many others, Fürst noticed that Litten's brown eyes shone through the glasses with "a sharp and penetrating effect." From "ten miles away" one could mark Hans Litten as an intellectual. But without the glasses, his eyes "were the eyes of a dreamer, which looked more inward than outward."[6]

In her later years his still-grieving mother would remind anyone who listened that "Hitler's first victims were Germans," and there were many reasons why, almost from the beginning, the Nazis condemned Litten to imprisonment in a concentration camp, hard labor, prolonged interrogations, beatings, and torture. To the Nazis Litten was half-Jewish, as he was the product of what Germans in the early twentieth century called a mixed marriage. In politics he stood far to the left. And he was a lawyer, a profession for which the Nazis had scant regard.

But above all it was Hitler's personal fear and hatred that landed Litten in the concentration camps, and this fear and hatred stemmed from the handwritten summons of April 1931. For when Hitler appeared in court on May 8, Litten subjected him to a withering cross-examination, laying bare the violence at the heart of the Nazi movement. The Eden Dance Palace trial exposed Hitler to multiple dangers: criminal prosecution, the disintegration of his party, public exposure of the contradictions on which the Nazis' appeal was based. It was only through luck that Hitler survived with his political career intact.

The Litten who emerged in the 1930s was a fanatical warrior. In trial after trial, appeal after appeal, he waged a ferocious and single-minded legal battle against the Nazis, using all of the tools available to a lawyer—raising evidence, filing charges, speaking in and out of the courtroom—not only to expose the Nazis' programmatic violence but also to hold their leaders accountable for it. In the last years before Hitler's dictatorship Litten became one of the most prominent anti-Nazi activists, a frequent speaker at public meetings in Berlin, and a contributor to left-leaning periodicals such as *The World Stage* (*Die Weltbühne*) and the *Workers' Illustrated News* (*Arbeiter Illustrierte Zeitung*).

In the worst years of the Great Depression, which by some measures hit Germany harder than any other country, Litten fought the Nazis without thought for his financial or even personal security. The fuel on which he ran was a deep and burning conviction. At best, his law practice broke even. At other times, especially in his last year of freedom, he lost money. To take the cases he believed in, he subcontracted less urgent matters to other lawyers, often paying those lawyers more than the clients paid him. He was only ever a step ahead of creditors and the tax authorities.

Litten's resistance to the Nazis went on after the "seizure of power" of January 30, 1933. Although he was one of the first to be arrested after Hitler was made chancellor, Litten fought back even from the concentration camps. When camp guards beat incoming prisoners, he protested, and was nearly executed on the spot. When a Nazi officer demanded that he confess to sending "innocent" storm troopers to prison, Litten refused and was beaten. When camp prisoners were ordered to put on a ceremony celebrating some Nazi anniversary, Litten read a poem with the provocative title "Thoughts Are Free." When

Gestapo officers and storm troopers tortured him to reveal secrets about his clients, most of them Communist activists, Litten tried to take his own life to avoid betraying his clients' confidences. His captors revived him.

Throughout his five-year imprisonment, Litten was an unfailingly generous and loyal comrade to his fellow prisoners. He shared the food packages and the money his family sent him. A one-man university, he taught his friends, most of them working-class young men who had never had a chance at higher education, about literature and art. When Jewish prisoners at Dachau were locked in their barracks for weeks at a time—a punishment known as "isolation" because it kept them away from the "Aryan" prisoners, while imposing on them the most thoroughly communal existence—Litten kept them sane by reciting passages from the works of favorite authors, all stored in his photographic memory, and lecturing on a wide range of subjects. He worked at translating medieval German poetry into modern German, read Dante in Italian and Shakespeare in English, and mulled over a groundbreaking book on the poetry of Rainer Maria Rilke. His dedication to his fellow prisoners and his passion for the life of the mind were also forms of resistance, humane, stubborn, and unrewarded.

Prisoners who were with Litten and survived, like the clients on whose behalf he had fought, cherished his memory. That he was among "the noblest men I have ever met" was a typical assessment, often repeated. Some of his friends responded with a nobility of their own. In late 1933, Litten's friends Max and Margot Fürst risked their lives to organize Litten's escape from the Brandenburg concentration camp. Margot had just turned twenty-one.

Litten's life became enmeshed with the lives of the most important men in the Nazi regime. Hitler considered Litten's cross-examination so important that he brought his own stenographer with him to court. In later years Litten's imprisonment pushed Hitler repeatedly into the kind of position he most hated: having to make a public decision that might turn out to be unpopular. Litten's advocacy posed a threat to propaganda chief Joseph Goebbels and Nazi Germany's "second man," Hermann Göring. The ambassador and later foreign minister Joachim von Ribbentrop had to deal with influential lobbyists in Great Britain who campaigned for Litten's freedom. Litten's mother forced SS leader

Heinrich Himmler, as well as justice official and later senior judge Roland Freisler, Reich President Paul von Hindenburg, and Justice Minister Franz Gürtner, to respond again and again to her lobbying for his release. Rudolf Diels, who became the first chief of the Gestapo, proved to be the decisive link between Litten's activities before 1933 and his fate after Hitler came to power. Why these powerful men feared and hated Litten reveals a great deal about them and the nature of the Nazi regime.

M ax Fürst called Litten's story a tragedy, and so it is. And like all tragedies it is also redemptive. But it is not a simple story. Litten was born in 1903 into the Germany of Kaiser Wilhelm II, reached adulthood in the turbulent years of the Weimar Republic, and died during Hitler's dictatorship. The wars and revolutions, and the recurring political, social, and economic chaos of those years, forced all Germans into repeated and wrenching decisions about public and private conduct: how to choose from among the welter of ideologies on offer in Germany's febrile politics, from all the blueprints for a new society or a return to a (supposedly) older and more virtuous one; and how to live in a society that increasingly forced the individual to choose between competing loyalties, between morality and expediency, even between morality and survival. Litten was passionately engaged in German politics from his student days on, and in the last years before the onset of Hitler's Reich he became as prominent as any political lawyer in the country. He faced every dilemma that could arise in a principled man's fight against unchecked power.

Inevitably he did harm as well as good; there was no other way. The harm was not only to himself. His work exposed his close friends to mortal danger; it tore apart and ultimately destroyed his family. Some of his political choices were harmful as well. Litten was not, as some later tried to paint him, a defender of the democratic system of the Weimar Republic. He was a revolutionary. Sometimes, especially early in his career before the battle against the Nazis became his primary cause, his targets were Social Democrats, the only unapologetic defenders of democracy in the Weimar Republic. When Litten tried to prosecute Berlin Police Chief Karl Zörgiebel for the murder of demonstrators, or defended a libel case by arguing that the Social Democratic Defense Minister Gustav Noske was a "scoundrel and a villain," he helped to weaken the democratic state in the face of Hitler's challenge.

Litten knew the choices he faced. He chose his enemies and how and when to fight them. He chose the clients whose battles he would make his own. For the most part they were working-class young Berliners from Wedding, Charlottenburg, and Neukölln—the neighborhoods most ravaged by the economic and political crises of the 1930s. These were the areas where unemployment could exceed 50 percent and where, consequently, there was a large pool of the disaffected and dispossessed to swell the ranks of the Communist Party's fighting organizations, the Red Frontfighters' League and the Combat League Against Fascism.

Nothing forced Litten to become the champion of the downtrodden. His was a prominent and privileged background. His mother, Irmgard, came of a family that had long produced Lutheran pastors and high-minded university professors, among the most honored professions in Germany at that time. His father, Fritz, was a law professor who rose to be dean of the law faculty at the University of Königsberg and later rector of the university. The Litten house was a center of Königsberg society, and the Littens regularly played host to generals, barons, and counts. When Hans finished his legal education, his pedigree and intellect assured him the kinds of job offers law graduates usually dream of, from the most powerful private firms and the most prestigious ministerial offices. He could have pursued wealth, comfort, and professional respectability. Had he made these choices he might not have been subject to persecution by the Nazis, at least in the regime's earlier years, and since later Nazi laws defined him as a *Mischling*, or a person of mixed blood, he might even have survived the Third Reich while living in Germany. In the weeks between Hitler's ascent to the chancellorship of Germany and Litten's arrest, he could easily have left Germany for safety abroad. Friends and family warned him of the danger he was in and pleaded with him to go. He chose not to.

He chose to be Jewish as well. Because his mother was Lutheran and his father a convert, Litten was raised in the official German Evangelical Church. His two younger brothers never identified with the family's partly Jewish heritage. Hans did—extravagantly, defiantly. Max Fürst wrote that Litten wanted to be Jewish in the same way that he wanted to fight for the workers of Wedding and Neukölln: he wanted to be on the side of the underdog. Eva Eichelbaum, another of Litten's friends from his Königsberg days who also later became a Berlin lawyer, made the same point when she remembered his decision to join a Jewish youth group.[7]

This book tells Hans Litten's story, focusing on his courtroom battles with Hitler and the National Socialist Party before 1933 and on his imprisonment in the years after 1933. But at every turn I look at Litten's life and his work in their broader context: the terrible predicament of German Jews in the early twentieth century, the rich stew of politics in the age of Weimar, the fascinating and doomed culture of Weimar Berlin, the nature of the criminal courts in which Litten worked, the growing dimensions of Hitler's terror, and life in the concentration camps of the 1930s. As a famous political prisoner Litten was the subject of several campaigns, public and private, for his freedom, and by the late 1930s his story had become entangled in the dilemmas of Anglo-German relations in the era of "appeasement." After the Second World War, Litten's memory became a sometimes bitter issue in the divided Germanies.

At the broadest level this book takes on two themes. The first involves the way criminal justice functioned in Weimar Germany and how the rule of law collapsed in the 1930s. Some historians argue that the horrors of justice under Hitler were simply a product of a long history of antidemocratic, antimodern, and anti-Semitic conduct and beliefs on the part of Germany's judges. Others posit that the beginning of Hitler's rule in 1933 marked a dramatic break with the legal culture of the preceding years. Neither version is correct. Hans Litten's trials between 1928 and 1933 show that the outcomes of particular trials did not, and could not, lie only in the hands of judges, however politically right-leaning those judges may have been. In Weimar Germany, the press, expert witnesses, the police, various levels of governments, political parties, interest groups, and certainly prosecutors and defense lawyers all had a powerful impact on what happened in the courtroom, often bringing randomness rather than consistent bias to judicial verdicts. Hitler's ascension in 1933 was merely one of a series of points in an arc of the rule of law in Germany. The slide into increasingly arbitrary rulings by Germany's courts (and of authoritarian practices by Germany's police) had begun before 1933, following years of remarkable progress in Germany's legal system. On the other hand, the Nazis could not expunge all of the deeply ingrained habits of a legal system immediately upon taking power. Such habits lingered, often with bizarre incongruity, through the first years of Hitler's rule. As Hans Litten had been a central player in criminal law in the democratic Weimar Republic, so he became one of the first and most visible victims of Germany's slide into lawlessness as the 1930s progressed.

The second theme involves a meditation on the moral consequences of political action. The story of Hans Litten and the people who were close to him (especially his mother, his brothers, and the Fürsts) is, fundamentally, a morality tale: it centers around the question of how to act in the face of injustice.

On some level, no historian looking back across the gulf of many decades can hope to answer the question "Why did they do what they did?" The answer lies in the innermost thoughts of people long dead. Hans Litten's niece Patricia Litten, reflecting on her own family's history, put it well: "The terrible thing is that we can all only speculate about history; we have fragments that are, so to speak, verifiable, and then there are a great many dark spots where one must speculate, instinctively."[8]

The task is made yet more difficult by the contradictions of Hans Litten himself. The man who so passionately took up the Judaism his father had rejected also felt a strong attachment to the cult of the Virgin Mary. The man whose deepest political and religious commitments were communal was also an eccentric individualist who liked to say that two people would be one too many for his political party. The man who described himself as a revolutionary socialist, and who was capable of the most strident and impassioned political rhetoric, was shy and awkward and, to cap it all, could be deeply upset by the slightest change in his private life. The man who was beset by many fears and phobias—including crossing streets—was also capable of extraordinary physical courage.

And yet many of Patricia Litten's "fragments" remain, and part of this book seeks to explore and to answer the question of why Hans Litten and his friends chose the battles they fought and the sacrifices they made. The answers lie in a mixture of religious faith, political conviction, Prussian duty, even family loyalty and conflicts. Some parts of this mixture arose out of problems and conditions specific to Germany in the early twentieth century. But some are as timeless as Shakespeare's meditations on the uses of power that lie at the heart of *Henry IV* and *Henry V* or the family jealousies of *King Lear*. These works were among Litten's own favorites.

At the beginning of the twenty-first century, Hans Litten, long neglected, is once again having a moment. Since the 1980s the German Association of Democratic Lawyers and the European Association of Lawyers for Democracy and World Human Rights have given a prize for human rights advocacy in his name; the 2006 winner was an American, Michael Ratner, president of the Center for Constitutional Rights. Since 2001 the German Bar Association has had its head office in Berlin in a building called the Hans Litten House, which stands on Hans Litten Street. Articles about Litten appear with some frequency in German professional legal journals. Why Litten should become the patron saint of German and, increasingly, world lawyers is an important question. But it is not the main reason I wanted to tell his story. The reason lies in the power of that story's moral qualities and in its mixture of historical importance and Shakespearian timelessness. Litten's was a very twentieth-century life, in the causes that animated him and the fate that befell him. Partly Jewish, partly Christian, deeply in love with his native Prussia and a committed internationalist, a political radical with his own quirky brand of cultural conservatism, erudite and philistine, arrogant and wracked by insecurities—few people could embody their country more than Hans Litten embodied twentieth-century Germany. At the same time, the moral quandaries that Litten and his friends faced, perhaps even the political crisis into which they were thrown, have all the enduring power of tragedy.

Hans Litten himself wrote about the "double edge of the deed," the impossibility of taking righteous action without doing harm. His life and his work forced him and others, repeatedly and with ever-increasing severity, to confront the question of how much to risk when morality becomes a life-or-death matter. The redemptive side of this story lies in the frequency with which he and his friends and family chose the dangerous answers over the safe ones.

PART I

The Whole Person

The Litten Court

Connoisseurs of irony can find much to ponder in the stories of Hans Litten's childhood.

His godfather was Franz von Liszt, celebrated professor of criminal law in Berlin, a younger cousin of the pianist and composer. Liszt was famous for his ideas on prison reform. He abandoned the classic liberal belief in fixed and finite sentences for criminals, believing that those who would always be a danger to society should be locked up indefinitely. This was the man who held the future concentration camp prisoner in his arms during the baptism.[1]

By his own account, Litten thought "very intensively about death" from the age of five. To comfort him, his mother would tell him that when the time came, if he were very good, he could ask God if, instead of dying, he might take a journey, far away, perhaps to Egypt. The words sank in: Litten could recall them nearly thirty years later—as Hitler's prisoner.[2]

Hans Litten was born in the town of Halle on the River Saale, on June 19, 1903. His father, Fritz Julius Litten, was a thirty-year-old junior lawyer; five days after the birth of his first son Fritz gave his inaugural lecture as a member of the law faculty at the University of Halle. Five years later Fritz Litten followed "the call," as German academics say, to a position as a full professor at the University of Königsberg, which for him meant a return to his family's East Prussian homeland.[3]

The story of the Litten family was typical of the rising German Jewish middle class of the late nineteenth century. Consciousness of that rise, and constant fear of its reversal, shaped how Fritz Litten lived his life. Having finally made it in the Kaiser's Germany, Fritz shared a credo with many German Jews of his generation: *Nur keine Rückfälle*— "Just no relapses." Successful German Jewish families knew that they were only several generations removed from a time in which Jews were mostly poor, their movements legally restricted and subject to the kind of indignity reflected in the log of an eighteenth-century Berlin gatekeeper: "Today there passed six oxen, seven swine, and a Jew." Fritz's father, Joseph Litten, was a businessman who dealt successfully in grain and wood, later founding a bank. Joseph was also, as a plaque at the synagogue recorded, chairman of the lay council of the Königsberg Jewish community. Fritz studied law in Leipzig, Freiburg, and Königsberg, earning his doctorate in 1895. He went on to do military service as a one-year officer trainee, typical for well-off young men in Imperial Germany. To enter the officer corps, however, Fritz had to convert to the official Evangelical Church. Conversion, which in pre-Nazi Germany made most, if not all, things possible for Jews, also opened the door to the academic career of which he dreamed.[4]

Fritz Litten's personal success, his strict adherence to the commandment "Just no relapses," and the anxiety of the social climber who wished his origins to be forgotten determined the lordly manner in which he carried himself. He built a large house, which became known as "the Litten Court." When the hyperinflation of 1923 wiped out his wealth (by November of that year the German Mark had fallen from a prewar value of just over 4 to the U.S. dollar to 4.42 trillion to the dollar) Fritz was undeterred. He told his wife, "I have no intention of changing our style of living; I shall simply earn more." And he did, through writing for the press and working from time to time as an arbitrator and as counsel to the German state railways. Hans Litten and his two younger brothers, Heinz Wolfgang, born in 1905, and Karl Reinhardt, known as Rainer, born in 1909, grew up in comfort and privilege.[5]

Professionally Fritz went from triumph to triumph. In 1912 he was named dean of the Königsberg law faculty. After the First World War he was appointed rector, equivalent to president, of the university. His politics were nationalist-conservative, another expression of "Just no relapses." "I was trained in the outlook of a Prussian officer and state official," he later wrote. He spoke proudly of his four years of service "in the field" during the First World War, for which he was awarded the Iron Cross First as well as Second Class, and retained the title of "Captain of the Militia (ret)." Shortly after the Battle of Tannenberg, at which the short-winded Russian advance into East Prussia was halted in 1914, Fritz Litten arranged an honorary doctorate for that battle's nominal commander, the "savior of East Prussia," Field Marshall Paul von Hindenburg. (Later, when Hindenburg was president of Germany, his path would intersect with the Littens' in a very different way). Fritz proudly called himself "educator of princes," as he had taught the grandsons of Germany's last emperor. He once told Max Fürst that he would gladly become a legal advisor to the Vatican, for then he would attain the rank of cardinal and the Swiss Guards would have to salute him with their daggers. "He said that in jest," said Max, "but he was serious about social climbing." Fritz was friendly with a circle of prominent conservative figures, among them the man who would become Hitler's first army minister, General Werner von Blomberg, and the future leader of the Nazified German Christian Church, Pastor Ludwig Müller. His wife later concluded—with a tone of barely concealed disgust, testifying to the tensions that would wreck the family in later years—"There was no denying the fact that my husband was a prominent figure.... [He] was often called in jest the 'uncrowned king of East Prussia.' Those who value such things would say that his was a brilliant career." Kurt Sabatzky, Königsberg representative of the largest German Jewish organization, the Central Union of German Citizens of the Jewish Faith, recalled that the Litten home was one of the centers of Königsberg society. Sabatzky could not help adding, however, that Fritz's stance in "Jewish matters" was "questionable": "He was a renegade, and loved to insist on the Christian character of his house."[6]

From time to time in the late 1920s and early 1930s, when elite members of East Prussian society gathered at the Litten Court, a guest would offer condescending sympathy to Frau Irmgard Litten about the "machinations" of her "misguided" son, the Berlin lawyer. They misjudged her. "There would be a nervous silence as the small, gentle woman began to argue that laws and regulations must not be employed just for the benefit of the ruling classes, but for ordinary people as well; that was what her son represented, and she was proud of it." Fritz Litten would try to change the subject.[7]

Irmgard Litten, born Irmgard Wüst in Halle in 1879, liked to say that hers was an old Swabian aristocratic family that had gone from producing marauding knights (*Raubritter*) to producing pastors and university professors. "The great majority of my forbears," she wrote, "were pastors; all, from the beginning of the seventeenth century and earlier, were Swabians; and most of them were fearless soldiers of

God." The difference between her family and her husband's was starkly apparent. Irmgard's father, Albert Wüst, was a professor of engineering at the University of Halle. A specialist in agricultural machinery, he was said to be easygoing in manner and progressive in his politics, especially regarding the rights and social position of workers. Her mother, Wilhelmine, was known in the family as an expert on art. The father's open-minded politics and the mother's passion for art, as well as the sense of entitlement of an established family, decisively shaped their daughter and, through her, the three Litten boys.[8]

Irmgard Wüst and Fritz Litten were married in September 1900. They had met at the University of Halle in 1898, where Irmgard, who chafed under the myriad restrictions on a young woman's life, dared to attend lectures. Her knowledge of art history was such that in a different age she might have become a scholar. Her independence and interest in politics might have led her into public life. The Königsberg chapter of the German People's Party once invited her to give a lecture on women in politics. She began with a long appreciation of Rosa Luxemburg, the revolutionary socialist leader who was murdered in the upheavals of 1919. When the chairman of the meeting objected, Irmgard asked if one could possibly deny that Luxemburg was the most important woman in German political history. The People's Party did not invite Irmgard to give any more speeches.[9]

Hans Litten's personality emerged early. First there was his astonishing memory: as a four-year-old he could recite long passages from the Grimms and restate conversations in their entirety, often enough an embarrassment for the parents. He composed poems, too, faithfully transcribed by his indulgent mother. He was an "early developer," far ahead of his fellow students, always able to do his schoolwork without the slightest effort. The youthful promise was abundantly fulfilled: the adult demonstrated an intellectual power that stunned all who met him. He seemed able to hold in his memory everything he had ever read, and he could recite hour on hour the works of favorite authors, such as Rainer Maria Rilke. He read Shakespeare in English, Dante in Italian, and Cervantes in Spanish. He studied Hebrew, Sanskrit, and the music of the Middle East.[10]

The young Hans also revealed a passionate religious feeling. Irmgard told of how her sons were thrilled to hear stories of "the Christ

Child who came to earth in order to bring peace to the world." They built a toy crib with the Holy Family, the three kings, and the shepherds and their flocks. "Little Hans wanted as many animals as possible. 'Why are there no *wild* animals?' he asked. 'Because they would kill and eat the others.' 'But not in the presence of the Christ child,' he said. 'He came to bring peace!'" And Hans was an instinctive democrat. According to Irmgard, the family's cook often complained that the young master was too friendly with the street sweeper and addressed beggars as "sir"—a deference he never showed to aristocratic guests at the Litten Court. He took promises seriously. "If anyone had frivolously made him a promise that could only with difficulty be kept, Hans would never leave his side, constantly repeating, with a look of reproach: 'But you promised; you must do it!'" Irmgard's recollections, written after Hans's death, are certainly tinged with sentimentality and with a didactic point. But the Hans Litten they convey—emotionally drawn to the underdog, believing passionately in promises and reproachful of those who would not keep them, utterly serious about the laws of God and man—foreshadows the adult Litten who crossexamined Adolf Hitler and suffered in Hitler's camps.[11]

Irmgard believed that her Wüst inheritance had decisively shaped her eldest son. It was she who brought to the Litten family the virtually religious faith in the importance of art and learning so characteristic of middle-class Germans at the beginning of the twentieth century. In his memoir of his own upper-middle-class Prussian Jewish family, the historian Fritz Stern stressed the importance of *Bildung*, or education and cultivation, to this kind of German, noting, "It was assumed that this cultural heritage, or patrimony, molded one's code of behavior, the values one professed and tried to live by.... *Wissenschaft* [scholarship] had a moral character, implying a total seriousness. For many, *Bildung* and *Wissenschaft* became twin deities." Hans Litten, even in his most radical moments—perhaps especially then—was entirely a product of this high-minded milieu. Perhaps one is never more a product of one's environment than when one rebels against it.[12]

Irmgard Litten wrote that one of her clerical ancestors "was so pugnacious, so extreme in his demands upon the righteousness of his flock, that the authorities, regarding him as impossible, sent him to Russia, to preach to the Germans on the Volga, where he built up a flourishing community." The young Hans, she added, "often reminded me of this ancestor, both in appearance and in character." While her family had long supplied high clerics to the kingdom of Württemberg, there were among them "adherents of eccentric sectarian ideas of early Christianity," who found themselves in conflicts of conscience with the official Church. Irmgard was convinced that her own intellectual independence and high-mindedness had strongly affected Hans and his two younger brothers. "I taught them that material interests must never be allowed to control one's actions; that one must be faithful to one's own convictions with fanatical obstinacy; that a compromise was never possible." She added that she had never realized what a lifelong handicap such an attitude would be.[13]

But from his earliest days Hans Litten was very far from being simply the "Franciscan type" that his legal colleague Rudolf Olden called him. Litten was an East Prussian patriot, his patriotism compelled, he said, "by the stronger logic of the landscape." Here, too, Litten embodied the refractory character of his homeland. An old stereotype of Prussia, confirmed for many by two world wars, is of a land of militarism and humorless, unblinking discipline. Elements of the stereotype have a basis in the historical record. But there has always been another side to the story. In the seventeenth and eighteenth centuries Prussia was a land of religious toleration, ruled by kings with a pragmatically enlightened approach to immigration. In the nineteenth century Prussia's universities led the world. In the Weimar Republic Prussia became, in the words of the historian Dietrich Orlow, the "unlikely rock of democracy." Its capital, Berlin, was a left-leaning city; Litten's hometown of Königsberg was a center of enlightened political and philosophical currents. The philosopher Hannah Arendt, a Königsberg friend of Litten's and Max Fürst's, once told the historian Joachim Fest, "In my manner of thinking and making judgments, I am still really from Königsberg." The same was true of Litten.[14]

Irmgard Litten remembered that at the beginning of the First World War, the eleven-year-old Hans was "as enthusiastic and militaristic as any other German boy," a claim borne out by the notebooks preserved with Litten's papers in the German Federal Archives. One is emblazoned "World War 1914: A People in Arms against a World in Arms." It is filled with patriotic doggerel bearing such titles as

"Hindenburg, the Liberator of East Prussia" and "The Hero's Death of the *Emden*" (a battle cruiser lost early in the war). Other notebooks contain poems, such as "England, England *unter alles*." Perhaps these prepubescent scribblings were merely compulsory school exercises, the kind imposed on children in all countries in all wars. But Irmgard kept them.[15]

Apart from showing a precocious grasp of international politics, these notebooks point to the character of the adult Litten in other ways. Max Fürst remembered Litten's great capacity for hatred: "I said that his burning hate was his German side." This may also have been a quality Litten inherited or learned from his strong-minded mother. Years after she had fled Germany, Irmgard wrote passionately of her hatred for Hitler's Reich. On one occasion in 1933, as she waited in the corridor outside the office of a secret police officer, an SA man sauntered past. "The look I gave him must have mirrored my thoughts very clearly, because a man . . . whispered to me: 'When one has such hate-filled eyes, it's better to keep them closed.'"[16]

In 1915 Fritz Litten took up a commission as a captain of the reserves and went to the front. Irmgard, left to look after the three boys, also took care of wounded soldiers. As the war dragged on, a gulf opened up between the patriarch and the son he had once called "the crown prince." A wartime photograph tells the story: a uniformed Fritz poses with a paternal arm around his eldest son; Hans, his face grave, tries to wriggle away, his shoulder dropped so as not to touch his father. Fritz Litten would later attribute what he considered his son's waywardness to his own wartime absence during Hans's "most important years of development": "I was . . . without influence on his upbringing, and so I lost control of him." Irmgard agreed, if with a different accent: "It was perhaps a misfortune for [my three sons] that during the years of the war—since my husband was at the front all the time—the education of the children was left entirely to me." If at first the war had allowed Hans to demonstrate not only his patriotism but his seriousness about following rules—the minister of food supply told Irmgard that Hans was "the only German who unconditionally obeys my regulations"—after the second year of the war he began to notice the injustices and inequalities in German society which the war exposed. "I did not bridle my tongue," said Irmgard, "and I believe what he heard and saw at this time gave him the first impetus to his socialistic and pacifist attitude."[17]

The hardest things to recover from the past are the unspoken assumptions. To grasp the full resonance of what Fritz meant about his absence during Hans's "most important years of development," or of Hans's independent views on the war, we have to recapture those pre-1914 central European assumptions governing the relations of parents and children. Here again Fritz Stern provides a clue: in the early twentieth century, parental guidance among the middle class of central Europe was "an expression of a secular-rational world in which the responsibility for moral education fell on the parents." Parental certainty mirrored "the prevailing sense of a world in order." In his moving evocation of the lost world of prewar Vienna, Stefan Zweig recalled the overwhelming social and cultural power age conferred, such that it was practically a scandal when the thirty-eight-year-old Gustav Mahler was named director of the Vienna Court Opera. Young professionals strove to grow their beards and move ponderously for fear that otherwise they would look too young and "unreliable."[18]

Fritz came home from the lost war in December 1918 embittered and even more authoritarian in his inclinations. He found his eldest son in no mood to pursue a legal career, wishing instead to devote himself to the study of literature or art history. Fritz had based his life on "Just no relapses." Now his eldest son *was* the relapse. And so it went, step by painful, downward step. If the father had suppressed his Jewish heritage for the sake of his ambitions, the eldest son would make a point of going to synagogue on the Sabbath with hat and prayer book. For his *Abitur*, the high school certificate for those planning to attend university, he would study Hebrew as his special subject; he would delve into Jewish mysticism and seek out friends from Königsberg's Hassidic community. Later, when Hans's professional activity brought the attention of the right-wing press down on his father, Hans would mock Fritz's reticence, as in this typically scathing letter: "That you are a Jew was an open secret in Königsberg—the *People's News* was in the habit under certain circumstances of registering the fact that the name of your father stands on the table of honor at the Synagogue, and as early as 1919 a democratically-minded leader from the anti-Semitic [German] People's Party had congratulated the party on its tolerance for letting a Jew appear as a speaker." When students debated whether to hang a portrait of Field Marshall von Hindenburg in the Royal Wilhelm Gymnasium, Litten's intervention almost got him expelled: "I was always in favor of hanging him." Only Fritz Litten's influence kept Hans in school. The chagrin of the social-climbing father, who had arranged Hindenburg's honorary degree, can easily be imagined.[19]

Fritz Litten had no time for the arts. "Talk to my wife about art," he would tell guests at the Litten Court, "she doesn't understand anything else." He had no respect for the intellectual abilities of his two younger sons and did not care what they did for a living. As far as he was concerned, they could devote themselves to "breadless art," and they did. Heinz studied law but wrote a doctoral dissertation on "The Modification of a Theatrical Work through Performance" and went on to become a theater director. Rainer, strikingly handsome and, as Max Fürst wrote, "the least complicated and the most able at life" of the Litten boys, was on the verge of becoming a major star of the German stage and screen when the Nazi takeover wrecked his career.[20]

With Hans it was different. On him rested Fritz's hopes of founding a dynasty of distinguished jurists. Fritz Stern writes of "the effectiveness of the patriarchal model" and "the comfort of following in one's father's footsteps or of having one's footsteps followed." This was a social norm among the German middle classes, and Fritz Litten, "in his enthusiasm for his own profession," as Irmgard wrote, was determined that Hans would study law. But there was also a pressing practical consideration. Although Fritz eventually recovered from his financial losses in the hyperinflation of the early 1920s, he felt that the family could not afford to have its eldest son take up a low-paying career in the humanities. Hans, however, did not show the slightest interest in the law. He voiced his contempt for legal study in his diary: "When the ox in paradise got bored, he invented jurisprudence." To protest the paternal demands, Hans sought a job at the Königsberg docks. Fritz eventually compromised as far as permitting Hans to study art history alongside law.

Hans enrolled at the University of Königsberg in the summer semester of 1921, where he avenged himself by attending his father's lectures and engaging him in debates, much to the delight of the other students. The feud with his father did not prevent him from becoming a brilliant law student. Upon graduating in 1924, he served his required apprenticeship as a judicial clerk, or *Referendar,* in and around Königsberg. Aided by his intellect and photographic memory, he passed his two state bar exams with impressive grades and was officially enrolled as a lawyer at Berlin's Court of Appeal, the *Kammergericht,* in the autumn of 1928. Perhaps the father-son feud sharpened Hans's skills as a courtroom advocate. As the German defense lawyer and historian of the bar Gerhard Jungfer has written, conflict with the father can sharpen "love for intellectual battle, love of argument, the culture of argument. Argument limits power, clarifies the fronts, compels clear positions, develops the intelligence, courage, and creativity"— altogether, as Jungfer puts it, "good conditions for becoming a defense lawyer."[21]

Fritz Litten's regret at forcing Hans to study law grew in steady increments. When Hans began defending Communists and other leftist activists in Berlin, Fritz demanded that he change his last name to protect the family honor. Hans agreed, but the Prussian Justice Ministry did not. The father's regrets would only grow as his eldest son's fame coincided with the approach of Hitler's Reich.[22]

The Black Mob

E very Sunday," wrote Max Fürst, "early in the morning, one could see small groups of young people at the train stations, each group in their particular clothing, often with a small flag of their own choosing, assembling to go out into the open country." These young people were the Weimar Republic's reincarnations of the pre–First World War *Wandervögel,* or "Migratory Birds," Germany's proto-hippie youth movement. "We hiked in the woods near Berlin; we swam in the moonlight in the lakes; we read Martin Buber and Bellamy's *Utopia*; we discussed Socialism and Zionism and Marxism and Freudianism; we disagreed with and we loved each other," recalled Gisela Peiper, one of Litten's friends from the time. Wolfgang Roth, a young Berliner who moved in the same circles, recalled it more sardonically:

"Long hair, shining [*leuchtende*] eyes and a lot of sentimental romance, everything old-German—whatever that was, or was supposed to be—campfires and songs with the guitar, and having a 'connection' with a girl—holding hands in roadside ditches, worshiping the moon and catching a lung infection."[23]

In 1919 the Central Union of German Citizens of the Jewish Faith had formed a Königsberg chapter of a youth group called the Comrades. The point of the Comrades was to keep young German Jews away from the Zionist youth movement; the Central Union described this task officially as preparing its members "for the difficult tasks in Germany." The Central Union had been founded in 1893 and developed into the largest Jewish organization in Germany. Its name made a political point: "We are not German Jews," it proclaimed. "We are German citizens of the Jewish faith." The initial Comrades meeting at the Königsberg Jewish Youth Home was packed, and branches of the group soon appeared in other towns in the region. In the spring of 1920, representatives of such Jewish youth groups from all over Germany met in Berlin and laid the groundwork for the Bund, the national organization with which German Jewish youth groups of all kinds would soon be affiliated.[24]

But soon after its formation, the Königsberg chapter of the Comrades was hijacked by the young Max Fürst—who was in the process of breaking with the expectations of his middle-class family by apprenticing as a furniture maker and embracing revolutionary socialist politics—along with his sister Edith and several others of like mind. Under these new leaders the group slipped the reins of the Central Union and became politically radicalized. Hans Litten was now a frequent guest at the Comrades' "home evenings." "With [Litten's] strong intellect and his great knowledge," remembered Erwin Lichtenstein, one of the founding Comrades, "he won ever more influence in the group and, without belonging to the group, developed into one of the most important Comrades." Fürst and Litten together would remake the organization in their own mold.[25]

The existence of a distinct Jewish German youth movement was a product of the precarious place of young Jews in the Weimar era. However much some of the ideals of the German youth movement were shared across confessions, the foggy romanticism of the non-Jewish

"Migratory Birds" could easily slide into nationalism, from whence it was but a half step into anti-Semitism. Max wrote that young Jews "did not fit in any of the German hiking associations" (revealingly, even in the 1970s, he accepted as self-evident that "German" and "Jewish" were mutually exclusive terms). Furthermore, he and his friends found that they had little in common with the Socialist working-class youth. He found the Central Union's "endless emphasis on the 'German'" embarrassing, yet he was not religious, and certainly not a Zionist. As we shall see, Litten was troubled by the same existential uncertainties. Perhaps it was the special position of Königsberg as a border town, a German island in a Polish and Lithuanian sea, that inspired the Königsberg Comrades to resist the imposition of rigid religious or ethnic qualifications for membership. What became known as the "Königsberg line" on German Jewish identity within the movement ran: "We are Jewish because of our heritage, and we speak German." ("And that not always correctly," was Litten's sardonic addition.) The Comrades meant this underplaying of their German side as a barb against the Central Union, to whose supporters it also seemed "monstrous" not to acknowledge and draw upon one's Jewish heritage. Postmodernists before their time, they opposed any definition that would have excluded stateless and Polish Jews who might wish to join them. For Hans Litten the definitional question was personal: as the son of a Gentile mother he himself was arguably not Jewish, a point other youth movement activists sometimes made against him.[26]

Someone from a very different place and generation, when encountering descriptions of what the Comrades actually did with their time, would likely be astonished to find that this was an autonomous *protest* movement rather than a worthy, adult-sanctioned, extracurricular activity. The members of the Comrades were another example of rebels indelibly stamped by their culture. These young people were early twentieth-century, middle-class, central European Jews, who believed fervently in the formative qualities of art and science. Max Fürst described the Königsberg Comrades' activities in the group's newspaper in November 1923: "In the most recent evenings we have discussed the individual areas of struggle," including "alcohol, nicotine"—which they were *against*—"vegetarianism, clothing, nudism, dance." Still to come were "the woman question, profession, settlements." Then there was the "history course," in which the members were to learn history "as it was," and not in the propagandized form in which German schools delivered it. Subgroups concerned themselves with studying the Talmud or the writings of Walter Rathenau, the German Jewish foreign minister who was murdered by right-wing extremists in 1922. For a special treat, mostly on Friday evenings, there were literary readings: the works of Martin Buber or Else Laske-Schüler. "These are our parties," said the eighteen-year-old Max. In his memoirs he waxed rhapsodic over the excitement of these earnest discussions: "We called it a 'discussion fit for a king' when we succeeded . . . in jumping out of our own skins, in letting ourselves be carried away by the opposing argument. . . . It was intoxicating for us, stronger than any narcotic." Of course, there were also the hikes: weekend outings around Königsberg, longer expeditions to the Kurish Spit, the long sandbar connecting the East Prussian and Lithuanian coasts.[27]

The Bund, the all-German federation of Jewish youth groups, was always an uneasy alliance. The dominant faction was known as the "Ring." The Ring's answer to the conundrum of German Jewry was to assimilate as closely as possible with German nationalism; like the non-Jewish German youth movement, the outlook of the Ring was influenced by the mystical nationalism of the poet Stefan George and his circle. The Ring emphasized self-discipline, education, and clean living: the "Boy Scout" virtues, as Fürst dismissively called them. Set against the Ring was the Circle, more intellectual and more self-consciously Jewish in its concerns. After Hitler came to power, a successor group to the Circle devoted itself to the development of a kibbutz in Palestine, which, as the Kibbutz Hasorea, sill exists.[28]

The third group, which Hans Litten and Max Fürst founded in 1925, evolved out of the Königsberg chapter of the Comrades. Its name, the "Black Mob," came from a song about a revolutionary troop of the German Peasants' War of 1525. This war—part of the turmoil following Luther's Reformation and, as Max wrote, "one of the few revolutions which arose out of German soil"—offered these young radicals an appealing mixture of romance and revolutionary example.

Hans and Max were mutually complementary leading figures. Max, handsome, easygoing, charismatic, always armed with his guitar, dubbed by many parents "the pied piper of Hamlyn," was the practical leader. The more reserved and cerebral Hans was the theorist. Recognizing his friend's gifts, Hans dispatched Max, newly minted as a journeyman furniture maker, on a tour of Germany in 1925 to campaign for the Black Mob within the Bund, and active Black Mob chapters developed in the places where Max spent most of his time. Max was painfully conscious of how he had inspired so many people to political action. After Hitler came to power, a large number of his recruits suffered and died in the concentration camps. In the 1970s Max confessed, "Today I would be absolutely unable to find the courage to intervene so drastically in people's lives."[29]

Early in 1926, the Black Mob's manifesto appeared in the Bund's newspaper. "The Black Mob is here," it announced, and outlined its agreement with and opposition to—much more of the latter—the other factions in the Bund. The Black Mob's goal was to prepare its members for adult life; this meant, above all, preparing them for political engagement. It was not enough to focus on individual development, as the Ring believed. Although it did not seek to impose "the socialist idea" on its members, the Black Mob was explicitly revolutionary: "We cannot be satisfied with a Senior League [Aelterenbund] which leaves society uncontested." The point of a youth movement was to "lead its people ... to deeds." The manifesto closed with a very Littenesque call to duty: "We need everyone for whom the youth movement is not a game, but an obligatory demand [verpflichtende Forderung]."[30]

Although its influence endured, the life of the Black Mob itself was short. The combination of nonpartisan radicalism, ambivalence to Jewish religious observance, and aggressive recruiting among the members of the other Bund factions quickly aroused hostility in those other groups. Added to this was Hans Litten's considerable talent for provoking quarrels. All of this came to a head at a meeting of the leaders of the Bund in 1927, at which a motion was tabled to expel the Black Mob. One delegate denounced "the yoke" that Litten had "imposed" on members of his group. Litten's hardly convincing rejoinder was that his organization had a leadership (Führertum), and that one was "obligated to obedience before a leader." At the end of a lengthy meeting with heated debate the result was 95 votes for expulsion and 59 against, with 24 abstentions.[31]

A year later, the Black Mob itself broke up. It had been troubled by an inner division between the exponents of class and those of generational struggle. Litten was the leader of the latter group; for him, in the generational struggle, "the ideas of the youth movement" went "farther" than the "struggle for socialism." But more to the point, the original core of the Black Mob had grown up. Adult life awaited, and with it, inevitably for these highly engaged young people, adult political commitments. One had either to form a political party or to join one; both ran against the nonpartisan ethos of the Black Mob. Max Fürst was so distraught at the breakup that for days he wandered the streets of Berlin, contemplating suicide. Litten saw things more simply: those who had driven the Black Mob to break up were just "traitors."[32]

The Grizzly, the Camel, and the Seal-Bear

The Hans Litten who summoned Adolf Hitler to testify could not have been what he was nor done what he did without the friendship and loyalty of Max and Margot Fürst.

Max Fürst and Litten met in the autumn of 1920. "It was a wonderful time, that time in which I got to know Hans," Max wrote in the late 1930s. Not that they took to each other right away. Max had already heard about the son of the famous professor: his radical politics, his great talents, his father's love for socializing with east Elbian barons and counts. "My mind was then already made up, and I said . . . 'just wait until real life hits you.'" Immersed in his apprenticeship, Fürst had nothing but "contempt for all intellectuals." He and Hans disagreed about the direction the Comrades should take: serious discussion group or hiking club? And if this were not enough, they were, as Max recalled, "always in love with the same girl." One day while hiking it came to a "wild brawl." But then, sitting on the edge of a field, they started talking about "our eternal love for east Prussia and our views on each other." So began a deep friendship that would end only with Litten's death, a friendship that would be sustained in the days after Hitler's takeover with a courage and loyalty usually limited to children's adventure stories and seldom encountered amid the terror of a brutal tyranny.[33]

At first the prospects for a love affair between Max Fürst and the very young Margot Meisel seemed just as unpromising. Max and Margot met on a youth group expedition in 1926. Margot saw Max playing his guitar and pointed him out to a friend: "I'll take that one." She was only fourteen, a student at a girls' high school at Nikolsburg Square in central Berlin, and came from a prosperous and distinguished family. Her father was a successful businessman who had arrived in Berlin by way of Hungary after the collapse of the Habsburg Empire. Her uncle was the composer Edmund Meisel, who wrote music for the films *Battle Cruiser Potemkin* and Walter Ruttmann's *Symphony of the Great City* and for some of the plays directed by Erwin Piscator.[34]

Already at fourteen Margot Meisel had the fiercely independent and resourceful character that would make her an effective partner for Hans Litten (and his champion in later years). Gisela Peiper remembered her as "wise beyond her years." Max called her an "extreme individualist." Margot could not bear to take public transit to work, "sitting between sleepless people and badly shaved men." So she walked, three-quarters of an hour each way, and with the money she saved she occasionally took a taxi. Later, when she was being held in solitary confinement in the police prison at Alexander Square, she knew that Max would be astonished "that I, Margot Fürst, have requested a transfer" out of solitary confinement to "common custody [*Gemeinschaftshaft*]." The teenage Margot did not like going to school and brought books along with her to read covertly during the lessons. If the teacher caught her and confiscated a book, she always had another in reserve. When she had had enough of classes she would, with serene self-confidence, leave by the teachers' entrance, politely greeting those coming the other way. No one ever stopped her. From a young age she rejected labels. Once, after listening to a pioneering feminist talk about "we women," Margot burst out in exasperation, "I'm no woman"—a statement that, as Max dryly noted, was "demonstrably untrue."[35]

Willful she certainly was, but Margot was not at all lazy. When she found work she believed in she devoted herself to it body and soul. Her aesthetic sense matched her work ethic. She once wrote of a friend:

The whole difference between Sina and me comes down to this: she loves the rich summer of the south, and I on the other hand love the spareness of East Prussia. I always have the feeling that in the splendor of the south there is already too much over-ripeness, while at home there is only ever a hint of how the summer could be; there is so much promise there. And I don't like to be satisfied [*satt*].[36]

Max Fürst was a handsome young man with curly dark hair and a sardonic smile. Gisela Peiper described him as "a very gentle person but of great inner strength"; when he played his guitar "he could hold everybody in his hands." Another friend of the time described him as "radiating joy, health and energy." It was Peiper who asked Max to look after the young Margot Meisel, who had "difficulties" with her parents. Margot's involvement with the Berlin group of the Black Mob had led to a quarrel; she had moved out of her parents' house and was living with her grandmother. Max did not see why he should be saddled with her. But when he complained that he had too many letters to write, Peiper suggested he take on Margot as his secretary. He agreed, and Max and Margot would be together for over fifty years.[37]

When Hans Litten came to Berlin in the autumn of 1927, he, Max, and Margot began sharing an apartment in August Street, near Alexander Square. At first Litten was not happy with this arrangement. He had been looking to room with Max alone. "I would prefer it, Fräulein Meisel," he told Margot, "if you would not disturb Max so often." But Litten's attitude to Margot soon changed. He was, Max noted, as prone to self-dramatization as to stiff formality. One day he announced that he had fallen in love with Margot, continuing his old pattern of falling in love with Max's girlfriends, and he declared his feelings to Margot as well. But somehow things turned out well. Hans and the Fürsts would room together until 1933, and their relationship, personal and professional, never wavered.[38]

Max and Margot married in November 1929, shortly after Margot's seventeenth birthday. Their daughter, Birute, nicknamed "Mop," was born the following May, and Hans and the Fürsts moved into a larger apartment on Koblank Street (today Zola Street), near Bülow Square (today Rosa Luxemburg Square), where they would remain until after the Nazi takeover. Max opened his first furniture workshop on George Street, under the elevated railway tracks. Margot worked initially for a film company writing promotional materials, but after the birth of Birute she went to work as Litten's secretary.[39]

Litten and the Fürsts developed a "family language," in which they all took on nicknames from animals. Hans was the "Grizzly Bear." Max was the "Camel," "on whose humps one can load all cares." Margot was the *Robbenbär*, or "Seal-Bear," from a poem by Christian Morgenstern listing fanciful names for the months of the year. *Robbenbär* represented November, the month of Margot's birthday. "Margot proved herself to be a good animal-tamer," said Max. She alone knew how to bring Litten out of his frequent depressions. Later, looking back on their time together, Hans wrote to Margot of how she had calmed him so that he "could still work within modest limits."[40]

They worked hard. Max's workshop consumed so much of his time that Margot called it "the whore." Even when still at the film company Margot often worked at night typing documents for Hans. Litten was the most driven of all, and his work habits set the tempo for the household. "He worked without interruption," said Max. In August 1931 Litten wrote that he left his apartment "mostly at seven" in the morning, and came home only "late in the evening." Irmgard Litten recalled that she was never able to visit Hans in Berlin for very long because "he was on the go from early in the morning until late in the evening, and when he did spare me a few hours he always had a feeling that he was neglecting his clients." Even at night, said Max, "he dreamed pleadings."[41]

On a typical day Litten would rise very early, eat a quick breakfast, and take the subway to the criminal courthouse in Berlin-Moabit, the northwest Berlin district that, as home to the two busiest criminal courthouses in Germany and two prisons, had become a byword for criminal law. In the afternoon he would usually go to his office near Alexander Square to work and to hold his office hours; only the very large cases, such as the Eden Dance Palace trial, would keep him in Moabit in the afternoons as well. In the evenings he would attend political meetings or rallies, often as a featured speaker. Even then his day would not be over. He liked to return to his office late in the evening to work. "He was inexhaustible," Margot recalled, working often until two in the morning, sometimes until four. She would leave some warm food for him in the kitchen of the Koblank Street apartment.[42]

The routine grew only more grueling after Margot went to work as Litten's assistant. She and Hans would often not return from the office until the small hours. "In the intoxication of work, Hans, who was otherwise so considerate to everyone, neglected his own needs as well as those of others," recalled Max. He never allowed himself a vacation, seldom taking even so much as a day off. One Sunday, after weeks of hard work, seven days a week, Margot hesitantly suggested that, instead of working, the three of them could go out together somewhere. Hans looked at her "with round, astonished, slightly reproachful child-eyes, and the sad 'you don't want to work?' was heart-rending." Margot remembered that Hans had asked the question as if it were "completely unbelievable" that she would not want to devote a Sunday afternoon to the legal briefs. The innocence and the reproach recall the attitude to promises Irmgard noted in him as a boy. Somehow, though, Litten continued to deepen his knowledge of art and literature and to work here and there on his projected book on the poems of Rilke.[43]

Saturday evenings and Sunday mornings were the only times the Fürsts found that neither "the whore" nor "(if at all possible) Hans" could come between them. They would go out to the countryside or go to a movie or stroll through Berlin. Leisurely Sunday breakfasts, Max wrote, were "the best hours that we had with Hans." In the afternoons they would go to the Rosen-Café on Rosenthal Square, which had the benefit of a gramophone and sound barriers. There they could safely discuss the confidential aspects of Litten's trials.[44]

The closeness of this relationship and the long work hours inevitably led to tensions. Max recalled that life with Hans was "wonderful, but not without dramatic aggravations." Litten was intensely moody, and the Fürsts had to work hard to keep him on an even keel. Max remembered, "I often thought of [Saul and] David as I sang away Hans' gloomy thoughts and depressions with the lute." Later, under the pressures of work and family, Max lost patience with Hans's moods, and Margot increasingly took on the task. "I was probably a terrible friend [to Litten] in the last days," said Max. "Often I was annoyed that Margot was so drawn under his influence and into his work and really had no time for me." There is no evidence that any romantic attachment between Hans and Margot complicated the domestic arrangements, although Max did write of a "gray November day in 1931" when Margot once again came home very late from the office, making him "sick with displeasure and annoyance over Hans and her." Margot's future plans were likely to cause further tensions in the household. In the early 1930s she was making efforts to catch up on her education. Her plan was to get her *Abitur*, the certificate qualifying a student for university, and then study law so that she could take over the civil side of Litten's practice. Hannah Arendt had not only encouraged Margot to continue her education, but also tutored her in Greek and Latin. The Third Reich permanently sidelined these plans.[45]

Litten's relationships with women were, as Margot herself put it, "complicated." To Max and Margot it seemed that Hans placed women into three distinct categories. There were "Madonnas before whom he knelt"; Margot suspected that his Madonna complex owed something to his veneration for his own mother, coupled perhaps with his hatred of his father. At the other extreme were "whores," "by which he did not mean the streetwalkers who carried on an honorable profession." The third category was made up of "female comrades." As Max recalled, Litten not only tended to fall in love with Max's girlfriends, but he also had an unrequited crush on Max's youngest sister, Hanna. Gisela Peiper thought Hanna Fürst represented Hans's Madonna ideal. Peiper had firsthand experience with Hans's idealization. Riding in a cattle car once during a youth movement expedition, she lay on the floor to rest, eyes closed. Thinking she was asleep, Hans said to someone nearby that "next to Hanna Fürst" Gisela was "the only other true Madonna we have."[46]

Hans did manage one partially requited love affair. In the early 1930s he fell in love with a young woman named Sulamith Siliava, and she became the fourth member of the Fürst-Litten household. Sulamith's father had been an actor at the Jewish Theater in Warsaw before moving his family to Berlin. In Berlin he could not support the family with his theatrical earnings; most of their income came from a stall at the Saturday market. Sulamith's husband, the photographer Walter Reuter, described her as very well read. Less generously, Max recalled her as a "somewhat plump" woman who had "broken out of a Turkish harem."[47]

It was clear to Margot that Litten had placed Sulamith in the Madonna category. Despite, or perhaps because of this, and despite the fact that the Fürsts had long wished for Hans to find a girlfriend, they found Sulamith "unbearable," lazy, imperious, and self-dramatizing. She tormented Hans constantly with threats of suicide. To cap it all, the relationship was not exclusive: Sulamith was also already involved with Walter Reuter. Hans and Walter were friends and knew of each other's relationship to Sulamith—something of a pattern for Litten. "The three of us often sat together until late at night at the Café Rosen at Rosenthal Square.... Mostly we talked about art and politics," Reuter recalled. Litten was remarkably generous to his rival. On one occasion Reuter left Berlin in despair, seemingly over Sulamith's connection to Litten. Litten sent him money to come back. Another Litten pattern was mixing work with friendship and romance. Reuter began working regularly for the artistically innovative and politically radical *Workers' Illustrated News* (*AIZ*), and Litten often gave him tips about events or people who might be worthy of a photographer's attention. In 1931 Reuter managed to infiltrate the infamous Berlin squad of Nazi storm troopers, "Storm 33," which by then had become Litten's particular target and was based in Charlottenburg, where Reuter had grown up. Reuter took shots of some of the storm troopers, which duly appeared in the *AIZ*, with accompanying text by Litten.[48]

Later, after his arrest, Hans kept up a steady correspondence with Sulamith, from which we can make several inferences about their relationship. A letter from Hans dated June 1935 goes out of its way to avoid conventional sentimentality, but also reveals a genuine emotional commitment. Sulamith had vented her grief at her separation from Hans and declared her hope that someday they might have a child together (she was married to Reuter by this time). "Dear creature," Hans replied, "I cannot possibly answer your sad little letter in the style and at the length that you would like. First, short and matter-of-fact answers to your four questions: (1) I still know what you look like. (2) I think a lot about you. (3) I seldom dream about you (but also seldom or never about other people who mean a lot to me). (4) I still love you." But by that time it was clear enough to Hans, if not to Sulamith, that they did not have a future.[49]

You Must Change Your Life

In a 1924 essay entitled "Youth and Modern Art," Litten quotes in full Rainer Maria Rilke's "Torso of an Archaic Apollo," a poem that celebrates the profound effect of a work of art, ending with the injunction: "You must change your life."[50]

For Litten, the poem expressed "the only view of art that is permissible for a youth conscious of its responsibilities"—a sentiment that conveyed the essence of Hans Litten, in whose thinking religion, art, and politics always merged to create an unyielding sense of duty. This was one of the spurs that drove him to prosecute Nazis. The other spur was his unremitting fury at his father.[51]

Irmgard Litten believed the young Hans's sense of justice was a legacy from her Lutheran clerical ancestors. Others also thought that a religious moral outlook lay at the base of Litten's character. The Berlin lawyer Rudolf Olden called him a "Franciscan." The radical pacifist intellectual and Litten's cellmate Kurt Hiller wrote in 1935 that Litten was "the most unselfish and helpful of comrades...a true Christian by nature, and also by conviction." Litten's "involved and baroque ideology," said Hiller, stemmed from a mixture of socialism and Catholicism. A few years later, Hiller wrote that Litten "had a complex world view," composed of, among other elements, "primitive Christianity and anarchism," which, he argued, have "a fluid border with one another." Alfred Dreifuss, who was imprisoned with Litten in the late 1930s, recalled that "this crystal-clear dialectician" was "filled with a fervent medieval Madonna cult, which went far beyond the 'religious.'" Litten once asked Dreifuss to light a candle for him at Munich's Asam Chapel if he were ever released. He wrote to Sulamith in 1936 about a novel set in the fourteenth century and written in "the spirit of medieval religiosity" that was "very close to me in its world view." A letter to his mother included a discussion of a portrait of the Madonna in the rose bower, showing that "Mary is the cause of the roses, as in the line 'then the thorns bore roses.'" Hans wanted a photograph of the painting for a friend "who knows that the dead grove of thorns really bears roses when Mary passes by with the child next to her heart—something most people in our century no longer know."[52]

However, long before Litten had formed his own version of medieval Catholicism, he carried on an ostentatious affair with the Judaism his father had abandoned. In his final year of high school he chose Hebrew as an elective subject and began to go to the synagogue. He took up Jewish mysticism and went so far as to visit the small Hassidic synagogue in Königsberg. Kurt Sabatzky, the Central Union man in Königsberg, remembered seeing him in the synagogue on Yom Kippur and asked him point blank, "How do you stand on religion?" Litten replied, "I live in my parents' house, where they don't want to know anything of Judaism." Though he had been confirmed in the Evangelical Church, this was purely a "legal matter." "By conviction," he told Sabatzky, "I am a Jew with all my heart."[53]

Litten's attachment to Judaism, taken together with his mother's conspicuous evasiveness about his Jewish heritage, has led to controversy. Sabatzky argued that it was "a serious historical deficiency" that in her writings Irmgard Litten "did not have the courage to say that her son was pursued with all the hate of the Nazis, not just as an alleged Communist, which in reality he was not, but also as the Jew Litten." Why, he wondered, was "this otherwise very brave woman so unforthcoming in this connection?" Sabatzky did not seek to answer his own question, but in fact the answer was clear enough. Irmgard Litten's memoir of Hans, *A Mother Fights Hitler*, was published in Great Britain during the Second World War. Irmgard herself wrote in 1951 that "on the advice of experienced anti-fascists" she had intentionally designed the book so that "it could not fail to have an effect even on conservative readers." This was a careful way of saying that conservative readers would be more impressed by Litten's Christianity than his Judaism.[54]

At the same time, as the recollections of Kurt Hiller and Alfred Dreifuss show, Litten's attachment to Christianity was every bit as real as his commitment to Judaism. His religious faith accommodated complexity. The words of the prophets, he told Max Fürst, just like works of art, were simultaneously involved in this world and the other. The moment they found "earthly expression" they instantly became bound by the laws of matter and reflected the economic, social, and psychological circumstances of their creation. For both art and religion there could only ever be "approaches," never "definitive proof."[55]

Max Fürst had some shrewd things to say about his friend's attachment to Judaism. In a 1939 letter to Irmgard, he remembered that one of the first things he had learned about her son was that, unlike his father, Hans insisted on his Jewishness "at every opportunity." The father-son feud was not the only explanation for this. Max believed that Hans took after his Christian mother much more than his formerly Jewish father. Once, as Hans was insisting on his Jewishness, Max wrote, "I pressed: that everyone emphasizes most about himself what he is missing." The remark made Hans angry, itself a confirmation of its accuracy.[56]

Many years later Max offered another explanation for Hans's Jewish identity: "He wanted to be a Jew as he later became the advocate of the workers," he wrote, because Litten "stood on the side of the downtrodden." Eva Eichelbaum, who knew Max and Hans through the youth movement, and as a lawyer in Berlin worked with Hans in the 1930s, recalled in the 1990s that anti-Semitism "was blooming" in East Prussia, "as always," just as the Comrades were being formed. "All the more remarkable was it for me that Hans Litten joined, of all things, a Jewish group. Why? He was a half-Jew. . . . Hans Litten counted himself among the Jews."[57]

In any case, it was the political principles Litten derived from his faith that mattered. That the source of his political and legal actions was his religious faith seems beyond question, even if that faith remains mysterious and controversial. Max and Margot Fürst, who knew Litten as well as anyone, insisted in later years that his politics were separate from his faith. But in the late 1930s, Max also wrote of Litten that "he was a Marxist and he was religious, and both determined his actions," and Litten's own writings are saturated with religious ideas.[58]

Litten believed in "the calling of the twentieth century to religion" and counted himself among the adherents of the "strong religious tendency" within the youth movement. This was not mere rhetoric. "Religion is responsibility before God," he wrote. "Think that through to the end!" In a 1925 essay, he warned members of the youth movement against abstaining from political action for fear of losing their souls. "Man cannot live without guilt," he insisted; "therefore we must have the courage to accept guilt and responsibility." There is an unmistakable connection here: religion is responsibility before God; political action requires the courage to accept both responsibility and guilt. His unbending sense of duty drove him to seek prohibitions of tobacco, alcohol, and social dancing in the youth movement. Those who had joined for fun and games could leave, he said, "and we will be glad to be free of them." Those who stayed needed to understand that the movement demanded "the whole person," which meant that it demanded sacrifices. Litten's writings often play on the contrast between outward conduct and inner belief, the latter much more important than the former. A true believer, he wanted only true believers around him. "Laws can regulate only outer actions, and all outer actions are worthless when they do not arise from inner necessity."[59]

The course of Litten's later life flows almost inevitably from the words of this twenty-year-old law student: responsibility before God and before one's fellow creatures; the duty to act, heedless of the consequences; the uncompromising allegiance to an idea, the involvement of the whole person; the "inner necessity"; almost, perhaps, the will to martyrdom—all are here.

If a rigorous conception of personal and social responsibility was one wellspring of Hans Litten's choices in life, his long-running and extraordinarily bitter feud with his father was another. "These three Litten sons," says Hans's niece Patricia Litten, "had a gigantic problem with this father." Aside from "all the historical connections," she added, the Litten story was a family tragedy. But as much as Hans raged at his father, he could not escape him: "He studied a subject he hated" because, even for Hans, "a father's word weighed so heavily." In Patricia's view, pursuing the law became for Hans a form of revenge. "I have the feeling that he took the path that he did not least in order to get back at his father once and for all." Or, as her husband, Johannes Blum, adds, "to beat him with his own stick." If so, Hans's revenge was calculated with exquisite shrewdness. For Fritz, the law was a path to acceptance into the most elite reaches of Prussian society. For Hans, it was a lever of revolution. In the face of Fritz's "Just no relapses," Hans took as clients the poor and destitute—willing himself to be the relapse.[60]

In his Black Mob days Litten insisted that the struggle between generations took precedence over the struggle between classes, and generational conflict was a constant theme in a number of articles he wrote for the anarchist newspaper *Black Flag* in the late 1920s. One of the defining legal-cultural events of that time in Berlin was the Krantz trial of 1928, in which the seventeen-year-old high school student Paul Krantz was charged with the murder of two young men after a night of heavy drinking and sexual jealousy involving the sister of one of the dead men. Litten thought this tragedy and its legal ramifications boiled down to "The Old Against the Young," the title of a Black Mob leaflet reprinted in *Black Flag*, which either came from Litten's pen or was at least strongly influenced by his ideas. "This trial," it read, "is only one episode out of [this] battle, which is carried out daily and hourly in a thousand forms and under a thousand masks." The old relied on a set of institutions to "gag and suppress" the young: schools and parents' associations, the justice system and the press, medical and "pedagogical" experts. Whatever transgressions young people might commit paled in comparison to the massive and systematic crimes these institutions inflicted on them.[61]

Indeed, Litten always wrote as if lurking somewhere behind anything he disliked or anyone he opposed was "the old Litten." When another young man was convicted of murder, Litten wrote that "*Rage-drunk fathers*" had generated, if not the verdict, "then at least the mental framework, out of which the verdict becomes explicable" (my emphasis). Young people had an absolute right to self-determination—this from a young man whom paternal will had obliged to study law rather than philology or art. It followed that the worst thing Litten could say of another youth movement activist was that he had dared to "work together with elements we are fighting, such as the parental house."[62]

Litten's contempt for the norms of middle-class family life could be positively toxic. In another *Black Flag* article from 1929 he wrote about several teen suicides that, "devoid of piety as youth is," occurred on Christmas Eve, "the evening of the year on which bourgeois family hypocrisy tends to reach its peak," when all "fall movingly into each others' arms, glance with 'misty eyes' toward the Christmas tree and mime for an hour 'harmonious family life.' " The tone hardly suggests fond memories of the joys of Christmas *chez* Litten. In another suggestive passage he argued that the elimination of corporal punishment was irrelevant to the real abuse young people endured in schools and reformatories. "There are psychological abuses that are a hundred times worse and long-lasting. . . . I know children who have never received a blow, but through ingenious psychological abuse have been made defective for life."[63]

The Hans Litten who comes through such writings is shrill, intolerant, puritanical, and humorless. He liked to quote Nietzsche—"It is the task of youth to 'philosophize with the hammer' "—and there is something pretentiously Nietzschean about his stance in these writings, as well as in his later trial work: that of the lone truth-teller surrounded by knaves, fools, cowards, and traitors. As a student and a judicial clerk Litten went to political meetings simply to voice scathing criticisms of the speakers (later, often a featured speaker at such meetings himself, he voiced scathing criticisms of the other speakers). His treatment of those who angered him could be blistering, even when they were friends or colleagues. In a 1927 letter to the leader of the Bund, Julius Freund, he characterized Freund's views on school reform as an "indicator of the rapidly progressing liquidation of the youth movement, as it is now being systematically carried out even in our Bund under your responsible leadership," and denounced the "scorn (concealing a bad conscience)" with which Freund attacked those "who have not gone along with the general betrayal of the youth movement." In 1929 Litten was incensed by a critique of the playwright Peter Lampel from a Social Democrat who charged Lampel with being, among other things, gay. "This excess of filth is really only possible in Germany. In no other land would it be possible that such a woman could open her mouth without the entire meeting, irrespective of party affiliation, rising up and spitting in her face."[64]

And yet Litten's strident poses must be understood in the light, as he himself might say, of his whole person. His political grandstanding and his trial work owed much to his tendency to self-dramatization. Margot Fürst said in an interview that Litten "had a flair for the dramatic . . . contemplative conduct was not his style." Self-dramatization was certainly an element of his summoning Hitler as a witness, his repeated efforts to prosecute Berlin's Police Chief Karl Zörgiebel, and the steady crescendo of conflict with courts and judges that dominated the last year and a half of his career. It played a role, too, in his imprisonment, especially in the first year and the last.[65]

A great gulf separated the public and private Hans Litten. "It is especially difficult for me to express myself at all personally," he wrote, and indeed, for someone so merciless in his dealings with opponents, he was painfully awkward in normal social situations. In a letter to Sulamith, he describes how several characters in the novel *Lost Earth* by the expressionist writer Alfred Brust "sit together at dinner, and within a few minutes turn deep red from embarrassment at 'being there at all,' because they are all of 'a stolid temper' and therefore cannot even begin a conversation." Litten believed this to be "a particularly characteristic inherited trait of our East Prussian landscape." Max Fürst wrote that despite his gifts Litten was tormented by feelings of unworthiness and inferiority. Margot recalled that this fierce advocate of youthful independence did not dare to address his law partner, Ludwig Barbasch, with the informal "Du," but rather stayed with the polite "Sie" and used "Herr Colleague" instead of a first name because Barbasch was eleven years Litten's senior. Max observed that this passionate revolutionary "did not like any changes" in his private life and was traumatized by moves from one apartment to another.[66]

Litten's unworldliness sat oddly with his toughness as a trial lawyer. He was, as Margot put it, "helpless with everyday things." He was almost incapable of crossing a street, suspecting that every car was trying to kill him. On the other hand he was slow to perceive real dangers, because, as Max recalled, "he had long since thought through all presumed dangers and the defense against them." Litten often failed to recognize signs of inebriation and would try to talk a drunk into behaving reasonably. Margot told a story about his reaction to a popular song of the 1920s, which told of "drinking away grandmother's house," along with "the first and second mortgages." One day Litten and the Fürsts heard the song being sung by someone who was himself slightly tipsy. Hans stopped to lecture the singer on his misstatements of mortgage law.[67]

He preferred books to people. "He had absolutely no understanding of people," Margot remembered. He could not bring himself to ask his own secretary to perform the most routine office tasks, sometimes summoning Margot from the Aafa film company to sharpen his pencils or make him a mocha. "He needed someone who could comfort him," said Margot. Nonetheless Litten's unwavering belief in education and self-improvement could overcome his shyness. He had a touchingly serious faith in popular education. Before his Assessor exam, he and Max would spend entire days at the café Mocha-Efti in Alexander Square drafting articles for youth movement newspapers. The prostitutes who frequented the café would sometimes grow curious about what the young men were writing so earnestly. "Since Hans could never refuse enlightenment when anyone asked for it, he read them our philosophical articles, or whatever we had just written. . . . They listened very seriously and thanked us politely."[68]

Margot Fürst told a story that underscored both Litten's reverence for books and his Prussian self-discipline. Once Litten flew into a rage about something or other and picked up a pile of books on a table in order to slam them down again. But because he could not actually bring himself to inflict such wanton violence on his books, he checked himself at the last second. "Rigor," said Margot, "was one of his characteristics."[69]

In politics Hans Litten stood rigorously far to the left. He saw the "proletarian class struggle" as the only means by which "humanity can be freed from the curse of the present social order." This belief, he continued, was drawn from Marx. Being a revolutionary involves an acceptance of political violence. Litten went so far as to say, "I am a radical socialist; I have rejected putting the Bund on a pacifist foundation."[70]

But Litten's brand of socialism was resolutely nonpartisan; indeed, his individualism rendered him an unsuitable member of any party. "Two people are too many for my party" is a remark often attributed to him, one that suggests a good degree of self-awareness. To his law partner, Ludwig Barbasch, Litten was "a fanatic left-wing man, who struggled always for his own opinion, and hated nothing more than the word 'opportunism.'" Litten claimed, as Rudolf Olden remembered, that he stood "far left of the KPD [the Communist Party of Germany]," and indeed Litten voiced contempt for the policies and the leadership of the KPD while dedicating himself to the party's rank and file. Some of this contempt stemmed from his dislike of the Party's constant, often purely expedient ideological shifts; some of it had to do with a rejection of the Party's slavish dependence on the Soviet Union, so that it could not "act freely in the interests of German workers," as Margot Fürst later put it. Sometimes Litten's quarrels with the leadership involved more practical matters. The Communist Party leadership, Margot recalled, really wanted political trials to create "inside Comrades" (*Sitzgenossen*), martyrs whose sentencing would expose the corruption of capitalist "justice." From this standpoint, Litten's efforts to secure acquittals were counterproductive. Indeed, Barbasch recalled hearing many complaints from Communist Party members about Litten's refusal to toe the line. "Leading persons" in the Red Aid, the Party's legal support group, asked Barbasch to intervene with Litten so that he would at least not air his differences so publicly. "Litten was very much excited about the demands of the 'Bonzen' [party bosses]," Barbasch wrote, "and threatened to lay down all the cases given to him by the Red Aid movement." A breach was avoided only through the intervention of friends. Berlin's political police, always zealous where the Red Aid was concerned, were well informed about these differences. In September 1932 one of the directors of the Red Aid told an undercover police agent that Litten was "very unpopular" with them and complained of "endless quarrels." The Red Aid even thought (most misguidedly) that "until just a few years ago [Litten] was still a Zionist."[71]

As little as he respected the leaders of the KPD, Litten had even greater contempt for the other major German working-class party, the Social Democratic Party (SPD), the pillar of the democratic Weimar Republic. "The quintessential party of lack of political principle" was one of his kinder characterizations. The SPD was an "international" party that had voted to fund a capitalist world war; it was a workers' party that counted among its leaders the "bloodhound" Gustav Noske, "who caused 15,000 workers to be murdered." These SPD "conversions" were, he believed, a product of pure opportunism, a turn to the stronger side. "Their conversions have always brought them something."[72]

Litten was no friend of the Weimar Republic, and it would certainly be wrong to see his legal activism as a defense of the democratic republic in the face of the Nazi menace. He denounced the Republic's capitalism and mocked its weakness, its "enormous comedy." "At that time, at the end of the Weimar Republic, we were against democracy," wrote Max Fürst, a statement in which the "we" can be taken to include Litten. In the 1990s Margot recalled that neither she nor Max nor Hans ever voted during Weimar. "We took the position that politically effective work could not be done with elections."[73]

If it is clear enough what Hans Litten was against, what was he for? He had a faith in collective actions at odds with his individualism, and indeed with some of his more elitist tendencies. "We are not alone in the world," he admonished members of the Bund in 1925. "Our actions or failures to act are connected with a thousand threads, forward and backwards, to the organism of the society in which we live." The individual was "powerless against the laws of social development." He dismissed Freudian psychology as an "individual solution of the 19th century." It was a mistake to attempt to heal psychological problems that were really products of social conditions. Individual troubles might even serve as a "spur" to "revolutionize the bourgeois order." Only ideas, or works of art, that were in some way products of a community had validity. He introduced his essay "Youth and Modern Art" with the apologetic disclaimer that it was "in part from me, that is, from one individual person, and thus is necessarily dilettantish and unsystematic."[74]

In his magisterial biography of Adolf Hitler, the historian Joachim Fest speculates that the most quintessentially German quality of the National Socialist movement was its perverted idealism: its uncompromisingly radical embrace of the power of an idea over reality, and its consequent hostility to reality. Though he dwelled at the opposite end of the political spectrum, Litten shared these qualities. Ludwig Barbasch recalled that Litten preferred an "idealistic cultural view, in which the principle of selection was prevailing," to the Marxist doctrine of material causes for historical events. As with the Nazis of Fest's description, Litten held this view with a fervor that could easily slide into authoritarianism. "Before us stands an image of human beings that is to become reality," Litten wrote in a 1926 essay on artistic education. "Knowledge only has purpose for us insofar as it serves education in accordance with this image. The enrichment of knowledge out of pure interest is an irresponsible waste of time." On another occasion he wrote, "A lack of consciousness of rank order is a sign of intellectual superficiality," leading to a failure to grasp "that the errors of the great are more important than the truths of the small." As always with Litten, religious imperatives were never far from cultural or political ones. Art was not there to serve people, he wrote; the "correct" idea was that people were to serve art. "In today's society, art, just like divine service, is degraded as an enjoyment or a means of education. One goes to church to 'be uplifted' or for moral improvement, but not to serve God."[75]

"Correct" and "incorrect" were in fact the crucial evaluative categories for Litten. A youth group member who had been on a tour Litten led through the Bamberg Cathedral remembered that "a girl spoke admiringly of how beautiful something was." Hans replied sternly that "beauty" was not a concept. A thing was either "correct" or "incorrect." Sometimes, however, beauty could transcend category. Gisela Peiper remembered Hans's explanation of the figure of Christ outside the Lorenz Church in Nuremberg: "Look, feel it! This is suffering, but the breast bones also have the form of the arch." The figure of Christ, he said, combined "the suffering and the spiritual intent." After the Second World War, Peiper, by then Gisela Konopka, returned to Nuremberg and found that the church had been destroyed by bombing—all except the side walls and the Christ figure. "I saw it in the evening glow with the red sun touching the suffering body. There, to me, was Hans again."[76]

Litten & Barbasch

Litten's second state bar or Assessor exam in the spring of 1928 was an ordeal both for him and for Max Fürst. Litten had completed his required clerkship at a court in Königsberg at the end of August 1927. Two months later he moved to Berlin to prepare for the exam—or at least that was the idea.[77]

The Assessor exam had an oral and a written component. Berlin candidates for the oral exam were summoned to the Prussian Justice Ministry, where they appeared before a commission consisting of judges, law professors, and senior civil servants with legal training. For the written portion the candidate was supposed to demonstrate a mastery of substantive areas of law as well as an ability to marshal arguments in the solution of a particular legal problem. The candidate was given precisely three weeks to submit the finished essay.[78]

Litten spent most of his preparation time for this ordeal sitting with Max in the café Mocha-Efti drinking endless cups of coffee and writing his "polemical essays on politics, art and life." He had a pile of books from the library that he resolutely ignored. Meanwhile he tormented Max with constant complaints that he would never be able to cope with the work and that "all this legal stuff was idiotic anyway." If Max tried to press him to study, Litten would "withdraw into depression and could not be spoken to any longer." This behavior, according to Max, was entirely typical for Hans and was based on the "feelings of inferiority and depression which he had before every action, whether an exam or a trial." On the other hand, Litten would compensate for his periods of lassitude and despair with superhuman bouts of hard work. He himself claimed that he was manic-depressive. Margot recalled that Litten's moods "alternated frequently," and on days in which he was in "poor form" he "despaired of the entire world."[79]

Combined with adroit handling from Max and Margot, Litten's intellect and memory came to the rescue. Two weeks before the essay was due, Max forced a "fierce argument" with Hans. "I threatened to move out and leave him alone." Hans was furious, but he went to a typing service and dictated his essay off the top of his head. The paper was graded "Good"—a high and rare distinction in the German grading scale. Then, before the oral exam, he went back to the same routine: protesting that he would never be able to pass, and then rallying at the last minute. He passed the exam on May 23, 1928, with a grade of "Fully Satisfactory," a notch below "Good." Litten thus achieved the rank of Assessor, but, as he had no desire to become a servant of the state, a judge, or a prosecutor, the Prussian Justice Ministry gave him a formal release from state service at the end of June. "His conduct in and out of office was beyond reproach," the ministry recorded in his file. On September 22 he was admitted to practice as a lawyer at the venerable Kammergericht, the Court of Appeal for the city of Berlin and (in those days) the surrounding province of Brandenburg.[80]

The years of education and professional training were over, and the Black Mob was a memory. It was time for Litten to decide how, where, and with whom to practice law. His talents and his pedigree ensured that he had no lack of options. He turned down offers from the Ministry of Justice and from prosperous private lawyers. He declined even a well-paid half-time position, explaining to Irmgard that he could not waste "even a moment." Litten worked briefly for the Communist Party, doing the kind of paperwork that even a revolutionary organization requires if it is going to rent office space and hire employees. But both the nature of the work and of the employer ensured that this was hardly a more congenial place for Litten than the Prussian bureaucracy. Instead, through friends, he found his way to Ludwig Barbasch, a radical socialist lawyer and stalwart of the Red Aid.[81]

Barbasch was born in Berlin in 1892, the son of a small manufacturer. Max Fürst recalled him as a revolutionary "with bourgeois meticulousness and the solidity of a bookkeeper." As a student Barbasch worked in the office of Karl Liebknecht, hero of the German radical left (and a Berlin trial lawyer). He had just completed his legal education and passed the first bar exam, the *Referendar* exam, when war broke out in August 1914. Barbasch volunteered for military service and served throughout the war, seeing combat in 1915 and 1916. His last post was at a flight training school in the small northern state of Mecklenburg-Schwerin. He joined the Independent Social Democratic Party—the party of those on the far left who had broken with the mainstream Social Democrats in opposition to the war—and after the war he became a minister without portfolio in the new Socialist administration of Mecklenburg-Schwerin. In January he participated in a coup that sought to cast aside the coalition of majority and independent Social Democrats and create a more radical government. The coup failed. Barbasch was arrested by the local Workers' and Soldiers' Council, one of the many such institutions that had sprouted all over Germany in the revolutionary climate of 1918–19. The Council initially sentenced Barbasch to death, but then, after twelve days, let him go.[82]

Barbasch returned to Berlin to resume his legal career. To do so he needed to complete his clerkship, and given his revolutionary record it was not certain that the state would allow him to do so. After some consideration, the president of Berlin's Court of Appeal gave Barbasch a position at a court in the small Brandenburg town of Prenzlau. Soon Barbasch was giving rabble-rousing speeches, advocating the establishment of a Soviet-style system in Germany. He was transferred to Königsberg, apparently in the belief that he would do less damage there. He managed to finish his clerkship and pass his Assessor exam at the end of 1921, whereupon he returned to Berlin and opened a law practice. When he wrote to the Prussian justice minister formally requesting his release from the justice department, he noted forthrightly that "to remain further in state service would be irreconcilable with my (Communist) political convictions." Barbasch became a member of a splinter group called the Communist Workers' Party, a group that, drawing inspiration from Rosa Luxemburg and opposing the centralism of Stalin, saw itself as standing to the left of the KPD.[83]

Barbasch left a record of his first meeting with Litten, in awkward but serviceable English, that says much about both men. It was in the late summer of 1928; Litten, the newly minted assessor, "desired to enter an office in which he had an opportunity to defend political criminal cases." Barbasch wanted to be relieved of precisely this part of his practice because he wished to concentrate on labor law, "of which I was becom[ing] a specialist." They had a long conversation about politics. Litten said that he had come to Barbasch because Barbasch was one of the few left-leaning lawyers who was a member of neither the Social Democratic Party nor the Communist Party. Litten explained that he could never work with a lawyer who belonged to one of the main Socialist parties because "he was a strict opponent of every centralized organization."[84]

Litten and Barbasch did not agree on everything. "His point of view was, for me, a very strange mixture of different incoherent elements, which I did not share at all," Barbasch recalled. "But I recognized his strong ethical feeling and his endeavour for truth, so that I did not attach great weight to our differences of opinion." For all of his political radicalism, Max recalled, Barbasch was a tolerant man, "otherwise he could hardly have gotten along with his unruly partner," who was, besides, eleven years his junior.[85]

In September 1928 Litten and Barbasch established a joint office in the Molken Market, moving in 1931 to King Street, next to Berlin's "Red City Hall" (so named for its bricks and not for its politics) near Alexander Square. "It was not a pompous office," Max Fürst recalled. "It rather reminded me of a bank in the truly old style." Entering the office, one was in a room divided by a wooden barrier, in which two secretaries worked, along with the office manager, who was in fact Barbasch's father: a "lively little man" with "beard and mistrustful eye." There were separate, very small offices for Litten and Barbasch themselves. "The whole thing looked thoroughly commonplace and bourgeois; certainly one would never suspect that in the other two rooms resided a couple of revolutionaries." But then, as Max noted, "no matter how idealistic, in the end even a lawyer's office is a business."[86]

A good part of the business that Litten conducted at Litten & Barbasch, especially before 1931, must have consisted of the sort of mundane work—wills, divorces, contracts—with which most lawyers pay their bills. This work is largely lost to the historical record, but we have a few indications of how much of it there must have been. Max recalled that even before Margot went to work as Litten's secretary, Litten would often call her in to his office in the evening to dictate documents to her, especially for the divorce cases. Litten considered it "out of the question" to dictate such delicate matters to the other secretary, although she was older than Margot. Max's recollection that Hans earned good money from his practice in 1929, as well as his passing reference to Margot's intention to study law so that she could eventually take over Hans's civil cases, also suggest that there was a large volume of this routine, nonpolitical work.[87]

Soon, however, the balance of Litten's practice shifted to the less lucrative political cases. Margot recalled that after 1930 Litten was "almost completely" occupied with criminal cases for the Red Aid, which inevitably meant, given the Red Aid's own shaky finances, that the payments were meager and slow to arrive. Unlike most prominent Berlin lawyers, including the politically active Alfred Apfel and Rudolf Olden, Litten was willing to work for little or no fee. The receipts were seldom enough to cover his costs; he struggled to make up the balance with those wills and divorces. Until early in 1930 Litten was still drawing an allowance from his father; then their steadily deteriorating relationship closed off this avenue as well.

The more his fame as a political lawyer grew, the less time there was for other cases. Often he would ask other lawyers to stand in for him for minor appearances. Two of the friends who helped him in this way were the pioneering female lawyers Eva Eichelbaum, whom Litten had known in Königsberg, and Hilde Benjamin, sister-in-law of Walter Benjamin and later East German justice minister. Margot reported that while Litten was occupied for most of 1932 with the huge Felseneck case, he farmed out all of his files to another lawyer, paying him more than the Red Aid paid Litten for Felseneck. After Litten was arrested in 1933, his mother had to settle his arrears of office rent.[88]

Litten's letters from the early 1930s paint a lively picture of his precarious finances. While in the middle of the Eden Dance Palace trial, Litten asked his mother to send him the rest of the money due to him from his grandmother's estate "as quickly as possible." He explained that "because of the big trial the smaller sources of income fell off, since I hardly had time this month for other cases." Although he would earn a good fee for the Eden Dance Palace case it would "probably only cover [my] debts and the cost of the move (we have to move our office next month)." On another occasion, he wrote that "the swine" from the department of revenue had accepted his application for a deferral. "I can't collect my outstanding debts with the same methods as the revenue department," he told his mother, "otherwise I would be punished with at least three months in prison for loan-sharking, and expelled from the legal profession for dishonorable conduct." In the same letter, he wrote of another upcoming trial of Nazi storm troopers for the killing of a worker named Riemenschneider. He would be acting for the private prosecutors. But "there probably won't be any money, since the court won't appoint me any more and the Red Aid is broke." He could not give the case to any other lawyer, as Nazi murders were his "specialty." "In short," Litten concluded, "everything looks great."[89]

The Red Aid of Germany (*Rote Hilfe Deutschlands*) was founded in 1924 as the German chapter of an international organization urged by the new Bolshevik regime in the USSR. Although managed by Communists, the Red Aid claimed to be a nonpartisan organization whose goal was supporting "proletarian class-warriors, who are arrested because of politically motivated actions or because of their political beliefs," along with "the wives and children of those arrested, [and of] fallen or invalided class warriors." The Red Aid's first leader was Wilhelm Pieck, later president of East Germany, followed by the

Communist Reichstag deputy Clara Zetkin. But support for its work also came from many liberal and Social Democratic artists and intellectuals, such as Albert Einstein, the writer Kurt Tucholsky, and the artists Käthe Kollwitz and Heinrich Zille. The novelist Heinrich Mann wrote, "Many innocent men...have only the Red Aid. The Red Aid is above all a civilizing work, to counteract the barbarism that threatens us."[90]

Around three hundred German lawyers took on clients at least occasionally for the Red Aid. They were not in it for the money. At a time when the Reichsmark (RM) was valued at a little over 4 to the U.S. dollar, the Red Aid paid its lawyers 40 RM per day for ordinary trials, 80 for a trial in the jury court. Certain kinds of appeals could also bring in 80 RM per day, and there were miscellaneous payments for preparing documents, visiting clients in prison, and for meals and overnight expenses. But the Red Aid was chronically short of funds, and in November 1931 lawyers had to agree to a "temporary" 50 percent reduction in the tariff. Information compiled by the secret police after the Nazis took over shows that the Red Aid paid Litten 665 RM in 1930 and 2,815.15 RM in 1931; Barbasch received a total of 5,288.90 RM. From this money the two lawyers had to pay their employees and run their office, as well as eat.[91]

His dedication to his work made Litten a hero to his clients. One of his early clients, a man named Bernhard Behnke, left an account of his first meeting with Litten, offering a striking picture of how this shy and cerebral son of a privileged family earned the admiration of the tough young Berlin workers who formed the bulk of his client base. Behnke, then a teenager, was arrested one May evening as he and a group of friends marched singing through the streets of Friedrichshain. A squad of police stopped them and charged them with breach of the peace. Some of the young men claimed the police had beaten them. They were told that they would be put through an expedited trial; for the older boys the likely outcome would be three months in jail, for the younger ones 300 Mark fines or three weeks in jail. The Red Aid got wind of the arrests and sent Litten to represent the young men. Litten was able to argue the case down to small fines for all the boys, which were in any event not imposed as the case fell under the terms of an amnesty. More than fifty years later Behnke vividly remembered the impact Hans Litten made on these vulnerable young workers:

At the time I did not yet know him personally. He seemed surprisingly youthful, slender, lively, and was completely informal. He greeted us and introduced himself as our attorney from the Red Aid. I had always imagined a lawyer very differently.... He spoke to us in a comradely way, addressed us as young comrades and was immediately using "Du." His natural, friendly manner immediately won him our trust.... Thus I got to know Hans Litten as a person who knew what he wanted, and on whom we workers could rely.[92]

The political cases Litten took on in his first year of practice dealt in various ways with the revolutions and counterrevolutions, coup attempts, and political assassinations of the turbulent years between 1918 and 1923. His first commission from the Red Aid was to represent men imprisoned after the "Central German Uprising" of 1921, arguing for their release under the terms of an amnesty. Next came work on behalf of the printer and publisher Ernst Friedrich. Friedrich put out the weekly newspaper the *Black Flag* (*Schwarze Fahne*) that mixed anarchist politics with irreverent humor. In July 1928 he devoted an entire issue of his paper to Gustav Noske, the former defense minister in the first postwar Social Democratic government. The banner headline was "Noske: The Murderer Laughs." Noske had earned notoriety in early 1919 by organizing the brutal suppression of revolts by revolutionary groups to the left of the Social Democrats, the Communists, and "Spartacists." "Someone has to be the bloodhound," the unabashed Noske had explained. Friedrich spoke for a broad current of opinion on the German left when he wrote that "to every feeling person" Noske must seem "a scoundrel and a villain." A few days later, Noske filed a request to prosecute Friedrich for libel. In October the public prosecutor issued an indictment.[93]

Foreshadowing the method he would use against Hitler, Litten, twenty-five years old and in the first months of his legal practice, decided to defend Friedrich by summoning Noske himself to confirm "that in his former capacity as supreme commander and Reich Minister of Defense he committed a number of actions that justify his characterization with the expressions 'scoundrel' and 'villain.'" Litten's motion to summon Noske explained that in 1917 and 1918, Noske had "used" his position as a Social Democratic Reichstag deputy, given to him through "the trust of the proletariat," to lobby potentially revolutionary sailors to keep up their faith in Germany's war effort. Thus Noske, the "workers' representative," had helped to prolong the "slaughter of proletarians, called the 'World War.'" "Anyone who so acts," Litten concluded, "is, in the eyes of the revolutionary proletariat, a scoundrel and a villain." When revolution broke out across Germany at the end of 1918, Noske "set himself at the head of the movement, with the intention of choking it as soon as possible." Again came the conclusion: "Anyone who so acts, is, in the eyes of the revolutionary proletariat, a scoundrel and a villain." On January 6, 1919, Noske was named the new Social Democratic government's supreme military commander. "In this capacity he suppressed the German proletariat with a brutality that had not even been used against the so-called 'external enemy' in four years of mass slaughter." "Anyone who so acts," came the now slightly modified refrain, "is not only in the eyes of the revolutionary proletariat, but in the eyes of every humane person, a scoundrel and a villain." And so it continued. The motion was signed with the proud, looping signature "Litten. Advocate."[94]

The motion was a kind of declaration of independence. Litten was giving notice that he would be a new kind of lawyer. German trial lawyers of the early twentieth century were no different from lawyers in any other time and place in believing that their job mostly demanded the gentle art of persuasion. Erich Frey, one of the most eminent criminal defense lawyers in Weimar Berlin, boasted, "I always preferred the foil to the heavy sword, and certainly to the wooden hammer." Even in political cases, the lawyer Rudolf Olden wrote, Berlin lawyers were more likely to rely on the traditional arsenal of lawyers' tricks, emotion, or "vocal extravagance" than fierce polemic.[95]

Hans Litten was never this kind of lawyer. His radicalism, according to Olden, was not a matter of form; it was a matter of substance: "Questions and requests for evidence...sometimes seemed to encompass remote subjects, even the whole structure of the state, when the case seemed only to be about a street brawl." One could hardly expect a German judge of the Weimar era to read without irritation the phrase "revolutionary proletariat," and provoking judicial annoyance seldom benefits a lawyer's client. Nonetheless, once he had analyzed a case and found a legal avenue—often an innovative one—to support his client, Litten never bothered with Frey's foil. He spoke always as a man who knew he was right, and his advocacy was, in every sense, revolutionary. Everyone at the criminal courts in Berlin-Moabit knew it. "An uncomfortable opponent—yes, that he was, but he did not see it as his task to be comfortable," said Olden. "At the height of his work in Moabit, I once sought to persuade Litten that he might be a little less intransigent, sometimes let things go and not always push things to the limit; otherwise we would not have him long in Moabit, and we could really use him. He replied that he was convinced that in any case our legal system would not last much longer, and for that reason alone he saw no grounds for concessions. I have to admit he saw what was coming more clearly than I did."[96]

Gustav Noske's libel case against Ernst Friedrich went to trial on March 14, 1929. The court found that Friedrich's words were insulting and that the truth of their content was beside the point and convicted him of libel. However, the judges took into account as mitigating factors "the origins of the defendant in proletarian circles" as well as "the politically hostile stance of the defendant to the complainant." The court gave Friedrich one month in prison.[97]

Litten paid for his aggressive defense of Friedrich with his own first (but far from last) clash with authority. The Berlin Lawyers' Chamber (the bar's official ruling body) formally reprimanded Litten for having made Noske's libel of Friedrich "his own," thus abusing his position as defense counsel. Records show that Prussian Justice Minister Hermann Schmidt also thought that Litten's motion "far exceeded tolerable limits," and he sought, unsuccessfully, to have Litten prosecuted criminally for it. The pattern for Litten's brief career was set. He would not follow Olden's advice; he would not live carefully. He would push every argument to the edge and make enemies of prosecutors, judges, police, and colleagues, as well as the brown-shirted Nazis and their leader.[98]

May Day

In the middle of 1929, Litten became involved in a series of cases that were to shape the rest of his life. These cases were also connected to the violence of Weimar's early years, though in a different way from

Friedrich's battle with Noske. One of the legacies of the Noske era was an enduring hatred between the major parties of the German left, the Social Democrats and the Communists. May Day 1929 would give Litten ample opportunity to show that he shared the Communists' contempt for the Social Democrats.

The fate of the Social Democrats in Weimar is a sad lesson in the dilemmas, compromises, and even betrayals inherent in the exercise of power by reasonable people in an unreasonable time. In 1929 the Social Democrats were the dominant party in the governing coalition in Prussia and, briefly, the leading party in the Reich government as well. Control of the state of Prussia brought with it control of Prussia's vital administrative positions, such as the office of Berlin police chief, which in 1929 was held by the Social Democrat Karl Zörgiebel. Since 1889, May 1 had been the day for workers' demonstrations, a fact to which Berliners might have expected Social Democrats to be sensitive. But the rising tide of political violence, especially from the right, meant that, as Zörgiebel himself proclaimed, demonstrations would constitute an "immediate danger to public security." A prohibition of all open-air demonstrations had been in force in Berlin since December 1928. Zörgiebel decided that he could not permit the left what he had forbidden the right, and he did not provide an exemption from the ban for workers' marches on May 1. Relishing a chance to embarrass the Social Democrats, the Communist Party announced that it would defy the ban.[99]

Germany's interior ministries suffered from growing paranoia in the run-up to May 1. Police informants across the country attended Communist meetings, public and private, and reported on speeches, plans, and threats. A nervous memo of April 23 from the Reich commissar for the supervision of public order to the Reich minister of the interior reported that the notorious revolutionary Max Hölz had announced he would go to Berlin for May 1, "where we will fight for the streets, cost what it may." The Reich commissar urged that "particular attention" be paid to this declaration. Two weeks before, a police informant in Stuttgart had submitted a report on a speech Hölz gave there in front of eighteen hundred people. "A wild fanaticism shone through all of his words," said the agent, who also noted that Hölz "found lively agreement from the majority of his hearers as he reported cynically on the acts of terror he had committed."[100]

Hölz's words suggest that the paranoia of the officials had some foundation. Through informers officials knew of the Communist Party's internal decisions. A KPD memo of March 30 that found its way into a police file noted the "particular significance" of May 1 and went on to ask district committees to report on plans for all "factories, unions, and mass organizations" in their districts. The Berlin police also knew of a resolution from the Central Committee of the KPD on "Guidelines for the May 1 Campaign," which spoke of plans for the "breach of the prohibitions of the bourgeois state," with the goal of giving May 1 "the character of a revolutionary proletarian fighting-demonstration."[101]

The mutual hatred between the two wings of the socialist movement, spawned by the bloody events of the German revolution in 1918–19, led directly to this atmosphere of intransigence and fear. In the weeks before May Day, accusations of "dictatorship in Prussia" clashed with assertions that "the KPD needs corpses" in the parties' respective newspapers. Before the First World War, the kaiser's authoritarian police chief had warned Berlin's workers, "The street is only there to serve traffic." Communists in 1929 mocked Social Democrats for adopting the same tone. Afterward Zörgiebel wrote self-servingly that "all signs," including "the daily ever more presumptuous writings of [Communist newspaper] the *Red Flag*," had shown that the Communist leadership was determined to incite violence between demonstrators and police. Therefore, he said, he had called for "calm and level-headed actions."[102]

It did not work out that way. On May 1 the police went out in force to the working-class districts of Wedding and Neukölln. When some inhabitants gathered in small groups, the police intervened with grossly disproportionate force. Violent confrontations erupted between demonstrators and police. In the course of May 1 and 2 the violence escalated. Firing blindly into crowds and even buildings, the police killed thirty-three people and wounded over a hundred more, many of them bystanders. As the journalist Carl von Ossietzky wrote in the *World Stage*, the dead and wounded were victims of the "prestige battle between the Social Democratic and Communist parties." Two journalists, one of them Australian, were among the victims. Reports of police officers killed or wounded that day were conspicuous by their absence.

Numerous witness accounts and reports in centrist papers with no interest in aiding Communist propaganda left no doubt that the "blind rage of the unleashed police war machine has become—we cannot avoid this conclusion—a public danger."[103]

Police witnesses told a different story. The Berlin political police, Department IA at the Alexander Square police headquarters (the "Alex," in Berlin argot), gathered statements from officers who had "attended the Communist demonstrations." Most were evasive and indirect, with heavy reliance on the passive voice. One officer claimed that demonstrators on Köslin Street fired and threw stones at the police. In response, "the uniformed officers made use of their weapons." After about twenty minutes the shooting was over, and "Köslin Street was made free for traffic once again." The same officer claimed "shots were fired" that evening at police officers from the rooftops of Köslin Street, Wieden Street, Wedding Street, and Reinickendorf Street, and "the fire was returned by the officers." If the accounts of demonstrators firing at the police were anything other than official fabrications, it is conspicuous that every bullet fired at a police officer seemed to miss its target.[104]

The Fürsts and Litten felt it was "obvious" that they should participate in the demonstrations that day. "Measured by today's standards," Max recalled, it was "an extremely peaceful demonstration." But the police presence was "massive": "Everywhere we were attacked by hordes with rubber truncheons." A police officer swung at Margot (then sixteen), but Max was able to ward off the blow. Hans did not get away so lightly. In the early afternoon, as he stood by the entrance to the Münz Street subway station near Alexander Square, he saw a policeman beat a man to the ground and kick him. Litten rushed to the beaten man, identified himself as a lawyer, and began taking down information. The police officer turned his attention to Litten, and as Litten himself rather laconically put it, "abused me considerably with his rubber truncheon." Max thought that in the heat of the moment, and absorbed in his work, Litten had not even noticed he was being beaten. Litten took down the names of the victim and several witnesses and spent the rest of the day walking around Berlin observing and recording the events. That evening, near the Schönhausen Gate, a security police officer fired several shots at him, "without any provocation and without warning, without hitting me."[105]

A report prepared for the Prussian Justice Ministry at the end of 1929 revealed that in the two Berlin court districts principally involved, nearly three hundred demonstrators had been charged with offenses as a result of the May demonstrations, with a little under fifty receiving some kind of punishment, mostly fines. "A number of investigations against police officers were launched," the report noted. "However all of them were stayed." In twelve of these cases it had "not been possible" to identify officers; in the rest there was no evidence of any criminal action.[106]

This official stonewalling provoked a response from a coalition of writers, journalists, lawyers, and politicians of the center and the left. Within a few days, such prominent figures as the writers Heinrich Mann and Alfred Döblin, the statistician E. J. Gumbel, the lawyer Alfred Apfel, the KPD parliamentarians Ottomar Geschke and Arthur Gohlke, the editor of the left-liberal magazine the *Diary* Stephan Grossmann, and the Neukölln district councilor and physician Dr. Schminke, all joined forces to form the Committee for the Public Investigation of the May Day Events. The committee had space in the Apfel & Beck legal offices on Frederick Street, with regular office hours for witnesses daily from 3 to 7 p.m.[107]

A police informant left a detailed report of this committee's first meeting on May 15. There were, the agent recorded, about forty persons present—the big names listed above (although Heinrich Mann was unable to attend the first meeting) and others, "almost all intellectuals," including "representatives of the press, a few physicians and 3 district councilors." Despite the diversity, the agent continued, "the fundamental tendency of the matter was, as became clear in the course of the meeting, communistic." Stephan Grossmann opened the meeting by saying that the committee was a "spontaneous expression of the will of morally and justly thinking men against the bloody terror of May Day." It was now the task of the committee "to seek the truth" about May Day through "objective and conscientious work," to identify the guilty parties and to bring them to justice. Dr. Schminke said that he had observed the autopsies of seventeen victims, which had proven that every one had been shot by the police, many of them "while fleeing." Another member of the committee reported that 150 witnesses had already been interviewed at Apfel's Frederick Street office and transcripts made of their evidence.[108]

Although the police informant described him only as a "lawyer of unknown name (of whom I know however that he appeared recently in the Köpenick Local Court as the defense counsel of a Communist disturber of the peace)," the next speaker was Litten. Litten announced that he had raised an indictment against the police chief. The account shows that Litten had already formulated his legal strategy for litigating May Day cases. Zörgiebel's demonstration ban was itself illegal, Litten argued; it followed that everything the police did to enforce the ban was tainted by the same illegality. Under the terms of the Criminal Code, the killing of civilians by police officers was therefore nothing other than murder. Furthermore, anything that civilians had done to defend themselves against the police amounted to "self-defense in the full legal sense." This argument would have to be "in the foreground" in the coming trials of "the victims of the police."[109]

The difference between Litten and his peers, even liberal and Social Democratic members of the Berlin bar, became clear when Alfred Apfel warned the gathering that Litten's indictment of Zörgiebel was nothing more than "action in the heat of emotion." Such individual actions were understandable, said Apfel, but nonetheless out of place. It was necessary to wait and "calculate coolly, until the case is ready." Apfel feared that the prosecutors, having once rejected Litten's case, would feel they had established a precedent. The participants, however, agreed to continue investigating May Day. A passage marked with multiple underlining in the police report records that a public meeting would be called, at which witnesses would be questioned before an audience.[110]

It was as a member of this May Day Committee that Litten made his debut as a public speaker at a political forum in Berlin, in Spandau, on July 5. Chairing it was the writer Erich Mühsam, who, along with other prominent members of the May Day Committee—Ossietzky, Schminke, and Apfel—would later share stages of Litten's journey through Hitler's concentration camps. Witnesses to the events of May 1 were produced and then testified as if they were in court. After these examinations, Litten, identified again as "a young lawyer whose name was not given," spoke of how police in Munich had forbidden meetings similar to those of the Berlin committee on the basis that they amounted to the first stages of a coup. He talked about the cases of two women who had been shot by the Berlin police, "whereby he emphasized the lack of conscience of the authorities, who had given the porter Koppen [next of kin of a victim] a settlement of 20 Marks compensation."[111]

Following his strategy of holding the leaders accountable and letting the followers go, Litten officially requested that the prosecutors' office charge Police Chief Zörgiebel with incitement to murder in thirty-three cases. Unsurprisingly, the prosecutors refused the request. Equally unsurprisingly, Litten appealed.[112]

Litten claimed, as Zörgiebel would "presumably not deny," that the police chief had not only upheld the ban on demonstrations for May 1, but had also ordered the security police to use truncheons and live ammunition against demonstrators. No one could dispute that firing live ammunition at people constituted "an intentional premeditated killing or an attempt at such," and beatings with rubber truncheons amounted to the infliction of grievous bodily harm. Thus the only question was "whether in the present case [Zörgiebel] acted illegally or not" in giving his orders.[113]

Litten's argument demonstrates that he was, almost in spite of himself, a master of the unconventional but inventive and penetrating legal interpretation, one who could manipulate and recombine the standard patterns of legal argument to startling effect. Legal commentaries left no doubt that a police measure was legal only when it "follow[ed] from policing considerations," which meant that under Prussian law Zörgiebel was entitled to order only "necessary measures" for upholding public peace and security or for the prevention of a public danger. But Litten argued that Zörgiebel had admitted to issuing the prohibition out of purely *political* considerations. He had uncovered Zörgiebel's admission in an article published in the *Berlin Daily News* on May 2. Zörgiebel had written that the ban was necessary in light of the difficulties of forming a government at the national level— clearly not the kind of "police" measure contemplated by Prussian law. Litten cited a case in which a court had held that the mayor of a town of nine thousand inhabitants must be presumed to know the legal limits on policing. The Berlin police chief, said Litten, must be at least as well informed as a village mayor.[114]

Litten also argued that the enforcement of the ban should stand in some reasonable proportion to its desired result. Killing thirty-three people could hardly further public peace and security. He suggested that the very frequency of police shootings on May 1 pointed to the existence of a secret order from Zörgiebel to fire on demonstrators; at the very least, the *absence* of an order *not* to shoot constituted unpardonable negligence. Litten's conclusion was personal; he was not raising the charge against Zörgiebel on behalf of any client. "My entitlement to an application for a judicial decision," he wrote, "arises out of the fact that I am among those injured through [Zörgiebel's] conduct." He described how on May 1 he had been beaten and shot at by police officers. Here Litten was acting for himself.[115]

On October 14, the 3rd Senate of the Court of Appeal rejected Litten's petition. Litten had based his case on the claim that the police shootings and beatings revealed a pattern of violence ordered from the top, arguing that intent shows itself nowhere more clearly than in pattern. The court responded by narrowing the issues to the point of absurdity. Litten had no standing to bring his petition because "in the two cases in which the applicant himself claims to have been unlawfully injured through the actions of the police" no criminal action could be attributed directly to Zörgiebel. The court observed that Litten had made no attempt to charge the "actual culprits indicated here, the police officers." Zörgiebel could be criminally liable only if he had incited the officers to attack Litten or assisted them in doing so. As for Litten's alternative claim of negligence, the attacks on Litten were, following Litten's own account, the intentional infliction of grievous bodily harm and intentional attempted homicide. It was legally impossible to hold Zörgiebel liable for *negligently* inciting such *intentional* actions.[116]

Litten also acted as defense counsel for many of the demonstrators charged after May Day with breach of the peace or resisting arrest. Some of these cases kept him busy until 1931. In every case Litten followed the maxim "The best defense is a good offense." He continued to hold Zörgiebel and the police accountable for the violence of May Day, but he varied his tactics, accusing Zörgiebel in open court of being guilty of thirty-three counts of murder and challenging Zörgiebel to sue him for libel—bait that Zörgiebel was smart enough not to take. But in the last of these cases Litten got a Berlin court to say that it was "doubtful" that Zörgiebel's ban had been appropriate, and that police squads and their lower-level leaders had committed "considerable excesses" on May 1.[117]

Litten's work on the May Day cases had serious consequences. The evidence that he brought forward discredited Karl Zörgiebel and the entire Social Democratic administration of Berlin and Prussia. But Litten's choice of opponent made this a dangerous victory. As the Social Democrats lost their hold on Berlin's workers, the Nazis waited in the wings.

There was a personal side to this as well. From his very first cases, Litten had attacked powerful men. Not many young lawyers would have had the nerve, or the ability, to do what he did. His actions flowed directly from his own mixture of moral certainty and political radicalism, his insistence on the engagement of the "whole person." It is also hard to resist the conclusion that Litten used the law to go after powerful men because here too, behind Gustav Noske and Karl Zörgiebel and (soon enough) behind Adolf Hitler, he saw the shade of his detested father.

Just as there were personal grounds for Litten's work, there were personal consequences. His two-year battle against Zörgiebel had earned him the lasting hatred of the Berlin police. He would feel the consequences.

PART II

Crossing Hitler

The Witness

Friday, May 8, 1931: everyone agreed that it would be "Moabit's great day." "Without doubt," predicted the tabloid *World in the Evening*, "one must reckon with a great sensation." "Exciting day," the Nazi Party propaganda director and Berlin party boss Joseph Goebbels noted in his diary. Early in the morning, police cars were lined up outside the huge Berlin criminal courthouse at the corner of Turm and Rathenower Streets. Police were everywhere: two units inside the building, one outside. Squads of National Socialist storm troopers were there too. As the morning wore on, their number rose into the thousands; the endless cries of "Heil Hitler!" echoed from the stone walls of Gründerzeit apartment blocks. The *8 O'Clock Evening News* featured a photograph of these "unemployed Nazis" on its front page, noting that they had been ordered to Moabit for a "spontaneous people's demonstration." The police managed to push them off Turm into the narrow side streets, where they had to content themselves with yelling at passersby and, some said, getting into brawls with each other.[1]

On the steps of the courthouse press photographers besieged the grand entry doors. No one could enter without a special permit. Even the great daily newspapers were granted only one entry card each.[2]

Three days before, a small group of senior officials had met to discuss security arrangements. Afterward, a prosecutor reported confidently to the Prussian justice minister that all the necessary measures had been taken, "especially insofar as the personal security of the witness Hitler is concerned."[3]

The personal security of the witness Hitler had been on the minds of these officials since May 2, when the court had acted on Hans Litten's request and formally summoned the leader of the National Socialist German Workers' Party to testify at the Eden Dance Palace trial, the trial of Konrad Hermann Stief and three other Nazi storm troopers for attempted murder. Shortly after Hitler received the summons, a secretary from Goebbels's office phoned the court to say that "the

Communists" were planning to attack Hitler as he entered the courthouse. Several days before Hitler's appearance, court officials therefore told the press that Hitler would be examined at eleven o'clock, following two other witnesses; in fact, they scheduled his appearance for nine o'clock sharp. That morning, the victims of the storm troopers' assault were examined for concealed weapons at the courtroom door. And shortly after nine o'clock, Hitler, along with his adjutant Lieutenant Wilhelm Brückner, was smuggled into the courthouse through a passage closed to the public that connected Turm Street to the holding cells and to the older criminal court building on Alt-Moabit, a long block away.[4]

For this appearance Hitler chose a plain dark blue suit instead of a brown storm trooper's uniform. The only sign of his political role was the small Nazi pin in his buttonhole. As they made their way to Courtroom 664 on the third floor, Hitler and Brückner could not see the crowds of police and storm troopers gathered outside. But the spectators' gallery was packed. Many of Berlin's most prominent officials and politicians were there, but, according to several papers, most of the spectators were storm troopers and members of the Nazi Party. The presiding judge, Superior Court Director Kurt Ohnesorge, lectured the noisier spectators about decorum, but the defendants were undeterred. When their Führer entered the courtroom, they leaped to their feet, raised their arms, and shouted "Heil Hitler!"[5]

Judge Ohnesorge pounded his fist on the table. "I have strictly forbidden demonstrations here," he said. "I least of all expected the defendants to disobey this order. If it happens again I will impose the most severe disciplinary penalties."[6]

In spite of the tight security, one "unauthorized" person had managed to get into Courtroom 664—not an SA thug or an enterprising reporter, but nineteen-year-old Margot Fürst. With the same self-possession that had gotten her out of tedious high school classes and later would keep her safe even from the Gestapo, Margot had stuck a file under her arm and told the police she had to bring it urgently to Advocate Litten's attention. Once inside the courtroom she stayed to watch Hitler's examination. In the file was a single sheet of paper with one line: "A greeting for the Grizzly Bear." Litten read the sheet with a "dignified and straight face," Margot recalled.[7]

After Judge Ohnesorge had lectured the witnesses on the significance of the oath, everyone but Hitler was led out of the courtroom to a nearby waiting room. At ten minutes past nine, Judge Ohnesorge turned to Hitler and intoned formally, "You are summoned here as a witness by request of counsel for the private prosecutor."[8]

Political Soldiers

By May 1931 Adolf Hitler could already look back on a twelve-year career in German politics. He had been a figure of real importance, however, for only eight months.

His biography is mostly common knowledge now. A soldier of the Great War who, in nearly four years at the front, was never promoted past corporal because his regimental officers thought he lacked the leadership qualities to be a sergeant, Hitler gravitated after the war to Munich, which was becoming the center of Germany's mushrooming radical-right political scene. Briefly employed by the army to scout the new parties and factions, he discovered a group called the German Workers' Party, founded by a locksmith named Anton Drexler. Hitler's intervention at one of the Party's meetings impressed Drexler, who pushed Hitler to join, as in fact did Hitler's superior officer. Soon audiences in Munich discovered that Corporal Hitler had one overriding talent: as he put it, "I could 'speak.'" This talent, and the force of his personality, soon brought him the leadership of the little German Workers' Party, which he remade according to his own wishes, adding the modifiers "National Socialist" to the Party's name. At first Hitler believed he could lead the party to a revolutionary overthrow of the shaky Weimar Republic. In November 1923 he made his bid for power, in the "Beer Hall Coup," working alongside several prominent conservative Bavarian politicians and the First World War general Erich Ludendorff. The coup was a failure. Hitler was fortunate to escape with nothing worse than a brief prison sentence for high treason, from which he emerged at the beginning of 1925.[9]

The mid-1920s were not a good time for Germany's radicals. After the runaway inflation of the early 1920s, the German economy recovered and began to return to prewar levels of prosperity. The prosperity brought a stabilization of the democratic system and an increase in votes for the centrist political parties. In the parliamentary elections of 1928, Hitler's National Socialist Party won only 2.6 percent of the vote; in "Red Berlin," dominated politically by the Social Democrats and the Communists, only 1.5 percent. The Nazis were a fringe party, their leader merely one more rabble-rouser.[10]

The outcome of the 1928 election was a "grand coalition" of democratic parties led by the Social Democrat Hermann Müller. Prussia, Germany's largest state, with three-fifths of the country's population, was likewise under the rule of a coalition led by Social Democrats. But by the fall of 1928 the ranks of the unemployed in Germany were beginning to grow, and the worldwide economic crisis that hit a year later proved a godsend for Hitler's movement. In that year Hitler joined a campaign launched by the conservative Nationalist Party against an American-led plan to restructure Germany's reparations payments to the victors of the First World War. The association with the Nationalists gave Hitler a veneer of respectability. At the same time, the revolutionary edge of Hitler's party, its violent contempt for the bourgeois certainties of nineteenth-century Europe, promised the only hope for many of the workers, shopkeepers, and unemployed youth who bore the burdens of recent German history. As its name implied, the National Socialist Party held out the promise, however spurious, of a more egalitarian and socially conscious nation. This held a powerful appeal in a Germany that expected the state to care for its citizens and that had become increasingly democratized since the end of the nineteenth century. The more the traditional parties seemed overmatched by the challenges of the twentieth century, the more the Austrian demagogue gained in popularity. On September 14, 1930, Germans went to the polls and this time gave the National Socialist Party nearly 6.5 million votes and 107 seats, 18.3 percent of the seats in Germany's parliament, the Reichstag. Literally overnight, the face of German politics was transformed. Not yet even a German citizen, the Austrian corporal was the coming man.[11]

With new prominence came new problems. The ideological appeal of the Nazi Party was a mass of contradictions: nationalist and "socialist," working class and bourgeois, populist and elitist, modern and antimodern. The Party sought a "community of the people" from which huge segments of the people were to be violently expelled—Jews most conspicuously, followed by members of the Socialist and Communist Parties, habitual criminals, the mentally handicapped, and (a little later) gay men. It wanted to restore the health of Germany's industrial economy and the power of its armed forces while returning people to the traditional rural life. But no contradiction was as fundamental and as politically dangerous for the Party as that between "legality" and "illegality."

After the ignominious failure of the Beer Hall Coup, Hitler concluded that the National Socialists could gain power in Germany only legally, through the very parliamentary elections they openly despised. This new legal strategy, however, put the Party in a bind. There was nothing in the Nazi Party's platform, including its anti-Semitism and militarism, that had not been common fare on the German far right for decades. Some Nazi demands, for revocation of the Treaty of Versailles, imposed on Germany in 1919 as the price of surrender in the First World War, and union with Austria, were standard across the spectrum of Weimar German politics. However, what set the Nazis apart were their youth and their use and advocacy of violence. No other political party was as young; even the leaders were in their thirties or forties (Hitler himself turned forty-two while the Eden Dance Palace trial was in progress). And no other party had an auxiliary army as fierce and as fast-growing as the brown-shirted SA or "Storm Sections." The SA tripled in size in the course of 1931, from 88,000 members in January to 260,000 by the following December.[12]

The young men who were pouring into the SA in 1931 had been born around 1910. Their whole lives had been shaped by war, revolution, economic crisis, and social upheaval. They had never known peace, security, or general prosperity. They belonged to a generation that faced unusually high levels of unemployment and poor access to higher education and apprenticeships. The police official Rudolf Diels, a man who, despite, or perhaps because of, his involvement in many of the Nazis' crimes was an uncommonly sharp-eyed observer of them, caught the essence of the SA men in his memoirs:

> They called themselves "political soldiers." Élan and audacity were their dogmas. . . . Ignorance of the noble and valuable things of culture had made them hostile to culture; the destruction of all social connections had made them rootless. With many, going berserk was overcompensation for their measureless weakness, their camaraderie a product of their fear of being alone.[13]

In smaller German towns it may well have been that the function of the SA was (as it always claimed) purely propagandistic: to stage parades and provide security at Nazi meetings. But the big cities, above all Berlin, required a different approach. "Berlin needs its sensation like a fish needs water," wrote one influential Nazi leader. "That is what this city lives on, and any political propaganda which does not recognize it will fail to hit its target." The man who wrote these words had been named the Party's Berlin boss, or *Gauleiter*, in the autumn of 1926. His name was Joseph Goebbels.[14]

Goebbels wasted no time in demonstrating what he meant by "sensation." The role of the Berlin SA was to move into working-class neighborhoods, dominated politically by the Communist Party and the Social Democratic Party, and get control of the streets through virtual gang warfare with the Communist Red Frontfighters' League and the Social Democratic Reich Banner Black-Red-Gold. Soon after his arrival in Berlin, Goebbels ordered a "propaganda march" through the solidly working-class district of Neukölln. He made a point of speaking at the Pharus Hall in the even redder district of Wedding. With incidents such as the beating of a pastor at a Nazi meeting and a brawl between SA men and Communists at the Lichterfelde-East train station, the level of political violence in Germany's capital began a steady escalation to what would become a full-blown civil war by the summer of 1932.[15]

But relying on the young toughs of the SA presented an ever more serious dilemma to the calculating politicians in Hitler's inner circle. The storm troopers tended to put as much emphasis on the "socialism" as the "nationalism" in their party's name, and their rhetoric was often hard to distinguish from that of the parties of the left. The Neukölln SA leader Reinhold Muchow wrote in 1926, "Berlin National Socialists almost without exception devote their energies to the conquest of the German workers (they are fed up with the bourgeoisie of all descriptions)." A few years later, after Hitler had become Germany's dictator, the members of the Berlin SA unit "Storm 33" (to which the defendants in the Eden Dance Palace trial belonged) looked back on what they called the "time of struggle" and recalled that although they had fought hard against the Communists, they would not forget their struggle against "the thoughtlessness and cowardice of the middle class," which neglected "the economic needs of its national comrades so long as things were going well for itself"; which "cravenly left the streets to Marxism"; whose lack of political instinct meant that it had "failed even to recognize the danger of the Jews"; and all in all was "fundamentally just as hostile to us as was the Red Front."[16]

As the Nazi movement began to gain electoral support after 1929, this angry, hateful, and semi-articulate SA radicalism sat ever more uneasily with the electorally oriented "legalism" of the Party leadership. The tension between the revolutionaries of the SA and the tacticians of the Nazi Party headquarters in Munich led to repeated crises—before and after Hitler himself came to power. Such a crisis formed the crucial backdrop to Hitler's appearance in Moabit on that May morning.

The crisis centered around the SA leader for Berlin and Eastern Germany, the former police captain Walter Stennes. Stennes had had a checkered career, typical of the men who joined the Nazis in the early days. Born in 1895, the son of a minor official, he was educated in military schools from the age of ten. When war broke out in 1914 he won a commission in an infantry regiment. He served throughout the war, mostly at the front—although he had a brief spell working with "higher staffs"—and was wounded four times. Unable, like so many veterans, to settle down to civilian life after the war, he organized one of the first "Free Corps" units. The Free Corps were squads consisting mostly of recently demobilized veterans along with students frustrated at having missed combat, on which Germany's first postwar Social Democratic administration relied to suppress its more revolutionary enemies. From there Stennes moved to the command of a tactical squad with the Berlin Security Police. In 1923 the Reich government asked him to command the "passive resistance" to the French occupation of the

Ruhr district. Later, as he wrote mysteriously in a 1928 biographical sketch, he was "active with confidential commissions" as an intelligence officer with the Ministry of Defense. He joined the Nazi Party in 1927 and soon became the leader of all SA troops east of the Elbe River.[17]

Stennes was one of those SA men increasingly discontented with the Nazi Party's efforts to woo middle-class voters with a program of ostensible legality. The first signs of trouble appeared in the spring of 1928, when Stennes claimed that the SA should be fully independent of the political leadership. Resentments boiled over again just weeks before the elections of September 1930, when the Party refused to put three SA men on its list of parliamentary candidates. Anger over this slight joined frustration with the chronically weak finances of the SA. Stennes traveled to Munich to express the grievances of the northern SA personally to Hitler; Hitler would not see him. As a result the Berlin SA moved into open rebellion. It refused to provide security for an election rally on August 30, and SA men vandalized the Berlin Party headquarters. Hitler was forced to travel to Berlin to meet with Stennes and with much of the rank and file of the Berlin SA. With his usual rhetorical pathos, he was able to save the situation—a promise of improved funding for the brownshirts helped—but the essence of the conflict, violent revolution versus a veneer of legality, could not be so easily or permanently mended.[18]

Meanwhile, shortly after the dramatic election success that September, Hitler affirmed his commitment to legality as a witness before Germany's highest court, the Imperial Supreme Court in Leipzig. Three army officers were on trial for plotting to commit high treason. The officers had tried to convince their comrades that the army should support a Nazi coup. The prominent Nazi lawyer Hans Frank (later the governor of Nazi-occupied Poland and, later still, one of those hanged at Nuremberg) summoned Hitler to testify that the National Socialist Party had no plans to overthrow Germany's democratic government by violent means. Hitler insisted that the SA served only as a bodyguard for Party leaders and as a propaganda arm: "We have from the first day forward trusted in the advertising power of the healthy idea; we are a purely spiritual [geistige] movement," he told the court. Certainly a movement that drew in "tens of thousands of young and temperamental members" could not be held responsible for the individual actions of those members. Nonetheless, he had done all he could to keep the SA from becoming militaristic, "as difficult as that is for a people which possesses an inner love of arms," especially when the Party's Communist opponents came out with the slogan "Beat the fascists wherever you find them!" The climactic moment of Hitler's evidence came when the presiding judge, Senate President Alexander Baumgarten, read out a quote attributed to Hitler from an article by the Neukölln SA man Reinhold Muchow. According to Muchow, Hitler had said, "Heads will roll in the sand in this struggle, either ours or the others'. So let's make sure that it is the others'." Hitler assured Baumgarten that Muchow merely "had his eye on the great spiritual revolution in which we find ourselves today," and insisted that he had no plans and had given no orders for a coup. But he added ominously, "I may assure you: when our movement wins its legal struggle, there will come a German Supreme Court, and November 1918 will find its retribution, and heads will also roll."[19]

In the months that followed, Hitler maintained this awkward dance, espousing legality while also trying to throw the SA enough red meat to keep its frustrations in check. In February 1931 he wrote that the SA was "no moral institution for the education of upper-crust girls, but rather a band of rough fighters." At the same time, he sent a steady stream of orders to the SA to be patient with the party's legal course. On February 18, for instance, he warned the SA of "provocateurs" who sought to "push the SA into the role of the attacker" to provide a pretext for the suppression of the movement. In March, speaking to an SA meeting in Munich, Hitler said, "I am accused of being too cowardly to fight illegally. For this I am certainly not too cowardly; I am only too cowardly to lead the SA into machine-gun fire." And yet he also told the men that they must learn "to defend [themselves] with the fist," and he closed by urging them to raise their right fists and swear to him that "with the fist the new Germany shall arise."[20]

Hitler and the Munich Party leadership were also working hard to limit the influence of the Berlin SA in general and Walter Stennes in particular. In September 1930 Hitler ordered that important eastern regions—North Saxony, East Prussia, and the city state of Danzig—be detached from Stennes's territory. A second order forbid all SA leaders to give speeches on behalf of the Nazi Party, an order that was aimed not only at Stennes but also at another popular SA leader from Silesia. Stennes refused to comply with these orders, even when SA Commander Ernst Röhm was dispatched from Munich to bring him to heel.[21]

Matters came to a head on April 1, 1931, when Hitler sacked Stennes as the OSAF-Ost, or supreme SA commander in the east. At first Stennes thought he could persuade Hitler to change his mind. He sent Hitler a telegram asking about this possibility, to which Hitler replied sternly, "It is not for you to inquire, but rather to obey my orders." The Berlin SA leaders declared their solidarity with Stennes, and Stennes led SA units in occupying the Berlin Party offices and those of Goebbels's own newspaper, the *Attack*. The next day, the Berlin SA leadership published an attack on Hitler's "un-German despotism" and "irresponsible demagogy." Goebbels confided to his diary that the Party was passing through its "most serious crisis" yet.[22]

He might have added that it was *his* most serious crisis as well. Goebbels occupied an awkward and anomalous position in the Nazi Party. In a movement of grizzled war veterans turned political gangsters, he was a failed intellectual whose clubfoot had kept him out of combat in the First World War. This predicament left him with a serious inferiority complex. Rudolf Diels wrote that for any theater director, Goebbels "could have served as the very image of the classical mask of Mephistopheles." But "from his face shone soulful, gleaming eyes, from which knowledge of beauty and greatness beamed.... The contradiction between his nature and brilliant gifts and his bodily constitution unleashed in his soul a constant antagonism."[23]

There were two poles in Joseph Goebbels's world. Like many frustrated intellectuals in politics, he was a true revolutionary, siding emotionally with Stennes and the SA in their battle with the Munich leadership. "Long live legality!" he wrote sarcastically in his diary on March 29, as the Stennes revolt was brewing. "Makes me want to puke." A month before, he had written a careful note of a pact with Stennes: "We are making an alliance. SA + me. That's power." He noted that Göring had reproached him for standing too close to Stennes, and his diary entries played constantly on the gulf within the Nazi Party between "Munich" and "Prussia," which he equated to the gulf between socialism (as he understood it) and reaction: "The Party must become more Prussian, active and socialist," he wrote on April 28 in a typical entry.[24]

But the other pole was his fanatical personal loyalty to Adolf Hitler. Goebbels's inner conflict ensured that there would always be some doubt about his role in the Stennes revolt. The Berlin political police believed he had been wholly on Stennes's side and jumped back to ostentatious displays of loyalty only when it became clear to him that the Stennes revolt would fail. According to police sources, the Munich leadership was well aware of Goebbels's near betrayal, and his position in the Party had consequently been weakened. Goebbels's most bitter rival within the Nazi Party, Hermann Göring—perhaps because after 1933 the records of the political police fell into his hands—gladly shared this belief, as did Göring's subordinate Rudolf Diels, who became the first head of the Gestapo: "Even Goebbels had ridden two horses," Diels wrote after the Second World War. But the more plausible interpretation is that advanced by Goebbels's biographer Georg Reuth, who argues that although Goebbels was emotionally on the side of the northern, "socialist," revolutionary, and antibourgeois Stennes people, his devotion to Hitler ensured that he could never go into open revolt. Either way, however, Goebbels had reason to be afraid of Stennes and what he represented in the Party—reason, indeed, to fear any and all exposure of the divide between the Nazis' "legal" and "revolutionary" wings. Goebbels's balancing act would turn out to be a key factor in the Eden Dance Palace trial.[25]

For Stennes's revolt did fail. On April 4, the Nazi newspaper the *Nationalist Observer* printed Hitler's statement on the Stennes revolt. As he did so often, Hitler drew a political moral out of an interpretation of his own life experience as the man who, a product of poor parents and without benefit of a university education, had been "drawn through the hardest school of life, poverty and misery." Yet he had founded a movement "for the salvation of the nation" at a time when "all of those intellectuals who cannot do enough in socialist phrase-making," the "con-men [*Possenreisser*] of salon-bolshevism and salon-socialism," were nowhere to be seen. SA men would be expected to recognize in this a reference to Stennes and his faction. Hitler dealt cleverly with the regional tensions that underlay the Stennes revolt: "Herr Stennes must know best of all that Prussiandom was and is not a geographical but a moral concept." All Nazis were Prussians, said Hitler, no matter where they came from. But "the Prussians are above all those National Socialists who know the meaning of loyalty and obedience, and not [those who are] mutineers!" He reminded the Party faithful that in Leipzig he had sworn the Party to legality, and he would not allow Stennes to make him "a perjurer." He closed with an attack on Stennes's capabilities, which he would very soon regret making: "Herr Stennes himself has, in his entire life, accomplished no more than the formation of a few pitiful roll-commandos." Yet Stennes had seen fit "in the moment of the greatest success of our movement" to oppose the leadership and thus to "deliver the party to ruin."[26]

Hitler's appeal succeeded. Only a few hundred SA men followed Stennes out of the Nazi Party. But the bitterness lingered. And along with Adolf Hitler, Walter Stennes had been summoned as a witness at the Berlin courthouse on that same May morning in 1931.[27]

The Eden Dance Palace

The Eden Dance Palace trial grew out of a grimly typical Berlin story of the early 1930s. It was this very typicality that Hans Litten wanted to demonstrate in order to make a political point about National Socialist "legality."

Even as Nazi political fortunes rose in the early 1930s, Berlin remained unpromising territory for the Party and its SA. The city had been a bastion of the Social Democrats since the 1890s. During the First World War it had been the center for liberal and Socialist politicians who opposed Germany's war effort and pushed to democratize the country, and in 1919 it became the birthplace of Germany's Communist Party (KPD). In the national elections of 1930 the Communists emerged as the most popular party in Berlin, winning 27.3 percent of the city's votes; the Social Democrats were right behind with 27.2 percent. Against this solid left majority the Nazis had to content themselves with 14.6 percent of the vote. Certain neighborhoods—such as Wedding, north of the city center, with its massive electronics factories and textile works, as well as Friedrichshain in the east, Neukölln toward the southeast, and parts of Charlottenburg in the west—were Communist strongholds: Wedding voted 43 percent for the Communists in 1930, Friedrichshain 38 percent, Neukölln 34.9 percent. These were the Berlin districts where the Great Depression struck most cruelly; the KPD drew its greatest support from the unskilled, the unemployed, the unwanted.[28]

The Nazis met the challenge of "conquering" Berlin head on. When the Berlin SA emerged in 1928 from a one-year ban following the deadly Lichterfelde-East brawl, it embarked upon a new strategy for gaining support in those grim KPD districts. Taverns had long been central to working-class culture. The SA moved to take them over, generally making arrangements with the tavern keepers to guarantee a minimum sale per month and driving out customers sympathetic to the SPD or the KPD. These taverns became known as "Storm taverns," homes to particular SA units, or "Storms." From these Storm taverns the SA men would go forth, night after night, looking for members of the Communists' Red Frontfighters' League or the Social Democrats' Reich Banner or Iron Front, sometimes even members of more conservative groups, such as the veterans' organization known as the "Steel Helmet," loosely associated with the Nationalist Party. This was politics as gang warfare, bearing more than a passing resemblance to what went on in contemporary Chicago. Newspapers brought daily reports of the dead and wounded from these street battles, which, as in gang warfare, had an intimate, neighborhood quality; the SA men, like their opponents, were usually from the neighborhoods in which they fought. Often, these tough young men switched from one gang to another, sometimes even from one side of the political spectrum to the other. In 1932 the Berlin police reported that over half of the men in some SA Storms were former Communists. Everyone, therefore, knew his neighbors' political affiliations. The SA's gritty image, the promise of camaraderie, and the uniform appealed to rootless young men. At the same time, because the victims of SA violence almost always came from the ranks of the political left, the Nazis could present the "struggle" of the SA as a defense against forces highly unpopular with the German middle classes. At the end of 1931 the *Attack* wrote of how "in Charlottenburg the red mob terrorizes the streets" and described what it saw as a typical nightly incident, as around a "calm Storm tavern" suddenly "shots whip through the nighttime streets, men in their prime are taken away, wallow in their red blood.... And the bourgeois sticks his head in the sand—has heard nothing, has seen nothing of what our boys suffer—and for him, too."[29]

The Storm tavern for Berlin's SA Storm 33 was called the Old Town, or Reisig's Tavern, after its owner. Reisig's Tavern was at 20 Hebbel Street in the western district of Charlottenburg, near the famous palace, but in an area so poor it was also known as "Little Wedding" after the famous slum. On the evening of November 22, 1931, about thirty people were in the tavern, almost all of them members of the Storm. A few short blocks away at the Eden Dance Palace, a regular haunt of left-leaning political groups, two different parties were under way. On the ground floor was a dance put on by a union of bakers and pastry makers. On the upper floor the hiking and social club Wanderfalke 1923 was holding a party.[30]

Neither Reisig's Tavern nor the Eden Dance Palace (despite its pretentious name) was a fancy place. Their grimness and squalor were altogether typical of Little Wedding. Later, the members of Storm 33 would give depositions before the examining magistrate, and their testimony spoke eloquently of the blighted lives that had led them to join the SA and to frequent such establishments. The lead defendant, Konrad Stief, twenty-two, already had two prior convictions for theft. He had attended the basic primary school (*Volkschule*), and had then been employed as an unskilled worker, most recently as a domestic servant, earning a net pay of 37 Marks per month after paying 55 per month for room and board. He had joined the SA in May 1930. Rudolf Wesemann, who at twenty-five had a prior conviction for the unauthorized carrying of a firearm, had trained as a mechanic but had been unemployed since a metalworkers' strike earlier that year. He claimed not to be receiving any relief payments due to his participation in the strike. He had belonged to the Nazi Party for five years and the SA for two years. Twenty-one-year-old Max Liebscher had dropped out of the parish school to train as a mason; now unemployed, his last job had been at the Siemens Building Union, where he earned 70 Marks per week. He had been a member of Storm 33 since the elections of the previous September. The comparatively elderly Albert Berlich—he was forty-two—had a different kind of story, but one also typical of recruits to the Nazi movement. He had served as an infantryman since the beginning of the First World War but was discharged as a result of a "serious stomach and intestinal ailment." He had been completely unable to work since 1926. He drew a military pension of 71 Marks and an invalid's pension of 22 Marks monthly. Berlich had been a member of the NSDAP for two months and had attempted to join the SA. He had prior convictions for embezzlement and begging.[31]

The SA men had composed a story to explain what happened at the Eden Dance Palace on the night of November 22, 1930. At around 9:30 that night, two members of Storm 33, one of them Liebscher, claimed to have been attacked as they passed by the Eden Palace by men "dressed in their Sunday best." Liebscher retreated to Reisig's Tavern and told the other SA men what had happened. Aroused to righteous indignation by Liebscher's story, about twenty storm troopers from the tavern hurried to the Eden Dance Palace. They forced their way into the building and went first to the ground floor room, where the bakers' party was in progress. The storm troopers clearly knew whom they were looking for—another sign of the personal nature of the political warfare on Berlin's streets, casting doubt on the SA defense that the raid was a spontaneous response to an attack on storm troopers by unknown opponents. When the Nazis reached the bakers' party one of them looked around and exclaimed, "They're not here! They're up above!" The SA men then ran up the stairs to the main hall, which at the time held an estimated 120 people from Wanderfalke 1923.[32]

The Wanderfalke people had been forewarned: a few moments before, two men had run into the hall shouting, "The Nazis are coming!" Witnesses reported that the dancers took the news calmly, with cries of "Music, keep playing!" and "Keep dancing!" Twenty-four-year-old Willi Köhler testified that he was "just about to ask a girl to dance" when he "noticed that something was up in the anteroom." Köhler testified that he saw Stief, Wesemann, and Berlich in the doorway of the hall. A few shots were fired into the room, he said, but he could not say who the shooter was. He saw another young man, twenty-year-old Norbert Budzinski, fall, and then Köhler himself was shot in the left wrist. Budzinski's wound—he was shot in the stomach—was described as "extremely life-threatening" by the doctor who treated him. At the time of the trial the bullet remained lodged near his spine, and he was unable to work. Walter Braun, twenty-four, was also shot, but, like Köhler, his injuries were comparatively minor.[33]

After firing the shots, the Nazis left the Eden Palace as quickly as they had come. The porter managed to telephone the police before being clubbed in the face by a passing storm trooper. In fact, two officers had seen the storm troopers heading for the Eden Palace and were already on the scene as the Nazis fled.[34]

The police and judicial investigations determined that Konrad Stief had been the leader of the attack. He, Berlich, Liebscher, and Wesemann were charged with the shootings of the three Wanderfalke men. Stief denied everything. He claimed that he had been at the Storm tavern until about nine o'clock and then gone home. On the way he passed the Eden Dance Palace, where he heard a disturbance and was arrested when he went to "see what was happening." Berlich, who was also arrested on the spot, claimed that he had been a guest at the Wanderfalke party. Liebscher admitted that he had been at the Eden Dance Palace but denied any involvement in the violence; Wesemann denied he had been there at all.[35]

"Murder Storm 33"

The Eden Dance Palace attack launched a three-month spree of SA violence in Charlottenburg. In the small hours of January 1, 1931, men from Storm 33 attacked and seriously wounded the brothers Erich and Robert Riemenschneider. Later that month, in a brawl outside Reisig's Tavern, men from the Storm stabbed to death a worker named Max Schirmer; and on February 2 they stabbed and then shot to death one Otto Grüneberg. The left-wing press began referring to the unit as "Murder Storm 33."[36]

For most of 1930 and 1931 the leader of Storm 33 was Fritz Hahn, a native Berliner, born in 1907. Hahn joined the SA shortly after his nineteenth birthday. As the *World in the Evening* reported sardonically, "By day he works quietly and modestly in the Commerce and Private Bank under Jewish management. By night he is the most notorious Nazi-chieftain in Berlin." In February 1931 Hahn was arrested in connection with the killing of Grüneberg, and in March he was picked up again for the attack on the Riemenschneider brothers. However, the prosecutor, State Advocate Paul Stenig, only filed charges of breach of the peace against him, and the Berlin Court of Appeal ordered Hahn's release. A judge intervened and ordered that Hahn face attempted murder charges for the assault on the Riemenschneiders. On July 11 the state prosecutor's office charged Hahn and four other members of Storm 33 with taking part in the "public formation of a mob, which with its combined strength commits acts of violence against persons"— the language of paragraph 125 of the German Criminal Code. Prosecutors deemed Hahn the "ringleader," which involved a higher penalty. Stenig did not attempt to rearrest Hahn, however, and by the time the case came to trial Hahn had vanished.[37]

This contrast between the savagery of Storm 33's tactics and the indulgence with which official Berlin seemed to treat the group formed an essential part of the background to Hitler's appearance in the Eden Dance Palace trial. This trial was not the first time Hans Litten had confronted members of Storm 33 in court. On March 31 the jury of Berlin's Superior Court III had begun hearing the trial of Paul Markowski and five other members of Storm 33 for the murder of Max Schirmer. Defending the SA men were the prominent Nazi lawyers Curt Becker and Dr. Otto Kamecke. Paul Stenig, the specialist in political trials for Berlin's Superior Court III, led the prosecution, as he would in the Eden Dance Palace trial. Litten joined the Markowski trial only after the evidence had been heard. Although the brutality of Schirmer's murder and the guilt of the defendants were clear, Stenig had asked for sentences of only one year's imprisonment against one of the SA men, who was still underage, and two years for each of the other five. Litten described what happened in a letter to his parents: "I had a great fight with Stenig. I had joined in . . . after Stenig's final pleading, with the declaration that his mild sentencing requests would be taken in the affected circles as an incitement to further murders. Success! Return to the hearing of evidence, Stenig raised his requests; the court even went beyond them." One of the storm troopers, Kurt Becker, was convicted of stabbing Schirmer and sentenced to five years' imprisonment for unpremeditated murder. Four other SA men received sentences ranging from one year to three years for inflicting grievous bodily harm. One was acquitted for lack of evidence.[38]

One of the results of the Markowski case was an enduring and bitter enmity between Litten and Stenig. Over the next two years these men would fight a kind of duel, despite often finding themselves, as in the Markowski and Eden Dance Palace cases, theoretically on the same side. Theoretically: as Litten wrote to his parents while in the thick of the Eden Palace trial, Stenig was "definitely none too comfortable" in the role of prosecuting Nazis alongside Litten. In the summer of 1932 Litten would characterize Stenig as "the fiercest Moabit opponent of proletarian defendants"; Stenig would denounce Litten repeatedly, publicly and privately, as a "dangerous irritant" in the justice system. Yet after 1933 they would both become targets for the Nazis.[39]

Like Litten, Paul Stenig was from East Prussia; in earlier days he had been a guest at the Litten Court in Königsberg. Newspaper artists' sketches show a beefy, balding man, with several chins, a hawk nose, and a severe expression. Litten and Stenig had known each other since 1920, when Litten was still in high school and Stenig a law clerk. Born in 1894, Stenig had volunteered for military service in August 1914 and served with distinction throughout the war. He was promoted to lieutenant and earned the Iron Cross Second Class. After the war he resumed his legal career, working for most of the 1920s as a judicial clerk and then a prosecutor in East Prussian provincial towns. In 1929 he was transferred to Berlin, and in October 1930, at the age of thirty-six, was named to the very visible position of political prosecutor at Superior Court III.

There was no doubt that politically Stenig stood far to the right. As a young judicial clerk he had been praised for his volunteer work with anti-Polish groups in East Prussia. But he was wholly engaged by work on the trials that came his way and did not belong to any political parties or lobby groups. He "is devoted with body and soul to his prosecutorial profession," said one official, and "throws himself completely into the individual matters entrusted to him." At the outset of the Markowski trial, in an article titled "New Faces in Moabit," the *Berlin Stock Exchange News* had written that there was something "uncommonly fresh" about the style of the "robust and rather temperamental" Stenig, who possessed the gift of quickly bringing his listeners round to his own point of view, even when they were "among the ranks of the defense counsel or the defendants." In later years even former opponents would speak respectfully of Stenig. One described him as "a knowledgeable man on criminal and procedural law, a quick-witted fighter and a diligent worker."[40]

In the Eden Dance Palace trial, the three wounded men—Budzinski, Braun, and Köhler—retained Litten to bring a private prosecution alongside the state prosecutor's case. In theory the trial was about determining whether any of the four defendants had shot the three victims. In practice the real meaning of the trial went far beyond the simple question of who had fired at whom. Litten was determined to use the trial to make a broad political point: that the violence committed by Storm 33 was an essential element of the Nazi program, carried out on orders directly from Hitler.

In the wake of the Stennes revolt, Litten happily took advantage of the tensions between the SA and the Nazi Party, revealing how well disaffected Nazis kept him informed. Midway through the trial, in a written request to ask questions of Storm Leader Fritz Hahn, who appeared as a witness, Litten claimed that "on April 24, 1931, in the afternoon, there was a meeting of Storm 33" at which members of the Storm had threatened Hahn that they would "spill the beans" on his involvement in another murder if he did not break with Stennes. In court Litten made the point explicit. "The witness Hahn is a Stennes follower," he said. "Two Hitler people threatened him that if he defected to Stennes, they would testify that Hahn was the murderer of the worker Grüneberg." For this Litten referred not only to "confidential information" he had received, but to "the reaction of the witness Hahn to my suggestion." According to the *Red Flag*, Hahn "visibly changed color" when Litten raised these questions.[41]

Litten was in fact working behind the scenes with the lawyer for the four Nazi defendants, Curt Becker. Becker himself was a Stennes follower, and therefore supported Litten's intent to use the trial to discredit Hitler, Goebbels, and the whole political leadership of the Nazi Party. For his part, Litten knew that the rank and file of the SA came from the same pool of workers as the Communists whom he represented, and he believed that the desperate men of Storm 33 could not be judged in the same way as their Party's cynical leadership.[42]

Leaks were not Litten's only source of information, however. Just a few days after the attack on the Eden Dance Palace he had organized a public meeting at a Charlottenburg assembly hall called the Turkish Tent. Anyone who knew anything about the SA assault was invited to come forward and "testify." Litten presided over the meeting and questioned the witnesses. As the Eden Dance Palace trial progressed and the young lawyer began to pose a greater threat, the Nazis fought back by attacking his professional ethics. It was improper for a lawyer to hold such a meeting and to shape the witnesses' evidence to suit his case. A "question and answer game, carried out with witnesses on whose testimony the fate of the defendants could hang, can lead to the gravest conflicts," read an editorial in the *Attack*. On April 30, presiding judge Ohnesorge directed Litten to testify about this meeting. Litten duly removed his black robe and entered the witness box. Under oath he acknowledged that the occasion had been less a protest meeting than an investigation. The "witnesses" were asked to step up to the podium and give their version of events; then Litten questioned them about what they had seen. One of the supporting judges asked Litten whether "as a lawyer" he did not have "serious doubts" about this kind of proceeding. Somewhat defensively, Litten explained that the Red Aid had urged him to hold the meeting. "I made all of the witnesses aware that they were not now standing before a court, but rather before a proletarian tribunal. However they had to testify exactly as they would in court. Beyond that, I advised the witnesses that they would certainly have to testify in court later, probably under oath." What Litten had done—which amounted to coaching witnesses on the content of their testimony—was as much a breach of professional conduct for a German lawyer in 1930 as it would be today. ("You just can't do that," as the eminent lawyer Gerhard Jungfer said of Litten's conduct in a 2006 interview.) It was the tactic of someone who, as Max Fürst wrote, always felt that he was fighting the last battle.[43]

Litten's behavior formed only one of the threads in the pattern of the Eden Dance Palace trial as the court prepared to hear from Hitler. Many Germans, especially those on the center and left of the political spectrum, wondered whether this time the state would hold Nazi leaders accountable for their Party's violence. The tensions between the SA and the Nazi Party simmered; important Nazis, perhaps Goebbels most of all, feared what would come of refighting the Stennes revolt in a courtroom. The Party leadership worried about how much the revelations of the Berlin SA's systematic violence would undermine its carefully constructed claim of legality. A few years later Rudolf Olden described the "difficult task" that Hitler faced in his testimony. To protect himself from a possible prosecution he had to "affirm loudly that he would use only constitutional methods in his political struggle." However, he had to do this in a way that would convince the SA that his affirmation was "a sham," a "successful fraud on the wealthy donors." It was, Olden wrote, not easy to "lie in such a complicated way." Hitler was caught between Litten and Stennes. A few days before Hitler's testimony, Stennes's newspaper, *Workers, Peasants, Soldiers*, announced that the evidence would reveal whether Hitler had perjured himself in Leipzig or made false accusations against Stennes in print. "In any case it will be determined that [Hitler] has lied, one way or the other."[44]

"The Boss comes today," Goebbels wrote in his diary on May 7. With characteristic sensitivity to the theatricality of the moment, he noted, "He must play the witness tomorrow in the Eden Palace trial." His worry seeping through, Goebbels added that this was "embarrassing, since Stennes has also been summoned." When Goebbels wrote the next day, "I am anxious for today's results," for once the propaganda chief was not lying.[45]

Roll Commandos

In the spring of 1931 German newspapers were full of stories about criminals. In Düsseldorf a notorious serial killer named Peter Kürten was about to be executed. In Berlin, the trial of Charlie Urban for the murder at the Mercedes Palace Theater began in May. On April 3 the *Berlin Morning Post* noted that the hit play *Preliminary Investigation,* written by the prominent lawyer Max Alsberg, had marked its 125th performance at the New Theater by the Zoo to enthusiastic applause, especially for its author (even Goebbels liked it, apparently overlooking Alsberg's Jewish heritage); it would soon be made into a film. On

May 12 came the premiere of Fritz Lang's first sound film, *M*, a lightly fictionalized story of a Berlin serial killer. This fixation on criminals—especially on serial killers—had its political side. Lang had wanted to call his film "Murderers among Us," a title that had alarmed a studio executive sympathetic to the Nazis. The film dealt with the ways fear, paranoia, and violent rhetoric could incite crowds to commit atrocities against selected scapegoats. The *Berlin Morning Post* thought Lang's film a product of the "darkest" part of "today's Berlin." An ironic confirmation of this assessment comes once again from Goebbels, who went to see the movie on May 21 and praised it enthusiastically: "Fabulous! Against the humanity-rubbish. For the death penalty! Well made. Lang will be our director someday." Berlin's mass press and general public, however, had all but ignored the Eden Dance Palace trial. It was only Hitler's appearance that now brought the case into the headlines.[46]

While Litten had been fighting his legal battles against Gustav Noske and Karl Zörgiebel, Germany's political landscape had changed beyond recognition. In the spring of 1930, the Weimar Republic, which in the late 1920s had been functioning tolerably well as a parliamentary democracy, had begun to slide into a condition of de facto dictatorship. A group of powerful men, operating behind the scenes but with the ear of Reich President Paul von Hindenburg, came to the conclusion that as a parliamentary democracy shaped by Social Democrats, Germany would never recover its economic strength, shake off the Treaty of Versailles, or reassert itself as the preeminent European power. At the center of this circle was General Kurt von Schleicher, head of the army's political office, who in the early 1930s became the Iago of German politics, always scheming and whispering in powerful ears (appropriately, the name Schleicher means "creeper"). Schleicher engineered the collapse of Chancellor Hermann Müller's "Grand Coalition" government in the spring of 1930, and Müller's replacement as chancellor by the far more conservative Heinrich Brüning, who came from the right wing of the Catholic Center Party. The real significance of the shift from Müller to Brüning lay not in the leaders' respective ideologies, however, but in Schleicher's plan for how Brüning was to govern. Rather than relying on a majority in the Reichstag, Brüning's administration would be supported by emergency decrees that President Hindenburg could issue under Article 48 of the Weimar Constitution. With these decrees

Brüning could rule largely independently of parliamentary approval, opening the door to an authoritarian system of governance. This alarming trend was compounded by the dramatic surge in Nazi votes in the elections of September 1930.[47]

It seems to have been this Nazi success that led Litten to reverse the political direction of his legal work. After the September elections and the Eden Dance Palace attack of November, Litten moved away from attacking Social Democrats such as Noske and Zörgiebel. The powerful man he was after now was Hitler.

When Hitler finally reached the witness stand in the Eden Dance Palace trial, presiding judge Kurt Ohnesorge got right to the point. "The claim has been made by counsel for the private prosecutors," Ohnesorge explained to Hitler, referring to Litten, "that Storm 33, to which the four defendants belong, is a 'roll commando.' He claims this roll commando was deliberately organized with the goal of carrying out planned and premeditated killings, and that this plan was known to the party leadership and approved by it. Do you know Storm 33? Do you know its leaders?"[48]

Ohnesorge held the rank of superior court director (*Landgerichtsdirektor*), the highest level of trial judge in the Weimar legal system. Superior court directors presided over jury courts and the most important civil trials, typically backed up by supporting judges at the lower ranks of superior court counselor (*Landgerichtsrat*), superior court judge (*Landrichter*), and recent graduates still holding only the status of assessor. Because a jury court tried the Eden Dance Palace case, Ohnesorge and his two supporting judges also had with them on the bench six "jurors." As a result of a 1924 reform, however, these were not jurors as in Britain or America, sitting and deciding separately from the judges. They sat with the judges and shared in all deliberations, but they were ciphers; the point of the reform had been to ensure that the judges could intimidate and control them.[49]

German criminal procedural law, then as now, assigned the presiding judge a dominant role in questioning a witness. This was why Ohnesorge and not Litten opened the questioning. But this was merely a matter of form. Litten had summoned Hitler and outlined the direction of the examination; Ohnesorge was, therefore, merely serving as a mouthpiece for questions that were really Litten's.

Hitler responded to the first question by giving a speech he would give at a political rally. It was "absolutely impossible" that any Berlin SA Storm had been formed to act as Litten alleged. The Nazi Party, Hitler insisted, "utterly rejects violent methods." The SA served only to protect the party "against the terror from the left" and "to carry out propaganda functions." "I have already explained," he said, "that the National Socialists are fundamentally legal." Though he had no love for the Constitution of the Weimar Republic, he knew that any attempt to come to power against the Constitution would only lead to "unnecessary bloodshed," which, for Hitler, would amount to a breach of the "blind trust" his followers had placed in him as leader.[50]

Without any prompting, Hitler turned to the matter of Walter Stennes. It was laughable, he insisted, to suggest that Stennes had formed roll commandos on the instructions of the Party. When Stennes held a position within the Party he had commanded twenty thousand men. The very size of this "mass" proved that it could not be a roll commando. "Now some within Party circles have accused me of being a coward, a conformist [*verspiesst*], a party boss, a bourgeois. Naturally I have defended myself and I have pointed to my success, which is seen in the building up of a gigantic organization of millions. Before he entered the Party Captain Stennes had two hundred men."[51]

Simply by bringing up Stennes and the roll commandos Hitler had placed himself in jeopardy. In an article in the *Nationalist Observer* published on April 4, as he tried to rally the Party against Stennes, Hitler had noted snidely that "Herr Stennes himself has in his entire life managed to accomplish nothing more than forming a few wretched roll commandos." Hitler's language suggested that he had at least known if not approved of Stennes's activity. Ohnesorge asked him, "In what sense did you use the term 'roll commando' in your article? The private prosecutors base themselves on your article. Did you mean that these roll commandos had orders to kill people?"[52]

Hitler tried to evade the question, claiming that when he wrote of roll commandos he had been referring to what Stennes had done before joining the Nazis. Hitler repeated that Stennes had failed to build up anything more than a few small, miserable organizations. "But even in this context," said Hitler, "I did not use the word 'roll commandos' in the sense that is imputed to me here."

Ohnesorge pressed the point: "I find the expression at least prejudicial."[53]

"Naturally I did not know," said Hitler, "that one day I would be nailed by a lawyer for this expression." He tried to find a way out. "The concept 'roll commando' has taken on an absolutely ridiculous meaning here," he said. He explained that the term came from the Western Front. It originally referred to a small section of men who had the job of "rolling up" an enemy trench. The military source seemed to cast an incriminating light on the SA's approach to its political enemies, but Hitler tried to emphasize that a roll commando therefore could refer only to a small unit of ten men, thirty at the most, and that the term "obviously in and of itself has nothing at all to do with the elimination of people." "The SA is forbidden to commit violence or to provoke it," he continued. "But in a case of self-defense it is hard to say where the line is between self-defense and attack. When an SA man is pursued for months by Red murderers..."[54]

Ohnesorge interrupted Hitler: "I ask that you refrain from using this expression," he warned. Hitler continued: "When an SA man is pursued for months, I can imagine that in an emergency he would fail to recognize the moment of self-defense. But if an SA man really oversteps the boundary of self-defense, you can't hold a person responsible for that. Not once has the leadership of the Party given out the slogan: 'Beat the opponent to death! Beat the Communists to death! Beat the SPD to death!' Those kinds of expression have only been used by the other side." (In 1929 and 1930 the Communists had, in fact, used the slogan "Beat the Fascists wherever you find them!")[55]

Ohnesorge tried to summarize the gist of Hitler's evidence: "So you say you are not conscious of using the term 'roll commando' in the manner in which you have been accused by the private prosecutors, and most especially not to refer to Storm 33?" Again Hitler's response was conspicuously evasive: "I do not know Storm 33." Ohnesorge pressed on: "You are also unaware whether any kind of plan, as is claimed by the private prosecutors, existed among the members of Storm 33?"

"That I consider to be absolutely impossible."[56]

It was at this point that Litten stepped in. By all accounts his manner was cool and reserved. When fellow lawyers like Rudolf Olden, Hilde Benjamin, and Götz Berger talked about Litten's way of handling a case, they always mentioned his memory, his knowledge of the law, his preparation (Litten always retained the contents of all the case documents in his photographic memory), and his persistence. "He gave up none of his rights, even the most minor," remembered Olden. "His way of asking questions was calm and measured, but very penetrating."[57] Calm and measured his questions may have been, but they were not any less dangerous for that.

"You have nonetheless raised the accusation," said Litten, "that Captain Stennes did not accomplish anything more than the formation of a few miserable roll commandos. Anyone would have to take this to mean that Captain Stennes had set up roll commandos within the National Socialist movement." Litten held up Hitler's *Nationalist Observer* article.[58]

"I did not mean to make any such accusation against Stennes," replied Hitler. "I did not mean to say that he worked illegally within the party. I only meant to explain that if I wanted to refute the criticism that was made of me by Stennes and the other radical leaders, I would have to leave the legal path, and I will not do that under any circumstances." Striking his own chest with his fist, Hitler insisted, "The legality of the party would only be placed in question if I were to approve roll commandos."[59]

"According to your testimony, you were afraid of Stennes," Litten stated coolly.

"Not of his forming roll commandos, but of the hopes and wishes that were in Stennes' newspaper, which you can read there," Hitler replied, referring to Stennes's new paper, *Workers, Peasants, Soldiers*, its very title a Socialist-sounding contrast to the violent monikers of other Nazi papers, such as the *Attack* and the *Stormer*. Later in the year Stennes's paper was taken up as the SA supplement to a paper edited by another Nazi apostate, Otto Strasser, who had also broken away from Hitler's movement because it was insufficiently Socialist and revolutionary: Strasser's paper was called the *German Revolution*.[60]

"So you were afraid of Stennes' illegal ideas?"

Sensing that the young lawyer was trying to trap him, Hitler took an evasive tack. "I am not in a position to judge them," he replied.

Litten stuck stubbornly to the question of roll commandos. "Did you not accuse Captain Stennes," he asked, "of appointing an SA leader in Danzig, who formed roll commandos and even broke up your own party meetings?" Hitler had made this accusation in his *Nationalist Observer* article.[61]

"But that has nothing to do with this case," Hitler protested. He continued to argue, somewhat irrelevantly, that Stennes's activities in Danzig proved his incompetence. Further, he said that Danzig SA men had been given permits for their weapons. He would not say more unless the public was excluded from the courtroom, because it was a matter of national security.[62]

Ignoring Hitler's comment, one of the supporting judges interjected, "You have characterized the expression 'roll commando' as blurry and fantastically misunderstood. Now I don't understand how you can *reproach* Captain Stennes with the formation of roll commandos."[63]

Hitler's response was again contradictory: "I used this expression in an article that I wrote in protecting the interests of the movement. Had I known the expression 'roll commando' would be interpreted as it has been in this trial and used against me, I would not have used it."[64]

Litten's other main line of questioning had to do with the Party's approval of statements by Goebbels. In January 1930, following the killing of a Berlin SA man (and pimp) named Horst Wessel, Goebbels had written in the *Attack* that the killers "must be beaten to pulp and muck." Nazi propaganda went on to trumpet Wessel as the Party's leading martyr. Litten asked Hitler about Goebbels's language: "You said that no violent actions are carried out by the National Socialist Party. But didn't Goebbels come up with the slogan 'The enemy must be beaten to a pulp' "?[65]

"That is not to be taken literally!" Hitler protested. "It means that one must defeat and destroy the opponent organizations, not that one attacks and murders the opponent."[66]

"For now I do not want to cast doubt on the honesty of your oath in Leipzig," said Litten, "but I am asking, does your struggle for power involve only the struggle against the state as it now exists, or does it also involve the struggle against the organizations of the working class that are opposed to you?"

"What does the struggle for power consist of?" Hitler began rhetorically. "It consists of defeating parties opposed to us. And of the struggle for the great masses. So if we use legal methods in the struggle against the state, we will use them in the struggle against the opposition workers' organizations also."[67]

Litten wanted to show Hitler the exhibits, which were weapons allegedly owned by the four defendants. Hitler brushed this off with the vague comment that sometimes a wrench or something similar might be found on an SA man. It was understandable if a man whose life was under constant threat took to carrying such a weapon. "I know what the fear of death is," he said.[68]

Curt Becker, the defense lawyer for Stief, Wesemann, and Liebscher, now stepped in with some questions about Stennes's relationship to the Party. Hitler may not have known that Becker was a Stennes man. According to *Voss's News*, when Becker rose to question Hitler, the Führer turned to him with "a friendly smile," apparently under the illusion that Becker would ask questions that would "give him the opportunity to sparkle." Once Hitler began to realize that Becker was not there to help him, his expression grew darker and his voice rose. He "stuck his hands in his pockets, than clasped them behind his back, then folded them across his chest; he was in a dilemma." Becker's questions amounted to a defense against Hitler's insinuations that Stennes was a police informer and therefore was trying to provoke the SA into committing criminal acts. Becker went on to suggest that the legality of the National Socialists was a sham, and he invited Hitler to prove it was not. Hitler replied that the SA was not armed: "I intervene when I hear of a weapon, and the leaders responsible are expelled from the party." Continuing with what some of the papers called "highly energetic political speechmaking," Hitler argued that if Germany was oppressed by an individual, by a conqueror like Napoleon, he would be prepared to follow a revolutionary course. But Germany was oppressed by a spiritual conqueror. To be liberated, the German people had to be conquered spiritually—in other words, through a legal political and propaganda campaign.[69]

By this time Hitler's testimony had already lasted two hours. He had remained standing while being questioned. The four defendants had likewise remained standing, a practice common at the time for defendants in German criminal courtrooms. Ohnesorge invited the four SA men to sit, but they refused. "Upright and zealous, genuine SA men," said Goebbels's *Attack* approvingly. "They showed their Führer that even in the slammer they were not to be brought low."[70]

Litten had three more questions for Hitler that, before asking, he had to submit in writing for the court's approval. The first challenged Hitler to characterize an organized assault by fifteen or twenty SA men with firearms as self-defense arising out of fear of Communist attack. The third involved the allegation that at a private meeting in October 1930, Hitler had promised Reich Chancellor Heinrich Brüning that he, Hitler, would dissolve the SA were he invited to join Brüning's administration.[71]

But it was Litten's second question that gave Hitler the most trouble. In 1927 Goebbels had published a small pamphlet entitled *The Nazi-Sozi*, whose purpose was to instruct Nazi Party recruits. If the Nazis could not in the end come to power through parliamentary elections, Goebbels had written, "then we will make revolution! Then we will chase the parliament to the devil and found the state on the basis of German fists and German brains!" The passage was cut from the second edition, brought out by the Nazi publisher Franz Eher in 1929. But it underlay Litten's question: Had Hitler known about this passage (which Litten cited precisely) when he named Goebbels the Party's propaganda director?[72]

It took the court three-quarters of an hour to decide to allow the second and third questions. Judge Ohnesorge put Litten's second question to Hitler: "Herr Hitler, you heard the question about appointing Herr Goebbels as Reich Propaganda Director. What do you have to say about that?"

"I cannot say under oath whether I knew Goebbels' book at that time," Hitler replied. "The thesis in Goebbels' book is entirely without value for the Party, since the pamphlet does not bear the Party emblem and is also not officially sanctioned by the Party. Only what is officially sanctioned has validity. Goebbels was appointed because of his extraordinary ability for propaganda, and must stay within the guidelines which I, as Party leader, give him."[73]

"Is it correct," Litten asked, "that Goebbels had already been made Party boss [*Gauleiter*] of Berlin in 1926?"

"I cannot confirm the date." (It was, in fact, correct.)

"Must it not be so, that something which a man like Goebbels says outside of his official Party position exerts an extraordinary influence on the members of the Party who read his pamphlet?"

Hitler replied with platitudes. "Our movement is a continuous melting pot," he said, "to which people come from all camps, from the Communists to the German Nationals." No party should be judged by an individual member; it should be judged only by its official policies. Hitler insisted once again on the Party's "granite-hard" commitment to legality.[74]

Litten could not be so easily deflected. "You didn't discipline or expel Goebbels, but instead made him Reich Propaganda Director," he pointed out. "Mustn't Goebbels' example rouse the idea in the Party that the program of legality hasn't gotten very far?"

According to the account in *Voss's News*, Hitler began to stutter and appeared to "search convulsively for an answer" that would cover him without too obviously abandoning Goebbels. He could only repeat that the Party operated legally and that this applied to Goebbels as well. "[Goebbels] is in Berlin and can be called here any time." Pressing the point, Litten asked if Goebbels had been forbidden to disseminate his pamphlet.

"I don't know."[75]

"And are you aware," Litten continued, "that numerous SA men and Party members, especially in northern Germany, hold to Goebbels' program of illegality?"

"If that were the case," said Hitler, "these people would have left me a month ago. Because a month ago they were all asked if they were in agreement with the course of one hundred percent legality. The result was overwhelming." Hitler turned to the judges and asked that the Party's investigation committee, the leader of the SA, and all the Party's district leaders (*Gauleiter*) be summoned to confirm what he had said. Ohnesorge ignored the request and asked Litten's third question: "Did you promise Reich Chancellor Brüning to dissolve the SA in the event of your joining the administration?" According to one account, Ohnesorge helpfully explained to Hitler the drift of Litten's question: it would suggest, he told Hitler, "that you yourself saw the SA as something illegal."[76]

According to the reports, Hitler was now "extraordinarily excited," and it is easy to see why: at a moment in which he had barely surmounted a crisis with the SA, any suggestion of willingness to betray his private army could be politically disastrous. "I insist," said Hitler, "that Brüning has not offered me any participation in his government, nor have we asked for any participation on the basis of any sort of concession. Dissolving the SA would mean for me the end of the Party. The SA men are the first men of the Party. To ask me to dissolve the SA in order to join a government would amount to asking me to commit suicide or asking my Party to commit suicide."[77]

In his memoirs, published long after the Second World War, Heinrich Brüning confirmed that he had met with Hitler in the fall of 1930 but said nothing of an offer to disband the SA. One of the many democratic politicians who went into exile in the United States during the Nazi years, Brüning had no reason to hold back information that would discredit Hitler.[78]

Becker, too, pressed Hitler to comment on allegations concerning meetings between Nazi and German army leaders at which the topic was the abolition or reorganization of the SA. When Becker asked point blank if "a reorganization of the SA" was presently under way, Hitler replied that the reorganization of the SA was a permanent condition. New members always had to be taught to feel 100 percent members of the Party and not to follow "the spirit of the Free Corps."[79]

Litten pounced. "In your opinion, what is the spirit of the Free Corps?"

Hitler explained that the "Free Corps spirit" was the belief that "a change in the fate of the German nation" could be brought about by placing physical strength at the disposal of a particular government. "The National Socialist knows that the fate of the nation depends on a complete spiritual transformation of the German people."

"Do you also include the notorious crimes and killings that were committed by the Free Corps as part of this spirit?"

Hitler became enraged. "I refuse to acknowledge that that kind of thing happened. The Free Corps committed no killings. They defended Germany."[80]

The court took a short recess, during which the *Attack*'s correspondent claimed to see Litten talking with Becker in the corridor: "It is very clear to us that [Litten] received 'his information' in this conversation," wrote the Nazi reporter, as interested in discrediting the one as the other. Litten's line of questioning after the break seemed to confirm the point. Just two weeks before the 1930 elections, Hitler had been faced with the first act of the Stennes revolt and in response had gone on a public relations tour of the SA taverns in Berlin. According to some reports, heavily armed SS men escorted him (the SS, later the most powerful organization in Nazi Germany, began as a small corps of body guards within the SA). The success of this campaign was mixed: at least some of the Storms had greeted their leader with icy hostility. Litten asked Hitler if it was true that armed escorts had accompanied him on these visits.[81]

This question, too, made Hitler furious: "That is complete lunacy!" Apparently unconscious of the pun, he went on, "In all the taverns I was greeted with stormy enthusiasm." His remark provoked laughter in the spectators' gallery.[82]

It was now 12:45. Hitler had been testifying for over three and a half hours and looked, according to *Voss's News*, "rather exhausted." The court broke for lunch. Hitler strode out of the courtroom. Playing sarcastically on Hitler's remark about "stormy enthusiasm," the *8 O'Clock Evening News* noted that there was no chance of "stormy appearances of any kind" during the break, as Hitler repaired to a private waiting room. Walter Stennes was standing in the corridor as Hitler passed; he ostentatiously turned his back on the leader from Munich.[83]

After the break the court took up the questioning of Stennes and the former commander of the Berlin SA, Ernst Wetzel. Rudolf Olden described Stennes as "a slender young man, agile like a lieutenant, but with some gray among the brown hairs, a man who makes an honest impression . . . one who speaks simply, who does not have the silver tongue that is seductive to some and disgusting to others." Stennes said that he had known nothing in advance about the attack on the Eden Dance Palace and did not know if it had been planned. SA formations, he explained, "have not forged such plans." He also denied having formed roll commandos within the Nazi Party. There was, he said, a "crass disproportion" between the Party's organization and its propaganda. The message the "ordinary" SA man would take away from a Nazi rally diverged sharply from the discipline the Party sought to impose on him. Stennes meant that the Party preached violence to its SA while posing as legal to middle-class voters. The ordinary man, naturally, paid the price of this hypocrisy. Stennes claimed that he had tried to impress the SA's plight on the Party leadership, to no avail.[84]

Stennes stood down, and Wetzel took the stand. Forty years old and, like Storm 33's Fritz Hahn, employed as a bank clerk, Wetzel also testified to long-standing SA grievances against the political leadership. "We SA leaders," he told the court, "take the position that the leadership remains responsible for what the individual men do." The men were not responsible for the violence of Germany's growing civil war; the guilt lay with "those who in speech and writing inflame the passions of the crowd." SA leaders, he said, had known for six months that Hitler, contrary to his earlier beliefs, had committed himself to legality. "We believe that he is serious about it," Wetzel added, "even if Goebbels tried to make his oath in Leipzig seem ridiculous to us." This was a striking piece of testimony, underscoring the murky role that Goebbels had played in the Stennes affair. Ohnesorge intervened abruptly: "That is not relevant to the case."[85]

Litten chose this moment to raise new questions for both Stennes and Wetzel dealing with the SA's attitude to the Nazi policy of legality and the responsibility of the Party's leadership for violence. A brief conference took place between Hitler, the Nazi Party's leading legal expert, Hans Frank, and Hitler's lawyer, Otto Kamecke, at the end of which Kamecke strongly opposed Litten's requests, arguing that Litten was abusing his position. The *Berlin Daily News* reported that by this time Hitler and the other National Socialist leaders present had been "seized by a considerable nervousness." The ground for this nervousness, the *Daily News* believed, lay in the fact that in the morning session "Hitler's protestations of legality had gone extraordinarily far." The court rejected all of Litten's questions, dismissing them as irrelevant, along with his request to summon a senior official from the Prussian Interior Ministry.[86]

Litten now asked that Hitler be brought back to the witness box. "Do you still maintain," he asked the Führer, "what you said in the morning session: that if you had followed Stennes's course you would have had to leave the path of legality?"

"I said the following," Hitler replied carefully. "I am a dutiful guardian of my Party's interests. The view that Captain Stennes puts forward in his paper would lead me to leave the path that I have taken."

Hitler still wanted to have it both ways so as not to antagonize the SA. "But I have to insist that it must be left to Captain Stennes to refer to his goals as legal. That is a matter of opinion."[87]

Litten returned to Goebbels's pamphlet *The Nazi-Sozi* and asked whether it was correct that it had now been published by the Nazi Party and that 120,000 copies were in print. Kamecke objected to the question. Litten made clear his intent with a startling revelation: "I have just learned," he said, "that this pamphlet is sanctioned by the party, that it is sold at all Goebbels' meetings, and that it is available in all party bookstores, contrary to Hitler's declarations about legality."

Even Ohnesorge seemed to be impressed by the dilemma now facing the witness. "Herr Hitler," he said, "you in fact testified in the morning session that Goebbels's text was not an official party publication."

"Nor is it," replied the Führer with growing heat. "A text becomes official if it bears the printed seal of the Party. In any case it is the Propaganda Chief who must be heard on these things, and above all—"[88]

It was here that Hitler lost all composure. It has been said that he was prone to outbursts of uncontrolled fury at those moments when he felt circumstances moving beyond his control. Talking to the Fürsts after the trial, Litten said that Hitler had "screamed like an hysterical cook." Hitler turned to Litten, his face deep red, and yelled: "—above all, Herr Advocate, how can you say that that is a call to illegality? That is a statement that can be proven by nothing!"

Unfazed, Litten moved in for the kill: "How is it possible that the Party publisher took over a text that stands in clear contradiction to the Party line?"[89]

We need to imagine how Hitler must have felt at this moment. This was a man who liked to call himself the leader of a movement of millions, surrounded by a cult that revered him as a virtual messiah come to deliver Germany from defeat and humiliation. He had triumphed in the elections of the previous fall and now presided over the fastest growing political party in Germany's volatile political environment. Now he was being pushed to the wall by an irritatingly persistent young lawyer. For all Hitler and his inner circle knew, the future of their movement might hang on what Hitler said in this Berlin courtroom. Litten's question forced him to face the contradictions that lay in his protestations of legality. Disavowal of the revolutionary spirit of the SA would arouse the storm troopers' suspicions, never far below the surface, that Hitler would betray them someday. It would play into the hands of the Stennes faction and possibly splinter the National Socialist movement. On the other hand, embracing illegality would jeopardize the electoral strategy that Hitler had followed with such success since the failure of his 1923 coup. Hitler had tried evasion, rhetoric, and extravagant rage. Nothing had worked.

And now, while he might have been wondering how to field Litten's latest question, Ohnesorge saved him.

"That has nothing to do with this trial," said the judge.

It was Litten's turn for outrage: "I can only say that the court now ..."

"I must ask that you not criticize the court," said Ohnesorge, cutting off Litten's protest.[90]

Hitler's dangerous moment had passed. Litten sat down.

The Oath

One more issue remained: the question of whether or not Hitler and the other witnesses should be sworn in. In German trials witnesses are usually given the oath after testifying, rather than before, as in an American courtroom. The oath then "strengthens" the testimony. If the court has significant doubts about the honesty of a witness, it may refuse to have the witness sworn, which correspondingly devalues the testimony.

State Advocate Stenig wanted all three of the day's witnesses— Hitler, Stennes, and Wetzel—to be sworn. Litten thought that Stennes should be sworn, but not Hitler or Wetzel. He argued that Stennes's testimony had cast the veracity of Hitler's into great doubt, a claim that brought Hitler to his feet in rage, demanding to intervene. (The official protocol records dryly that Hitler, along with the lawyers, "was heard on the matter.") Litten cited an example of Hitler's unreliability as a witness. "What does the abbreviation 'SA' mean?" he asked. Litten explained that Fritz Löwenthal, another lawyer, had accused Hitler of perjury, when as a witness at an earlier trial Hitler had testified that SA stood for "Sports Section" rather than "Storm Section."[91]

"I have explained the development of the term on earlier occasions," said Hitler. "We spoke earlier of a 'Hall Guard Section' [*Saalschutzabteilung*], then of a 'Sports Section' [*Sportabteilung*], and since the great hall battle in Munich in 1921, of a 'Storm Section' [*Sturmabteilung*]."

"Then why haven't you brought a libel suit against Advocate Löwenthal?"

"I have been slandered and insulted for five years. I have no time and no desire to carry out all of these trials."

After brief deliberation, the court gave Hitler, as well as Stennes and Wetzel, the oath. The protocol records that with the agreement of all parties, the three witnesses were excused at 6:09 p.m. and the trial adjourned until the morning of May 11. The great day in Moabit was over.[92]

A Snag with Hitler

I waited the whole day with a pounding heart for the outcome of Hitler's testimony," Goebbels wrote in his diary the next day. "It worked out. Stennes was very tame and—O Wonder—swore an oath to legality. With this he decapitated himself." Despite the defiant tone, Goebbels's diary also reveals that both he and Hitler had grasped how damaging Litten's questions on Goebbels's pamphlet had been:

A snag with Hitler: My "Nazi-Sozi." There was an incriminating [*verfänglich*] sentence there. In the evening we're sitting at the Kaiserhof [Hotel] and then it occurs to me that this sentence was cut from the 2nd edition. Rejoicing. Hitler positively dances for joy. It vindicates us. Hitler and I will write a salty letter to the court. . . . The day that began so gloomily ended up brightly and well. You have to have luck.[93]

This diary entry is a striking confession. "The day that began so gloomily" and ended with Hitler "positively danc[ing] for joy" are evidence of how much Litten's questions had shaken the Nazi leaders. Goebbels and Hitler wasted no time drafting their complaint. The court received the letter on May 9. "As I take it from today's press announcements regarding the examination of Adolf Hitler in the trial of *Stief et al.*," Goebbels wrote, "the Jewish lawyer Litten attempted to demonstrate the illegality of the National Socialist movement through citing a sentence from my pamphlet 'The Nazi-Sozi.'" The sentence in question, Goebbels continued, was supposed to show that he advocated coming to power through violence. The "Jewish lawyer Litten" claimed that the pamphlet was published by the Nazi Party's official publisher and was "distributed by the thousand" at Nazi rallies. But it was clear "to every unbiased person" that the phrase "we will make revolution" referred to "a spiritual transformation and not an unconstitutional coup." In any case, the Party's publisher had not printed the first edition of the pamphlet, and Goebbels had deleted the incriminating sentence "years ago on my own initiative" as it "gave rise to many misunderstandings." "The Jewish lawyer Litten," Goebbels concluded, "has made himself guilty of an obvious deception of the court through his irresponsible claims. I leave the judgment of this to the public. I will permit myself to publish this letter in the press as soon as it is in the hands of the court." And indeed, Goebbels's letter appeared in the *Attack* the next day, under the headline "Half-Jew Litten and the 'Nazi-Sozi.'"[94]

The *Attack* put a bold face on Hitler's examination. It recorded that Litten and Becker had "asked many questions of the witness Adolf Hitler," but that they were "matters of insignificance." Those who had actually been present in the courtroom might have been surprised to read that Hitler's responses to Litten's questions were "succinct and unambiguous" and that Hitler had proven "that neither lies nor slanders can break up the victory march of our movement." Goebbels's diary more accurately reflects his worry about the impact of Hitler's testimony, but the propaganda director also shrewdly observed that "Stennes lost the trial." Goebbels realized that Stennes could not keep his hold on the "revolutionary" elements of the SA while himself proclaiming allegiance to legal measures. With perhaps more optimism than assurance, Goebbels wrote that the Party's legality "is once again tolerably grounded.... Who won't believe it now..."[95]

While Nazis proclaimed Hitler's appearance a success, it was clear to most other observers that he had been caught on the contradictions of his movement. Naturally the impression that Hitler made depended on the audience. Mining class as well as regional prejudices, the *World in the Evening* likened Hitler to "an Austrian-Czech master-butcher" and an "oily barber." The *Berlin Morning Post* summed up the results of Hitler's examination: "The leaders swear to their legality, but the subordinates are to a great extent independent and claim for themselves the right of self-defense—as they understand it." The *Voss's News* columnist Moritz Goldstein noted that Hitler had sworn once again to his legal intentions: "Who can say how he means it, and if he means it in a certain way, how he will mean it in the future?" But if the subordinates began to rebel against the hypocrisy at the top, "perhaps the scales would fall from their eyes."[96]

The shrewdest contemporary observer of the case was Litten's fellow lawyer Rudolf Olden, also a political editor at the *Berlin Daily News*. Olden went straight to the paradoxes that Hitler's examination revealed. "Hitler swears and swears to his legality," Olden wrote. Although it was true that Hitler had not spoken of heads rolling, as he had the previous fall in Leipzig, "few believe him. Does he actually want to be believed?" The answer, Olden thought, was that the "nationalist masses" did not believe and did not want to believe Hitler's protestations of legality, preferring the "revolutionary phrases they have been fed for years." It was those who *did* believe in Hitler's fidelity to the Constitution who now "turn[ed] from him in disappointment"—men like Walter Stennes and Ernst Wetzel. Olden's summary: "Yesterday in Moabit two revolutionaries put the screws to the former revolutionary." The "representatives of the proletarian and the national revolution"—he meant Litten and Stennes, or at least "the forces that stand behind them"—wanted to send a message: " 'Don't believe him any more,' they want to say to the masses, 'he is telling the truth.' Because then, so they calculate, he will lose the masses." Olden closed his essay with a rhetorical question: "Had Hitler already sworn too much?" He answered with a chillingly prophetic verbal sigh: "No, the people do not catch on that fast."[97]

Verdicts

The rest of the trial was, inevitably, an anticlimax. When it resumed the following Monday, the court heard a few witnesses summoned by the Nazi defendants; even the *Attack* thought their evidence was of little consequence. The same day State Advocate Stenig began his closing address, speaking for three hours and continuing the next day. Although Stenig accepted that the attack on the Eden Dance Palace had not been planned and that the storm troopers lacked the deliberate intention to kill necessary for first-degree murder convictions, he asked for convictions and for heavy sentences for lesser offenses: against Stief, for serious breach of the peace, attempted second-degree murder, and unauthorized carrying of a weapon, five years and six months in a penitentiary with five years' loss of civil rights; against Wesemann, for serious breach of the peace and attempted second-degree murder, five years in a penitentiary and five years' loss of civil rights; against Liebscher, for serious breach of the peace, two years six months in prison; and against Berlich, for serious breach of the peace and serious bodily harm, two years in prison.[98]

Then it was Litten's turn to speak. He began by expressing sympathy for all "revolutionary workers," whether they sided with the Nazis or the Communists. But underscoring his central message, he referred to the SA as "systematic murderers of workers" and insisted that twenty defendants should be before the court, not four. He argued that the Nazi witnesses were dishonest as a group, and that on May 8 Hitler had perjured himself at least four times. He closed with sentencing requests more severe than Stenig's: he wanted six years in a penitentiary for each of the defendants, for attempted first-degree murder and serious breach of the peace.[99]

Becker and Kamecke, for the Nazis, asked for acquittals. Kamecke, mirroring Litten's efforts to set the case in a wider political context, argued that the defendants were scapegoats for a government that could, if it wished, ease the economic crisis, but instead "demanded that political victims be punished for the failure of its economic policies."[100]

The court convicted Stief, Liebscher, and Berlich of breaches of the peace and trespassing and sentenced each of them to two and a half years' imprisonment. "It is beside the point," said the judges, that "it cannot be proven that they themselves fired the shots. Because at the time the shots were fired they were—as stated earlier—ready, able and willing to support the shooter or shooters with physical force. They were also resolved for their part independently to attack the opponents in the justified expectation that they would receive help from others." Wesemann was acquitted.[101]

Ohnesorge was a careful judge. The written judgment in the Eden Dance Palace case revealed a thorough effort to weigh the conflicting witness statements and derive from them a reliable narrative of what had happened on the night of November 22, 1930. At the same time, the judgment was marked by a stubborn refusal to see the broader political importance of what the defendants had done at the Eden Dance Palace. It also devoted a great deal of attention to Litten's professional conduct.

With something of a judicial sigh, the court found that its "difficult task" was to "examine the testimony of the witnesses as well as that of the defendants for its inner value for the finding of a verdict." The court examined the internal consistency of each witness's various statements to the police, the magistrate, and the court, and then compared the different witnesses' narratives one with another. It found that the testimony of witnesses who claimed to recognize the four defendants as attackers contradicted not only the defendants' evidence but was also "to an extent mutually contradictory," and, still more, each witness's various statements were self-contradictory. On the other hand there were striking similarities in some of the facts various witnesses recalled; three witnesses, for instance, described Wesemann's sideburns. The judges did not draw the conclusion from such substantial agreement that the witnesses were simply telling the truth. Rather, "the court has arrived at the conviction that the observations of these witnesses were mutually influenced."[102]

How? The police had questioned a number of witnesses on November 28, six days after the attack on the Eden Dance Palace. But what the court characterized as a "Communist protest meeting"—Litten's meeting at the Turkish Tent at which he asked witnesses to "testify"— had taken place on November 26. The witnesses had come forward, spoken of what they had seen, and then answered Litten's questions. A large number of witnesses at the trial had spoken at this meeting. "The witness Litten," said the court, "confirmed the correctness of this account of events in the Turkish Tent."[103]

Such a proceeding raised "the most severe doubts" from the "point of view of an investigation of the truth." There was a danger that witnesses might be influenced by Litten's questions and in the end be unable to distinguish between what they themselves had seen and heard and the stories of other witnesses. (The witnesses were excluded from the courtroom until their evidence had been heard to avoid just such a taint.) "This danger," the court went on, "is all the greater when—as here—a politically united audience uses the protest meeting to pursue the goal of proving that members of a politically opposed group have committed a violent act." And certainly there was also the danger that "unscrupulous persons" would deliberately change their stories to fit those of other witnesses. Litten had argued that the Turkish Tent meeting made no difference; no court could ever exclude the possibility that witnesses would get together and compare and blend their stories. The court would have none of this; the meeting amounted to "an irresponsible enlargement of the sources of error." The testimony of the victim Walter Braun was a prime example. Examined in the Westend Hospital on November 23, he said he had not seen any of the attackers and could not identify them. Three days later, shown photographs of Wesemann and Stief, he claimed to be able to identify them as attackers. Examined by the magistrate on January 14, he gave an exact description of Wesemann, mentioning Wesemann's black shirt and sideburns. Köhler's evidence followed a similar pattern. In both cases, the court said, it could give their testimony little weight. In fact, the court found that it could place no weight on the evidence of any of the witnesses Litten had examined at the Turkish Tent.[104]

The critical question all along had been one of motive: Was the attack on the Eden Dance Palace a random action by young Nazi hotheads, or part of an organized campaign of terror? The court concluded that although Liebscher's story had filled the storm troopers with the desire to "to commit violence of some sort or another on the participants" of the Wanderfalke party, they had acted without any specific intention to kill their victims. Litten had argued that the attack was a plan for the "premeditated murder of revolutionary workers." But the court thought that all the evidence was against this. The storm troopers had had no knowledge of the layout of the Eden Dance Palace, and the court also found it significant that most of them had gone out into the November night without hats or coats.[105]

It was in discussing whether there were mitigating circumstances for Stief and Liebscher that the court came closest to dealing with the broader political implications of the case:

> Both defendants belong to Storm 33 of the NSDAP and—as must be believed—are in the midst of a bitter struggle with the members of left-radical political groups. This struggle has often led to violent confrontations. The court is not in a position to decide who bears the greater responsibility for these fights; it is in the nature of the matter that each group attributes the chief, or sole, responsibility to the other. Only from this inner disposition does it become comprehensible that the National Socialists answered a comparatively insignificant jostling with such disproportionate severity. This inner disposition, which governed the defendants in their behavior, must—even if it is one-sided and unjustified—be considered as a mitigating factor in sentencing.

The court found that "such an irresponsible, brutal action reveals a raw mentality which . . . requires a severe penalty." Nonetheless, it would not punish the defendants with the deprivation of civil rights—a common additional penalty in the Weimar legal system—as they "did not act from dishonorable motives."[106]

None of the parties to the Eden Dance Palace trial wished to leave the verdict as it stood. German law in 1931 permitted one level of appeal from a jury verdict. Such appeals lay to Germany's highest court, the Imperial Supreme Court, in Leipzig. The SA men, the prosecution, and Litten's clients all appealed.

There was really only one issue in the appeal: Would the Imperial Supreme Court acknowledge the broad political stakes of the trial, or would the justices, as Ohnesorge's court had done, minimize the case by focusing on trivialities? Remarkably, the Ohnesorge court had entirely neglected Hitler's evidence in its lengthy written judgment. Thus Hitler formed an essential element of Litten's appeal. In his appeal brief Litten noted that his question for Hitler, "whether the witness sees the actions of the defendants as an attack or as an overstepping of the bounds of self-defense as he understands it," had been rejected by the court. Litten argued that this was an error in law. In its verdict the court had failed to recognize that "internal" as well as "external" facts could be subjects of witness testimony. He argued that getting Hitler to define "self-defense" as the SA understood it was vital to the trial. If Hitler had testified that he considered the defendants' conduct to be self-defense, the "court's belief in the National Socialist claim of a Communist share in the responsibility for the constant conflicts" would have been shaken.[107]

Litten also made one argument ostensibly *in favor* of the SA defendants. The court had ruled that they were not to be recognized as "criminals by conviction" (*Überzeugungstäter*), a determination that would allow them better treatment in prison. Litten objected. "The private prosecutor," he wrote, "has a justified interest in being protected from a violent political opponent through the highest possible sentence, but on the other hand has no interest in defaming the opponent beyond what is necessary." It was clear enough why Litten chose to argue this point. It was another way for him to demonstrate the political agenda behind the Eden Dance Palace attack, which the court did not want to see.[108]

The Imperial Supreme Court heard the appeals on November 19, 1931, and made no significant changes to the trial decision. As Litten's essential argument in the trial was that the SA's actions were *political*, the most important passage of the Imperial Supreme Court's judgment dealt with the meaning and scope of a political trial. The "subject of the investigation and decision," said the high court, was "crimes and misdemeanors against the public order, life and bodily security, of the kind that occupy the courts in ever greater numbers." The Eden Dance Palace case, however, was not a political case "in the strict sense," although the "rage and hatred" of "party political agitation" lay behind what had happened. Whatever a party leader thought about the attack was, therefore, beside the point, as was the issue of whether the defendants' party had set itself "the goal of fighting for power with illegal means." Questions touching on such matters—Litten's questions—were irrelevant. The laws of criminal procedure were not to be "misused" for the purposes of "creating a sensation, to advertise for any kind of institution, a business operation or a party, or to create difficulties for third persons and to expose them before the public." There could be no clearer rejection of Litten's case against Adolf Hitler, the National Socialist Party, the SA, and the threat that they represented.[109]

The Double Edge of the Deed

In 1925, in one of his passionately polemical essays, Litten took to task those who thought members of the youth movement should abstain from politics. Their disdain, said Litten, stemmed from a fear of responsibility: "The recognition that every deed that does good must do harm somewhere else, this recognition of the 'double-edge of the deed'...leads many people of the young generation to swear off acting at all." Litten believed that anyone who avoided acting for fear of guilt failed to recognize that guilt could flow from inaction as well. "Man cannot live without guilt," he concluded; "therefore, we must have the courage to accept guilt and responsibility."[110]

Litten's words were prophetic. For he paid a high price for his cross-examination of Adolf Hitler. So did others, especially other members of his family. With the Eden Dance Palace trial, the "Litten family tragedy," as Hans's niece Patricia Litten calls it, moved toward a climax: the trial brought on the final break between father and son.

This round of the Hans Litten versus Fritz Litten feud went back to the beginning of 1931. In February, Prussian authorities had launched an investigation of Fritz for tax evasion, alleging that he had hidden funds in foreign bank accounts. Fritz had in fact set up a bank account, in Danzig—since the end of the First World War an international city under the management of the League of Nations—which he designated a "scholarly support account." As Fritz explained it to the tax authorities, the purpose was to allow the capital to grow until the interest would suffice to support ongoing research projects. The Königsberg State Financial Office nonetheless saw the account as an "untaxed private asset" and, after an investigation that included a search of the Litten home, assessed a heavy fine against Fritz (not altogether reliable sources reported the fine as being as high as 6,000 Marks). But there was no public prosecution, and Prussian authorities found no reason for disciplinary action against Fritz in his capacity as a professor (and therefore a Prussian civil servant).[111]

At best this episode reflected no great credit on Fritz Litten. But his enemies—Nazi and other far-right activists and journalists in Königsberg—now sought to blow it up into a major scandal. A few months after the Eden Dance Palace trial an anonymous denunciation was sent to the disciplinary court for Prussian civil servants. Hints regarding the contents of Fritz Litten's lectures, and the claim that the denunciations had to be kept anonymous because "a few students who are closely connected to us" were approaching their state bar exams, suggest that it came from right-wing Königsberg law students. The denunciation closed militantly, in language redolent of Nazi speech-making: "What is not sound must fall. And it *will* fall."[112]

Right-wing newspapers in East Prussia began following the story eagerly. One, the *East Prussian Observer*, ran a banner headline with inch-high letters: "Professor Litten's Peculiar Tax Affair." After referring, essentially accurately, to the existence of the account in the Danzig bank (without, however, mentioning its purpose), the paper continued:

> It is simply impossible to mention this matter without linking a few considerations to it. From his teaching activity at the university and the commercial college, Herr Professor Litten, who incidentally comes from a very rich Königsberg patrician family, draws a considerable income.... It must therefore astonish us that such a man, blessed with wealth and fortune and called upon to defend the law, should commit tax evasion. What gives the case a piquant flavor is: Professor Litten is held to be a man of extreme national sentiment, conservative in his political and scholarly views, who carries on lively social contacts with the east Prussian aristocracy and the aristocracy of finance.[113]

This came at a time, the article continued, that international confidence in German finance was at a low point. (Indeed, in the autumn of 1931 the world financial system as a whole was in a parlous state: a series of bank failures beginning in Austria had contributed to a run on the German Mark and the British pound, causing further headaches for the embattled Heinrich Brüning and precipitating a change of government in Great Britain.) "And at the same time that Germany's statesmen travel around the world and are zealously concerned with dispelling the ever greater mistrust in our country, a pre-eminent, famous representative of German scholarship invests his money abroad, thereby emphasizing: I myself have no more confidence in Germany." "There are many more patriots in Germany," the paper concluded, "who—when they recite the slogan about giving blood and treasure for the fatherland—always mean only the blood and treasure of others."[114]

Fritz Litten himself had no doubt that such scathing attacks were retaliation for his son's professional activity. In June Hans Litten wrote to his father, beginning with an apology that "burdens of work" had prevented him from answering his father's letter "in the matter of Hitler." In his anger at Hans's work in the Eden Dance Palace case, Fritz had cut off all financial support to his eldest son. Hans indignantly defended his work in the case as "less of a political than a general-legal sort: representing the interests of people who are sitting ducks for organized murder bands, to whom German judges act as accomplices." If Fritz wanted to "draw economic consequences" from this work there was nothing more to be said, since Hans had not asked for money for a year. The letter goes on to bring the effects of Hans's work on his father's life into sharper focus. Fritz had complained of being "denounced" as Jewish in the right-wing press—an uncomfortable development for a man who had converted to the Evangelical Church and wished nothing more than to be fully accepted in aristocratic Prussian society. Fritz had also complained that press attacks had hurt his position with the conservative German People's Party: "I cannot imagine how vulgar attacks in the Hitler press could have such serious consequences with the People's Party," wrote his son. "You yourself, in our last conversation, insisted how little influence the Hitler-party and its opinion has on the People's Party." In what was probably an excess of self-dramatization, Fritz had said that he would have to leave Königsberg. "If you really have the intention of leaving East Prussia," Hans replied truculently, "I ask that you let me know as soon as your decision and the time of your departure are determined. I would then immediately arrange my discharge from the Berlin Court of Appeal and my admission to the Superior Court of Königsberg."[115]

In the fall of 1931 Fritz broke off all further communication with his eldest son. He later wrote, "All my warnings and efforts to get him away from his political-ideological insanity were without success." Hans had become, said his father, a "fanatical and unscrupulous defender of Communists," which was unbearable for a father who had "fought against Marxists" most of his adult life. Fritz went so far as to forbid Hans to visit the family home in Königsberg.[116]

Some of Fritz's rage must have been attributable to the wreck of his own career, for wrecked it certainly was. The attacks on him over Hans's activity, coupled with the tax affair, were accompanied by, or perhaps stimulated, a decline in his health. At the end of 1931 he retired, after submitting to the Prussian Ministry of Education three different doctors' reports attesting to his inability to continue working. One of the reports came from the University of Königsberg's professor of psychiatry, suggesting that it was most of all stress that lay behind his sudden need to retire. Fritz was fifty-eight years old.[117]

The other members of the Litten family also had to endure the consequences of Hans's work. Brothers Heinz and Rainer would ultimately be driven from promising theatrical careers and from Germany itself; Irmgard would wear herself into exhaustion and premature old age. Max and Margot Fürst would suffer in a different way, as we shall see. Hans Litten's niece Patricia recalled that her father, Rainer, whose stage and film career was starting to achieve spectacular success in the early 1930s, found himself by 1934 with "no other choice but [to emigrate], because of Hans's work." This meant that for the rest of his life he was saddled with a heavy burden: genuine admiration for Hans's heroism mingled with the knowledge that Hans's work had "strangled" his own career. Rainer was "somehow always in the slipstream [Windschatten] of this overpowering brother, who did so much damage ... but naturally also aroused so much admiration in him," she said. Rainer died of emphysema; for Patricia it was the only thing he could possibly die of. "He literally suffocated" on guilt and resentment.[118]

But it was Hans Litten who suffered the most. One consequence of the Eden Dance Palace case was renewed professional trouble. In a report to his superior on July 26, 1931, Paul Stenig noted that the jury court's acquittal of Wesemann was based largely on its doubts about the effects of Litten's public meeting at the Turkish Tent. It was open to the public prosecutor to consider bringing charges against Litten, but Stenig thought there was no need to do this, as "the Lawyers' Chamber is going to make this event the subject of a discussion." In the end nothing came of it for Litten, but it was hardly the last time that his aggressiveness in court would land him in trouble with the bar.[119]

Much more serious was the vindictive hatred that the Nazis began to direct at him—a sure sign of his success. Where before the *Attack* had contented itself with passing references to the "counsel for the private prosecutors" or "the Communist lawyer," it now wrote of "this comic peddler," an "anarchistic lawyer," a "half-Jew with unshorn hair." "What are all the pudgy little half-Jew's legalistic tricks supposed to mean, next to the clear words of Hitler?" was the *Attack*'s revealingly defiant question. It dismissed Litten's questions about Goebbels's pamphlet as an exercise in quoting out of context in order to produce "another sensation" for "the Jews," and because Litten had not mentioned the pamphlet's second edition he had "therefore deliberately lied."[120]

But whatever he said for public consumption, Goebbels was far too canny not to recognize the damage Litten had done. "We still have plenty of worries," he wrote in his diary on May 10. "The press is outdoing itself with lies about Hitler's examination. But we will defend ourselves."[121]

Goebbels would have to defend himself as well. Suspicions regarding his ties to Stennes lingered in Munich. In a file of press clippings held by the Nazi Party Archive, someone made a note later in 1931: "Between Goebbels, Koch (East Pr.), Rust, Otto Strasser, Gregor Strasser and Schulz things are going on that require observation. This group wants to move closer to socialism, which at the moment has a great effect on the masses, and gradually cut out Hitler and Munich."[122]

Hitler least of all thought the day had gone well. During the summer and fall of 1931 the Führer was repeatedly reminded of one danger to which the young lawyer's questions had exposed him: the threat of a perjury prosecution.

What would have happened had Ohnesorge not stopped Litten's questioning at precisely the point where Litten confronted Hitler with the Party-official status of Goebbels's pamphlet? As Ohnesorge reminded him, Hitler had claimed the pamphlet was not official; Litten was able to show that it was. But that was not the only perjury threat that Hitler faced. On May 12, a Berlin journalist named Helmut Klotz, editor of Stennes's paper *Workers, Peasants, Soldiers*, officially requested that the Berlin prosecutors bring perjury charges against Hitler. The reason: in response to some of Litten's questions, Hitler had made various claims about an SA leader named Fricke, among them that Fricke had participated in breaking up an SA Christmas party in Danzig. Klotz's request was not dismissed out of hand; senior Berlin prosecutors launched an investigation. State Advocate Stenig was asked to make a statement about Hitler's testimony; Stenig recalled that Hitler had testified about Fricke in response to Litten's questions, but could not remember the content, especially since the matter was "irrelevant to the proceedings." Hitler, back in Munich, was asked to explain himself to the examining magistrate, which he did in a letter dated August 6, 1931. This letter constitutes the only direct statement we have from Hitler on the examination of May 8 and on Litten personally. Among the striking facts that emerge from the letter is that Hitler had had his own stenographer present to take down the day's proceedings—another sign of how seriously he took the case, and in later years perhaps an aide-mémoire of his hatred of Litten.[123]

In the course of an "hours-long examination," Hitler complained, "the defense counsel, Advocate Dr. Litten [Hitler spelled it Lütten], continually deviating from the question at issue, put countless questions to me, which were from the outset completely impossible to answer from my own knowledge." It was obvious, Hitler continued, that he could have known anything about the content of Litten's questions only from information supplied to him by other people. Hitler had repeatedly told the court that "official party decisions cannot be examined by me for their correctness down to every last detail"—another deflating admission from the man who billed himself as the great leader. The rest of Hitler's defense amounted to a demonstration that, though he had made vague allegations against Fricke in his early April *Nationalist Observer* article, he had not repeated the allegations under oath. The Berlin prosecutors accepted this entirely underwhelming assertion of innocence. (Even at this late date, the police were not exactly sure whom they were dealing with; a letter asking after progress in Hitler's case refers to "Artur Hitler.") In October, senior Berlin prosecutor Benno Köhler wrote to Klotz to say it could "not be proven" that Hitler had committed perjury in his May 8 examination. The chief prosecutor at Berlin's Superior Court I reported to the Prussian justice minister in late August that "following a detailed investigation" of the allegations Hitler had made against Fricke, a charge of perjury could not be maintained because Hitler "had insisted in his examination he based his answers on reports and statements from third persons."[124]

It is impossible to know what effect a conviction for perjury in late 1931 or early 1932 would have had on Hitler's political fortunes. A conviction for treason in 1924 had, if anything, helped him; the platform he gained at his famous 1924 trial in Munich contributed to making him an important national figure. The Nazis, leaders included, were accustomed to prison time and skillfully exploited their sentences to pose as martyrs to an unjust system. On the other hand, a perjury conviction, devoid as it is of the trappings of honor that can accompany a dissident's treason conviction, might have hurt Hitler particularly with the middle-class voters who were increasingly turning to him in the early 1930s, and a jail sentence, even a short one, would have deprived the Nazis of their most potent speaker for the flurry of crucial election campaigns in 1932. And so the perjury prosecution remains one of the tantalizing "what ifs," taking its place alongside the others: What if Litten's questioning of Hitler had contributed to driving a deeper wedge between the SA and the party? What if more Germans had noticed and been alarmed by the patent dishonesty of Hitler's game with "legality"?[125]

All of these dangers for Hitler—the perjury charge, the splitting of the movement, the loss of support—were *possible* outcomes of Litten's advocacy in May 1931. For the sake of these possibilities Litten ran the risks that he ran, accepting the "double edge of the deed"; for their sake he brought down terrible consequences on his family, his friends, and most of all on himself. For Hitler certainly knew how much danger Litten had put him in. On top of that, Litten had humiliated him, and Hitler had a long memory for humiliations.

Here again important evidence comes from the memoirs of Rudolf Diels. Soon after Hitler had come to power in early 1933, and soon after Diels had become the first chief of the Gestapo under the new Prussian Interior Minister Hermann Göring, Göring handed Diels a thick file and asked, "What do you have to say about this?" Written on the file were the words "Hitler Perjury." The file contained records of the Social Democratic Interior Minister Carl Severing's efforts to prosecute Hitler for perjury for, Diels wrote, the "oath of legality which Hitler had sworn in the high treason trial against the officers Scheringer and Ludin in 1931 before the Imperial Supreme Court in Leipzig." A conviction could have opened the possibility "not only to carry out the deportation of Hitler," but also to saddle him with a lengthy prison sentence. Diels's signature was on many of the memos and reports, and Göring had presented the file to him as a grim warning. "If the contents of this file become known," Göring told Diels, "you will be killed in the street."[126]

Diels was either wrong about the date of the trial or about its identity. The Leipzig trial occurred in 1930. No documents survive pointing to an investigation of Hitler for perjury in that case. On the other hand, as we have seen, documents *do* survive from the perjury investigation arising out of the Eden Dance Palace trial, and those documents make no mention of an earlier case. It is therefore likely that the file Göring showed Diels grew out of Litten's examination of Hitler. Even if Diels had the trial correct and the date wrong, his account underscores the seriousness of the threat Litten's work had posed to Hitler, and the boundless lust for revenge that threat had awakened among the Nazi leaders.

Bülow Square

From the summer of 1931 to the winter of 1933, Litten's life was an increasingly grim battle with the Nazis, and with authorities who refused to share his assessment of the Nazi threat. In the course of this battle, Litten became the prime example of what one prosecutor called "underground influences" in the administration of justice in Weimar Berlin. How this came to be is an essential part of Litten's historical importance. Litten was a challenge to Germany's legal system. The way the system responded to him reveals its essence.

In early August 1931, the voters of Prussia went to the polls for an unusual election. The avowedly nonpolitical organization of war veterans called the Steel Helmet had launched a plebiscite in which Prussians were to vote on a dissolution of the Prussian Parliament and the holding of new elections, on the basis that the current Parliament was unrepresentative of the public mood at the beginning of the third year of the world economic crisis. All of the opposition parties in the Prussian Parliament—from the Nazis and the German Nationals on the far right to the center-right German People's Party to the Communists on the far left—joined to support the call for new elections.[127]

On the evening of Sunday, August 9, crowds gathered in Berlin to await the results. Communist supporters assembled at the Party headquarters, the Karl Liebknecht House in Bülow Square, very close to the Koblank Street apartment Litten shared with the Fürsts. When the plebiscite failed, receiving only 9.8 of the 13.4 million votes needed to force a new election, the mood turned sour and violence erupted between police and Communist supporters. The police tried to break up the crowds with truncheons, and several people were injured. But this time the police paid a price as well. Two police officers, Captains Anlauf and Lenk, were killed in an exchange of gunfire. The killer was Erich Mielke, who in later years would become the minister of state security of the (East) German Democratic Republic, and after the fall of the Berlin Wall would serve a few years in prison for this killing. But in the immediate aftermath of the shooting the Berlin police had another and, one suspects, more dearly held theory about the killer's identity.[128]

Litten was about to begin work on a major trial, and on that Sunday night he worked until 1 a.m. Max Fürst had a rush order, and he and Margot worked late at his shop. After leaving the workshop they went to see a movie, returning home in the small hours. Soon after that the police were at the door. A witness claimed to have seen Hans and Max at Bülow Square. The police arrested them and took them to the "Alex."[129]

Their interrogations lasted for hours. The police told Litten that a witness had seen him fleeing toward his apartment on Koblank Street shortly after the shooting of the officers. In fact, Litten had been in his office at the time of the shooting—but by himself. How to prove he had not been at Bülow Square? Although in later years Max did not remember it this way, the *World in the Evening*, which seems to have gotten its information directly from Litten, reported that Hans had walked home from his office with "a companion" who had been at the movies with his wife at the time of the shooting—which must have meant Max. Max had a tighter alibi, and Hans and Max were released around nine o'clock that morning. Who was the witness who had claimed to see them at Bülow Square? At the time Litten told the *World in the Evening* that he suspected a Nazi informer. Max wrote that the witness was "a rather crazy young man" who had once approached Litten to offer information about a case. Litten had determined with a few questions that the young man had nothing sound to offer. "This was now his revenge," said Max, "and the police"—their memories of Litten's campaign against Zörgiebel still fresh—"had only too gladly believed him."[130]

This conspiratorial alliance of Nazis and police would dominate the rest of Litten's life. At the end of May he applied for a permit to carry a handgun. Earlier that month the *Attack* had run an article headlined "With Knuckle-Dusters and Crowbars" that Litten felt contained "an open incitement to murder me." "As a consequence of my professional activities in and outside of Berlin," Litten explained in his application, "I am frequently obliged to walk home alone late at night." One night a group of about forty SA men had threatened him with walking sticks as he waited for a train at the Bellevue station in west Berlin. He had escaped them only by jumping onto a train at the last moment.[131]

Litten knew that he could not count on any official protection. The "triviality" of the sentences against the SA men in the Eden Dance Palace trial had only encouraged more Nazi violence, he wrote. The police were hopeless. There had been "insufficient police protection" at the Eden Dance Palace, as well as during the attempted murder of the Riemenschneider brothers, the murder of Max Schirmer, and the murder of Otto Grüneberg, he noted, listing only those crimes that could be charged to Storm 33. Indeed, police protection against Nazi violence tended to "fail so completely" that there seemed to be "method in this failure."[132]

The police refused to issue the gun permit, and Litten's appeal of their decision was also rejected. In response, Litten drafted a complaint to the Prussian interior minister, accusing the officials who had handled his application and appeal of "serious breach[es] of official duty," negligence in office, "intentional mockery of the applicant," and an "objective encouragement of National Socialist assassins."[133]

Interior Minister Carl Severing fought back. He sent a copy of Litten's September complaint to Justice Minister Hermann Schmidt with the request that Schmidt prosecute Litten in the lawyers' discipline court. Severing was of the view that the "highly insulting attacks" in Litten's complaint constituted a breach of professional duty. The request was passed along the chain of command to the chief prosecutor at Berlin's Court of Appeal and on to Berlin's Lawyers' Chamber, which found that Litten's complaint "contained serious libel" and requested an indictment. This charge was in time joined by another: after losing a trial in the fall of 1931, Litten accused the presiding judge of deliberately misrepresenting the defendant's statements and glossing over important contradictions in the evidence of the Nazi witnesses in order to arrive at a conviction. A trial on this charge was supposed to take place in September 1932, but Litten was busy with another case and the hearing was put off to early 1933. The shy young lawyer had given another powerful demonstration of his talent for making enemies.[134]

Richard Street

Litten's capacity for making enemies advanced in tandem with his growing influence on the conduct and the outcomes of political trials in Berlin.

After the Eden Dance Palace trial, Litten was involved in two more cases that grew out of Storm 33's violent spree of late 1930 and early 1931: the "Hahn" trial for the attack on the Riemenschneider brothers (although Hahn himself had fled, leaving his subordinates to face the court) and the case against Paul Foyer and others for the murder of Otto Grüneberg. The same court heard these cases in quick succession in August and September; the trials showed that Hans Litten's arguments about the SA were beginning to get through to some of Berlin's legal officials. The presiding judge, Superior Court Director Rambke, a conservative jurist who would go on to serve Hitler's Reich, opened the

Foyer trial by giving the jurors an overview of "the bloody deeds of Storm 33" that had thus far resulted in convictions. The *Attack* complained that Rambke's lecture had "pushed hard against the boundaries of what is procedurally permissible." Rambke asked Rudolf Wesemann—the defendant acquitted in the Eden Dance Palace trial, whom Litten summoned to testify in the Foyer case—if Storm 33 had formed roll commandos, sparking further outrage from the *Attack*. (Wesemann said he had never heard of such a thing.) Even Paul Stenig, serving once again as the prosecutor, asked for uncharacteristically high sentences: over ten years in a penitentiary for Paul Foyer.[135]

Rambke's court sentenced Foyer to five years and four months in a penitentiary for second-degree murder; two other defendants also received severe sentences. It was, the *World in the Evening* acknowledged, the first time a Berlin court had given National Socialists penitentiary sentences for the murder of a worker. Shortly after the close of the Foyer trial, Wilhelm Kube, a Nazi member of the Prussian Parliament, vented his spleen over the "unheard of conduct" of Stenig, who never missed an opportunity to "attack and insult" members of the Nazi Party and was "abetted" by judges like Rambke and Ohnesorge. During the Hahn trial the *Attack* had referred to "the Litten-Stenig alliance" (the existence of which would certainly have shocked the principals); covering the sentencing requests in Foyer's case, Goebbels's paper thought that because Litten was a "severe psychopath," he should be taken "even less seriously" than Stenig.[136]

In April 1932 Litten defended twenty-two men, mostly members of the Combat League Against Fascism, against charges that they had planned and carried out the murder of Heinrich Böwe, the owner of a Storm tavern on Richard Street in the hardscrabble district of Neukölln. The killing of Böwe had resulted from a Chicago gangland–style attack, in which a large crowd of demonstrators provided cover while as many as eight men fired indiscriminately through the windows of his tavern. Litten began by arguing that the attack amounted to self-defense, a working-class neighborhood's response to the danger a Storm tavern posed. But as the trial progressed, the arguments increasingly centered on the tactics by which the police had obtained confessions from some of the defendants. These arguments pitted Litten against a police officer named Kurt Marowsky.[137]

Litten claimed that Marowsky had extorted confessions and other testimony through lies, threats, bribes, and abusive interrogation techniques. So aggressively did he challenge both Marowsky and the magistrate who had conducted the preliminary investigations that the prosecutor, State Advocate Hans Volk, remarked, "It seems to me that the defendants have mistaken their role and that they think they are the prosecutors." (The *Red Flag* agreed with Volk.) A few months later Marowsky wrote that he had "the distinct impression" that Litten had tried "with all means at his disposal" to turn him into the defendant. "These methods of Advocate Litten's," said Marowsky, "have been well known to this department [the political police] for a long time."[138]

Marowsky fought back. He began to make counterallegations, such as that Litten had helped defendants formulate alibis and, in one case, escape to Russia. The most serious allegation arose in October 1932, months after the trial. By this point, as we will see, a wide circle of prosecutors, police, and judges were looking for any evidence of Litten's wrongdoing that might get him expelled from the legal profession. In late September Heinz Schüler, a witness in the Richard Street case, was arrested for another shooting in Neukölln. After his arrest he asked to be examined again in connection with Richard Street, as he had "important information" to give. The information was that Litten had encouraged him, and others, to commit perjury. Schüler's claimed motive for coming out with this information: "I want absolutely nothing more to do with Communism." The real reason probably had to do with the incentives the police could offer someone who had just been arrested. The officer who took Schüler's statement was Marowsky.[139]

In the meantime, Litten had scored a considerable success with the Richard Street defense. The court found no evidence that any of the defendants had fired at Böwe's tavern. Ten were acquitted of all charges; others received minor sentences. The court had proven especially receptive to Litten's argument that the false testimony given by various defendants and witnesses was a product of psychological factors, which was at least an indirect endorsement of his accusations against the police.[140]

All of this—Judge Rambke's acceptance of the serial nature of Storm 33 violence, Stenig's heavy sentence requests, the outcome of the Foyer case, and the acquittals in Richard Street—showed that in just over three years Litten had begun to have a serious impact on Berlin's criminal courts. Little wonder that this influence was accompanied by growing threats of violence from the SA and the constant machinations by police, prosecutors, and ministerial authorities to find some pretext to damage him, perhaps to drive him from the practice of law altogether. Both kinds of threat would only intensify during 1932.

They Know What They Do

In most times and in most places, to say that a prominent political lawyer had an impact on the courts would be banal. In the case of Weimar Berlin it is anything but.

Most historians have described the German legal system in Weimar as reactionary, antidemocratic, antimodern, and anti-Semitic. Such critiques focus almost entirely on the judges, and there were good grounds to view the Weimar judiciary with suspicion. In cases involving expressly political crimes—above all, political assassinations—judges tended to be far more receptive to the pleas of right-wing defendants, such as "shot while trying to escape" and "patriotic sentiment," than to those from the left. A lecturer in statistics at Heidelberg University, Emil Julius Gumbel, summed up this tendency in a 1922 book entitled *Four Years of Political Murder*, which gave birth to the slogan that has come to characterize Weimar justice ever since: "Mild to the right, hard to the left." Gumbel found fifteen political murders committed by activists of the left that resulted in eight executions and average prison sentences of fourteen years. In contrast, he counted 314 political murders committed by the right, of which only twenty-two had led to convictions, yielding average sentences of two months. The German judiciary seemed intent on slighting or damaging the republic in any way possible. Even the relatively calm middle years of the Weimar Republic, between the stabilization at the end of 1923 and the onset of economic and political crisis after 1929, were marked by what came to be called the "crisis of confidence in justice," a widespread feeling that the judiciary was politically driven.[141]

In 1931 a left-wing writer named Ernst Ottwalt published a novel that summarized the left's complaints about the German judiciary, *For They Know What They Do*. Though Ottwalt's book was fiction, the Prussian Justice Ministry took it seriously as a potentially dangerous criticism. An article in *Voss's News* summed up the novel's message this way: "The justice system of the German Republic operates unjustly and arbitrarily.... With judgments and decisions an illegitimate ruling class, the ruling class of Imperial Germany with the outlook of Imperial Germany, wants to defend its rule and its outlook against the new age and against the republic." *Voss's News* was skeptical, however, that Ottwalt had proven his point. It pointed out that a recent series of books had indicted the same justice system for being subverted by the democratic left. The reference was to *Justice Enchained*, written under a pseudonym by a Nazi sympathizer named Ewald Moritz.[142]

Voss's News was on to something. The Ottwalt-Gumbel picture of the administration of justice in the Weimar Republic was based on half-truths. Historians writing in more recent years have also tended to miss the extent to which the administration of justice varied regionally in Germany (and thus took on a very different quality in Social Democratic Prussia than in reactionary Bavaria) and evolved over time (and thus was very different in 1930 than in 1920). In the second quarter of 1931, for instance, following an emergency decree on political violence passed at the end of March, 2,027 of a national total of 3,418 "police actions" were directed at members of the Communist Party. If this still suggests an official preference for pursuing Communists, the disparity is far less than that reported for earlier years by Gumbel, and as the historian Heinrich August Winkler writes, "It was not necessarily because of the political bias of the police and the justice system that the Communists were the main targets of the emergency decree." This was, after all, the period in which "fortified struggle against fascism" was official Communist Party policy, involving not only boycotts, rent strikes, and demonstrations, but also "countless cases" of "individual terror" against Hitler's followers—such as the attack on Böwe's tavern.[143]

Indeed, according to data on political violence compiled by the Prussian Interior Ministry, the Communists were by no means getting the worst of the street battles, and the respective numbers of Communist and Nazi defendants reflected the amount of violence they actually committed. The ministry found, for instance, that in Berlin in 1931 208 Nazis were wounded, five died of wounds, one was murdered, and another was killed in "self-defense." By contrast, seventy-two Communists were wounded, five died of wounds, and three were murdered. The same source supplied data for culprits who could be "determined or assumed with certainty." In cases of wounds inflicted on Nazis, said the ministry, 253 Communists could be identified as culprits (along with five Stennes followers). In cases of wounds inflicted on Communists, 105 Nazis could be identified as culprits. In the first three months of 1932, 120 Nazis and 42 Communists were wounded in political brawls; 229 Communists and 40 Nazis could be identified as culprits. We can be certain that these statistics did not themselves represent any effort to whitewash the Nazis at the expense of the Communists, for they were gathered in part to serve as a basis for legislation banning the SA. A historical study of the political police in the last years of Weimar and the first years of Hitler's rule found a rough equivalence in political violence committed by left and right, as well as an equivalence in its police treatment.[144]

But if German justice in Weimar was not as "one-eyed" as many historians have claimed, this is largely because there really was a legal *system* and not merely a judiciary. The judges of the Weimar Republic were part of a system that included political institutions, parliaments, and justice ministries (in Prussia, controlled by solidly democratic politicians); a loud, extensive, and politically highly diverse press; a range of lobby groups; and, not least, the private bar. All of these could and did have an impact on what happened in the courtroom. An aggressive defense lawyer like Litten could draw not only on his rights to summon witnesses and to speak in court, but could also mobilize other components of the system, especially the press and lobby groups.

Weimar was a great age for progressive legal journalism, and Berlin-Moabit was the haunt of such gifted writers as Kurt Tucholsky, Walter Kiaulehn, and Moritz Goldstein (aka "Inquit"). The acknowledged dean of Berlin's legal reporters, however, was *Voss's* Paul Schlesinger, better known by his pseudonym, "Sling." Sling's eloquent essays and his impassioned campaigns for reform made him both respected and feared among Moabit lawyers and in the Prussian Justice Ministry. The star defense lawyer Erich Frey recalled that "Sling's word weighed heavily" with prosecutors, judges, ministers, and parliamentarians. A court president reporting to the ministry on a controversial trial in 1928 enclosed one of Sling's critical articles and remarked that in light of Sling's reputation, the ministry would have to respond publicly. The ministry introduced a number of reforms, such as issuing printed instruction cards for jurors and opening an official press office in Moabit, on Sling's recommendations.[145]

Judges and prosecutors complained incessantly about the glare of media attention in which they had to work. "Here in Berlin," read one article in the *Berlin Morning Post*, "the whole administration of justice plays out in immediate proximity to a watchful ministry, an ever-present general prosecutor, and a press which in any given case is ready to intervene." When an especially embattled criminal court judge asked for a transfer to a civil court, the court president wrote that it would be difficult to find a successor, as very few senior judges were enthusiastic about working in the criminal courts of Moabit. In a memo written in February 1933, the Berlin judge Superior Court Director Steinhaus noted that press attacks had been a fact of life since 1918 for every Berlin judge, "especially in the last few years." Steinhaus was no proto-Nazi. He was subjected to repeated and savage criticism from the right-wing press for his leniency and courtesy to defendants. His memo was a response to criticisms in the *Attack*, which by then was the voice of power, and so his words took courage.[146]

It was not just that judges in Weimar needed to be stoical and thick-skinned. The records of the courts and the Justice Ministry bear witness to the press's strong influence on personnel decisions. This was especially so after Hermann Schmidt, a member of the liberal wing of the Catholic Center Party and a former judge on the Berlin Court of Appeal, became Prussian justice minister in 1927 and brought considerable reforming energy to his department. Under Schmidt, the ministry began collecting complaints about judges and conditions in the courts that eventually filled many large files. Special charts recorded the names of judges who were the subject of press attacks, as well as when and where the attacks had appeared. In the Krantz trial of 1928, the manner in which the presiding judge questioned the star female witness, Hilde Scheller, about her sexual experiences drew a barrage of press criticism from across the political spectrum, as the president of the court later acknowledged. In his review of the case, the president argued, with paranoia typical of the Weimar years, that the real motive of these attacks was to "shake the authority of the state, especially of the criminal court, and in the end to destroy it." In another demonstration of the power of the press, in that same case Assistant Police Chief Bernhard Weiss had gone to hear the police interrogations of the defendant Krantz and Hilde Scheller. Asked in court to explain why, Weiss simply said, "The case had very much excited the public." When the trial was over the presiding judge took a sick leave and was then transferred to a civil court. He never led a jury court session again.[147]

Weimar also saw the formation of many liberal and left-wing legal associations and lobby groups. In addition to the League for Human Rights and Red Aid, whose support was so critical to Litten's advocacy, Berlin's liberal and Socialist criminal lawyers formed the Criminal Law Association, which often found itself in conflict with more conservative lawyers in the profession's establishment. The highly conservative judges' associations, the League of German Judges and the Association of Prussian Judges, had their liberal counterpart in the (admittedly much smaller) Republican Judges' League, which also published an influential journal, *Justice*.[148]

It was, however, the defense bar that was the most important means of bringing popular opinion into the courtroom and leading judges to make decisions they might not otherwise have made. The task of the criminal defense lawyer is to act in more or less permanent opposition to the state. Therefore, the degree of independence and power the defense enjoys in the courtroom is a reliable index of the broader degree of liberty, tolerance, and pluralism in the society as a whole. As German political culture had become steadily more open after the end of the Bismarck era in the early 1890s, the power of defense lawyers in German courtrooms had grown apace, reaching a high point in the later years of Weimar that would not be matched again until long after the Second World War. The great lawyers of Weimar—Max Alsberg, Erich Frey, Alfred Apfel, Rudolf Olden, Paul Levi, Ludwig Bendix, Johannes Werthauer, Max Hirschberg, and certainly Hans Litten—represented an array of collective brilliance that formed a fitting counterpoint to the artistic, literary, and scientific glories of Weimar Berlin, and it is to the advocates of that era that German lawyers today turn when they seek models of democratic engagement. Apfel, one of the most committed of them all, was paying tribute to the influence of lawyers in the courtroom as well as to the (much maligned) caliber of judges in Berlin's courtrooms when he wrote in 1931, "I am convinced that an acquittal could be achieved in at least half of all political trials, if the defense were carried out in a more legally precise manner." The number of judges and prosecutors who "keep an open mind about acquittals in political trials which are distasteful to them is larger than one commonly assumes." Even after 1933 the Nazis paid retrospective tribute to the effectiveness of these left-leaning lawyers, as well as to the journalists who often worked alongside them. At a conference held in 1936 on the theme "Jewry in Legal Scholarship," one law professor claimed that before the "transformation" (meaning the Nazi takeover) it was "frequently noticed" that "individual Jews, such as Sling or Alsberg," had become prominent in the criminal justice system, a challenge to "self-conscious Germans." This professor also found Litten to be one of the prime examples of the problem. Every one of the great lawyers listed above was Jewish, at least as far as the Nazis were concerned.[149]

The Weimar far right itself certainly felt that things in the courts were moving against it. Otto Kamecke, who, as we have seen, was one of the most prominent Nazi defense lawyers, wrote to Storm 33 leader Fritz Hahn's employer while Hahn sat in investigatory custody in 1931 to deliver a pessimistic opinion on Hahn's chances of being set free. "The jurisprudence in political trials has recently become uncommonly more severe," he wrote, "and the courts are easily inclined to convict even those who were only present at the scene of a brawl, even when they did not themselves participate in the violence." The far-right German Times listed in 1929 the kinds of actions that, in its view, could limit the career of a judge. If he acquitted "Feme judges" (members of right-wing murder squads) he would immediately be demoted to a minor post; if he insulted the left-liberal journal the Diary he would be transferred to a civil court; if he indicted a celebrity mobster he would be exiled to a small town.[150]

It is sometimes said that the Supreme Court of the United States follows the election returns. Something of the sort was true of Prussia under the solidly democratic coalition that governed until 1932, especially after Schmidt took over the Justice Ministry in 1927. But the proposition that the courts followed the election returns was a two-edged sword. In the course of 1932 it became clear that the dire economic and political crisis raised the danger of a rapid relapse into authoritarian government, and with it the collapse of the rule of law in Germany.[151]

Underground Influences

Seldom, perhaps never, has the capital city of an industrialized country seen in peacetime anything like the wave of crises that visited Berlin in the year 1932. In January there were reported to be 569,000 unemployed persons in the city. By March the figure was up to 606,000, an official rate of 52.3 percent. Siegfried Kracauer, a theorist of modern culture and the Berlin correspondent for the *Frankfurt Times*, wrote, "One sees the crisis now on every corner." The elegant Café Bauer had closed; the streets had been taken over by a "forest of beggars." The *Berlin Local Advertiser* reported in July 1932 that in the season just ended, the forty-three Berlin theaters had failed to sell even a third of their tickets; the great director Max Reinhardt had given up and gone back to Vienna; 104 movie theaters had closed. "Most of us," playwright Carl Zuckmayer recalled years later, "lived in these last years before the end of the Weimar Republic like peasants who make hay or reap grain while on the horizon the storm clouds pile up."[152]

Berliners were called upon to vote in five different elections that year: two rounds of a presidential election in March and April (in which old Field Marshall Paul von Hindenburg narrowly defeated the challenger, Adolf Hitler), followed closely by elections for the Prussian Parliament (in which the Nazis emerged for the first time as the largest party in Prussia, with 36.3 percent of the vote). At the end of May, the powerful clique led by Kurt von Schleicher convinced President Hindenburg to dismiss Chancellor Heinrich Brüning and replace him with the Rhennish aristocrat Franz von Papen. Papen's only claim to power lay in his family wealth and title; his lack of competence, experience, and knowledge of the world were exceeded only by his inexplicable self-confidence. As part of a deal for National Socialist acceptance of his administration, Papen agreed to lift the ban on the SA that the Brüning administration had reluctantly steeled itself to impose, and agreed as well to call national parliamentary elections for July, even though no election was due until 1934.

The lifting of the ban on the SA on June 14, 1932, set the stage for the most violent election campaign in German history. According to official statistics, eighty-six people were killed in Prussia in the month of July alone, with hundreds more wounded. The worst single event occurred in Altona, a suburb of Hamburg, on July 17, when between eight hundred and a thousand Nazis staged a march through working-class districts. A street battle developed. Some witnesses claimed to see people shooting at the Nazis from the buildings. Police were also fired at and returned fire. The result was twelve dead and fifty-four wounded.[153]

Altona's "Bloody Sunday" supplied a pretext for a move long planned by the circle around Papen. The democratic Prussian administration of Otto Braun and Carl Severing had stayed on after the April elections as a "caretaker" administration, since no working majority was possible in the new parliament. But the German Constitution gave the president the authority to depose a state government if it was unable to preserve law and order. Papen now claimed (aided by allegations from Rudolf Diels that senior Prussian civil servants were conspiring with the Communists) that "Bloody Sunday" made manifest the failure of the Braun-Severing administration. With Hindenburg's approval, he dismissed Braun and Severing, put Berlin under military rule, and personally took on the leadership of the Prussian government—a coup d'état under a fig leaf of legality.

In the Reichstag elections held ten days after the Papen coup, the Nazis surged to their highest vote share in a free national election: just over 37 percent, making them the largest party in the Reichstag. The hapless Papen could not assemble a majority out of the bitterly divided parliamentary factions. Hitler could have formed a coalition with the Catholic Center Party, but he refused, and Hindenburg refused to appoint him chancellor through the emergency powers that had supported Brüning and Papen. National politics seemed deadlocked.[154]

The Prussian Braun-Severing administration had been the "rock of democracy" in the Weimar Republic. With that rock gone the slide into dictatorship accelerated. The criminal justice system, the most sensitive barometer of the political climate, registered the changes. In August Papen obtained President Hindenburg's assent to yet another emergency decree, in which the remedy for political violence was the creation of "Special Courts" in the cities most affected, Berlin among them. In these Special Courts, speed and not justice was the goal, and it was to be achieved by stripping defendants of most of their procedural rights, including the right to appeal a conviction. Whereas homicide cases were normally heard by jury courts, the Special Courts consisted only of professional judges. Yet they could deliver draconian punishments, including the death penalty for anyone who committed homicide out of "political motives." In one of the first Berlin Special Court trials, the prosecutor State Advocate Hans Mittelbach argued that the purpose of the Special Courts was "to obliterate" the "elements hostile to the state." Mittelbach would go on to become one of the first officers in Hitler's Gestapo.[155]

To liberals and the left, the creation of the Special Courts was a crisis in the rule of law. The defense lawyer Erich Frey called the Special Courts "the tomb of the unknown defendant." Rudolf Olden wrote in the *World Stage* that it was one of the "worst phenomena of political life" that such "reforms" were carried out in secret by ministerial bureaucrats, without public discussion and without parliamentary approval. "A great people that allows its legal developments to be decided in secret chambers and imposed on it by decree—truly a sight at which one could despair of the future."[156]

For Litten, the creation of these courts represented a move by the "bourgeoisie" to adjust outdated legal institutions to the "intensified" state of class warfare. As prominent as any political lawyer in Germany by the summer of 1932, despite his youth (he was twenty-nine), Litten threw himself into a public campaign against the Special Courts. He spoke in the Schwinemünder Meeting House on September 2, and on September 5, under the headline "Litten Speaks," the *Red Flag* announced that he would speak in the Frankfurter Hof on Frankfurter Avenue on the theme "Special Courts against Workers." On September 15 Litten spoke at a "conference" sponsored by Red Aid about the Special Courts; speaking with him were Johannes Werthauer and Ernst Ottwalt, author of *For They Know What They Do*. He appeared at a protest meeting in Weissensee on September 19, while Ludwig Barbasch spoke at a similar event in Spandau. In late August Litten appeared as counsel in the first Berlin Special Court trial. His first argument was that the case should be transferred to a regular court, as the decree establishing the Special Courts was unconstitutional. His motion was denied. While Litten was trying this case, there was another Storm 33 shooting in Charlottenburg.[157]

The shooting arose out of another confrontation between SA men and members of the Combat League Against Fascism. Storm 33 had recently moved into the tavern at 12 Röntgen Street. On August 29, a group of Combat League men were on their way home from a meeting. As they rounded the corner of Röntgen Street they ran across a group of storm troopers in front of the tavern. An exchange of insults escalated into shooting. Three of the SA men were hit; one, Herbert Gatschke, was killed.[158]

The Nazis exploited Gatschke's death for its full propaganda value. Hitler, Goebbels, and Göring all attended the funeral on September 3. "If our dead," said Hitler, "will not have the good fortune to experience Germany's rise, then we have the duty not to commemorate them like the Germany of 1918, for then their deaths will have been in vain."[159]

On September 9 prosecutors charged nine men with the shootings. Five of them, including the main defendant, the Combat League's local organizer Werner Calm, faced the new charge of political murder, which carried the death penalty under the emergency decree of August 9. The trial opened September 20. Litten was there for the defense.[160]

In the course of the Röntgen Street trial, the Nazis outdid even themselves in attacking Litten. The Nazi lawyers Kamecke and Uhrland complained that Litten's lectures at public meetings and his private conversations with witnesses had "obstructed the investigation of the truth." When the court summoned Litten to testify about his practice, the *Attack* pounced. "Now, finally, our suspicion that this strange Mr. Litten is the intellectual father of all the contradictory Communist testimony is confirmed by the court as an obvious fact." Litten had, the *Attack* continued, done his clients no service. Now that the court had found "Litten's hair in its soup," it was clear that the defendants "had everything to hide." While it was clear that the real criminals had been caught, a "Jewish law-twister" was attempting "with the filthiest and most repellent methods" to cover up their "cowardly and underhanded deed." Litten's mockery of justice could not continue, the *Attack* argued. Either he had to "disappear immediately and voluntarily into private life," or lawyers of his stripe should be "expelled forever from the courtroom!"[161]

The evidence in the Röntgen Street trial unfolded along predictable lines. Litten's clients stressed the defensive character of all their actions. The Nazi witnesses presented themselves as innocent victims of Communist aggression. Most of the evidence from bystanders favored the Communists' account, telling only of shots fired from the Nazi side of the street toward the Communists. Litten efficiently discredited the few witnesses who told a different story, such as a Lutheran minister whom Litten forced to admit to his membership in the Nazi Party.[162]

The decisive evidence came from the ballistics expert Dr. August Brüning. From his examination of twelve bullet holes in buildings on Röntgen Street, Brüning concluded that all twelve shots had been fired from the Storm tavern. Furthermore, a comparison of a bullet found in a wall across the street from the tavern with the bullet that killed Gatschke revealed that the bullets had been fired by the same gun—in other words, not only had the Nazis been the aggressors, they had probably killed their own man. Undeterred, the prosecution claimed that the Communists had hidden in the Nazis' tavern in order to ambush the SA men.[163]

Indeed, the closing argument of prosecutor State Advocate Wagner had little to do with the defendants and everything to do with politics in the fall of 1932. He dropped the homicide charges against all defendants—meaning that their lives were no longer at stake—while still asking for heavy penitentiary sentences for Werner Calm and four others for serious breaches of the peace. Wagner asked that the remaining four defendants be acquitted. He complained bitterly of press coverage sympathetic to the defendants and hostile to the Special Court, the prosecution, and "against the so-called 'Murder Storm 33.'" Litten, working alongside this "agitation," had gone out of his way to create difficulties for the court and to allow the events in Röntgen Street "to vanish in a murky darkness." The preliminary investigations had yielded "very clear conclusions" about the case, but the trial had wiped them away. The reason for this lay in Litten's public meetings and his conversations with witnesses. A few witnesses had altered their testimony after such conversations. A number of organizations (Wagner chiefly meant the Red Aid) had worked tirelessly to bring "underground influences" to the courtroom. Wagner maintained to the end that the Combat League men had fired first and that there was no clear evidence that the SA men had fired any shots at all.[164]

Immediately after Wagner's closing argument the court ordered the release of all nine defendants from custody. News of the release spread through Berlin "like wildfire," reported the *World in the Evening*, and a huge crowd gathered outside the Moabit courthouse to greet the men as they emerged. They went on to a party in their honor held at the offices of the Red Aid, where they were photographed, fists raised in the "Red Front" greeting, along with Litten and his co-defender, Kurt Rosenfeld. Even before the verdict, the *World in the Evening* claimed the defendants owed their freedom "to the masses of the German proletariat," and above all to the Red Aid and the "selfless defense" by Litten and Rosenfeld. The *Attack*, on the other hand, noted with "outrage" that the Special Court did not hold the "Communist murderers" to be clearly guilty.[165]

The next day Litten and Rosenfeld gave their closing arguments. Litten asked that his clients be acquitted not just for lack of evidence, but for their demonstrable innocence. The judges were not willing to go that far. They acquitted all nine defendants, but managed to find that the Communists and the Nazis had both fired shots, and that it was impossible to say who had fired first. Although the court was more restrained than the prosecution in criticizing "underground influences," the written judgment complained that the defense and "the press which stands behind it" had dredged up every scrap of evidence that could assist its case—a strange but revealing criticism of a courtroom defense.[166]

The Röntgen Street trial demonstrated how much a broad range of political forces could affect the criminal courts of Weimar Berlin. The left celebrated the victory as an illustration of its influence. "Solidarity Victorious!" crowed the headline in *Berlin in the Morning*; a "powerful wave of proletarian solidarity" had crested in front of the court in Moabit. Litten, recalling Wagner's words about "underground influences," wrote, "The prosecutor's anger is understandable." Papers such as the *World in the Evening* and *Berlin in the Morning*, he continued, by keeping the "proletarian public" informed, had ensured that "numerous witnesses" came forward during the trial, making victory possible. The Red

Aid put out its own pamphlet celebrating its "mass defense" in the case—in other words, the way the printing of hundreds of thousands of leaflets, demonstrations by thousands of workers outside the court, and numerous public meetings had swung the case in favor of the defendants.[167]

Official sources supported the seemingly self-congratulatory Litten–Red Aid explanation of the victory in Röntgen Street. In a long letter dated September 30, 1932, as the Röntgen Street case neared its end, the Berlin police chief complained about the protest meetings and demonstrations the Red Aid had organized against the Special Courts—he singled out Litten's speeches as especially inflammatory—and concluded that by seeking to intimidate the judges they had determined the outcome. On September 16 a delegation appeared at the Prussian Justice Ministry and handed over a resolution calling for the abolition of the Special Courts and criticizing the indictment in the Röntgen Street case. These citizens were told, in best bureaucratic style, that the Reich and not the Prussian Justice Ministry was responsible for the Special Courts, and that in any case the Prussian ministry could not intervene in a case in progress. But the delegation returned on October 4 to complain about the handling of the Röntgen Street trial. This time the woman who led the delegation refused to accept any "not our department" answers. "The spokeswoman replied that she had the right to protest, and in her capacity as a taxpayer to be heard thereby. She then promised the submission of a written 'resolution' and took her leave along with the two other members of the delegation."[168]

Senior justice officials saw all of this as far more than a joke or an annoyance. They worried about the impact of the Special Courts on public opinion. During the Röntgen Street trial, Court of Appeal President Eduard Tigges and the deputy president of Superior Court I, among others, had observed the proceedings from behind the judges' bench. The Special Courts had been in existence for less than two months when nervous officials met at the Reich Justice Ministry to discuss what to do about them. Ministerial Director Leopold Schäfer told the meeting that the ministry—now in the hands of the Bavarian national conservative Franz Gürtner, who would go on to be Hitler's justice minister and remain in that post until his death in early 1941—wanted to limit the activities of the Special Courts, and eventually abolish them. The limitations on defenses were not consistent with the rule of law, he said, and the anger the courts aroused was itself counterproductive. Indeed, said Schäfer, since the abolition of the Special Courts was inevitable anyway, it would be better if it appeared to be a "voluntary act of the Reich government" and not "a surrender to the growing resistance." The Special Courts were abolished at the end of 1932, in a move that coincided with an amnesty for political prisoners.[169]

It was not just democratic public opinion, however, that had railed against the Special Courts. After a Special Court in Beuthen sentenced five SA men to death for an especially brutal murder, the Nazis turned their propaganda machine loose on the courts as well. The *World in the Evening* found another lesson in Röntgen Street. It observed that "the entire press left the room" as the young Nazi lawyer Uhrland gave his closing address. Had they stayed, the reporters would have seen the future. Undeterred by two weeks of unconvincing evidence, Uhrland asked the court to sentence the defendants to death—including one underage defendant, who, as a minor, was not eligible for the death penalty. Such was the legal competence of Nazi jurists. "That is their business," said the *World in the Evening*. "But the politics of the private prosecutors in this trial reveal the abyss of hypocrisy of the National Socialist Party, which appears to fight against the Special Courts, but here in Moabit wants to use the Special Court as a tool of its politics of revenge." Germany would soon be in the grip of that hypocrisy.[170]

Felseneck

H ans Litten's last big case—his last courtroom battle against the Nazis—came with the so-called Felseneck trial, which dragged its way through most of 1932.

The Felseneck case arose out of yet another attack by SA men on working-class supporters of the Communist Party. On the night of January 18, 1932, men from several SA Storms met at the Bergschloss tavern in the north Berlin district of Waidmanslust. When the meeting was over the storm troopers marched, under police escort, to the district of Reineckendorf-East. The SA story was that they wished to see some of their members safely home in an area in which they feared attack from the Communist Combat League Against Fascism. In fact, the SA went to carry out a raid on the Communist-dominated Felseneck "cottage colony."[171]

"Cottage colonies" were (and still are) a familiar part of the landscape of German cities. In most cases the colonies provided garden allotments for city dwellers. But in the 1930s it was also common for the poorest among the working class, especially the unemployed, to live permanently on such allotments. In 1932 there were an estimated two hundred thousand "small gardeners" (Kleingärtner) in Berlin; Reinickendorf alone could boast 236 colonies. There was nothing idyllic or quaint about these settlements. The Felseneck colony consisted of about a hundred tiny cottages, made of wood or even roofing paper, all of them "equally miserable," as a reporter for the Red Flag wrote. In the bleak winter of 1932 most of the workers who lived in the Felseneck colony were unemployed. This fact alone made it all but inevitable that the political sympathies of the colonists would gravitate to the Communists. There was also a history of violence between the SA and certain residents of Felseneck. The SA bore a particular grudge against Fritz Klemke, a recent recruit to the Communists. When the SA men marched to Felseneck on the night of January 18, they therefore went to demonstrate their strength, to punish the colony for its political sentiments, and in particular to kill Klemke.[172]

When the SA men reached Felseneck, however, they clashed with members of the Combat League Against Fascism. In the spasm of violence that followed, Klemke was killed, shot through the heart after being beaten to the ground. The SA also suffered: one of their number, the fifty-eight-year-old art instructor Ernst Schwartz, died from a stab wound. Although dozens of colonists were initially arrested for Schwartz's killing, the evidence increasingly pointed to one suspect: Karl Ackert, a thirty-four-year-old unemployed worker, Felseneck resident, and member of the Combat League.[173]

By January 20 the World in the Evening could report that the Red Aid had retained Litten to represent the workers arrested for the killing of Schwartz and for the private prosecution of Klemke's killers, and Litten argued that the SA had gone to the Felseneck colony on a mission of revenge, with the collusion of the Berlin police. Litten's perennial adversary, Paul Stenig, prosecuted the case, and Litten wasted no time tearing into him for claiming that it was a case of "a Communist ambush on SA men," an interpretation Stenig shared with the Berlin police and much of the conservative and even moderate press.[174]

Litten became a member of the Investigatory Committee on Swastika Terror, which once again began questioning witnesses and holding public meetings. On January 26 a squad of between two hundred and three hundred SA men broke up a meeting of this committee at which Litten was supposed to speak. Police Chief Albert Grzesinski prohibited a second meeting on grounds with which Litten was familiar: that "the so-called examination of witnesses" would influence their testimony and therefore "considerably disturb" the state's administration of justice and "endanger public order." Grzesinski, who was a Social Democrat, was much less concerned about the danger to public order posed by the fact that only a few of the SA men involved in the attack were in custody, and therefore free to agree on testimony with their comrades.[175]

The trial—of six storm troopers for the killing of Klemke and eighteen Felseneck colonists and members of the Combat League Against Fascism for the killing of Schwartz—opened on April 20, 1932, before a jury in Superior Court III. The presiding judge, Superior Court Director Bode, was leading his first jury court session.[176]

From the beginning the court heard evidence that not only seriously incriminated the SA, but cast the actions of the police in a dubious light. A storm trooper named Fritz Dorst admitted that Storm Group Leader Werner Schulze had ordered the SA men to march from the Bergschloss to Felseneck, and that the police had unaccountably pulled back as they neared the colony. Another SA man, eighteen-year-old Heinrich Villwock, reported that as the storm troopers approached Felseneck they were ordered to "attack in firing line," and that before they left the Bergschloss tavern Schulze had told them, "We have one more bit of business. If we meet any commies, bump 'em off and get out of there."[177]

Villwock also gave the court a detailed account of the execution-style killing of Klemke. Several SA men had beaten Klemke to the ground with steel rods, he said, when suddenly "a tall man in a dark coat" had appeared with gun in hand to shoot the unconscious Klemke. Several other Nazis confirmed the main elements of Villwock's story.[178]

Litten's own investigations soon led him to the identity of the tall man in the dark coat. Over three-quarters of a century later it is impossible to say with certainty that Litten's solution was correct. But it is highly probable.

The process of discovery began with infidelity. As Franz Schwarz, one of the Nazi defendants, was in custody, his wife had an affair with a man named Karl Böttcher, who had ties to the Red Aid. Frau Schwarz worked in the kitchen of an SA hostel. The rumor in SA circles, she told Böttcher, was that an SA man had followed a police officer into the Felseneck Tavern near the colony, where the officer wanted to make a phone call. While making the call, the officer had handed his service revolver and flashlight to the SA man, who had gone to the colony, killed Klemke, refilled the revolver with cartridges that Franz Schwarz gave him, and returned the revolver but not the flashlight to the policeman. Böttcher took this story to the Red Aid, and from there it found its way to Litten.[179]

The officer who had been in charge of the storm troopers' police escort was Theodor Oldenstedt. At first, under Litten's cross-examination, Oldenstedt denied ever giving a revolver or a flashlight to an SA man. But Böttcher's information allowed Litten to trap Oldenstedt. Wilhelm Grewen, a General Motors employee and SA sports instructor, admitted to the police that he had gone into the Felseneck Tavern along with Oldenstedt. When Grewen appeared as a witness he said that Oldenstedt had *handed* him his pistol while making the phone call. Grewen claimed that he had Oldenstedt's pistol for "only a few minutes." Litten confronted Oldenstedt with the contradiction between his story and Grewen's; Oldenstedt had testified that he had "forgotten" the pistol in the tavern and gone back for it when he realized he had forgotten it. Oldenstedt admitted that Grewen's account could be correct. What was more, after much hesitation, Oldenstedt admitted that it was "possible" that while he was making his phone call, Grewen, with the revolver, had gone somewhere else. On June 8 the papers reported that Oldenstedt, for whom things seemed to be going from bad to worse (he had been forced to surrender his notebook, in which Grewen's name appeared), had attempted suicide; this was later amended to his having a nervous breakdown. Some witnesses claimed that he had said in anguish that the murder of Klemke "left him no peace" and that he feared it would cost him his job. Oldenstedt did not deny making these statements, but he claimed he had been joking.[180]

Litten tried to get the police and the prosecutors to prosecute Grewen for Klemke's killing. In court on May 26 Litten gave Stenig's assistant the information about Grewen's role. The letter that the prosecutors claimed to have sent the police that morning—by pneumatic tube—went astray. Litten claimed that the police had deliberately given Grewen time to get away or to dispose of evidence; the prosecutors retorted that Litten was spreading a "deliberate falsehood."[181]

Months later, Chief Prosecutor Sethe wrote to Litten to say that the case against Grewen had been dropped for want of evidence. The date of Sethe's letter was February 28, 1933—the day after the Reichstag burned and the day Litten was arrested.[182]

But before then, the focus of the Felseneck trial had shifted. It became a case about Litten, and the rule of law in Germany itself.

"A Dangerous Irritant in the Administration of Justice"

The atmosphere in the Felseneck courtroom was tense even by the standards of Litten's trials. Litten believed that the prosecutors and the judges were conspiring to protect Grewen and the SA and to cover up the involvement of the police in Klemke's killing, and he did not hide his anger with Judge Bode and Stenig. Litten repeatedly accused Bode of unprofessional, even illegal conduct, peppering his remarks with contemptuous suggestions that Bode "did not understand my explanation," or "perhaps the point escaped you." Litten accused Stenig of lying and attempting to "sabotage the proceedings." Stenig responded by demanding that the court take "extraordinary measures" against Litten "not anticipated in the Code of Criminal Procedure."[183]

Into this atmosphere came the "Papen coup" of July 20. Litten lost no time in making a tactical point of the removal of the Braun-Severing government. On July 21 he asked that the Felseneck proceedings be adjourned. Because of what Litten called Papen's "coup d'état," the legitimacy of the Prussian government was in question, and it was not clear who could properly instruct Stenig and his assistant. The trial could not continue until the court obtained "a declaration from the two representatives of the prosecutor's office" stating "by whose commission they have appeared here." Even such a declaration, Litten argued, would not resolve the prosecution's legal difficulties. If Stenig and his assistant claimed that they were representing the "constitutional" Prussian government, they might be arrested at any moment; if they said they were working for the "coup" administration, their authority to act was at best dubious. After reading Litten's application, Chief Prosecutor Wilde at Berlin's Superior Court I decided only reluctantly that he could not charge Litten with libeling Hindenburg and Papen.[184]

The Papen coup was not the only conspiracy in the air in Berlin in the summer of 1932. Stenig had already hinted in court at an attempt to drive Litten from the Felseneck case. In late July the prosecution decided to salvage the case by finding a way to remove Bode and replace him with someone who would be tougher on Litten, and, if possible, to get rid of Litten as well. This decision would develop into one of the most revealing dramas of criminal justice in Berlin on the eve of Hitler's takeover. The forces arrayed against Litten—prosecutors, police, judges, and Nazi storm troopers, with their lawyers and their press—were an alliance of all the enemies Litten had made since 1928. Litten's last legal battle, then, was the logical culmination of his career.

The opening act came in a long memo written on July 28 by Chief Prosecutor Sethe to his superior at the Court of Appeal, accusing Litten of dragging out the Felseneck trial to unconscionable length by abusing his right to question witnesses, and criticizing Bode for allowing Litten such free rein. Bode had, in fact, showed great respect for Litten, praising his "skill and legal knowledge" in private conversations with the prosecutors. Bode had told Stenig privately that the Code of Criminal Procedure offered no remedy to a judge confronted with a lawyer as determined to raise questions and evidence as Litten was. Sethe also found it unacceptable that Litten had accused the police and the magistrates of falsifying examination protocols, the prosecution of falsifying investigation results and of seeking to protect the Nazis, and the court of failing to judge the matter objectively. In short, Litten was "a dangerous irritant in the administration of justice" who fought against the order of the state "without scruple."[185]

The point of Sethe's memo was that the trial should be adjourned and continued "under a more suitable president." Sethe also asked his superior to consider what other possibilities there might be for the prosecution to "save the wayward state of the trial." If other solutions could not be found, perhaps the prosecution should drop the case.[186]

In light of subsequent events, the conclusion of Sethe's memo was a carefully worded code. It is likely that senior prosecutors, possibly Sethe himself, approached Bode with the message that either he or Litten had to go, and that he should take a harder line with Litten. Sethe had a history of behind-the-scenes efforts to manipulate judges, often to the vexation of Justice Minister Schmidt and Prime Minister Braun. On August 11 *Germania*, the flagship newspaper of the Catholic Center Party, ran an article under the headline "Felseneck Trial—Without End," which drew on information clearly leaked by Stenig to deliver a fierce criticism of Litten's tactics, with the conclusion "The jury court should be able to defend its own dignity through the most severe disciplinary measures against unprofessional defense lawyers."[187]

Four days later Judge Bode's court expelled Litten from the Felseneck trial. Because Bode had repeatedly told Sethe and Stenig that the law did not allow him to do this, signs of the prosecutors' influence were all over the sixteen typed pages of the court's ruling. The court frankly admitted "that this measure, which is certainly unusual in a German criminal proceeding, cannot be supported by a specific and express provision of the Code [of Criminal Procedure]." But the court found that "there are consequences that so necessarily emerge from a given situation, that they do not need an express statutory rule." To cover its bets, the court also argued that there was a provision in the Code that permitted "by analogy" the same conclusion: paragraph 145 allowed the court to appoint a new defense counsel if the present defense counsel refused to carry on the defense. Certainly Litten had not expressly refused to the defend any of his clients, but "his behavior amounts to the same thing, because he refused to carry out the defense" as "the administration of justice requires." He had abused his right to ask questions, his only purpose was to generate "unscrupulous political propaganda," and his attacks on the police and the courts were false and outrageous. "The jury court has too high an opinion of the task of finding the law entrusted to it, to allow... the courtroom to become a playground of fanatical political passions." So it was that the court now saw it as its "well founded duty" to "expel Advocate Litten" from the trial.[188]

The controversy over Litten's handling of Felseneck and the court's response was the last crisis in the city's courts before Hitler's takeover. The attitude of the Nazi papers was no surprise: their demands for Litten's murder had become more open than ever. Typical was a headline in the *Attack* in early June: "How Much Longer May Litten Provoke? Bring the Anarchist's Dirty Work Home to Him!" Most of the liberal and left-wing papers cautiously supported Litten, stressing the lack of a statutory basis for the court's decision, and even politically moderate papers pointed out the disproportion in the court's responses to Nazi and Communist provocations. The *Berlin Times* noted that Litten had faced repeated violent threats from the Nazis without the court feeling any need to use its disciplinary powers, yet the same judges had now expelled Litten for engaging in political propaganda.[189]

Erich Cohn-Bendit, a left-leaning Berlin lawyer (and father of the famous '68er Daniel), poured scorn on the jury court's decision in the pages of the *World Stage*. Posing the question "Can the court expel a defense counsel?" was, he said, equivalent to asking "May the court play cards during the closing arguments, or may the prosecutor enhance the effect of his pleading by breaking into song?" Echoing a closing line from the great Berlin lawyer Max Alsberg, Cohn-Bendit wrote that the expulsion order was fit only to be torn up and tossed at the judges' feet.[190]

Litten himself gave an interview to the *Red Flag* the day after the expulsion order. He claimed that he had believed in Bode's objectivity until the day on which "Constable Oldenstedt's perjury was proven" and yet, instead of pursuing the issue, the court broke off the hearing at this "critical moment." Since then he had increasingly come to the conviction that the court did not want the case cleared up. He announced his intention to appeal the decision and was confident that "such an open perversion of justice" would not stand. Litten had words for Stenig as well, setting the expulsion issue in the entire context of

Litten's battles against the Nazis. He recalled, "I had my first clash with Dr. Stenig in the Storm 33 trials, because I had the impression that I was the only one concerned with solving the murders."[191]

When the Felseneck trial resumed on August 25, most of the other defense lawyers in the case, including, remarkably, the Nazi lawyer Ernst Plettenberg, declared that they "regretted [the court's] measure all the more as Herr Advocate Litten...always acted in the sincere belief that he was protecting the interests of his clients." Despite having received a letter from Bode telling him that he was forbidden even to enter the spectators' gallery, Litten made an ostentatious attempt to take up the defense once more. The guards blocked his path into the court, even when Litten, "with loudly raised voice," advised them that they were committing the offense of coercion and that Bode was guilty of a perversion of justice. Nonetheless, the judges probably thought they were rid of him when, to the surprise of many in the Berlin legal community, the Berlin Court of Appeal rode to Litten's rescue and quashed the expulsion order.[192]

For the prosecution, Litten's return to the trial was an unmitigated disaster. Litten suggested that his expulsion had become a "prestige question" for the court and the prosecutors, and so the prosecutors could not let it go. After the Court of Appeal decision they probably whispered in Bode's ear that he should respond by falling on his sword. On September 2 Bode and fellow judge Kuhlo gave notice of a "situation which could justify their removal" from the case. They did not bother to conceal their exasperation with Litten and the Court of Appeal. "In contrast to our view," they wrote, "that from an evaluation of the *entire pattern of Advocate Litten's conduct* in the trial his intention to disrupt the trial emerged plainly, the Court of Appeal...declared that the grounds which the jury court had set forth...were not valid." Under these circumstances no one could expect the defendants to retain confidence in their judges, and so Bode and Kuhlo believed they had to withdraw. The jury court ruled accordingly on September 3. Because only one supplementary judge was available, the trial could not continue. The whole painful business would have to start again from the beginning. The hollowness of the judges' concern with the defendants' confidence in their objectivity was captured by the liberal magazine *Tempo*, which observed that the judges had "achieved nothing other than . . . condemning the defenseless prisoners to a second trial, with all its physical and psychological torments, to further time in custody and a still longer test of nerves."[193]

Expelled

The dramatic turns of the Felseneck case in late August and early September seem only to have increased the determination of a broad group of authorities—police, prosecutors, and judges, aided by the Nazis—to drive Litten not only from this one case, but from the legal profession altogether.

The second round of the trial was due to begin on October 13, before a specially constituted jury court of Superior Court III under Superior Court Director Böhmert. On October 11, however, Stenig sent Böhmert a report of a magistrate's examination of one of the Nazi defendants in Felseneck—Franz Schwarz, whose wife had been responsible for the revelations about Oldenstedt and Grewen—in a separate political case. Schwarz, another former Communist who had gone over to the Nazis, claimed that on the day he testified in the Felseneck trial he had met in Aschinger's Restaurant with Karl Böttcher, Hans Litten, and "another lawyer." There Litten had pressed Schwarz to accuse Grewen of the killing. Litten supposedly promised that "nothing would happen" to Schwarz if he testified against Grewen; arrangements could be made to send him to Russia. Litten asked Schwarz to come by his office to talk further, which Schwarz refused, as he wanted "nothing more to do with the Communist Party." On October 13 Judge Böhmert informed Litten that Stenig had asked the court once again to expel Litten from the case, on the grounds that Litten was suspected of aiding and abetting the defendants. The opening of the trial was put off while Schwarz's allegations were investigated.[194]

It was, to say the least, a striking coincidence that this evidence emerged from a vulnerable defendant just when the prosecutors needed it. And in another remarkable move, although normally a magistrate would conduct a preliminary investigation, it was Böhmert himself who formally examined Litten, along with Erich Cohn-Bendit, who was the "other lawyer" Schwarz identified. Litten, Cohn-Bendit, and Böttcher all testified that although a conversation had taken place between them and Schwarz in Aschinger's, it was Schwarz who had approached Litten, and they roundly denied that Litten had encouraged Schwarz to testify in any direction (other than exhorting him to tell the truth) or had made him any offers.[195]

On Saturday, October 15, the three judges who would hear the Felseneck trial, Böhmert and his supporting judges, Krüger and Arndt, barred Litten from appearing in the second round of the trial. "According to the relevant jurisprudence of the Imperial Supreme Court, and modern legal doctrine," the court ruled, "a defense counsel... cannot participate, when the law forbids his participation in the interests of the objective truth." A lawyer who could not look upon a case with "unprejudiced, objective legal judgment," who broke all boundaries and made the case his own, who was suspected of involvement in the offense, was in some way an accessory, influenced the participants in the trial, or made untrue statements in court that "deliberately cast the facts in darkness," could not be permitted to act in court. The court believed that Litten was this kind of lawyer. In other words, the court chose to believe a Nazi thug who had already shifted allegiance from one side of the spectrum to the other, by his own account wished to switch back, and was a defendant in two trials, rather than three nonindicted witnesses, two of them lawyers.[196]

But the Schwarz story was not the only ground for Litten's removal. In September Litten had published an article on Felseneck titled "Courting Disaster" ("Zu Grunde gerichtet") in the *Workers' Illustrated News*. The article made claims about the first Felseneck trial that the court found objectionable. It was also accompanied by a photograph (taken by Litten's friend and romantic rival Walter Reuter) of Litten speaking to a crowd of Felseneck colonists. To the court this photograph caught Litten in the act of making "public and—as the caption of the picture betrays—one-sided and partisan pronouncements" calculated to influence the colonists "in a particular direction." Finally, the court anticipated that Litten himself would be called to testify about the Oldenstedt-Grewen story, and that the role of witness could not be combined with the impartiality German law expected of a defense lawyer, especially since the law required that witnesses be excluded from the courtroom while others were testifying.[197]

The weakness of the court's reasoning was apparent to most of the Berlin press. *Voss's News* said that it was wrong even in its point of departure: at issue was not the right of a defense counsel to be admitted to a courtroom, but the right of a defendant to retain the counsel of his or her choice. The distinguished lawyer Erich Eyck (later a biographer of Bismarck and an early historian of the Weimar Republic itself) wrote, "Certainly we do not approve of everything Advocate Litten has done, and of which the order accuses him." It was unprofessional for Litten to discuss the case in a restaurant with a defendant from the other party, and it had always been an unwritten rule that a lawyer should avoid "as much as possible" writing in the press about a trial in which he was engaged while that trial was in progress. But no jurist who read the court's order could conclude that there was sufficient evidence against Litten to justify opening a criminal case. The court's reasoning put defense lawyers in an impossible position, placing them under suspicion if they could not refute "accusations which any arbitrary person, even a bitter political opponent," raised against them. An accusation could thus force any lawyer from any trial, a serious threat to German justice.[198]

In a similar vein the *Berlin Daily News* warned lawyers that if they did not intervene in "the injustice that has been done to this lawyer," they would "saw off the branch on which they themselves sit." Less legal and more emotional was the *Red Flag*'s reaction on October 16: "Advocate Litten is a proletarian defense counsel, respected by the workers and hated by the fascists." The paper urged Berlin's workers to protest the Superior Court's decision and to "fight with the Red Aid for the release of all proletarian political prisoners!"[199]

Litten's expulsion was a consequence and an expression of the political and legal situation of Germany in 1932. Toward the end of the nineteenth century a more adversarial—one might say a more British or American—conception of the position of the defense counsel had come to hold sway among German barristers and characterized the courtrooms of the Weimar Republic. It was hardly a coincidence that this was the era in which the political culture of Germany was, in fundamental ways, moving closer to the Western democratic pattern.

But in 1932 the political parties gaining influence in Germany—the National Socialists and the Communists—were those most strongly opposed to parliamentary democracy and the rule of law. Their rise was in part a case of action and reaction; the more working-class support shifted from the (very law-abiding) Social Democrats to the Communists, the more middle-class voters were frightened into supporting the Nazis. The Papen coup toppled the last important government in Germany still firmly committed to democracy, and the second half of 1932 brought changes in crucial realms of the Prussian civil service, as democratic officials were purged and replaced with those more comfortable with authoritarian rule. The creation of the Special Courts in August, and the drastic scaling back of the rights of defendants that went with them, demonstrated how the authoritarianism of the Papen government could reveal itself in the administration of justice; lower level officials, such as the Berlin prosecutors, took their cues from the top. In short, the process by which liberalization of politics and the courts had moved in tandem since the 1890s began to go into reverse. As part of this process, so conspicuous a challenger of authority as Hans Litten had to be brought to heel.[200]

Litten appealed his expulsion once again, basing his argument on the claim that a conspiratorial clique of judges and prosecutors was seeking to remove him from the trial. His main target was Stenig, who from the beginning had been "the driving force in the numerous illegalities of the earlier jury court proceeding." Litten referred to the August 11 *Germania* article, for which Stenig was clearly the source, and he claimed that before the start of the second trial Stenig had told a group of lawyers and reporters that this time Litten would be gone in less than two weeks. Böhmert himself had confirmed the existence of the conspiracy in a conversation with Litten: "I am aware," Böhmert had said, "that there is a circle of persons here, who are not immediately involved in the trial, but interested in it, and who enjoy just such rumor-mongering." Nonetheless, Böhmert and one of the supporting judges, Superior Court Counselor Adolf Arndt, were, Litten wrote, possessed by "an extraordinarily strong aversion to the political tendency of the defendants represented by me," which they had made very plain in earlier political trials. The outcome of Felseneck would leave very little doubt that Litten was correct.[201]

Sethe, who responded to Litten's appeal on behalf of the prosecution, predictably denied all of Litten's allegations. "I see no reason," he wrote, "to respond to the kind of tone and evidence which Advocate Litten considers appropriate." When Stenig had said Litten would be excluded from the new trial within fourteen days—Sethe admitted Stenig's statement—the prosecutor had meant only that Litten's exclusion would follow if he maintained the tactics of the first trial.[202]

The Court of Appeal ruled again on Litten's exclusion on October 28. This time the prosecutors won. If in fact Litten had tried to influence Schwarz's testimony and that of the residents of Felseneck, such behavior was improper for a defense counsel. The court made a broader claim as well. "At the stage of the main trial," it held, "the court alone determines the nature and extent of the investigations, so that neither the prosecution nor the defense counsel are justified...in conducting this kind of investigation, to say nothing of withholding, entirely at their discretion, all knowledge of them from the court." A defense lawyer was absolutely forbidden to meet with witnesses or defendants who were not his clients without permission of the court. Litten had breached this rule; the court added ominously, "Whether this conduct fulfills the requirements of the criminal offense of acting as an accessory can be left aside."[203]

Litten responded nearly a month later in the pages of the *World Stage*. He wrote, "Contemporaries who, in the midst of the class struggles of the 20th century...still see in the Court of Appeal the stronghold of a metaphysical justice ruling over the struggling classes, have been disappointed." The ruling amounted to nothing more than "an emergency decree abolishing the defense counsel." He closed with a phrase reminiscent of his youth movement days, when he had written that "a youth movement that takes its task seriously must be political." Now, in the autumn of 1932, he wrote, "A legal profession that takes its task seriously...must proclaim it a professional obligation to work against this ruling."[204]

Despite his politics, Litten drew some support from the legal establishment, which recognized the broad political stakes in the shackling of a defense counsel in the criminal courtroom. The Berlin Lawyers' Chamber convened a special meeting on November 21 to discuss the case. The chairman, Dr. Ernst Wolff, was obviously uncomfortable with Litten's politics and courtroom tactics. The bar, he insisted, would not deal with any particular "Litten case," but what had happened to Litten could happen to any lawyer. The question was really one of the "freedom and independence of the entire legal profession," a statement that received the "lively applause" of the assembled colleagues. The essence of a lawyer's work was nothing less than the defense of personal freedom, and it had been a long time since freedom was "as threatened as under present conditions." The chamber passed a resolution calling for strict legal limits on a court's ability to expel a lawyer. One of the speakers in the debate was Ludwig Bendix, a zealous Social Democrat and prolific scholar of criminal law and legal theory. Bendix would very soon share with Litten the consequences of the rule of law's collapse in Germany.[205]

The Lawyers' Chamber protest met with some success. Under pressure from Court of Appeal President Tigges, Senate President Schönfeld, whose court had dismissed Litten's appeal, backtracked from his ruling. Schönfeld denied that the ruling said, or meant, that a defense lawyer could not undertake his own investigations. On Litten himself, however, Schönfeld was adamant: Litten's meetings "behind the court's back" were breaches of professional conduct. This answer was good enough for Ernst Wolff. Rudolf Olden, always the wisest commentator on legal developments in Berlin, wrote sadly in late November that the Berlin bar had been too passive in its defense of Litten. A free legal profession was, he said, "a liberal achievement," and its abolition would be a step backward into the absolutism of the eighteenth century. "That is forgotten by neither its friends nor its enemies," said Olden.[206]

The second round of the Felseneck trial got under way in mid-October, and if Litten was missing as a defense counsel, he was dramatically present in other ways. On December 1 he appeared as a witness, warmly greeted by his former clients. But even when he was not physically in the courtroom—Judge Böhmert barred him even from the spectator's gallery—Litten haunted the proceedings. Neither Stenig nor the Nazis seemed to know what to do with Litten gone; they needed him as a foil. The *Attack* wrote that Litten's replacement, Fritz Löwenthal, took over in the spirit of Litten. Because the Nazis wished to portray Litten as a tireless wire-puller, they attributed much of the evidence to him: a witness who testified in early December was described as "the sensation of Jews Litten and Löwenthal." When the trial reached closing argument in mid-December, Stenig's summation was devoted as much to Litten as to the defendants. With his alleged witness tampering and investigations, said Stenig, Litten had caused the first trial to collapse and had "made a farce" of the second.[207]

The closing arguments were not yet wrapped up when the Reichstag passed an amnesty for political offenses. The amnesty applied to all political crimes committed before December 1, 1932, for which the punishment was not greater than five years in prison. This meant in effect that the amnesty covered anything outside of homicide. The legislation also abolished the Special Courts. Its passage rendered the long Felseneck trial all but moot.[208]

The judgment in Felseneck was pronounced on December 22. It amounted to a whitewash of the SA, a lesser exculpation for the colonists, and an indictment of Litten.

The court rejected any notion that the SA had planned a raid on the Felseneck colony. To reach this finding the court had to reject such evidence as Villwock's claim that Storm Group Leader Schulze had exhorted his men to "bump 'em off and get out of there." The court rejected other evidence implicating the Nazis on the basis that the evidence was really Litten's—impressed upon unsophisticated witnesses.[209]

The court tentatively concluded that it was Karl Ackert who had "treacherously" stabbed Schwartz. Ackert "knew nothing of moral restraints" and had been carrying a knife of a size and shape that fit Schwartz's mortal wound. This was a reasonable conclusion on the evidence. However, the judges believed the evidence did not reach as far as certainty, and so they refused to convict Ackert.[210]

As for the murder of Klemke, the court thought two things were certain: the guilty man belonged to the SA, and he was not among the defendants. But the court thought it was "chronologically and spatially impossible" that Wilhelm Grewen could have had anything to do with Klemke's killing. It dismissed the story from Böttcher and Frau Schwarz as "chatter" from the SA kitchen; Oldenstedt's remarks about his guilt feelings over Klemke and his fears for his career were simply "not very clever."[211]

Inevitably the matter of Grewen drew the court back to Litten. After reviewing the evidence of both Schwarzes, Böttcher, Cohn-Bendit, and Litten himself, the court found that nothing contradicted Schwarz's assertion that Litten had urged him to make false statements against Grewen. The effort to solicit perjury from Schwarz raised the "urgent suspicion" that Litten was guilty of "aiding and abetting" his clients. Litten's extensive investigations were nothing but the "most severe imaginable threat to the uncovering of the truth." The author of this scathing indictment of Hans Litten was no ultrareactionary judge yearning for the lost kaiser or the coming dictator. It was Adolf Arndt, a leading Social Democrat, Litten's age, and, like Litten, the son of a successful Königsberg law professor who had converted from Judaism. It is likely that Arndt had also written the decision excluding Litten from the second round of the trial.[212]

So in the end the court could convict no one for the deaths of Klemke and Schwartz. Any other offenses came under the terms of the amnesty. After nearly a year of a trial fought bitterly in two rounds, with endless motions, appeals, public meetings, and demonstrations, all of the defendants went free.[213]

Inquit (Moritz Goldstein) in *Voss's News* recorded the verdict with satisfaction. The court, he thought, had shown fairness to both sides. The verdict not only corresponded to the present state of public opinion, it showed how the environment had changed since the previous January. "From the day of the deed to the day of the judgment, the wave of violence in Germany has risen sharply and then fallen again." The fall in violence had made the verdict possible, and the verdict in turn would contribute its share to calming the situation. The *Berlin Daily News* recorded an almost identical opinion. After a trial that had "put all other trials of the past year in the shade," the court had "acted in keeping with the action of pacification of the Reichstag and the Reich government."[214]

This mood of relief was typical among German democrats at the end of a turbulent year that had seemed likely to bring Hitler to power and yet in the end had not, and that had seen a civil war slowly cool. Few of history's ironies have ever been so grim.[215]

Threats

As 1932 came to an end, whatever hopes some Germans might still have entertained for their country, the people close to Litten were growing increasingly worried about him. The strain of Felseneck had worn him down. For a man of twenty-nine his health was poor. He had become very heavy and was beginning to suffer from heart trouble. One doctor urged him to lose some weight for this reason; a specialist at the University of Königsberg observed an irregular heart beat which, he believed, was not "organically" caused (in other words, not the result of a birth defect or previous heart disease), but rather the result of "functional disturbances."[216]

By the end of 1932 Litten was facing other threats as well, threats that were a direct consequence—and in their way a tribute—to the effectiveness with which he had fought the Nazis. Max Fürst wrote that Litten had "had the breath to keep up this struggle for three years." The deadly seriousness with which the Nazi Party, the SA, and prosecutors like Stenig and Sethe now sought to ruin Litten's professional future, and even threaten his life, was his reward.[217]

For deadly serious they now were. In the wake of Felseneck the authorities were in earnest about using a criminal conviction to drive Litten from Moabit. In late December prosecutors prepared to launch more cases against Litten for witness tampering in the Richard Street case. Kurt Marowsky, the subject of Litten's strenuous attacks in that case, was behind the allegations. These new allegations had surfaced in October, at the same moment that Schwarz's evidence had emerged to drive Litten from the Felseneck trial. The possibility of a prosecution over Felseneck hovered as well, and the professional discipline case arising out of the gun permit issue was still pending.[218]

Litten was now in constant danger from Berlin's storm troopers, whose methods were more direct than the prosecutors' or the bar's. Members of the SA had already attacked Litten in deserted streets, in a subway station, even, as Irmgard wrote later, "in a little café." Litten was now accompanied everywhere he went by a bodyguard of men from the Combat League Against Fascism. Irmgard begged him to leave

Germany, even temporarily. The family had rented a house in Czechoslovakia. Litten refused. "The millions of workers can't get out," he said. "So I must stay here as well." In January 1933 there came a new wave of arrests, and Litten had a full slate of clients. He would not abandon them.[219]

One man in particular had been watching Litten's career carefully since 1931. When Litten was arrested for the Bülow Square shootings, this man wrote the reports for the Prussian Interior Ministry. When Litten aroused the hostility of Interior Minister Severing, this man drafted the letters. When Litten's cross-examination exposed Adolf Hitler to the threat of a perjury prosecution, this man drafted those reports too. What was more, in 1932 this man, by his own admission, began leaking confidential information to Nazi leaders such as Hermann Göring and even became a "sponsoring member" of none other than Berlin's SA Storm 33. In December 1932, when the War Ministry discussed plans for mass arrests in the event of a civil war, this man was there to represent the Interior Ministry. And he was the man who prepared the political police arrest lists, containing the names of prominent Communist and Socialist politicians, left-leaning writers and artists—and lawyers. The man was Rudolf Diels. Diels worked in the political police department of the Prussian Interior Ministry in 1931 and 1932. In 1933 he would go on to lead the Gestapo.[220]

PART III

Toward Dachau

The Reichstag Burns

M y son was arrested on the night of the Reichstag fire." With this simple declarative sentence, echoing the opening line of Franz Kafka's *The Trial*, Irmgard Litten began her account of what happened to Hans Litten after Hitler came to power.[1]

Litten was not alone in being arrested that night. Many other politically engaged lawyers, among them Ludwig Barbasch and Alfred Apfel, were also taken into custody, along with around five thousand other people, mostly Social Democratic or Communist activists, writers, artists, and intellectuals. Most were soon set free again. Litten was not.

In spite of all the dangers Litten faced at the turn of 1933, the possibility that a lawless new regime would imprison him seemed remote. At the end of 1932 the National Socialist Party seemed to be disintegrating. In national parliamentary elections held in November, the Nazi vote had dropped for the first time since 1928. In December Gregor Strasser, the Party's able and popular organizational director and a man often linked to Walter Stennes, resigned after losing a long-simmering power struggle with Hitler, raising once again the prospect of a split between the Party's revolutionaries and its opportunists. On New Year's Day 1933 the *Frankfurt News* wrote that "the mighty Nazi assault on the democratic state has been repulsed"; *Voss's News* was confident that "the republic has been rescued." The New Year's Day cover of the *Workers' Illustrated News* featured one of John Heartfield's distinctive collages, showing Hitler and a battered swastika falling off a cliff. The Nazis themselves felt the wind going out of their sails. Some were close to panic. "The year 1932," Goebbels summed up on Christmas Eve, "has been one long run of bad luck." The playwright Carl Zuckmayer remembered the forlorn spectacle of the SA's New Year's march in Berlin-Schöneberg: "It was gloomy and half-hearted, like the weather," he said; "the passers-by hardly glanced at it."[2]

But in one of history's most devastating ironies, another high-level conspiracy was about to restore the Nazis' fortunes. The key figures were Kurt von Schleicher and Franz von Papen. Schleicher was the political general and virtuoso conspirator whose scheming had lead to the replacement of the last parliamentary administration under Hermann Müller with the first "presidential" Chancellor Heinrich Brüning in 1930; Schleicher's dissatisfaction with Brüning's concessions to the Social Democrats had led him to seek Brüning's replacement with the even more reactionary Franz von Papen in the summer of 1932. Like most elite conservatives in 1932, Schleicher and Papen believed that the fundamental political challenge of the time was taming the Nazis, using Hitler's following as the necessary mass support for an authoritarian regime, and thus permanently excluding the Social Democrats and Communists from power. And, like most elite conservatives, they gravely underestimated Hitler's ruthlessness and political skills. Papen thought that he could buy Hitler's support by reversing the ban on the SA and offering Hitler the vice chancellorship. But after the Nazis surged to a new peak of support in the elections of July 1932 Hitler demanded the chancellorship for himself, and neither Papen nor President Hindenburg was willing to grant him that. Schleicher, for his part, had assumed that he could manage the inexperienced Papen and was unpleasantly surprised to find that on taking office "little Franzie has discovered himself." It was Hitler's intransigence that forced the holding of elections in November; the outcome revealed that fewer than 10 percent of voters supported Papen's government. Schleicher seized the opportunity to persuade Hindenburg that if Papen remained in office there would be a civil war that Germany's small army could not control. Hindenburg grudgingly accepted that the only alternative to civil war was a Schleicher administration, and so in early December "the creeper" became the chancellor.[3]

It was Papen's bid for revenge on Schleicher that brought about the last act of this political theater. Brooding over Schleicher's betrayal, Papen concluded that becoming vice chancellor under Hitler would give him the real position of power. In negotiations in January Papen convinced both Hitler and Hindenburg (who was fond of Papen and had been sorry to see him leave the chancellor's office) of the rightness of this solution to Germany's political quandary. And so it was that on January 30, 1933, Adolf Hitler became chancellor of the German Reich, heading up a cabinet with Papen as vice chancellor and with most of the other key positions in the hands of establishment conservative figures rather than Nazis.[4]

As 1932 turned to 1933, "daily life went on" in the apartment at 1a Koblank Street. Like the jaded pedestrians of Zuckmayer's memory, Litten and the Fürsts paid little heed to the "howling formations" of SA men yelling "Jews out!" or "One-way street to Palestine." Litten's practice was as busy as ever, and although Margot was pregnant once more, she was obliged to work "unceasingly." "She could have used more rest and care," Max remembered, "but neither Hans nor I could give it to her." Hitler's appointment as chancellor made little impression on them. So many "awful governments had come and gone," Max recalled. They assumed that no new German government could be any worse than the ultrareactionary Papen administration.[5]

In the small hours of February 18—Hitler had been chancellor for just over two weeks and had called yet another election, promising his supporters (accurately) that it would be the last—Margot gave birth to a son. Like Birute, the boy received a Lithuanian name, Elnis. Litten kissed Margot's hand in congratulation and regretted that he would have to do without her work for "at least a few days." Two days later, Max and Margot, Litten, Ludwig Barbasch, and some of Litten's and the Fürsts' friends from the Black Mob held a meeting around Margot's bed. Barbasch said it was time for all of them to get out of Germany; Litten especially was in danger. Once again Litten refused to go. "It is always difficult to argue against courage and ideals," Max recalled sadly.[6]

On the evening of Monday, February 27, Max rode his bicycle to see a customer. "As I crossed 'the Linden' I knew something was happening: racing fire engines, ambulances, and signs of fire. The customer already knew what was going on, and on the way home I made a wide detour, so as not to get caught in any demonstrations. Hans came home late and knew no more than I did."[7]

Historians still argue about who exactly set fire to the plenary chamber of the Reichstag building. Was it a Nazi pretext to crack down on the Social Democratic and Communist opposition, as most non-Nazis assumed at the time? Or did the Dutch Communist Marinus van der Lubbe—a mad Lee Harvey Oswald–like figure, whom the police found shirtless in the blazing building and yelling "Protest!"—act alone? After three-quarters of a century the only certain thing is that Hitler used the fire to advance from a still shaky chancellorship at the head of a coalition to a real dictatorship.

One of the changes the Nazis had already made was to reform Berlin's political police in a manner more to their taste. Hitler's righthand man Hermann Göring, now Prussian interior minister, chose Rudolf Diels to be the new head of Department 1A, the political police at the Alex. To emphasize the separation of 1A from the rest of the Berlin police, Göring ordered the department to move from the Alex to a former art school on Prince Albrecht Street. In April the department also acquired a new name. Göring did not want to call his new force the Office of Secret Police (*Geheimes Polizeiamt*) because the natural abbreviation GPA was too similar to the USSR's GPU. Instead, it was called the Office of Secret State Police, or *Geheimes Staatspolizeiamt*. The post office came up with the abbreviation "Gestapa"; the organization would eventually become infamous as the Gestapo.[8]

On the night of February 27, as the Reichstag burned, Diels was summoned to meet the Führer there. He found Hitler, he recalled, "leaning his arms on the stone parapet of the balcony and [staring] silently into the red sea of flames." Göring told Diels that this was "the beginning of the Communist revolt," but before he could continue, Hitler burst into one of his trademark rages. "There will be no mercy now!" he yelled. "Every Communist official will be shot where he is found! The Communist deputies must be hanged this very night. Everybody in league with the Communists must be arrested!" Diels assured Göring that orders would go out for "the arrest of those Communist officials" whose imprisonment "had been intended for some time."[9]

Diels returned to the Alex. "There it was buzzing like a beehive," he wrote. Squads of security police in steel helmets with rifles at the ready stood at the entrance to the building. Police officers clutched lists of suspects, "ready for ever and a day." The first cars with "astonished arrestees, dragged out of their sleep," were rolling up to the Alex's entrance.[10]

Litten would soon be among those "astonished arrestees." At 4 a.m. the police came to 1a Koblank Street and took him into "protective custody."[11]

Sonnenburg

At first the whole thing did not seem so alarming. After all, Litten had been arrested before. The Fürsts and Irmgard Litten were relieved it was the police who came to Koblank Street, and not the SA. "Actually very decent of the government to protect its opponents in this way from the brown hordes," was Irmgard's reaction. Max recalled that the arrest proceeded more calmly than in 1931. The police allowed Litten to bathe unhurriedly. A search of the apartment revealed nothing more incriminating than a few drawings of Naumburg Cathedral, in which Litten had carefully traced the transition from Romanesque to Gothic. The police confiscated these "highly suspicious" sketches.[12]

That night the Alex was filled with the representatives of liberal, Socialist, Communist, artistic, literary, journalistic, and legal Berlin—everyone and everything that the Nazis hated and feared. One of the prisoners was the journalist Egon Erwin Kisch, whose account gives us an idea of what Litten experienced:

> The benches on both sides of the corridor are occupied; "cultural bolshevism" is crammed together in the space between them. Everyone knows everyone else, and every time someone new is dragged in by the police, there are greetings all around.... The policemen who seal us off from the other side of the corridor are young fellows, already with the "special constable" swastika on their armbands. They seem very excited. Their jobs are new to them; they try all the harder to cover their uncertainty with loutish behavior.... Names are called out, groups form, "to the right," one is taken down to the police cells. We are thrown into an underground communal cell; 47 men must find a place there.... Everyone seeks out a neighbor, next to whose spot he folds his mattress into a pillow.... Everyone tells how his arrest was.[13]

Most of Berlin's left-leaning political lawyers were arrested that night or soon after, or else, like Max Alsberg, Kurt Rosenfeld, and Rudolf Olden, managed to escape Germany after receiving a timely warning. Ludwig Barbasch was arrested along with his younger partner. Kisch wrote of that night at the Alex that the first person he saw was the lawyer Alfred Apfel. "Fine, I think, fine that he is there, he can intervene immediately for me. 'Hello Dr. Apfel, I've been arrested.' 'Me too,' was all he said."[14]

Later that day Hitler's cabinet met and approved a decree known formally as the Decree of Reich President von Hindenburg for the Protection of People and State, better known as the "Reichstag Fire Decree." The first paragraph suspended the civil liberties contained in the Weimar Constitution, retrospectively legalizing the arrests of the previous night, as well as the imprisonment without trial of anyone the regime deemed a political threat:

> Restrictions on personal liberty, on the right of free expression of opinion, including freedom of the press, on the right of assembly and association, and violations of the privacy of postal, telegraphic and telephonic communications, and warrants for house searches, orders for confiscations as well as restrictions on property rights are permissible beyond the legal limits otherwise prescribed.[15]

From the Alex, Litten was taken to the old Spandau Municipal Prison on Greater Berlin's northwest fringes. Irmgard held back from visiting, or even writing (the frequency of letters was limited), so that Margot could stay in contact with him. Margot, still recovering from the birth of Elnis, threw herself into salvaging Litten's work and trying to find a lawyer to work for his release. "Several times I found her at home as she simultaneously nursed the baby, spoke on the phone and made notes," Max recalled. "She was exhausted to the point of collapse."[16]

The members of Berlin's political bar were themselves now in too much danger, if indeed not already dead or under arrest, to risk taking over Litten's practice or to represent him personally. Nonetheless Margot found a safely conservative lawyer for Litten and Barbasch. These two also found support from a more official quarter. On March 3 Ernst Wolff, the chairman of the Berlin Lawyers' Chamber, wrote in protest to what was now Hermann Göring's Interior Ministry. The lawyer who was acting for Litten and Barbasch had told Wolff that the grounds for their arrest were "not yet known." He also did not know if Litten and Barbasch, and their colleague Apfel, had been taken into protective custody or if they were in "investigative custody." Wolff noted that, according to press reports, these lawyers had been arrested for representing Communist defendants; he referred specifically to Röntgen Street and Felseneck. The chamber could not evaluate the accuracy of such reports. But Wolff protested the state's assumption that a lawyer necessarily shared his clients' political convictions. Apfel was in fact released eleven days after his arrest—a release owing, so Apfel believed, to erroneous reports of his death in the foreign press, which the new regime was glad to prove wrong. As for Litten and Barbasch, the extent of the Interior Ministry's indulgence was to allow the Lawyers' Chamber to arrange new representation for their clients. This concession seems to have come after some pressure from the Justice Ministry.[17]

At the beginning of April word reached Irmgard, Max, and Margot that Hans had been moved to the "concentration camp"—a new word in German—at Sonnenburg. Built in the 1830s, Sonnenburg was an old penitentiary that Prussian authorities had closed in 1931 due to worsening sanitary conditions. The wave of arrests in early 1933 forced such old prisons back into service. The new Prussian justice minister, the fanatical Nazi Hans Kerrl, designated Sonnenburg the special prison for Communist leaders who were being held pending trials for high treason. Many of the guards were members of Storm 33.[18]

Litten arrived on April 6 with a group of fifty-two other prominent anti-Nazis. In his first letter from Sonnenburg, he wrote that he was well and that there was no special significance to the change of location. His second letter was different. He spoke of his will, and asked Max to sell all of his books, as he would not be needing them any longer. Rumors about the terrible abuse of prisoners in protective custody were beginning to spread in Berlin. Soon there were more than just rumors.[19]

Among Litten's fellow prisoners at Sonnenburg was the radical writer Erich Mühsam, who had enjoyed a brief political career in the short-lived Socialist republic in Bavaria in the spring of 1919 and paid for it with nearly six years in the fortress-prison of Niederschönenfeld. Mühsam's wife, Zenzl, managed to get to Sonnenburg to visit him. She found him "horribly beaten," such that "I could hardly hide my shock from him." His glasses had been broken, his teeth had been knocked out, and his beard cut off. Back in Berlin Zenzl reported to Irmgard Litten that it was Mühsam and Litten whom the SA guards most seriously abused. The SA had beaten Hans so badly that none of the prisoners saw him anymore. Townspeople in Sonnenburg had witnessed prisoners being beaten with rubber truncheons and kicked with hobnailed boots, and they, too, said that Litten was among the worst treated. A Sonnenburg prisoner who was later released wrote, "Whether Litten will get out alive I cannot say. He himself begged [Gestapo officer] State Advocate Mittelbach...just to put a bullet in his head, because he could not bear this bestial mistreatment." Another prisoner later told Irmgard that on one occasion SA men hauled Hans out of his cell at night. "Now you're going to be shot," they told him. But they wanted a souvenir. "You will be photographed at the very moment of the shooting." They put revolvers to each side of his head, the flash went off, the picture was taken. But there were no bullets.[20]

An inventive ring of prisoners managed to smuggle reports out of Sonnenburg. At the center of this ring was a former KPD Prussian parliamentary deputy named Erich Steinfurth, assisted by prisoners whom the Nazis had put to work in the camp office. There the prisoners got access to confidential reports, which they transcribed. Steinfurth sent the reports to his wife in letters written in invisible ink. One of these reports concerned Litten. "With the second transport [to Sonnenburg] on April 6," said the report, "came 60 men by train." The SA immediately beat the prisoners, concentrating on Litten, Mühsam, and Carl von Ossietzky, the journalist and Litten's old comrade from May Committee days. "Litten was beaten with rubber truncheons at the train station, because he wanted to take off his coat so that another prisoner could wear it," the report continued. Later, at the prison, Litten and the others were singled out for more beatings. "A civilian official and an SA man led the prisoners into the building; as they did so, Litten complained about the beatings. The SA man immediately drew his revolver to shoot. The official pushed him back...for this reason later there was a tremendous quarrel. The official was accused of not having freed himself from the Social Democratic past." Later Litten was beaten to the point that he could no longer walk, and then nearly strangled. On April 9, the report concluded, Litten tried to kill himself by slashing his wrists.[21]

Litten was able himself to get information about his treatment to Irmgard and the Fürsts through coded language in letters. In a letter to Margot, under cover of instructions for fictitious cases, Litten wrote that "Bär" (a version of his nickname) "must finally be allowed to terminate his lease. He is on such bad terms with the other residents that they constantly attack him when he comes home at night. They have repeatedly beaten him in life-threatening ways." A client named "Perthier" (another of Litten's nicknames) needed to make his will, as he was dying. Litten was also concerned about the case of "Hali" (he had often signed his youth movement articles this way), who had already made several attempts at suicide. Hali's father "has high connections, and with these can certainly help him get to a more reasonable place. He gets on terribly with his son, but you must make clear to him that it is a matter of life and death."[22]

The Littens did of course have "high connections." Irmgard was able to turn to a Who's Who of the German elite for help. She began with Hitler's war minister, Werner von Blomberg, who had often visited the Littens in Königsberg. Blomberg, probably out of naïveté rather than ill will, calmed Irmgard's suspicions. "He is a defeated opponent," Blomberg told her, "and naturally he must be put in custody to render him incapable of resistance." Blomberg thought Litten's very status would serve as protection, if only because mistreating such a man would have a poor effect on public opinion. Nevertheless Blomberg promised to call the authorities at Sonnenburg and to speak to Göring.[23]

Fritz Litten prided himself on being an "educator of princes," and it was to the royal Hohenzollern that Irmgard turned next. She went to visit Prince Wilhelm, son of the Crown Prince Wilhelm and grandson of the last German emperor, Wilhelm II. Prince Wilhelm was sympathetic but said that he had no influence and was himself in danger, as he had been a member of the "Steel Helmet," which the Nazis considered reactionary. What about the Crown Prince's brother, Prince August Wilhelm, Irmgard asked? August Wilhelm, known as "Auwi," had been an early convert to Nazism. But Prince Wilhelm replied that the family had broken with Auwi over his politics. The Crown Prince himself would be willing to help, said Wilhelm, but he would likely not have any influence either; in any case, he was on holiday in Italy and was hard to reach.[24]

Not that all of Irmgard's efforts were in vain. Rudolf Diels wrote later about the "hair-raising rumors" about Sonnenburg that came to his ears at the time, and of the "complaining relatives of Communists who reported on their missing or maltreated sons and brothers." He was referring to Irmgard Litten and Zenzl Mühsam, among others. In the chaotic transitional conditions of early 1933, a number of prosecutors were seconded to the secret police. One of these was Hans Mittelbach, a man of Litten's age whose path Litten had crossed already in the Felseneck case. Diels put Mittelbach in charge of all concentration camp prisoners in Prussia. After the rumors and the terrible letters from Hans, Irmgard Litten pressed Mittelbach to investigate conditions at Sonnenburg, warning that she would bring all of her social influence to bear and dropping the name of General von Blomberg.[25]

Mittelbach did go to inspect Sonnenburg and recorded in a memo to Diels what he found there. The "well-known Communistic personalities" Litten, Mühsam, Ossietzky, and others had been abused on their arrival, he said. His memo confirmed that some of the prisoners' spouses, as well as townspeople in Sonnenburg, had witnessed this. Mittelbach was "forced to conclude" that some prisoners, including Litten and Mühsam, had been "abused to a very great extent." He had found Litten in a cell with a broken window "with a completely puffy face and swollen left eye." Diels also went to have a look at Sonnenburg and found conditions as bad as he had been told. In his 1949 memoir he wrote that he ordered Mittelbach "to bring Ossietzky and the no-less-dreadfully beaten Litten" back to a Berlin hospital; Mittelbach himself recorded at the time that he had "immediately arranged" for Litten's medical treatment in Berlin. Whether or not Mittelbach or Diels really gave such an order "immediately," the results were certainly not immediate. Mittelbach's memo was dated April 10; the account of Sonnenburg smuggled out by prisoners suggests that Diels's visit had taken place April 7. But it was not until April 25 that Mittelbach brought Litten back to Berlin. At any rate it is clear that Mittelbach drove Litten in his own car to the prison at Spandau and called the Littens to say that Irmgard could visit Hans there.[26]

"Coordination"

The last election was held on March 5, 1933. With the SA and police turned loose on the meetings and rallies of other parties, civil liberties suspended by the Reichstag Fire Decree, and most of the Communists and many Social Democrats in concentration camps, Hitler was confident that this time he would win a clear majority. The election results were a disappointment to the Nazis. Their vote surged to a new high, nearly 44 percent, but this meant that they could control the Reichstag only in coalition with the Nationalists, who won 8 percent. Hitler's main objective was the passage of an "Enabling Act" by which the Reichstag would delegate its powers to his administration for four years. As a constitutional amendment, the passage of such a bill would require a two-thirds majority. When the newly elected Reichstag met in the Kroll Opera House on March 23 Hitler got his law. The Communist deputies were absent, either in concentration camps or in hiding, and the large numbers of storm troopers posted around the opera house intimidated the Liberal and Catholic Center deputies. Only the Social Democrats voted against the law, parliamentary leader Otto Wels daring to tell Hitler, "No Enabling Act can give you the power to destroy ideas which are eternal and indestructible." With a stroke Hitler had freed himself from the control not only of the Reichstag, but also of old President Hindenburg and the circle of aristocrats and military officers who had put the "Bohemian corporal" in office, confident that they could control him.[27]

Drastic changes to the fabric of life in Germany followed quickly on the passage of the Enabling Act. Within a few months all political parties other than the National Socialists were outlawed, as were labor unions, professional organizations, and any other association not expressly affiliated with the Nazis. The Nazis called this process *Gleichschaltung,* or "coordination." They also "coordinated" the governments of all the German states—along with the courts, the bar, and the judiciary.

In March 1933 Hans Kerrl, a former Justice Ministry official and Nazi Prussian parliamentary deputy, assumed the office of Prussian justice minister. Under Kerrl's administration the "coordination" of criminal justice in Prussia proceeded rapidly. Jewish judges and prosecutors were transferred to civil courts or dismissed. On April 1, in an action connected to the infamous (but not very successful) boycotts of Jewish businesses on that day, units of the SA occupied all Berlin courts in a "defense action" and refused admission to all lawyers or journalists who were of "Communist or Marxist orientation or Jewish background." The next day the *Berlin Daily Observer* noted, "The absence of Jewish lawyers yesterday led in a series of cases to adjournments," and it hoped that in the coming week "appropriate measures" would allow the courts to operate smoothly once again.[28]

Measures, appropriate or otherwise, were indeed on the way. On April 7 the government issued the notorious Law for the Rehabilitation of the Professional Civil Service, along with a companion ordinance, the Law on the Admission to the Legal Profession. Paragraph 3 of the Civil Service law specified that "officials who are not of Aryan origins *are* to be placed in retirement," and paragraph 4 provided that "officials who by their previous political activity do not offer the assurance that they will at all times without reservation stand up for the national state, *can* be dismissed from service." "Non-Aryan" was defined in a subsequent regulation as being "from non-Aryan, especially Jewish, parents or grandparents." In the event of "mixed" parents or grandparents, it sufficed for non-Aryan status "if one parent or grandparent is not Aryan."[29]

The priorities of the Nazi regime emerged clearly from the different language of paragraphs 3 and 4, the "are" and the "can," although paragraph 3 made an exception for officials who had served at the front in the First World War or lost a father or son in combat, or held an official position before August 1, 1914. The Law on the Admission to the Legal Profession provided that lawyers who fell under the definition of non-Aryan could apply for readmission to the bar if they met the seniority or war service exceptions. Lawyers who had any connection to the Communists, however, were simply to be expelled from the profession. A few days later Roland Freisler, newly installed as state secretary in the Prussian Justice Ministry, later infamous as the presiding judge of Hitler's People's Supreme Court, explained the new laws to the *Berlin Daily News*. The regime wished to avoid "unnecessary hardness" with the regulations, Freisler insisted, but at the same time any lawyer who "had engaged in support of Communist activity" was going to be disbarred.[30]

These laws provided the pretext for a thorough purge of Berlin's courts, accompanied by all of the absurdities and ironies of Nazi rule. Prosecutors and judges who faced the loss of their jobs now tried to claim that under the democratic "system" they had only been following orders, while resisting in their hearts and subverting democratic policies where they could. A "non-Aryan" prosecutor pointed out that he had won the Iron Cross in combat and had "fought against Marxism and eastern-Jewish immigration," while attempting to "prevent unjust and unworthy prosecutions of National Socialists." He was dismissed anyway. Chief Prosecutor Benno Köhler, a frequent adversary of Litten's, and who, as we saw, had declined to prosecute Hitler for perjury in 1931, argued that he had always done his duty with no thought of politics. He was "thoroughly nationally inclined" and had "served the new government for seven months in this most difficult time." His three children had long been in the Hitler Youth or its related organizations. His credentials were to no avail; the new masters fired Köhler too.[31]

Berlin Nazis hated few Moabit prosecutors more than Paul Stenig. In a fit of rage, Goebbels had once told his lawyer, Otto Kamecke, "This man will have to be marked for later." "Later" came in the spring of 1933. The new rulers put Stenig "on leave" in late March. Stenig fought back with the same tenacity he had shown against Communists, Nazis, and Hans Litten. Indeed, Litten was his trump card. "In the [Felseneck] trial," he wrote, "I fought a hard battle against the former advocate Litten, whom I recognized as a dangerous irritant in the public administration of justice." Stenig congratulated himself that because of his "ceaseless efforts" and "after overcoming numerous obstacles" the "expulsion of Litten as a defense counsel was brought about." When Nazi officials approached him for confirmation of this story, the Nazi lawyer Reinhard Neubert stressed Stenig's "essential contribution" to the exclusion of the "evil Communist lawyer Litten." Otto Kamecke, Hitler's counsel in the Eden Dance Palace trial, who probably remembered Goebbels's rage, was cooler in his comments, saying little beyond the observation that Stenig was "definitely not a National

Socialist." The general prosecutor argued that Stenig's fierce court-room battles against Nazis did not amount to "political activity" in the sense of paragraph 4 of the regulation. At worst, perhaps Stenig could be transferred to a judicial position. Even the Berlin Nazi Party office endorsed this recommendation. And yet, in September 1933 Stenig was dismissed from the Prussian justice service for "political unreliability."[32]

The Nazis also had scores to settle with the German judiciary, and some Berlin-area judges, perhaps defensively, went out of their way to display enthusiasm for the new regime. On April 20 there were birthday celebrations for Hitler at several courts, including the criminal court in Moabit. In August 1933 the *Berlin Local-Advertiser* reported on the ceremonies to open the new session of the jury court in Potsdam. The presiding judge, Superior Court Director Dr. Pusch, after accepting the "German greeting" (the Hitler salute) from all present, gave a speech in which he celebrated the return to authoritarian practices in the criminal law. But the most revealing sign of the attitude of German judges was reported by the paper *Monday* on March 20, 1933. Officials at Berlin's Superior Court I, it was said, had voted to request the return of the two portraits of Emperor Wilhelm I to the jury court rooms, where they had hung before the revolution of 1918.[33]

This outburst of royal fervor eloquently illustrated judges' failure to understand what Hitler was bringing them, and the accommodation between judges and Nazis was always awkward. Hitler himself had long maintained a strong dislike of jurists. German judges, conservative and authoritarian as most undoubtedly were, had been trained to under-stand the law as a fixed, orderly, and predictable scheme of rights and responsibilities. There was no way to reconcile such a view with the radical and irrational lawlessness of the Nazis, or with the doctrine that there was no law but the "will of the Führer." The enthusiasm that some judges showed for the new regime in 1933 was usually qualified by hints of unease. When the presidium of the League of German Judges passed a resolution in March 1933 greeting "the will of the new government to make an end of the enormous poverty and destitution of our people," it added a plea: that the independence of judges to decide cases only according to "law and conscience...must remain!"[34]

Since at least the time of Bismarck the freedom of the German criminal defense bar had faithfully reflected the openness of the entire political system. Thus the private bar was as much a target for the Nazis as were the judges and prosecutors. Here, too, "coordination" came in the second half of March and the beginning of April. The board of the Berlin Lawyers' Chamber collectively resigned; reliable Nazi lawyers took their places, among them Neubert and Kamecke. In April 1933 there were upwards of eighteen hundred lawyers in Berlin whom the Nazis defined as "of non-Aryan origins." With their outlook formed by anti-Semitic propaganda stressing Jewish cowardice, the Nazis had expected perhaps forty "non-Aryan" lawyers to meet either the seniority or military exceptions to expulsion from practice; in fact, about twelve hundred of the eighteen hundred "non-Aryan" lawyers were readmitted, until 1938, when those who had not yet emigrated were finally disbarred. But left-wing lawyers, Jewish or not, were finished. Some fled, like Max Alsberg to Switzerland or the flamboyant Erich Frey to Chile. Leo Plaut, who had been assigned the defense of Litten's clients in Felseneck after Litten's expulsion, tried to save his professional existence Stenig-fashion by pointing to his work in that trial: Litten himself, said Plaut, had accused him of "going over to the National Socialists," a judgment that Plaut now tried to flaunt. But Plaut was a practicing Jew, and the First World War had ended before he could get to the front. His appeal to Felseneck did him no more good than it had done Stenig.[35]

Even prominent Nazi lawyers did not fare well in the Third Reich—revealing again the fundamental hostility of the Nazi regime to the rule of law in all forms, including its own. Curt Becker from the Eden Dance Palace trial was convicted of homosexual activity and sent to a concentration camp in 1936; Hitler and Goebbels's lawyer, Otto Kamecke, met a similar fate in 1938; Ernst Plettenberg, chronically in trouble for various forms of minor corruption, was disbarred in 1933. Alfons Sack was arrested in connection with the infamous "night of the long knives" at the end of June 1934, and although he was released, he was often in trouble with professional authorities in the years that followed. Sack died under somewhat mysterious circumstances at the end of the war, a man, as journalist Walther Kiaulehn wrote, who "knew too much." Only Reinhard

Neubert went on to success, holding down senior positions as head of the Berlin Lawyers' Chamber and the Reich Lawyers' Chamber.[36]

Litten was clearly finished as a lawyer long before his former Nazi adversaries had had time to run afoul of the Third Reich. His Justice Ministry file records the steady closing in of authority, with the usual Nazi mixture of cruelty and punctilious observations of regulations. The general prosecutor at the Court of Appeal reluctantly concluded that Litten could not be prosecuted for aiding and abetting his Felseneck clients. He had probably done what he had done for political reasons and was therefore covered by the December 1932 amnesty. In the meantime, Litten had received the form letter that followed the passage of the Law on the Admission to the Legal Profession. Dated May 6, the letter carried the signature of Roland Freisler. "You are accused," it read, "of having engaged in support of Communist activity." The reverse side of the page gave details: "the defense of Communists and the acceptance of fees therefore from the Red Aid," as well as "the making of contributions to the Red Aid." The letter gave Litten, "in accordance with section 4 of the regulations of April 25, 1933," the "opportunity to make a statement, and to bring forward any evidence to rebut" the charges "within a period of one week from the service of this order." On May 6, of course, Litten was at Spandau, recovering slowly from the torture and beatings he had received at Sonnenburg. In case he was still thinking of returning to the courts, the letter informed him that he was provisionally forbidden to represent any clients.[37]

There could be no doubt about the outcome. In June the Prussian justice minister notified the interior minister that "the admission of the Advocate Hans Litten to the bar of the Court of Appeal is withdrawn, in accordance with paragraph 3 of the Law of April 7, 1933." Paragraph 3 was the provision that applied to non-Aryans, but the other documents in the file show that Litten was expelled from the profession only on the basis of paragraph 4, the Communist activity clause, and indeed one form filed with the president of the Court of Appeal has "non-Aryan origins" crossed out, with the reason for the expulsion that Litten had "engaged in support of Communist activity." The justice minister helpfully noted that with Litten's expulsion from the bar, "the disciplinary proceeding launched against him is rendered moot."[38]

Spandau

S pandau was, in the words of the journalist Egon Erwin Kisch, who was there with Litten, "an old prison town." He remembered reading the prison memoirs of an adventurer named Matthison, who had sat in Spandau two hundred years before; the legendary highwayman Christian Andreas Käsebier had done time there as well. "Perhaps Matthison had slept on the same mattress...perhaps Käsebier had used my hand towel," wrote Kisch. Now, like the Alex, Spandau catered to an altogether different crowd of prisoners: intellectuals, artists, journalists, lawyers, Socialist and Communist politicians, physicians, even clergymen—all of those who made up the "other Germany." The political conditions of early 1933 had caused the inmate population to rise: the prison pastor Paul Lemke noted that whereas there had been an average of 150 prisoners at Spandau in 1932, 300 more arrived in March 1933.[39]

Spandau was a far better place than Sonnenburg for the "other Germany" to be. The Berlin lawyer Ludwig Bendix described Spandau as the "humane realm" of Prison Inspector Hohwedel, a former Social Democrat. Hohwedel's administration showed that it was not possible, even under Hitler's regime, for an entire legal and penal system to sink into barbarism both rapidly and simultaneously. Hohwedel greeted Bendix and the other prisoners who arrived with him in late June 1933 with a reassuring speech, letting them know that "protective custody did not place in question the personal honor of those affected." The prisoners could wear their own clothes and receive weekly food packages; before Bendix arrived even the delivery of flowers and phone calls had been permitted, although these privileges were later revoked. Hohwedel told Bendix that he had intervened in a number of cases with Hans Mittelbach to try to get "his" prisoners released.[40]

Soon after arriving at Spandau, Litten wrote to his mother that his health was "unchanged," but "I am working now nonetheless, since the doctor has expressly permitted it and I want to use the time." He was studying tomb paintings (*Grabmäler*) of the popes, and he had a number of specific requests for books on the subject. Although Litten was supposed to be held in solitary confinement, Hohwedel had arranged for another prisoner with artistic interests to spend the days with Litten pouring over the art books; as Bendix recalled, arranging suitable cellmates for his prisoners was one of Hohwedel's preoccupations. Prison records show that Litten subscribed to *Voss's News*. He spent much time in discussion with the Dominican father P. F. M. Strathmann, imprisoned for his pacifism. Strathmann saw himself as a "modern theologian," believing that theology should be grounded in science. With this disposition it is easy to see how he and Litten would find common ground.[41]

When Irmgard Litten was finally able to visit Hans at Spandau, she found him cheerful. He praised her for her lobbying efforts; Mittelbach, he said, had saved his life. Hans told his mother that he thought "this situation"—Hitler's regime—would probably last five years. Outraged, she responded that it could hardly last six months; a guard muttered, "Not even; a lot can happen in six months." Irmgard secured permission for a visit for Hans's thirtieth birthday on June 19, although the regulation month since her previous visit had not passed. She was asked, "Do you really think we would send you away on your son's 30th birthday, without your having seen him?" Max, along with Margot and their daughter, Birute, received permission for a birthday visit as well. Max and Hans would never meet again.[42]

But the relative kindness of the guards could not alter the hard facts of Litten's condition. When Margot first visited Litten at Spandau, she found him changed beyond recognition. He wore "the expression of the hunted" and constantly looked over his shoulder. Irmgard catalogued his injuries: his face was so swollen that the shape of his head seemed to have changed; "everything seemed oddly crooked." He suffered from severe headaches; he had sustained serious injuries to his legs; his jaw was cracked and many of his teeth had been knocked out; he had lost some sight in one eye; probably the bones under the eye were broken, but only an X-ray, unavailable at Spandau, could confirm this. In June Litten wrote his mother that there was little the doctor could do for him. "He has prescribed pain-killing tablets for me, but I am supposed to use them as little as possible, because they attack the stomach." His injuries from Sonnenburg could "only be brought in order with the passage of time." He complained that he suffered from anxiety attacks—"heart spasms"—which were worse than the head-aches. He had suffered from these "even on the outside last year," and nothing could be done for them, as they were "purely nervous."[43]

Litten managed to pass Margot a note containing the key to a code that he used in his letters. The first letters of the fourth word in each sentence would, strung together, contain the "real" message. The first thing Litten did with the code was ask for enough opium for an over-dose: if he was going to experience anything like Sonnenburg again, he wanted a sure means of escape. With some difficulty, the Fürsts secured the opium and smuggled it to him in a pound of butter.[44]

Diels's List

Most of Litten's contemporaries, his colleagues at the Berlin bar as well as friends and family, assumed that he had been arrested solely because of the enmity of Adolf Hitler, stemming from the Eden Dance Palace trial.

Irmgard Litten, for one, had no doubt that Hitler's lust for vengeance was the driving force behind Hans's arrest. She described meeting the infamous Roland Freisler in 1933 to press for Hans's release. Freisler, she said, was "the only one of the high officials who treated me shamelessly." When she tried to justify Hans's defense of Communists, Freisler angrily dismissed her case with the remark, "In my eyes he is a completely unscrupulous man, for whom I will not under any cir-cumstances do anything." And yet, Irmgard also claimed that friends of Freisler's had told her that Freisler had tried to take up Litten's case with Hitler. With no result: Freisler had apparently told his friends, "No one will be able to do anything for Litten. Hitler's face went purple when he heard the name."[45]

Another of Irmgard's stories of Hitler's hatred involved no less a figure than Crown Prince Wilhelm. Irmgard managed to secure Prince Wilhelm's intervention in Hans's case by cleverly manipulating the Crown Prince's adjutant, stressing the prince's great popularity and voicing feigned astonishment that a prince of the royal house of

Hohenzollern could possibly be afraid to talk to Hitler about the fate of a prisoner. Aristocratic friends close to the Crown Prince told Irmgard later that Wilhelm had indeed spoken to Hitler about Litten. According to these reports, Hitler lost his temper. "Anyone who speaks on Litten's behalf gets thrown into a camp, even if it's you!" was his answer to the prince. Cautiously, Irmgard noted, "I have not been able to determine whether or not that is true."[46]

It was at least more likely to be true than the story about Freisler. A surviving Justice Ministry memo does confirm that Irmgard Litten met with Freisler, albeit in 1934 rather than 1933, and with all allowances for official language the memo confirms Irmgard's account of the tone and substance of the meeting. But it seems all but impossible to believe that the ruthlessly ambitious and fanatical Nazi Freisler would take the slightest chance of antagonizing Hitler by intervening with him on Litten's behalf. When he became a judge, Freisler did not shrink from sentencing former clients and friends, such as the former Berlin SA leader Wolf-Heinrich Count von Helldorf, to death. Freisler was also far from Hitler's inner circle and would have had little opportunity to talk to the dictator. Hitler personally disliked Freisler, who, according to some stories, had returned to Germany from his time as a Russian prisoner of war a convinced Bolshevik. Rudolf Diels wrote that he was once able to impress a point on Freisler because "I . . . had a closer and more frequent connection with his Führer than he himself did." The story of Freisler's intervention on Litten's behalf rested on hearsay, and Freisler himself, or his friends, had every motive to try to fob off the persistent Irmgard with the claim that he had tried to intervene with Hitler.[47]

In 1933 there clearly were Germans with more to fear than Litten from the wrath of Hitler. Of the key personnel from the Eden Dance Palace trial, it was Walter Stennes who was in the gravest danger. Diels reported a Hitlerian tirade from early 1933: "I have heard that this traitor Stennes is still alive and is being held prisoner. Such a man has forfeited his life!" The SS, which had found Stennes hiding in a hunting lodge north of Berlin, was unlikely to misunderstand such language. But Stennes was saved by the kind of jealousy and intrigue common among the leading Nazis. Göring was convinced—not without reason, as we have seen—that his rival Goebbels had sympathized with Stennes's revolt. So Göring intervened in Stennes's case, pried him loose from the SS, and let him go on the condition that he write out a statement implicating Goebbels, which Göring could hold for future reference. Stennes gladly complied, and Diels drove him to the Dutch border. He and his wife eventually found their way to exile in China.[48]

The fate of Albrecht "Ali" Höhler, the convicted killer of the Nazi "martyr" Horst Wessel, points in a similar direction, but with a less happy outcome. "If it was clear for anyone that he would not survive this time, then that was certainly so for the little pimp Ali Höhler," wrote Diels. Höhler was already in prison for the murder, but this was nowhere near good enough for the SA. One morning SA men took him from his prison on the pretext of transferring him to another one and murdered him in a forest. Diels claimed after the war that he had tried to initiate a normal homicide investigation but found the way blocked not only by Göring, but also by Freisler. Diels also claimed that the order to shoot Höhler came from Hitler himself. Had Hitler focused on Litten as he did on Stennes and Höhler, Litten would have been summarily killed in 1933.[49]

Hitler, as we will see, would later have a decisive impact on Litten's imprisonment, and there can be no doubt about the reason for his towering hatred. But the evidence suggests that in 1933 Hitler himself had only an indirect influence on Litten's arrest and imprisonment. To see who had direct influence, and to understand why Litten was arrested on the night of the Reichstag Fire, we have to return to Diels.

Rudolf Diels was born in 1900 in the Taunus region, near Frankfurt, to a prosperous farming family. His social background as well as combat experience in the First World War cemented his life-long political stance as a national conservative. As a student in Marburg he was briefly involved with a Free Corps unit and went on to membership in one of the notorious dueling fraternities that were once such a feature of German student life. Tall, handsome, and suave, Diels earned a reputation for prodigious drinking and womanizing and left college with the requisite dueling scars across his face. After two years of medical study he trained as a lawyer, passed his Assessor exam in 1924, and went into the civil service. He quickly developed an expertise in the combating of political radicalism, and by the early 1930s he was working in the political police division of the Prussian Ministry of the

Interior, with special responsibility for the Communists and other left radicals.[50]

Diels was, as a postwar West German official put it, a "shady character." Diels himself quoted with pride a liberal journalist who referred to his "nose" for "future political constellations." He was ambitious and nearly devoid of political principle: a democrat in late Weimar and the early Federal Republic, a conservative nationalist with the dueling fraternity and the men of the Papen and Schleicher governments, an enthusiastic Nazi from late 1932 who could write to Heinrich Himmler of his "great joy" at being named an officer in the SS. Diels also saw when it was time to jump away from Nazism, and jumped almost too soon, which cost him a stay in a Gestapo prison at the end of the war. But at the Nuremberg trials and later, this arrest emerged as another example of Diels's political adaptability; the first chief of Hitler's Gestapo was a prosecution witness at Nuremberg, not a defendant.[51]

But about one political passion Diels was consistent and sincere: from regime to regime he remained a burning anti-Communist. His post at the Prussian Interior Ministry, where he prepared reports on "Communist acts of violence [Ausschreitungen]," was not just a congenial one for the old Free Corps man, it was one that made him interesting to the fast-rising Nazis. By 1932 Diels, a member of the "Democratic Club" who had been brought into the Interior Ministry to strengthen the young pro-republican forces there, could see that his future lay in another political direction. Shrewdly foreseeing the impending Papen coup against the Prussian government, Diels leaked a distorted account of his superior's meetings with Communists to the right-wing press, and to Papen personally. Papen used Diels's story as evidence of the "treasonous" intrigues of Prussia's democratic administration, and thus one of the grounds for the coup of July 20, 1932. The result was a substantial promotion for the thirty-two-year-old Diels.[52]

But Diels could also see that Germany's political shifts would not rest at Papen. In 1932 he began supplying Göring with secret information about the Interior Ministry. Of greater significance for Litten's fate was that in 1932 Diels was in close contact with the "leading men" of the Berlin SA, who made him a "sponsoring member" of Storm 33. Thus Diels would have been hearing about Litten from Litten's most bitter enemies at just the moment that his work at the ministry was also forcing his gaze toward the young lawyer.[53]

For as Diels's fortunes rose in the course of 1932, his jurisdiction for the battle against the Communist Party and its related groupings, like the Red Frontfighters' League and the Red Aid, was steadily extended. He followed with close interest several matters involving Litten. A letter to the Prussian justice minister from August 1932, asking about the status of the professional discipline case against Litten over the firearm permit, bears Diels's signature. In October 1932 Diels sent the justice minister a copy of a letter by the Berlin police president complaining of speeches "bordering on the impermissible" that Litten, "resident at Koblank Street 1a," had recently made on behalf of the Red Aid. The letter went on to point out that Communist lawyers had spoken in the "numerous" Red Aid meetings held to protest the Special Courts, "especially the lawyer Dr. [sic] Litten, who has been much talked about recently in connection with the Röntgen Street trial."[54]

There is an even more telling link. In a statement given to investigators at Nuremberg after the war, Diels described his work in this period as the investigation of "political crimes and excesses." Political excesses, he explained, consisted of "murders, for instance the murder of the police officers Anlauf and Lenk in front of the Liebknecht House [Bülow Square] in Berlin in 1931."[55]

The importance of Diels's attention to Litten's role as a "Communist" lawyer and speaker at political meetings, as well as the obvious prominence of the Bülow Square shootings in his memory even after the war, emerges when we see the official reasons for Litten's imprisonment. Litten, of course, had been briefly arrested for the murder of Anlauf and Lenk, something Diels would certainly have known. Gestapo documents recording the reasons for Litten's detention in 1934 continued to claim that Litten had been "brought into connection with" or "wrapped up" in the Bülow Square murders—a fact that would have found its way into the Gestapo's records via Diels, and which points strongly to Diels's influence in Litten's arrest and detention. The same Gestapo documents record as "justifications" for Litten's arrest that he was "a notorious Communist defense lawyer a. speaker at comm. meetings." Again, the echoes of Diels's observations of Litten in 1932 are striking.[56]

Two other facts link Diels to Litten's arrest. The first is that Litten was arrested by regular Berlin police in the early hours of February 28. This means his name had to be on the arrest lists that the police had prepared for such a moment. The second is that it was Diels who drafted those lists.

The lists are admittedly a controversial subject. Exactly when they were drafted is a central element in the long-running controversy about responsibility for the Reichstag fire. Diels himself gave conflicting evidence on this question. But there can be little doubt about his involvement in the preparation of the lists.

In the years immediately after the Second World War, Diels was naturally anxious to minimize his own role. As a witness at Nuremberg, he wrote that the arrests after the Reichstag fire followed a plan that had been in place "for ever and a day," and that "lists for all conceivable cases had lain ready for years with the police in the land, according to which on cue any kind of film of arrests, searches and confiscations could be unrolled." In his memoirs he added the critical point, "The lists of the Severing police needed no supplement after the 30th of January 1933."[57]

Even before the Nazis, the Prussian Interior Ministry had kept ready lists bearing the names of activists on the extreme ends of the political spectrum. This point is confirmed by witnesses with no incentive to shade the facts, such as Robert Kempner, Diels's erstwhile colleague in the Interior Ministry, a Social Democrat of Jewish background who was forced into emigration under the Nazis and returned to Germany as a prosecutor at Nuremberg. Diels must have thought that by showing that the lists predated the Nazis he was clearing his own name, but in fact evidence points to his involvement in the preparation of lists in 1932. In November 1932, Franz Bracht, the man who had replaced Carl Severing as Prussian interior minister after the Papen coup, had issued a "Secret Decree" concerning "The Determination of the Addresses of Leaders of Radical Organizations." Given Diels's position in the ministry by this time, it is inconceivable that he would not have been involved in this project. On December 14 there was a meeting at the War Ministry to discuss plans for the event of a civil war between Communists and Nazis. The plans were to include mass arrests. The Prussian Interior Ministry was therefore represented at this meeting—

by Diels. In the context of Bracht's decree regarding addresses it is striking that the documents mentioning Litten that crossed Diels's desk in 1932 always noted that Litten was resident at Koblank Street 1a.[58]

It is most likely, then, that Litten's name had found its way onto the political police arrest lists by the fall of 1932. It is also possible that Litten's name was not added until after the Nazi takeover. Here again, however, Diels's role would have been decisive, for there is no doubt that he worked on the lists after January 30, 1933.

Diels's insistence at Nuremberg and in his memoirs that the arrest lists had "needed no supplement" after the Nazis came to power was an obvious defensive move. But at other times he told a different and probably more honest story. In February 1933 he admitted to Robert Kempner that he was in the midst of augmenting the lists, adding the names of "friends of ours"—meaning Social Democrats and Democrats, "a remarkable number of pacifists, people from the circle of the League for Human Rights," and Communists. Shortly before his sudden death in the autumn of 1957, Diels made similar confessions to several German reporters, who then published lengthy magazine articles based on his revelations. One of these stories, by the prominent journalist Curt Riess, ran for two months in weekly installments in the illustrated magazine the *Star*. Riess's story added a striking detail: it was Joseph Goebbels who had given the political police additional names for the lists after the Nazis came to power. When Diels died, a week after the publication of this detail, the *Star* noted that he had played a "definitive" role in Riess's articles.[59]

Rudolf Diels, then, functioned as a magnifying glass, concentrating all the rays of Nazi hatred onto Litten. He seems especially to have concentrated the hatred of those Litten had attacked or threatened in the Eden Dance Palace trial. Goebbels, of course, had as much reason to fear and hate Hans Litten as did Hitler and the men of Storm 33, and Litten would have been on any list of arrestees Goebbels sent Diels. In a speech on the dangers of Communism to the 1935 Nazi Party Rally at Nuremberg, Goebbels could still dredge up Litten's name for propaganda effect and use the Bülow Square shootings as an example of Communist terror. Later, Hitler's hatred would decide Litten's fate. But in 1933 it was Diels who transformed the story of Litten's battle against the Nazis into tragedy.[60]

"I Must Burden You with My Suicide"

In the middle of June 1933, Litten returned to Moabit as a witness in the perjury trial of Franz Engelhardt, one of the Röntgen Street witnesses. The *Attack* reported, "As Litten was brought forward, those who knew him before could not resist smiling." He had lost his "imposing, muscovite lion's mane," appearing before the judges with an "8 millimeter haircut and—absolutely contrary to his former habits—well-shaved." The *Attack* also quoted Litten's complaint that he was suffering from memory loss as a result of a head injury. An exile paper, the Prague *Social Democrat*, noted that in drawing attention to his head injury and memory loss, Litten "had been the first to get a court to take judicial notice of atrocity stories." "Everyone understood him," said the *Social Democrat*—everyone except the *Attack*, anyway. " 'It was absolutely the old Litten,' said 'coordinated' journalists at the time, not without admiration."[61]

Litten was in court again because Freisler and Justice Minister Kerrl were seeking to reopen criminal cases that they believed exemplified the corruption of the "System Era"—the Nazi code word for Weimar. Among these were many cases involving Jewish suspects. But there were also cases of "Communist capital crimes," such as the murder of Horst Wessel, the Bülow Square shootings, and, most fatefully for Litten, Felseneck. When Irmgard Litten met with Freisler, he used the allegations about Litten's conduct in Felseneck as justification for his continued detention. Early in 1934 the prosecutor and Gestapo officer Otto Conrady told Irmgard that "one must always reckon with the possibility" that a formal criminal proceeding would be launched against Litten for "aiding and abetting."[62]

The "protective custody" prisoners at Spandau were divided into two classes: the regular and the "prominent." Litten, along with Ludwig Barbasch, Ludwig Bendix, and Egon Erwin Kisch, was among the prominent. The main event of the day for these prisoners was the "free hour," when they could exercise in the courtyard. As most of the prominent prisoners were held in solitary confinement, this was their only opportunity to socialize. One free hour in particular, on the last

Hans (left), Rainer, and Heinz. (Courtesy of Patricia Litten)

Fritz Litten (in uniform) with his sons during the First World War. Hans is already wriggling away from the paternal grip. (Courtesy of Patricia Litten)

Irmgard Litten, around the time she published her memoir. (Courtesy of Patricia Litten)

Rainer Litten as a promising young actor at the beginning of the 1930s.
(Courtesy of Patricia Litten)

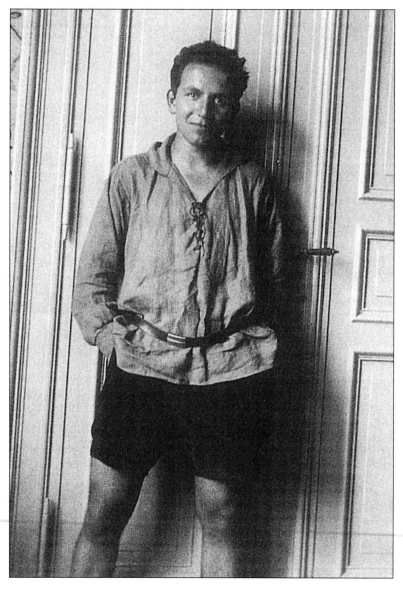

Max Fürst in youth movement attire. (Courtesy of Birute Stern neé Fürst)

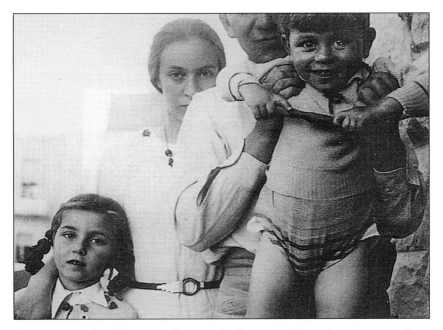

The Fürst family after emigrating to Palestine, 1935. Margot's eyes convey the determination of a young woman who, at twenty-three, had already served nine months in prison for trying to free Hans Litten. (Courtesy of Birute Stern neé Fürst)

Hans as a student, early 1920s. (Bundesarchiv)

The Bear in front of the Bear Fountain in Berlin, early 1930s. (Bundesarchiv)

Joseph Goebbels, Nazi propaganda director and Berlin party boss, speaking at a Nazi rally in Berlin, 1932. (Bundesarchiv)

Adolf Hitler in a Berlin courtroom for a case against Walter Stennes, early 1932. (ullstein bild/The Granger Collection, New York)

Hans Litten in the Berlin-Moabit courthouse with his Felseneck clients the day he was expelled from the trial, August 15, 1932. (ullstein bild/The Granger Collection, New York)

Rudolf Diels as head
of the Gestapo, 1933.
(Bundesarchiv)

Hans Litten, in a portrait drawn by a friend at Lichtenburg, 1934.
(Bundesarchiv)

day of June, was burned into Bendix's memory. Litten came late, and Bendix noticed right away a striking change in his "otherwise lively, intellectually animated face." Litten looked, he thought, as if he were filled with despair. "I cannot and will not ever forget this expression," said Bendix, especially after he learned the cause of it. Barbasch explained to Bendix that Litten had come to the free hour directly from a police interrogation. The officers were Kurt Marowsky, still bearing a grudge against Litten from Richard Street, and two SA men. They wanted Litten to confess that he had known from the beginning of the Felseneck case that Karl Ackert was guilty of Ernst Schwartz's killing. If Litten did not confess, the men told him, the "brown police" would go to work on him in the same way they had done at Sonnenburg. They left Litten to mull this over for six weeks. Everyone, Litten as well as Bendix and Barbasch, understood the gravity of the threat.[63]

On August 10 Litten's interrogation resumed. Irmgard arrived for a visit just before he was taken away. She heard her son's raised voice in the inspector's office: "Didn't you forward my letter to the Gestapo?... I'm being picked up by the same man who threatened me with abuse"—referring of course to Marowsky. Irmgard knew or inferred that the interrogation would deal with one of the Felseneck defendants, and she urged Hans to tell the Gestapo men whatever they wanted to hear. Litten told her that they did not just want him to breach lawyer-client privilege, but to testify to things that were not true.[64]

According to a female witness who could not be identified, probably Herta Hohmann, wife of Felseneck defendant Kurt Hohmann, a gang of SS men extorted Litten's evidence on August 10 through further beatings. The police records give a version of what Litten said that day—omitting the violence—which, in light of other testimony from Litten himself, and from Irmgard Litten, is likely accurate. Marowsky confronted Litten with Herta Hohmann's claim that she had visited Litten at his office during the trial and that he had told her not to worry, "we already know who Schwartz's murderer is," and that they would "wait and see, and if there is no other way we will give him up." Litten admitted that he knew that Ackert had stabbed Schwartz. He added, "Ackert made this confession to me rather late," although "since the beginning of the trial I had had clues that Ackert had to be the one who had stabbed Schwartz." The protocol of Litten's evidence closed with a formula that, under the circumstances, was an utter mockery: "The evidence I have given today is the pure truth, and I have given it freely and without influence from any side." After he had given this testimony, the police confronted Litten with Ackert himself, who, reportedly, admitted to killing Schwartz as well as to confessing to Litten during the trial.[65]

The police and the prosecutors now had the confessions they had sought for so long. There were yelps of glee from the Nazi press, and all the German papers, by this time no longer independent, gave the story prominent coverage. "Communist Confesses to the Murder of SA Man Schwartz," read a banner headline in the *Attack*, and in only slightly smaller letters, "Advocate Litten's Knowledge Revealed." The *Attack* reported that "the Communist lawyer Litten," who had "already been in a concentration camp for a long time," had confessed that he knew "already before the beginning of the trial" that Ackert was guilty. In fact, according to the August 10 protocol, even under torture or the threat of it, Litten had denied knowing of Ackert's guilt *before* the trial.[66]

The Felseneck investigations in 1932 had yielded plenty of evidence to suggest that Ackert had in fact been Schwartz's killer, and Litten was quite likely telling the truth about Ackert's guilt. But true or not, Marowsky and his thugs had forced Litten into a violation of lawyer-client privilege. The anguish this caused Litten's upright soul can be seen in a letter he wrote to Margot Fürst three days later. "My nerves are now really shot," he complained. "I hardly ever sleep any more. If I do fall asleep, I have the most awful dreams. Typically I have the craziest panic attacks at the slightest sound." He had seen the prison doctor, who prescribed tablets. Litten apologized for burdening the Fürsts with his sorrows. "It is the earlier experiences," he said, "which are now having after-effects."[67]

Two days later his torment had become unbearable. On August 15 Litten wrote seven letters: two to Gestapo officer Otto Conrady and one to the prosecutor's office at the Superior Court, recanting his accusations against Ackert and his own confession; one to his mother; one to Margot Fürst; one to Klaus Neukranz, the prisoner with whom he had been working on the tomb paintings of the popes; and one to Prison

Inspector Hohwedel. He could not tolerate leaving an accusation against a client, as well as a breach of professional confidentiality, on the record—but nor could he bear any more brutality at the hands of the Gestapo. There was only one way out. Between writing the first and second letters to Conrady, Litten decided to take his own life. To Hohwedel Litten wrote, "I very deeply regret that I must burden you with my suicide on the last day before the beginning of your vacation— it was unfortunately not possible to put it off." He asked Hohwedel to ensure that the other six letters reached their recipients, and with heartbreaking rectitude assured the director that even though he had no money with him for the postage, he was sure there was enough in his account to cover it. In a final chivalrous gesture toward the comparatively decent prison regime at Spandau, Litten wrote that he had been carrying poison with him since the previous autumn. "I hid it so well," he wrote, "that in spite of the most thorough searches it was not found either at my arrest at the police presidium or in Sonnenburg. The Spandau officials can therefore not be criticized for having likewise not discovered it." Unknown to Litten, however, the guards had been under orders to chain him at night and had refused to carry out the order.[68]

Early in the morning of August 16, Litten took the opium that the Fürsts had smuggled to him. The drug caused him to vomit, however, and after a while he realized that he was going to survive. He added a postscript to his letter to Hohwedel, dated "August 16, early": "Since the poison failed, I have to slash my wrists."[69]

He was found later that morning. His fellow prisoner and former colleague on the May Committee, Dr. Schmincke, was immediately summoned. Ludwig Bendix wrote that it was only Schmincke's intervention that saved Litten's life. The prison doctor recorded more soberly that Litten was "somewhat weakened as a result of considerable blood loss," but that he was "fully conscious" and his heartbeat was "comparatively good." He had slashes on the inside of his left forearm that he had given himself with a razor blade. Litten was rushed in an ambulance to the hospital at the holding cells in Moabit. The main concern of the prison report was with the consequences of this suicide attempt for the Spandau officials: the report noted that Litten had a razor because he had been given special permission to shave himself, but claimed that "in light of Litten's conduct up to now, a suicide attempt could not have been predicted." The prison officials did not doubt that the attempt was "meant seriously."[70]

Litten's time for martyrdom had not yet come. When Irmgard reached the prison hospital the doctor told her that he would do everything possible, as the state still needed Litten's testimony. Irmgard told him that under such conditions she would rather Litten had died. "When we have his testimony, he can do what he wants with himself," was the reply. Marowsky tried to interrogate Litten, but it was of little use. Litten told his mother, "If they had shot me everything would have been all right, but I couldn't bear the martyring and torturing any longer." He wanted further interrogations to be held at the hospital so that someone would hear his screams.[71]

From the hospital Irmgard and Margot went to the Gestapo and there met Otto Conrady for the first time. Conrady, the successor to Hans Mittelbach as the Gestapo officer responsible for all protective custody cases in Prussia, was a year younger than Litten. The son of a police official, he was a native Berliner who had been working as a temporary prosecutor at various Berlin courts since 1931. Irmgard Litten described him as "a good looking man, in keeping with the National Socialist idea of beauty, with a hard, ice-cold stare"; she especially remembered how his eyes turned green when he was angry. A picture in his personal file confirms her description: it shows an athletic young man with full lips, a cleft chin, and thick fair hair, cropped very short on the sides in military style.[72]

Conrady insisted that Litten's statement on August 10 had been true, his recanting false. Irmgard, outraged, insisted that her son had no motive to lie: he was a religious man, and he would not want to leave the world with a lie, "for which he would have to answer before God." Conrady replied that Irmgard was assuming that he did not believe in God, but in fact he did. "Then I am greatly astonished at your behavior," she said, "and I can only tell you this—I look forward to the moment when we shall stand face to face at the last judgment. Then our roles will be reversed—if there is a God." Conrady believed that Litten's suicide attempt was a ruse, that he had counted on being saved at the last minute. "I was there at the Felseneck trial," Conrady continued; "I know him." His eyes, said Irmgard, were "green with hate."[73]

She might have been glad to see a little of Otto Conrady's future. In January 1943, while serving with General Friedrich Paulus's Sixth Army at the Battle of Stalingrad, he was listed as missing. After the war a fellow soldier told a court in Stuttgart that Conrady had been taken to a prisoner of war camp near Stalingrad, where he died on April 12, 1943.[74]

Under the somewhat primitive prison medical care, Litten recovered slowly from the suicide attempt and from the earlier brutal treatment at Sonnenburg. He described his condition in a letter of September 7: "I get up every day for a little while, on the doctor's orders... but I always have strong dizzy spells and nausea. I have not had my eyes examined yet, because the walk to the examination is still too tiring for me.... I still want to put off dental treatment as long as possible, because the whole left side of my head is still very sensitive and at the moment—touch wood—the broken teeth are leaving me in peace. Also my nerves are so totally shot that as much as possible I want to avoid any assault on them." He complained of not receiving letters from either Irmgard or Margot, adding, "This endless uncertainty is appalling."[75]

Meanwhile, the police and the prosecutors had still not given up on the Ackert case. According to an official report of late September, Ackert released Litten from his duty of confidentiality on August 22— with what inducement is not recorded—and repeated his own confession, though he now denied ever having confessed to Litten. On August 23 the interrogators were back in Litten's hospital room to take another statement. This time Litten said that his statement of August 10 had been false. The truth was that he had strongly suspected, but not known, that Ackert had killed Schwartz—a qualified recantation, suggesting again that his August 10 statement had been at least substantially true and that the cause of his anguish was the breach of confidence and not the falsity of the statement. Litten's evidence closed with the statement, "The reason for my false confession is that I feared I would be physically abused if I made a true statement."[76]

Soon the point was moot. Ackert died in custody on November 23, ostensibly as a result of "cirrhosis of the liver, dropsy, and circulatory weaknesses." The prosecutor took the trouble to notify the justice minister that as a result of Ackert's death, the case against him would be stayed.[77]

Means of Escape

In late October the Gestapo sent Litten to yet another former penitentiary converted into a concentration camp. It was in the small
provincial town of Brandenburg, west of Berlin.[78]

Litten's first letter from Brandenburg contained the news (using a
new code that Margot Fürst and Heinz Litten had devised and managed
to communicate to Hans) that he was again being seriously abused.
Irmgard later learned the details from a released prisoner. Litten was
still weak from the blood loss and poisoning of his suicide attempt, but
had to suffer the same vicious "exercise" in the courtyard as the other
prisoners, while at the same time the Gestapo continued to interrogate him over Felseneck and even the Reichstag fire (a man who had
been with Litten in the Moabit hospital told the police Litten had
admitted harboring van der Lubbe). The horror of the interrogations
must nonetheless have paled in contrast to the abuse from the SS
guards. One prisoner saw guards driving Litten, "so befouled and
tattered that he was all but unrecognizable," across the courtyard with
"blows and kicks." When Litten seemed about to collapse, the guards
ordered him into a corner of the courtyard, where there was a small
cesspit:

> Holding his head over the puddle, Litten was forced to go
> down on his hands and knees. To prevent his body from sag-
> ging, Person [one of the guards] took his bayonet and held
> it point upwards under his victim's abdomen. Then both
> sentries alternately beat him with the flat of the bayonet on
> his back and buttocks. This continued until Litten collapsed
> and fell with his face in the latrine. Bellowed orders and kicks
> could no longer overcome his apathy. He was dragged out of
> the courtyard.

The prisoner added laconically, "After Litten had been dragged away,
the SS men attended to us."[79]

In his second letter from Brandenburg Litten asked for a large
quantity of cyanide, sewn into the sleeve of a new suit. But when
Irmgard had secured the poison and had a seamstress perform the

operation on a suit, she found that the jacket smelled so strongly of the poison that there was no way it could get past the guards. She gave up, and Litten understood. But suicide remained on his mind. Kurt Hiller, who was also sent to Brandenburg in October, recalled that a few days after his arrival, a "comparatively decent" SS man approached him and asked if he would be willing to share a cell with Litten to prevent him from killing himself. Hiller agreed, though without enthusiasm. He told Litten bluntly that the SS would hold him responsible if Litten killed himself; after some debate, Litten's sense of responsibility took over and he agreed that he would refrain from suicide attempts as long as he and Hiller were together.[80]

Hiller claimed to have had a restorative effect on Litten. They passed the hours in their cell in wide-ranging philosophical and literary conversations, which, Hiller wrote in 1935, "I shall never forget." Hiller also tried to persuade Litten that he should stay alive to continue his fight against National Socialism. After his release in 1934, Hiller told Irmgard that Hans felt he no longer had the strength for political action, and that "even if he should one day recover his liberty he would no longer be a very useful combatant." Nonetheless Hans promised Hiller that he would "do his very best."[81]

Litten's greatest asset throughout his imprisonment was his indomitable mother, whose tireless lobbying succeeded from time to time in ameliorating his conditions. Whenever she learned of abuses in the camps, nothing would stop her. She wrote to Rudolf Diels, she badgered Otto Conrady, she went to see the commandant of the Brandenburg camp, SS Hauptsturmführer (Captain) Fritz Tank. In November she managed to visit Hans at Brandenburg. She had another stormy session with Conrady, whom she told, "The most base, cowardly and dishonorable crime that there is is to abuse a defenseless person, and . . . anyone who tolerates this is not a bit better than these criminals." Hans's next letter contained the coded announcement that his treatment had improved. Hiller later told Irmgard that he and Litten were moved to another section of the prison, one for old people, invalids, and the sick: "Many others, who enjoyed special protection, found their way into these sections." Hiller said that the Gestapo had ordered that Litten not be abused. Even Commandant Tank was friendly to him after receiving this order.[82]

In his letter to Margot of August 13, Litten asked, "What is going on with the efforts for my release?" Irmgard had told him that although there were things she could do, she had decided to hold off because for now it was safer for Litten to remain in prison. "Sure that may be right," Litten wrote, "but now I ask you urgently to put aside all reasonable grounds and do everything you possibly can." Reasonable grounds would do him no good "if I go down the drain here." He added, "By the way, I recently learned by chance from my mother that you were only comforting me recently when you claimed that my remaining in Spandau was assured. Please do not do anything like that. I am ultimately not so crazy that you have to tell me fairy tales; besides, then I cannot rely on your news any more. So please, do not do that again, it is definitely no comfort for me."[83]

Under the impact of Litten's letters, the requests for poison, the suicide attempt, and the steady rumors of the abuse to which he was subject, Max and Margot Fürst began to think about solutions to Litten's nightmare more drastic than Irmgard's lobbying. A letter Margot wrote to Max a few months later, under conditions in which she had to choose her words carefully, shows how much she suffered from Litten's imprisonment: "I certainly know what it is," she wrote, "to be out there and to be thinking about someone who is sitting in here." After Litten's suicide attempt, Conrady refused to allow Margot to visit. Her response: "Then I will marry him. They can't forbid a visit from his wife." First, of course, Margot would have to divorce Max. Max agreed, "if it is good for Hans." Litten's move to Brandenburg foiled these plans, however. Margot urged Irmgard to think about bribery or some similar approach to get Litten out of Brandenburg, but Irmgard feared that such methods would lead only to her arrest, and then there would be no one left to carry on the "legal" lobbying efforts.[84]

"As we then saw," Margot recalled more than half a century later, "that there was no end in sight, and that all of the mother's efforts to use the influence of highly placed persons failed, I went illegally over the border to Czechoslovakia." In Prague she met with Franz Kafka's friend and executor, Max Brod, editor of the newspaper the *Prague Daily News*; in Geneva she saw the Fürsts' (and Litten's) old friend Hannah Arendt. "I dictated a ten-page-long report to Hannah Arendt over everything that I knew; she brought it to the International Jurists'

Conference and to the English and French press.... By then I was long home again." The limit of success seemed to be, as Max wrote, that Litten had become someone "who had to be shown" publicly to demonstrate he had not been murdered or tortured, which at least led to improvements in his treatment. By August 1933, when the Communist newspaper baron Willi Münzenberg and other émigrés in Paris published the famous *Brownbook* on the early stages of Nazi terror, Litten's name was prominent. The *Brownbook* recorded his arrest, and that of Ludwig Barbasch, along with the literary celebrities Ossietzky and Kisch and a number of Communist politicians.[85]

Such publicity from time to time forced Goebbels, after March 1933 no longer merely the Nazi Party's propaganda director but Germany's propaganda minister, to draw on his formidable rhetorical skills in defense of the regime. In the summer of 1933, for instance, he assured Prince Carl of Sweden, head of the Swedish Red Cross, "as I have assured myself on many occasions," that custody in the concentration camps was carried out "in such a humane manner as could serve as a model even for the most modern penal system." If Prince Carl were to visit Germany's camps he would find "healthy, well-nourished people, who want for nothing beyond their personal freedom." Indeed, said Goebbels, most of the prisoners, who came from "a proletarian milieu," enjoyed in the camps a "considerably higher living standard" than they had in freedom.[86]

Propaganda and marginal improvements in Litten's treatment could not satisfy the Fürsts. Margot moved on to yet another, and much more drastic, plan. "As we then realized that nothing had done any good, we decided to get him out of Brandenburg." In November 1933, Margot took the idea of escape to "a member of an anti-Nazi organization," who in early December sent two men to speak to her: "sinister characters" in SA uniform, as Max recalled, who claimed they had joined the SA to help opposition figures escape. Among their claimed (and, as it later turned out, false) successes was the rescue of Richard Scheringer—one of the officers tried for treason in the army trial of 1930, at which Hitler had first sworn in court to Nazi legality—who had gone over to the Communists after being sent to prison.[87]

At the first meeting with the Fürsts, the men collected 8 Marks to travel to Brandenburg for reconnaissance. They returned a few days later and met this time with Max and Margot and the Fürsts' friend Felix Hohl, who agreed to supply the men with weapons. On December 13 the men returned to discuss their plan for getting Litten out of Brandenburg. There was to be a Christmas party for the guards on the evening of December 16, a Saturday night. These men could arrange an invitation; around midnight, when the guards were suitably drunk, they would dress Litten in an SS uniform and smuggle him out of the prison. They would rent a car to drive him to Prague. Hohl would wait on the road between Belzig and Treuenbrietzen, until the car with Litten had passed, to ensure that Litten was on his way. On December 15 Margot gave the undercover men all of the documents from Litten's political trials, which she had hidden after his arrest. Litten was to take them abroad to publicize Nazi violence and lawlessness. Max and Margot were supposed to come up with 100 Marks for Litten's SS uniform and another 100 Marks for the car rental, "a sum that was certainly within reasonable limits, although it was not easy for us to come by." Kurt Hiller would be included in the rescue, "if possible."[88]

From the beginning, Max did not share Margot's enthusiasm for the plan. "I did not like these guys at all," he admitted. "I wondered what would become of the children and everyone who depended on us, if we too were arrested." But Margot insisted, and Max generously allowed, "She was right, too, because how could one live with the consciousness that Hans was sitting in the concentration camp and being abused? How could one take responsibility for passing up a chance to free him?" Irmgard Litten was also skeptical. She believed that any such attempt would be hopeless. Moreover, she knew that if she were caught doing anything illegal she would never be allowed to visit Hans again. The Fürsts agreed, and deliberately kept Irmgard uninformed.[89]

On Saturday, December 16, Max and Margot went to their cottage in Sachsenhausen, a village north of Berlin, where they had moved their children. Early Sunday morning a troop of SA men burst through the door, armed with revolvers and truncheons. Before anything happened, three-year-old Birute appeared and asked, "But my dood Max, why do you want to go away?" (The children always called their parents by their first names.) The SA men lowered their weapons and calmly informed the Fürsts they were under arrest.[90]

The SA men took Max and Margot to the new Gestapo headquarters on Prince Albrecht Street. It was only in the course of his interrogation—actually "more beating than questioning"—that Max was able to learn what had happened. Felix Hohl had also been arrested, confirming that the operation had been betrayed beforehand. Later, when he was able to talk to Hohl, Max learned that Hohl had been waiting at the crossroads when a troop of SA men fell on him. On his way to his next interrogation Max saw one of the undercover SA men, presumably the man referred to in the official documents as "the informer." By the time Hohl and the Fürsts were arrested, all of Litten's trial documents had been in Gestapo hands for two days.[91]

Margot, meanwhile, had been taken to the Alex, where she proved as adept as ever at working the system. On December 18 she was able to write to Bernhard Hartkorn, Max's partner at the workshop, beginning her letter bluntly, "Dear Hartkorn: Max and I were arrested yesterday." The following day she was even able to place a telephone call to her parents, and by her fifth day in custody she begged her parents to send "any kind of readable book (for instance, Shakespeare)" as the prison library contained only "entertainment novels." The indomitable Margot could handle even the Gestapo: seeing how awkwardly an officer typed her statement, she took over the work herself. Although she was considered to be dangerous and was mostly kept in solitary confinement, she told Max later that she was the only one of the female prisoners at the Alex who was never beaten. Margot's mother and daughter were able to visit her. "She had something of the invulnerability of Scheherazade," Max wrote; her prisoner number was 1001.[92]

All three—Hohl, Max, and Margot—were clever at divining how much the interrogators knew (and thus how much was pointless to deny), while at the same time not admitting other points that could be damaging, and, not least, using their own testimony as a way to inform the others of what to say and what not to say. On one occasion Gestapo officers read Max a transcript of Margot's testimony, which matched his on every point except that each had tried to shield the other. Later, Max had a chance to speak with Felix Hohl again, who convinced him to let Margot take the blame on herself. She was incriminated in any case, and if anyone had a chance of being let go, it was Max. The official documents show that Max and Margot admitted planning the escape and giving the undercover men the money, weapons, and documents. They denied only that others had been involved in the attempt. The documents also confirm that Max said he had not been directly involved in planning the escape, but had only known about it. Margot testified that "the plan for the escape had come from her."[93]

Max's memoirs suggest that he never knew just how much danger he, Margot, and Hohl were in. It was not until February 9, two days after Margot and Hohl had been moved to the holding cells at the courthouse in Moabit, that the Berlin general prosecutor opened a formal investigation against the three of them. The charges under consideration: attempted freeing of a prisoner, breaches of firearm regulations—and conspiracy to commit high treason. After relating the facts as the police knew them, the general prosecutor concluded, with a good deal of imagination, that the matter "was obviously a case of a grandly calculated Communist action," in which at present only a "small number" of participants could be identified. Litten's escape with his documents could have "no other purpose" than "to win over foreign public opinion, or at least the support of the world Jew-press, and thus to inspire the Communists in Germany and abroad to new and more determined treasonous activity against the Reich." This allegation was the basis of the treason charge. The Reich chief prosecutor, however, saw no sufficient grounds to launch a treason case. He invited the general prosecutor to undertake any "required measures" within his own jurisdiction—which meant prosecuting the lesser charges.[94]

In January Max was taken with a draft of prisoners to the new concentration camp at Oranienburg, ironically very close to where his children were living in Sachsenhausen. Here he suffered the same kinds of abuses and torments that Hans Litten had undergone at Sonnenburg and Brandenburg. Then, in February, he was suddenly released. Margot remained in prison, and there was no way of telling when, if ever, she would be free. She was permitted to write one letter per week. Max could, and did, write to her more frequently, although the censor at one point asked that he write more legibly.[95]

Alone in her cell, Margot struggled with a heavy burden of guilt. She was afraid, "and with reason," as Irmgard wrote, that the failed rescue had made Litten's terrible situation worse. At the same time, as her daughter, Birute, recalled, she felt "very guilty" that she and Max had been arrested. Her first letters from prison revealed a desperate desire for Max's forgiveness, "because she wanted to do it . . . and [Max] did what he did because of her."[96]

In her first letter to Max, written on December 28, Margot's anxiety is betrayed by the touching indirectness with which she approached her most urgent concern. Well into the second page of the letter, she wrote, "I am a little worried that maybe you are mad at me. But of course you love me, and after this we will both put back together what has come apart." She wrote consolingly that "everything will be all right," and that when they were free once more "you will in any case have a reasonable wife again, without the craziness of recent times." By January 16 she had still received no word from Max, and she was growing ever more worried about his state of mind. "I know," she said, "that in the moment that we see each other again, everything from before will be forgotten." Max was finally able to write to her on January 18. He assured her, "I will always love you, no matter what has happened."[97]

Max passed on to Margot whatever information he could about Litten, always disguised in the "family language." In one especially moving letter, written to buoy Margot's spirits after she wrote of the strain of solitary confinement, Max described how he would paint the walls of her cell; among the animals he would paint would be "a large, sad grizzly bear—well, perhaps I shouldn't write about him. He trots over and licks your little paw." Margot responded cheerfully, pointing out the vagaries of Max's spelling: "I believe the grizzly bear would be immediately transformed into a most roguish creature if he saw that he was supposed to be a 'grysly.'" When Max's brother-in-law was released from the Esterwegen concentration camp, where Hans was then being held, Max wrote, "He also brought me greetings from Mr. Perthier, who is doing well." On one occasion, he wrote that "there was also news from Joachim Behr," yet another, rather obvious, play on Litten's middle name and nickname. "He is doing all right. You do not need to worry about him."[98]

Even indefinite imprisonment and interrogation could not break Margot's loyalty to Litten. The officer who censored her letters exclaimed to Margot, "I can't understand how two such accomplished and cultivated people as you and your husband could have thrown yourselves away on such an inferior person as Litten!" This only enraged Margot. Her lawyer told Max that the prosecutor had dropped a hint: if Margot denounced Hans Litten as a criminal, "the situation could be improved." She refused. On one occasion she burst out in rage to a police officer, "You hate [Litten] so simply because you are envious and angry that so fine a man should be fighting against you. You'd be only too glad to have him on your side!" To which the officer replied dryly, "Granted. But he doesn't happen to be on our side."[99]

The first sign of hope in Margot's case came with an amnesty for political prisoners and for other offenders facing minor prosecutions that Hitler proclaimed in early August 1934. The amnesty contained exceptions: it did not apply to "high treason" or to actions "through which the manner of the execution or the motives" revealed a "contemptible cast of mind" on the part of the culprit. Margot, the former lawyer's assistant, saw the text of the amnesty decree and insisted in a letter to Max that her case was not one of treason (she did not know how nearly it had been), "nor do I have a contemptible cast of mind." It was not so simple, of course. Nazi legal thinking was more than equal to the task of finding that the amnesty did not apply to her, and in a later period of the Third Reich she and Max would certainly have faced death sentences. But a few days later came the news that Felix Hohl had been released. And even the prosecutor, as it turned out, was sympathetic to the young mother. When she promised him that in the future she would forget politics and devote herself to her children, he took advantage of the amnesty and stayed the case against her. In Nazi Germany, being acquitted of criminal charges was no guarantee of freedom, and only some lobbying by Margot's mother, invoking her husband's international business connections, kept Margot from being sent to a concentration camp. In September 1934 she was finally released.[100]

The Fürsts could do nothing more for Litten, but neither could they bear "to stand by doing nothing as he was slowly tortured to death." Warned in 1935 of their impending rearrest, they managed to secure visas for Palestine. In October 1935 they left Germany, not knowing when, if ever, they would return. They knew only, as Max later wrote, that one way or another the end for Hitler's Germany "would have to come with horror."[101]

Madonna in the Rose Bower

For long weeks after the failed escape attempt, the Brandenburg authorities denied Irmgard Litten all contact with Hans. Naturally she could not let on that she knew the reason. Through January and February she kept writing to him, letting him know that the Fürsts had been arrested (though not why) and later that Max had been released.[102]

Litten knew much of what was going on through other channels. The Fürsts had dropped hints about the planned escape in their ingenious code: "Hold on, flight is being worked on" and "Köpenickiade is being prepared," the latter a reference to the famous escapade of Wilhelm Voigt, the "Captain of Köpenick," who in 1906 used a fake captain's uniform to commandeer a squad of soldiers and rob the Köpenick town hall. After the Fürsts' arrest, Litten revealed the code to his interrogators. He denied having expressed a wish to escape, admitting only passive acceptance of the Fürsts' plans.[103]

Kurt Hiller later told Irmgard what happened to Hans in this period. In mid-December, a few days before the planned escape, the guards took Litten and Hiller to the cellar and confiscated Litten's letters. Hiller and Litten immediately guessed that the escape attempt was blown. Remarkably, however, the authorities still kept them in the same cell, and so they were able to agree on a story: Hiller had known nothing about the whole affair, while Litten had known but not approved. Litten's revelation of the code was supposed to support his claim of passivity. After his interrogation Hiller was taken to another part of the camp; Litten was held in solitary confinement. Kurt Ludecke, a dissident Nazi imprisoned at Brandenburg, recalled the transfer of Hiller and Litten to a "dormitory," and that after a time "Litten disappeared." "I know that he was held for weeks in a dark cell in the prison hospital, and then was taken away after the New Year."[104]

One letter fragment hints at Litten's deeper understanding of the Fürsts' rescue attempt and seems to ask a question about Max's state of mind after it. It is impossible to affirm the date or even the recipient of the letter, as it survives in a typed copy presumably made by

Irmgard. Litten describes what he calls an idea for a novel he has been considering:

> A woman between two men, whom she loves equally. The first, younger, returns the love, the second, older, not (perhaps he loves another woman, but that will play no role in the writing). There is no question of jealousy, because the younger man (I think of him as about 24) has a relationship with the older man (who I think is about 4 years older) of unconditional reverence (he has been decisively intellectually influenced by him, or perhaps received help in an especially difficult situation).... The normal, un-tragic course would be that the woman finds happiness with the younger man, while she gives up on the older man. The tragic conflict arises because the older man gets into some kind of terrible position (the details are not yet clear to me, but since the action naturally takes place in the Middle Ages, one can perhaps think of the prisons of the Inquisition) in which the woman can help him a little bit, but only if she separates from the younger man without hope of reunion. In this situation she decides for the older man. A mistake in the conception, perhaps, is that such a difficult decision is laid on the shoulders of a woman.... An unsolved problem for me is also the psychological situation of the younger man at the end of the action.[105]

The nature of Hans and Max's relationship, Margot's willingness to divorce Max in the late summer of 1933 so that she could continue to visit Hans, her role in pushing forward the escape attempt, the constant refrain in her letters from prison about asking forgiveness from Max, and of course Hans's description of the older man in his scenario as having fallen victim to something like "the prisons of the Inquisition"—this all makes the letter seem more than an idea for fiction. The reference to the "psychological situation of the younger man at the end of the action" is Litten's effort to learn whether Max was angry with Margot, or Hans, or both. Only the honesty of the cool disinterest in Margot is suspect. As we saw, Hans had a habit of falling in love with Max's girlfriends, and at one point confessed to Max that he had fallen in love with Margot; Margot recalled years later that Litten had told her this directly. In a letter Hans wrote at the end of November 1936 he referred to a postcard Max and Margot had sent him in 1932 of a portrait of the Madonna in the rose bower: "We had a special connection to the picture, because Margot, when she wore her hair in pigtails while traveling, bore such a resemblance to it—I always called her 'the little Madonna in the rose bower.'" That Litten would liken Margot to the Madonna speaks eloquently enough of his attitude to her. Margot's prison letters hint at strain in the Fürsts' marriage in 1933—on one occasion she wrote that the past year had not been "so very praiseworthy" for her—and the tension was likely over Hans. Although in his memoirs Max printed a selection of his moving and passionate letters to the imprisoned Margot, he admitted that at the same time he "occasionally had other girls" with him.[106]

Litten knew of the Fürsts' emigration. He may have known that his partner, Barbasch, had gone to Palestine as well. By 1934 the Nazis had destroyed the community in which Litten had lived—the world of cultured and literary, left radical and legal Berlin. The members of that community were dead, in prison, in exile, or beaten into servility. Hans Litten was, increasingly, alone.[107]

Long Knives

In the spring and summer of 1934 important shifts were taking place in the basic structure of the Nazi regime. The ranks of the SA had expanded dramatically since the movement came to power, from about 750,000 in February 1933 to over two million by the summer, and nearly three million by the beginning of 1934—four and a half million if the affiliated Steel Helmet members were counted in. These numbers worried the officers of the regular army, not least since it was well known that SA Commander Ernst Röhm saw his troops as the nucleus of a new national army. Röhm was also not shy about voicing the storm troopers' widespread frustration at the new state's loss of revolutionary momentum and their desire for a "second" revolution. In June 1933 Röhm wrote, "A tremendous victory has been won, but not *absolute* victory.... It is in fact high time the National Revolution stopped and became the National Socialist one." Privately he was scathing: "Adolf is a blackguard," he told Hermann Rauschning; "he is betraying us all." Hitler was forced to a decision: he could have the support of the SA or of the army, but not both. His answer to this quandary came in the "night of the long knives" on June 30, 1934, with the murder of at least eighty-five leading SA men, Röhm among then, along with many other people against whom Hitler had grudges, such as Kurt von Schleicher. Thousands more were arrested. After that the SA never again posed a serious threat to Hitler or to the army, or even constituted an important element of the Third Reich—an ironic outcome for so many of Litten's enemies. The disillusionment and despair in the ranks of the SA echoed that of the left the previous year. One SA man recalled sadly that after the Röhm murders, "the real revolutionaries drew the consequences and got out. Resigned to it."[108]

The timing of the SA purge had also had much to do with the failing health of President Hindenburg. The Nazis were anxious about what would follow Hindenburg's clearly impending death: it might provide the occasion for a conservative counterrevolution against the Nazis, perhaps centered around Franz von Papen, who was giving very critical speeches in 1934, or for the SA's long awaited "second revolution." Thus the purge was directed against both potential threats (one of the victims was known to be the author of a particularly pointed Papen speech). When in early August Hindenburg finally died, with the SA broken and the conservatives intimidated Hitler abolished the office of president and merged its functions into his own, under the new designation "Chancellor and Führer." All military personnel, and soon after that all civil servants, were required to swear personal oaths of loyalty to Hitler, rather than as before to Germany or its constitution. There were clear signs, especially in the wake of the SA purge, that the Nazi regime was settling down into a more stable kind of authoritarian rule. A large number of people who had been put into concentration camps in the first half of 1933 were released: a third of the entire camp population on July 31, 1933, alone. By May 1934 there were only a quarter as many concentration camp prisoners as there had been a year before.[109]

In April, as a byproduct of these shifts in power, Göring gave up effective control of the Gestapo. The SS leader Heinrich Himmler was named Göring's deputy, with Reinhard Heydrich as Gestapo director. This meant in practice that the Gestapo had passed into Himmler's growing SS empire and had become a national rather than a purely Prussian force. Rudolf Diels resigned and went to work as district president in Cologne. "Heydrich," Diels wrote, "dismissed my entire staff, which did not appear reliable to him. He arranged that the minister of the interior would not permit employment in the capital city for any of them. They disappeared into subordinate posts." But the size of the force increased dramatically under Himmler and Heydrich. Diels recalled that in his time there had been approximately two hundred officials working for the Gestapo in Berlin; by the end of 1935 there were fifteen hundred, and Prussian Finance Minister Johannes Popitz told Diels that under Himmler and Heydrich the Gestapo's annual budget jumped from 5 million to 40 million Reichsmarks.[110]

Otto Conrady was one of the Gestapo officers who became a casualty of the changes. At the end of April 1934 Göring wrote to the justice minister that "on the basis of fundamental considerations" Dr. Otto Conrady "cannot be employed further in the service of the Secret State Police. His remaining in Berlin is also not appropriate [angezeigt]." At the beginning of July Conrady took up new duties as a prosecutor in the western city of Hamm, from whence he begged Roland Freisler—without success—to be allowed to return to Berlin. A letter from the new Gestapo master Himmler notes that Conrady, like other ex-Gestapo officers, was to be removed from his former professional field and geographic area to ensure the "smooth working of the authority"; a letter from Göring's office went out of its way to counter any suggestion that the transfer was a reflection on Conrady's job performance. Thus the available evidence suggests that Conrady was an unlucky pawn. Irmgard Litten, however, told a different story. A well-connected lawyer told her she had "broken the necks" of both Conrady and Mittelbach. Other officials had noticed that Conrady always gave Irmgard Litten an hour of his time when she appeared at his office, although he refused to see anyone else. He had told colleagues that she was his "favorite case," and Zenzl Mühsam's account confirmed that he did not as a rule receive prisoners' relatives.[111]

The Führer's Clemency

After the long silence imposed following the failed rescue, Irmgard received a postcard from Brandenburg dated January 22, 1934: "I am well, so you don't need to be worried on my account," Litten wrote. "But please find out as soon as possible—perhaps through a lawyer—whether or not there is a criminal proceeding pending against me. I need this information as the basis for a possible petition for release." A Gestapo officer had advised him to hire a lawyer to prepare such a petition. Hans recommended that Irmgard approach a Berlin lawyer named Hans Dittrich, who had "already handled a number of these cases." He added, "Since the [Gestapo] commissar thinks such a petition could succeed, the matter is urgent for me." Just the day before, Litten had been moved again. He wrote from his new address: Esterwegen, Concentration Camp 2, Barrack 1.[112]

Esterwegen was part of a huge complex of prisons and concentration camps along the River Ems near the Dutch border, where the prisoners were set to work draining and cultivating the moors. The historian Nikolaus Wachsmann writes that survivors' accounts of the Emsland camps "paint a picture of brutal labor, random violence and sadistic torture," in which inmates were regularly beaten, kicked, whipped, set upon by dogs, their teeth knocked out; some prisoners were killed. The SS described it as "the most difficult to command of the German concentration camps, since it harbors without exception serious criminals, and lies physically in an extremely remote location surrounded by a reactionary population."[113]

Litten's East Prussian soul was able nonetheless to find some compensation in the grueling labor. "It is a comfort for me that I approve of the meaning of the work," he wrote his mother, "and above all the wonderful landscape: great wide plains, almost without trees, unlimited views in all directions. That is depressing for most people, but of course you know how I love such plains. It reminds me strongly of our East Prussian plains." On the other hand, the labor in the moors made him too tired to do any "intellectual" work in the evenings. He contented himself, he said, with reading a few lines of Hölderlin or

Shakespeare—"I have met someone here who has the entire English Shakespeare."[114]

In late February Irmgard Litten got permission to visit Hans once again. She arrived to find that he was in the infirmary. Hans explained that because of his heart spasms he frequently fainted. A few days before he had fainted while riding on a truck. He fell off, and the truck ran over his leg. He had been lying in bed for several days with what he described as "crazy pain" before the doctor so much as had his leg X-rayed. The next day he was sent to St. Mary's Hospital in nearby Papenburg. The X-ray revealed a fractured fibula.[115]

In the hospital Litten recovered slowly. Meanwhile Irmgard went months without further word from him. Not until the beginning of May could Hans write, "I am now already very well...everything has healed." He was no longer in constant pain, although he had difficulties walking; he could now do so only with a cane, and even this caused his foot to swell, an effect that the doctor told him would last "perhaps a few years." As always, the best clue to his mood was whether or not he was reading: "I would at the moment have time to read, but I hardly get to it, because I can concentrate so little that even reading the newspaper is difficult."[116]

Small wonder, then, that Litten's petition for release was an "urgent" matter. To assist Dittrich, Litten wrote out a long defense of his work as a lawyer and of his political views. He insisted that he had never been a member of the Communist Party "because of considerable political differences." Moreover, he had often stressed these differences in the courtroom and in public speeches. His political activities had never extended beyond his courtroom work and public speaking on "general political questions," and in the event of his release he would refrain from any political activity, as "any activity directed against the National Government [would be] madness."[117]

His final argument took on directly the hatred the SA bore him from trials such as the Eden Dance Palace case. "I have often encountered the view," he said, "that I had often acted especially hatefully toward the SA in court." In fact, Litten argued, no "Communist lawyer" had been as just to opponents as he had been to SA men. When he acted as a private prosecutor against SA defendants, he always followed the principle that he should never ask for a conviction unless it were one he would have arrived at as a judge. Furthermore, "in all these cases I have spoken passionately for the personal honor of my political opponents." Rather disingenuously, he cited his argument on appeal in the Eden Dance Palace case, in which he had asked that the defendants be deemed "criminals by conviction."[118]

Dittrich was a Nazi Party member and had to get special permission to represent Litten. In late March Irmgard received a brief note from him, returning what he called Hans's "exposé" of his political views with the comment, "I deeply regret that I am unable to assist you in this matter." Dittrich's refusal was part of a pattern. Again and again Irmgard found that lawyers were afraid to take Hans's case or were subject to threats if they dared to give her advice. Cutting out the freedom of action of defense lawyers was one of the ways the Nazis paid tribute to the influence the private bar had wielded in Weimar courts. In 1935 Werner Best, the deputy director and top legal officer of the Gestapo, explained the policy: "Under no circumstances may it be conceded that the application of protective custody could be turned over for examination and decision in any kind of judicial form." Allowing lawyers to get involved in the cases of concentration camp prisoners and the "consequent recognition of certain rights of these lawyers" would be the first step toward allowing the justice system to rule on protective custody. "The forms of procedure of the justice system," he said, "are, under present conditions, absolutely inadequate for the struggle against enemies of the state."[119]

Irmgard gamely went ahead and submitted the petition herself. But in June, just before Litten's birthday, she had to tell him that the petition had been rejected with the explanation, "At this time your personal safety could not be guaranteed." She tried to cushion the blow by suggesting that the uncertain conditions would soon pass and he could then be released.[120]

If Irmgard could not find a lawyer she would do it herself, and in 1934 and 1935 she lobbied Germany's leaders and tried to interest influential people abroad in clemency for Litten. She linked her efforts to symbolic occasions: Hitler's birthday, important state anniversaries, and the aftermath of particularly Hitlerian successes. "Eventually I was told that I would receive absolutely no more answers if I wrote so often.

One had the right to submit a petition for clemency every three months. So I limited myself to that."[121]

Her memoir makes clear how relentlessly she fought for Hans's freedom, or at least for the amelioration of his conditions. What she pushed to the margins of her book was that her battle was carried out under constant personal strain: ill health, poor finances, and a growing rift with her husband and the rest of her eminent social circle. Hints of the strain come through in her letters. Money became much tighter in the Litten family after 1933. Fritz had fled to Czechoslovakia after Hans's arrest and did not return to Germany until 1934. While he was gone the Prussian government stopped paying his pension. Irmgard wrote that he returned only because "the transfer and exchange of currency were becoming more difficult." But even in Germany Irmgard and Fritz lived apart. She took a smaller apartment in Berlin early in 1934; she wrote Hans that the new apartment was pleasant enough, "but when one pays half as much in rent, one must certainly become more modest in one's demands." Hans's letters reveal occasional confusion about whether he should write to "father's address" or to Irmgard's. Her social circle had changed as well; the generals and barons were gone. "I socialize now much more with young people than with people my age," she wrote in late 1934, "with whom I do not have very much to talk about."[122]

The Litten family did, however, have ties to President Hindenburg, who might have been expected to remember with gratitude the honors Fritz Litten had arranged for him at the University of Königsberg. So in 1934 Irmgard wrote to him, playing, with impressive rhetorical cleverness, on themes of motherhood designed to be congenial to an elderly officer who embodied his country's most conservative traditions: "A despairing mother turns to your Excellency with the request for clemency for her son." She dropped her husband's name as a subtle guarantee of the Litten family's political respectability. Deploying an argument she would use repeatedly, she insisted that her son's advocacy was a legacy of her "old and respected family of south-German pastors." This is why Litten had become a defender of Communists and why he "unfortunately" had experienced a "confrontation with the present Reich chancellor, who at the time had been summoned as a witness." The "Herr Reich chancellor," Irmgard Litten continued, "is said since that time to have considered Litten an especially dangerous Communist leader. I believe that here an incorrect impression has arisen." Hans, she insisted, had never belonged to the Communist Party and never been a political candidate; he had acted only as a lawyer. She catalogued Hans's sufferings in the camps—the abuse at Sonnenburg, the suicide attempt, the fractured leg at Esterwegen—stressing that when she visited him at Brandenburg late in 1933 his "psychological and physical state was that of a completely broken man." Hindenburg's state secretary Otto Meissner wrote Irmgard that Hindenburg had listened to the presentation of her petition with "the greatest personal sympathy and had passed it on with his support to the appropriate authorities." But "it was, like all my petitions, rejected." It is possible that Meissner was lying, and that he himself suppressed the petition so that it never got to Hindenburg. According to Rudolf Diels, Göring was blackmailing Meissner, so that Meissner operated like a shield, keeping from the president everything "that spoiled the picture of the orderly authoritarian state."[123]

Irmgard did not shrink from appealing directly to Hitler as well, sending a petition to him on April 18, 1934, two days before the Führer's forty-fifth birthday. Here again she played upon maternal and patriotic themes and added a good dose of flattery. "Your approaching birthday," she wrote, "gives me the courage to make an unusual request for a personal audience." She trusted in Hitler's "well-known chivalrous disposition toward the defeated opponent," and noted her own credentials as "a German woman for whom the fatherland comes before anything."[124]

The prospect of clemency from Hitler was not as fantastically remote in 1934 as it might have seemed at first glance. By August, with the threats from both the SA and the conservatives neutralized, Hitler felt secure enough to make gestures of conciliation toward his defeated enemies. He proclaimed an amnesty for political prisoners in honor of the late President Hindenburg. This was the amnesty that saved Margot Fürst. He also issued a decree on August 7 proclaiming his wish that "on the occasion of the amalgamation of the office of the Reich President with that of the Reich Chancellor" the pardoning of prisoners and the staying of prosecutions should not be limited to the regular criminal process. Instead, "to the extent possible, there should be releases from protective custody." Hitler ordered the state governments to examine all such cases on an expedited basis and to release prisoners "where the occasion for the imposition [of custody] was minor, or where from the duration of custody and the nature of the prisoner it can be anticipated that he will in the future no longer conduct himself with enmity toward the National Socialist state and its organs."[125]

When Irmgard heard of the amnesty she wrote immediately to Hitler. The Gestapo had told her that Hans remained in custody only because the state could not guarantee his safety if he were released. Irmgard parried this (transparently spurious) claim cleverly: "I consider this fear groundless in view of the authority of the present state leadership and National Socialist discipline." She also went directly to the point most likely to stand in the way of Litten's release. "I have the following fear," she said. "My son, as is well known, aroused your personal ill-will in a trial—if I am not mistaken, it was the so-called Kurfürstendamm trial" (she was, of course, mistaken). Irmgard hastened to add that she was convinced Hitler was too great a man to seek vengeance against a broken prisoner. "But I fear that some authority or other, in the mistaken belief that it is acting according to your wishes, might without further ado reject placing my son on the list of those to be amnestied." Perhaps, she continued, these were just "fantasies." But she dared nonetheless to ask that Hitler order the examination of her son's case "objectively and benevolently" in accordance with the guidelines Hitler himself had given.[126]

It was characteristic of the Kafkaesque absurdities of Nazi rule that the regime monitored its own human rights abuses with an extraordinary expenditure of bureaucratic effort. Hitler had ordered that reports on all prisoners be prepared by September, and they were: the Gestapo and other authorities had to evaluate and report on each protective custody prisoner and whether or not he or she should be released; if the prisoner was to be retained in custody, the Gestapo had to report on the grounds for the continued detention. Questions were asked, charts were prepared, information gathered, files filled.

Naturally many people linked with Litten were caught up in this process. The Gestapo recorded that Alfred Andree, one of Litten's Felseneck clients, "belongs to the Comm. rowdydom. Principally involved in the murder of Prof. Schwartz i.e. Felseneck case." The Gestapo decided that Andree's "protective custody must provisionally be upheld." The reason was in part the death of Ackert, which had spared Andree a long prison sentence. The Gestapo also refused to release Carl von Ossietzky, because it was certain "that in the event of his release Ossietzky would . . . leave Reich territory within 24 hours, and from abroad carry out atrocity propaganda in the strongest manner."[127]

Under the heading "Grounds for Custody" the entry for Litten read, "Notorious defender of Communists and speaker at Communist meetings. For years he attacked members of the National Socialist Party in the most hateful way and with the nastiest means in Communistic trials. Has also been brought into connection with the Bülow Square murder case (murder of the captains Anlauf and Lenk on August 9, 1931)." In the space provided on the chart for "further suggestions for release" the Gestapo noted simply, "After renewed thorough examination, in light of his previous anti-state activity of many years' duration, a *lifting of the protective custody is not approved*" (emphasis in original).[128]

As we have seen, this justification supplied a hint about the role Rudolf Diels played in Litten's imprisonment. The emphasis on Litten's standing as a supposed *leading* Communist was also fateful. The Nazis were far more reluctant to release the leaders than the rank and file. Diels recalled one occasion on which he tried to interest Göring in an amnesty for concentration camp prisoners. Outraged, Göring replied sharply, "If you release the functionaries, tomorrow you will have the illegal Red Frontfighters' League, the Red Aid, the underground propaganda once again. We must accept that ten thousand such people will remain forever behind barbed wire as enemies of the state." Litten's name appears on an attachment to a letter from Göring listing "prominent protective custody prisoners" in the company of Theodor Neubauer, a Communist Reichstag deputy and later underground resistance fighter, Ossietzky, and Walter Stöcker, another Communist politician. Finally, the comment about the attacks on Nazi Party members may be as close as a police officer wished to go to recording that one of Litten's main offenses had been attacking not just Party *members*, but the leader himself "in the most hateful way." The essence of this reasoning, a little more briefly stated, was repeated on the catalogue card that the Gestapo kept of all its protective custody prisoners and the reasons for their imprisonment. Here again was the reference to Litten as the "notorious defender of Communists," the attacks on Nazi Party members by the "nastiest means," and the shootings at Bülow Square.[129]

The Gestapo did not trouble to explain its reasoning to Irmgard Litten. For months she received no response to her petition. Eventually Hans-Heinrich Lammers, the state secretary at the Reich Chancellery, wrote that her petition had been sent to the Gestapo. Irmgard later received a curt note informing her that her petition disclosed no "sufficient cause" to release Litten from protective custody. She kept trying in 1935, but the responses were only variations on the same theme.[130]

For the most part Fritz Litten was conspicuously absent from efforts to free his son: perhaps a reflection of the gravity of their feud, perhaps, as Irmgard suggested in her memoirs, from purely tactical considerations. But Fritz made one, rather half-hearted effort. In July 1935, he, too, addressed a petition directly to Hitler.[131]

Fritz was careful to identify himself as a retired professor of law as well as a retired captain of the reserves and, below his signature, holder of the Iron Cross First and Second Class. He attempted to arouse Hitler's sympathy by emphasizing his own anti-Communism. He had "broken off all contact" with his eldest son and "forbidden him entry to the parental home" in the autumn of 1931, since all of his attempts to keep Hans from his "political-ideological madness" had been without success. Fritz wrote, "[I] considered the measures taken against my son in February 1933 to be absolute necessities of state, and have up to now undertaken nothing for him." To do so, "[I would have] set myself against my own human and political convictions." What followed was a strikingly ambivalent plea for his son's freedom. His wife had, he said, ruined her own health with the years of worry over her "lost" son. Taking over from her the drafting of a petition was the only way Fritz had been able to get her to leave Berlin for some rest. "Only for this reason," said Fritz, "do I dare to express to the Herr Führer and Reich Chancellor the respectful request to examine the matter once again and accordingly decide if a release of my son now, after 29 months of imprisonment, is consistent with the interests of the state."[132]

This curious petition could be taken two ways. The lack of sympathy might have been a rhetorical device. Or perhaps the ambivalence of the petition was real; so wide had the gulf become that Fritz could not bring himself to try to bridge it even under such extreme circumstances. Improbable as it may seem, the coldness with which Irmgard wrote about her husband in her memoirs (and even more so in her letters) and Fritz's conspicuous silence regarding any further release attempts suggest the latter.

Irmgard, however, kept up the fight. Her brother, the lawyer Reinhard Wüst, coached her for a presentation to Hitler's minister of justice Franz Gürtner. Gürtner promised to take up the case, but, as always, nothing happened. "I heard later from friends of Gürtner," Irmgard wrote, that "he had pursued my son's case with the warmest interest" but that he could "do absolutely nothing for him." A memo Gürtner wrote in August 1935 shows what he really thought about Litten. After noting that Irmgard Litten had met with him the previous year and asked for his intervention with Göring in Litten's case—"This wish was not met"—Gürtner went on to note all the factors that made Litten an enemy to the National Socialist regime. Among them were that he was a "half-Jew" and had billed the Red Aid for the "defense of Communists."[133]

Irmgard also petitioned the man who presided over the growing SS empire, *Reichsführer SS* Heinrich Himmler, in the process becoming almost friendly with Himmler's adjutant Hans-Heinrich Frodien. She succeeded in negotiating with Frodien for permission to visit Hans every three months. But this did not ensure any more sympathy from the Gestapo. A year after the Gestapo had refused him the benefit of the Hindenburg amnesty, an internal memo returned to the question of whether he should be released. The memo records that, at least as a matter of form, Litten's release was considered (and rejected) on a regular basis; the Gestapo kept Litten in prison in the interest of "public safety" as he was a "fanatical" and "leading" Communist intellectual. To emphasize Litten's importance to the Communists, the memo noted that "at present a great propaganda action is being organized by Jews and emigrant Communists abroad," which "alone proves that Litten is seen by his own people as an important member of the KPD." The Gestapo thought absolutely nothing of Hans's and Irmgard's promises regarding his lack of interest in politics in the event of his release: no such promise could prevent him from going abroad and joining the "Jews and the emigrants" in their "anti-state" activities. The memo was signed by Werner Best, the Gestapo legal officer so opposed to mixing lawyers and the rule of law with the fate of concentration camp prisoners.[134]

Through her other sons' theatrical connections, Irmgard Litten had become acquainted with the actress Emmy Sonnemann, the mistress and later the wife of Göring. So one of Irmgard's petitions made its way to Göring as well. Again it was rejected, and again sources from the Nazi side shed some light on how it must have been received. Rudolf Diels claimed that in late 1933 and early 1934 he pressured Göring to release more political prisoners. Göring was outraged as Diels recounted: "Set free this whole Communist rabble, give up with one blow this most beautiful achievement of the revolution, the physical elimination of the subhumans? Göring could not grasp it." Göring told him, in a statement that suggests the attitude he would take to a release of Hans Litten, "You know nothing of the wickedness of which the Communists are capable. They are fanatics, from whom one is only safe when they are under lock and key."[135]

Diels pressed his argument and Göring agreed they would take it to Hitler. Hitler's reaction was also revealing. His first question was "What do you want to do when these Communist leaders relapse?" Then, typically, he launched into a tirade. "When I hear of the excuses that one makes for these villains, these subhumans, I just don't get it," he raged.

> Much too much of a fuss is being made about this under-handed gang of murderers! Now we are putting them up carefully in camps, we are feeding and nourishing them, yes we even let them work. I will not have German soil contaminated by this scum. . . . Now this year, the year of the revolution, has gone by, and they are all, all still alive. They should have been made to disappear from the very first. I never left these Bolsheviks in any doubt about what we National Socialists were going to do with them. I wanted these guys put up against the wall and shot.

Diels added, "It was an absolutely unrestrained outburst. Flying arms, in a mixture of pathetic rant and wheezing groan, he abandoned himself to his wildest fantasies. There was much that I did not understand."[136]

The all but inevitable result of these rejections was that by the summer of 1934 Hans Litten had abandoned hope of an early release, and perhaps hope of any release at all. "I do not reckon on my release for the next few years," he wrote after the rejection of the Dittrich petition, and added a little later, "I am in any case—touch wood!—very calm since I have the certainty that release cannot be counted on in the foreseeable future." Talk of release and plans for release, which had been the main subject of his and Irmgard's letters in the first half of 1934, began to fall away. In the years to come, talk of freedom appeared in Irmgard's letters only around Christmas, when she would try to raise Hans's spirits for the coming year. At the end of November 1934 she wrote to him, "It would be wrong to vegetate in dull hopelessness. No one knows when the Führer's clemency will give you back your freedom." But Hans sank further into fatalism. It is often said that taking a long view historically serves as a comfort in terrible times. One of Litten's fellow prisoners remembered years later that "surrounded by death strips and daily scenes of destruction," Litten worked "incessantly" on "a draft, entitled 'On the Plan for the Coming World.'" "We are going through a short, insignificant pause," he wrote, sometime around 1937, "inconsequential for the further development, and which in a few decades one will no longer notice at all when one looks back."[137]

Thoughts Are Free

In the summer of 1934 Hans Litten was moved once again, this time to the concentration camp at Lichtenburg, in the Saxon town of Prettin. He arrived on June 13, writing to Irmgard, "The long journey was very beautiful, only the transport did not really agree with my leg." Litten would remain at Lichtenburg for just over three years. If it is possible to say such a thing, these years formed the more tolerable phase of his odyssey through Hitler's camps. Lichtenburg had the reputation of being a "comparatively good camp, to which primarily sick and invalid prisoners were sent." Ludwig Bendix, who had been with Litten at Spandau and Brandenburg, was at Lichtenburg as well. He recalled that Litten enjoyed a unique place in the camp, working as a master bookbinder with one or two assistants. He enjoyed "quite a few liberties," among them the maintenance of an "extensive book chest in which he kept many books of art and literary history and lent them freely to the comrades." Hans ordered these books through Irmgard, who, in trying to fill Litten's highly specialized orders, became well known to a range of antiquarian book dealers. Litten also ordered plenty of detective thrillers, which were useful for bribing the guards.[138]

A visitor to Lichtenburg—the old buildings still stand—will be struck by how small the prison really was and how claustrophobically narrow its courtyard. Perhaps this is why Litten, whose passion as a student had been hiking, sought a different kind of freedom and returned to his scholarly interests at Lichtenburg, despite the terrors and deprivations of life in a Nazi concentration camp. On October 21, 1934, he wrote Irmgard, "I now have so much ability to concentrate that I can once again do a little scholarly work. So I am asking for a book parcel, and as soon as possible. Please send, from the German-English Shakespeare edition, if available, the following volumes: All the history plays, *Hamlet, The Tempest, Measure for Measure, As You Like It, Love's Labours Lost, Pericles, Cymbeline, Lear.*" He also asked for books about the Naumburg Cathedral, Rilke's poems, the *Epic of Gilgamesh* "in the small Insel edition," and Shakespeare's sonnets as translated by Stefan George, noting that the last two items were already in his personal library. "By Christmas," he continued, "I hope to have progressed far enough that once again I can concern myself systematically with Dante." Some of his requests exhibited a simply astonishing erudition for a thirty-one-year-old who had dedicated his life to his law practice from the age of twenty-five and been imprisoned since the age of twenty-nine. He asked Irmgard, for instance, to find out if a book by Rudolf Borchardt on the relationship of Dante to the Provençal troubadour Arnaut Daniel had been published, because "in an essay from 1921 (as I recall) B. referred to his 'forthcoming treatment of Dante and Arnaut.' If the book exists, it might have been published by Rowohlt."[139]

In a postscript to the same letter, he continued in this characteristic vein of high-mindedness and Prussian diligence, "I have recently read a few excerpts from the Homer transcription by Rudolf Alexander, and thereby discovered that (after 13 years!) I finally have enough distance from school that I can read Homer again. For the sake of caution I will first read this very good translation, before I dare the original text. In my work plan I have scheduled the time after Christmas for this."[140]

Imprisonment did nothing to change the young man who had read his essays to curious prostitutes in the cafés around Alexander Square "because he could refuse enlightenment to no one." Litten wrote from Lichtenburg with great enthusiasm about a project to translate medieval German poetry into modern German as a reader for high school students. This idea grew out of a friendship he had struck up with a prisoner named Hans Cieslack. So often and so glowingly did Litten write of Cieslack's ability that Irmgard assumed Cieslack must have studied German literature at a university, an impression strengthened when a literature professor of Irmgard's acquaintance told her that it would be impossible to carry out the project without the necessary reference materials at hand, even for students in his seminar. But Cieslack was a mason by trade, in whom Litten had inspired a passionate interest in German literature.[141]

Litten's erudition commanded respect even among some of the SS men, who sometimes came to him for legal advice. One guard wanted Litten to represent him in court and was astonished when Litten told him he could not. "He [the SS man] had imagined that if an SS man wanted it, it would be permitted." Another assumed that such a learned man must also be wise in affairs of the heart and asked Litten's advice on his love life. Litten recommended that he read the poems of Rilke. The SS man did so, returning to Litten for explications of the more difficult passages. "Whether it solved his romantic problems," Irmgard wrote, "I have not been able to learn."[142]

The learned comments on art and literature that filled Litten's letters were also a kind of code, a way for the cerebral Litten to find access to emotional subjects. For example, he made much in his letters of Shakespeare's *Henry IV*. In 1935 he wrote, "I have recently read *Henry IV* three times; it now belongs...with *Hamlet*, *Macbeth*, *Coriolanus* and the *Tempest* among the five plays that I would select if I could have only five works of Shakespeare with me"—a favorite game among the prisoners, he added. At the heart of both parts of *Henry IV* is a bitter feud between an arriviste king whose rule is never secure and his talented but wayward son. The parallels to Fritz and Hans Litten are obvious, albeit without the heartrending reconciliation that comes at the end of *Henry IV, Part 2*. Both Littens may have yearned for such a reconciliation. Perhaps this is why the play spoke so strongly to Hans; perhaps this is why, among Hans's papers, is a card from Fritz depicting a fourteenth-century painting of the angel throwing the millstone into the sea, from the *Book of Revelations*. There are only three words written on the card in hand: "Heartfelt wishes! Father."[143]

Another favorite was Shakespeare's sonnets. Litten wrote to Sulamith Siliava that the sonnets were "particular favorites of mine, not just as literature but personally." The sonnets deal chiefly with the poet's love for a young man and his desire that that man have children; they deal with aging and loss; and with death. It is not hard to see how all of this would touch the imprisoned Litten, "not just as literature but personally." While there is no evidence of a sexual element in Litten's friendships with Hans Cieslack and another prisoner, Paul Libuda, with whom he became very close, the evidence from the letters definitely points to a romantic charge of the sort otherwise heterosexual men often find in all-male company—in boarding schools, or in the army, or in prison. Litten often wrote that he felt much older since his arrest. In October 1936 he wrote to Sulamith, "Of course you know that I have felt very old for a long time now.... That began very early for me. Even at the age of 18 Ibsen's *Master Builder* shook me, probably the strongest symbolic shaping of the problem of aging." Litten wrote his mother that he had recommended Sulamith read the sonnets because "that which separates us is there so well expressed." This Delphic utterance could have referred to Litten's relationship with Cieslack or his sense of aging; or that he felt it was too late for him to have a child with Sulamith; or, perhaps, that he knew he was soon going to die. Or all of these.[144]

What had been a passionate, if complicated, affair between Litten and Sulamith Siliava broke down under the stress of Litten's imprisonment. Sulamith had fled to France and then to Spain with Walter Reuter after Hitler's accession to power. There they eked out a living as street musicians and with Walter's camera. Their son, Jasmin, was born in October 1934. Yet in spite of separation and all the other complications, Litten's earlier letters from the camps reveal his love for Sulamith. In March 1935 he wrote that he was "madly delighted" by her letter of January 1 and with pictures that she had sent him. "I thought about you intensely and often during your pregnancy," he added. He reported that Cieslack wanted Hans and Sulamith to have children, "and since they would be a cross between Purring-Cat and Bear, he called them 'Purring Little Bear' and 'Growling Kitten.'" Sulamith replied, "Before I tell you about us, I must tell you that your friend Hans has given me a great shock. Do you know that 'Purring Little Bears' and 'Growling Kittens' are absolutely not imaginary animals? Your friend is clever and I believe that he belongs to you very much (I wish it very much). But I want to have a child with you! I have known that for a long time!" She insisted that he must know "as well as I do" that they would be together again some day and that "*our* child will play with Jasmin." She had already discussed this arrangement with Walter: "He not only agrees, he thinks it must happen. Are you as sure of that as I am? You must prepare yourself. What I mean is: be ready."[145]

Litten tried to lower her expectations. He told her that their having a child together was "not so simple." He thought that she was counting too much on his early release. "Please prepare yourself soberly and matter-of-factly for the fact that Jasmin will be at least 9 years old by the time we can have a child." In any case Litten thought he might be too old and ill by then to start a family. In early 1935 mysterious tones in the letters hinted at other strains in the relationship. In February he wrote Irmgard that he might not be able to write on the next scheduled occasion because he urgently needed to direct his permitted letter elsewhere. The problem seems to have been Hans Cieslack. "It would probably be better," he told his mother, "if you did not copy my letters in their entirety for Sulamith, but only in extracts. If, for instance, you copied my last, somewhat uncontrolled letter word for word (I hope you didn't) she will definitely be very unhappy *that another person means so much to me*. I can naturally write her about all this myself (will probably even do it), but in any case she doesn't need to learn that from a letter that is not for her" (emphasis added). In November 1936 he asked if Sulamith had answered his letter from the summer: "She will probably be very sad about it . . . but there is nothing I can do about it."[146]

Over time the tone of Litten's remarks both to and about Sulamith grew impatient. In November 1936 he wrote to Irmgard that "all that"—he meant Sulamith and Jasmin—"seems all so far away to me now." His letters returned again and again to their differences in literary taste. In December 1936 Irmgard wrote that Sulamith had sent Hans a Christmas present, a gift that was obviously important to her: "From Sulamith came the Rembrandt book *R.v.R.* by Hendrik van Loon, with the dedication 'to my beloved Bear, I am giving you this book because I find it magical. So it should belong to you. Christmas, 1936.'" Hans did not recognize, or want to recognize, what the expensive and beloved book might signify. It became a subject of grumpy complaint in his letters. In January 1937 he wrote, "If Sulamith has such a strong personal connection to the Rembrandt book and gave it to me for that reason then I naturally must try to read it on the side, although it is very far removed from my work."[147]

When he got around to reading the book Litten did not like it. He told Sulamith that he could "find no connection" to the book and that he could "scarcely imagine" what she saw in it. He was also irritated when Irmgard sent Sulamith a copy of Shakespeare's sonnets. This was, he reminded Irmgard, the book that expressed what separated him from Sulamith: "For that reason . . . I would not exactly choose that book as a gift. . . . I hope that she wanted another book from you." By July 1937, as Litten's condition was steadily deteriorating, he wrote Irmgard that he was "very pleased by your account of Sulamith," but he added, "My joy is not totally unclouded, as long as I must worry about a person who ultimately is much closer to me."[148]

Reading over Litten's prison letters again in the 1970s, Max Fürst concluded that they "show what human beings are capable of." As he reflected on the fact that Litten poured his spirit into the study of Shakespeare and Rilke and medieval poetry while enduring all the pain, terror, and humiliation of life in a concentration camp, Max asked—and who could doubt the answer—"Can there be a greater victory over need and despair than such letters?"[149]

But Litten's battles, and his victories, were not only intellectual ones. The man who had fought Hitler with such steely determination before 1933 had not vanished. His defiance showed itself in part in his generosity to his fellow prisoners. Released prisoners often told Irmgard of how Hans would buy them extra food, and of how hard he worked to ease others through the worst of concentration camp life. Litten's letters leave no doubt about the depth of his concern for those who were especially close to him. In September 1935 he wrote Irmgard about a friend of his named Gerhard, who had just been released. Gerhard, who loved children, was separated from his wife and young child. Litten had given him a photograph of Jasmin as a good-bye present. "I would be very glad," Litten wrote, "if Sulamith would write a few lines along with the picture."[150]

Ludwig Bendix said Litten was rumored to give most of the money Irmgard sent him to the poorer prisoners, and when there were collections for such things as Christmas packages for prisoners who received nothing from outside, "Litten always stood at the top of the list with comparatively high contributions." It was even said that he had imposed fast days on himself—another example of his own, eccentric Catholicism—as "atonement for the serious punishment or even execution of a former client, against whom the Gestapo had extorted his testimony," which again suggests that it was the guilt from his accusation of Karl Ackert in 1933 that drove him to his suicide attempt.[151]

But Litten also directly defied the SS and SA who ruled the camps on a number of occasions. He was almost shot at Sonnenburg for protesting the beatings of prisoners. There was another such incident at Esterwegen.

Among the surviving records of the Nazis' Justice Ministry is a slim manila folder marked, somewhat paradoxically, both "Secret" and "Historically Valuable." The documents pertain to the investigation of the SA man Heinrich Remmert, the commander of the Esterwegen camp from November 1933 until the SS took over the camp in August 1934. The folder contains a letter dated September 11, 1934, from the chief prosecutor in the town of Osnabrück, in whose jurisdiction the Esterwegen camp fell. The letter is to the Prussian justice minister in Berlin; it bears the subject line "Abuse of th. Advocate Litten." "In Barrack 2 of Concentration Camp II in Esterwegen was found the former Advocate Litten from Berlin," the letter began. In April 1934 Lieutenant Colonel (*Obersturmbahnführer*) Kiecker had visited Commandant Remmert in Esterwegen.[152] Remmert took Kiecker to Barrack 2 and called the prisoners to assemble. He ordered Litten to step forward and explain why he was in protective custody. Litten replied that he had defended Communists in court. Remmert ordered him to add "and sent innocent SA men to prison." Litten refused to say this and Remmert punched him in the face. The chief prosecutor's letter concluded with the note that "in accordance with instructions" he had not yet questioned the prisoners about this occurrence. He had already secured an order for Remmert's arrest from the court in Osnabrück. Ten days later Berlin forbid the chief prosecutor from proceeding against Remmert (Remmert was facing other charges, not related to the abuse of prisoners). On November 9 the chief prosecutor forwarded the documents in the case to Berlin and added, irony shining through the bald bureaucratic language, "Further to the report of September 11, 1934, it is noted that Litten is supposed to have sustained a broken leg in the camp." The chief prosecutor did not seem to consider this an accident.[153]

It is in connection with this investigation that we get the first officially documented hint of Hitler's direct involvement in Litten's case. The last item in the file is a note from the Prussian justice minister to the Osnabrück prosecutor: "The proceedings against Remmert for the maltreatment of Litten...have been dismissed by decree of the Führer and Reich Chancellor of November 29, 1934." The episode did no damage to Remmert's career. When the SS took over Esterwegen, he was accepted into the SS and transferred to a post at the Dachau concentration camp.[154]

There were other such examples. On one occasion, when the prisoners at Lichtenburg were ordered to celebrate a Nazi event, Litten organized a reading. He himself read a poem he knew from his time in the youth movement. A prisoner described the scene: "Consider: all around black uniforms, thugs; up front, standing on a small platform, a poor, crippled, tormented man. He suddenly reads a poem that in this context has an oppositional, no, a revolutionary, an incendiary effect." The poem that Litten read sums up his life at Lichtenburg. It is a famous example of the *Freiheitslieder* or "freedom songs" of the revolutionary era of the late eighteenth and early nineteenth centuries, with which advocates of liberty had challenged censorship and other forms of repression. It is called "Thoughts Are Free." The last stanza reads:

Though they shut me up
In a dungeon dark
All this is vain
Availing them nothing;
For then my thoughts
Shiver the bolts
And shatter the walls:
Thoughts are free![155]

On one occasion, when Irmgard visited Hans in Lichtenburg, he was able to tell her of some of the SS atrocities. She was disturbed by the calm way he told the story, and she wondered if he had lost his capacity for hatred and revenge. "I asked him anxiously: 'You will never forget that?' He, very quietly and calmly: 'No.' He held my gaze for just a moment, but this moment showed me the same unbounded desire for revenge, the same fanatical hatred, that I felt. How often have I seen this look in the eyes of former prisoners, when they speak of their tormentors." "I knew that none of them would be missing from my side when the day of vengeance came," she added.[156]

So Hans Litten lived and worked—on medieval poetry and Rilke, reading Shakespeare, Dante, and dozens of other writers, meditating on artists ranging from the Master of Naumburg to Franz Marc, and repeatedly showing a defiance that was all but superhuman—until the summer of 1937.

The Jew Block

Irmgard Litten had always proven both tireless and skillful when it came to keeping her son's spirits up. But in 1937 the task grew ever harder. That summer the alarming signals in Hans's letters began to multiply. On July 16 he asked Irmgard to cancel his subscriptions to the *Stock Exchange News* and the *German Future*, as they were no longer permitted in the camp. Three days later he wrote that he was sending her all of his books, "which we must send home by order." He added, "You can well imagine what that means to me." Another passage of the letter asked Irmgard to keep the various mementos he was sending back, such as a pocket inhaler his grandmother had given him shortly before her death, and candlesticks connected with "many beautiful memories" of the Christmases he had spent in Lichtenburg. "Although I have little hope of ever seeing these things again, I have not been able to bring myself to destroy them." When Irmgard went to the Gestapo to pick up her quarterly permission to visit Hans, the officer told her that all visits to Lichtenburg were canceled. Lichtenburg was being closed and the prisoners sent elsewhere.[157]

A little later Irmgard received a short letter from Hans on "Concentration Camp Buchenwald" stationery. He signed the letter "Hans" and not "Hans-Achim," a prearranged signal to Irmgard that he was being beaten or tortured. Litten's next letter, dated August 29, was also signed only "Hans" and written in a hand markedly shakier than that of the earlier letters. Litten had little to say, not even filling the regulation four pages, though the writing was larger than usual. It was clear that the relatively tolerable days, in which he had a job in the bookbindery and leisure time for his scholarly work, were over. On September 12 he wrote Irmgard that he had to cancel his subscriptions even to the Nazi papers he had been permitted in July.[158]

By 1937 the contours of National Socialist terror in Germany were once again in flux. The previous year Hitler had given the SS and the Gestapo a new mission for their concentration camps. The camps were no longer to be primarily tools for the suppression of political resistance— there was little enough of that left—but instead were to begin purging the "German race" of its "undesirables." The composition of the camp population began to change, and its numbers, after a drop in the mid-1930s, began to rise once more. By 1937 only a minority of camp prisoners were "politicals." The rest were habitual criminals, "anti-socials," gay men, and, increasingly, Jews, there not because they were Communist or Social Democratic opponents of Hitler, but for violating such strictures as the 1935 Nuremberg Laws, which outlawed marriage between Jews and non-Jews and criminalized all sexual contact between them. Political prisoners began to feel even more of a beleaguered, if superior, minority.[159]

A letter from late September contains what at first seems like the usual Litten touch: "A piece of the literary supplement from an old issue of the *Nationalist Observer* came into my hands," he wrote, containing "a review of several new books on the German middle ages. I took from it that according to recent research, Countess Uta was held prisoner after her separation from Burkard in a cloister near her home castle, and later in a Bavarian cloister (perhaps Wesobrunn?), where she is supposed to have died. Unfortunately I cannot cite the title and publisher of the book, because the beginning of the review was torn off." Irmgard got the point right away. A released prisoner had told her that when Litten wrote of Countess Uta of Naumburg he meant himself; Burkard was one of his friends at Lichtenburg. Countess Uta—actually an eleventh-century noblewoman named Uta von Ballenstedt, best known from the famous thirteenth-century statue of her in the Naumburg Cathedral—was originally from Lichtenburg, so the first cloister referred to the Lichtenburg camp, the second to the Dachau concentration camp, in Bavaria, near Munich. Saying that the top of the review had been torn off was an effort to frustrate any censor intelligent enough to become suspicious. It seems likely that Litten had been told, or heard rumors, that he would be sent to Dachau. And indeed, on October 17 he wrote from Dachau, where he had arrived the day before. A week later he noted, "On the journey here I had the great pleasure of seeing the towers of the Naumburg cathedral again in the distance."[160]

Dachau was not like the other German concentration camps. Prisoners who came from elsewhere soon found, as Ludwig Bendix wrote, "that in Dachau the wind blew from a completely different direction." A. E. Laurence (born Alfred Lomnitz), an economist originally from Breslau, passed through Dachau's gates in 1937. He and the other prisoners in his contingent were beaten savagely on arrival, including by "another political prisoner with the usual red insignia, but this one had the yellow patch of the Jew in addition." He jumped at them, wrote Laurence, "like an angry wild animal, trying to hit the tallest of us in the face and kicking others with his shiny jackboots." Laurence was astonished to be abused by a prisoner—and, as he recalled, "not just any prisoner," but Heinz Eschen. Eschen was the SS-designated "senior prisoner" of Dachau's 6th or "Jew" company, a fierce anti-Nazi who would play a central role in the last phase of Litten's life. Laurence would later come to understand that Eschen had reasons to act as he did, but at first it seemed to him that in Dachau the "great solidarity of all prisoners had been successfully breached." The SS had had managed to get their victims, including Jews, to hate and abuse each other.[161]

Litten came to Dachau with a small group of prisoners from Buchenwald. They had barely arrived when, according to fellow prisoner Alfred Dreifuss, "with lightning speed the news went through the camp that Hans Litten was there too." For those, like Dreifuss, who had known Litten in Berlin and remembered his "long, unrestrained hair," "kind eyes," and "gentle, fine artist's hands," Litten's appearance after four and half years of imprisonment was a shock: he was "pale and thin, distorted by the shaven head, the one leg dragging behind him." Fritz Rabinowitsch, another Dachau prisoner, remembered, "As we returned from work in the evening, we saw among the 'entrants' a form that walked slightly bent, wearing glasses that sat crookedly, pants wrongly buttoned up, jacket not properly worn." Heinz Eschen told Rabinowitsch that Litten would be joining the 6th company.[162]

Barrack or Block 6, home to the 6th company, would be the center of Litten's life at Dachau. Its prisoners were a varied group, united only by the fact that the laws of the Third Reich deemed them to be Jewish. "There were about 160 men in our barrack," Rabinowitsch remembered: teenage boys who had traveled the world as cabin boys or pages, old men from "some small town or other" who had been accused of seducing their "Aryan" maid or housekeeper—in other words, Jewish men guilty of "race defilement," a crime under the Nuremberg Laws. There were livestock dealers; "rag and bone men," mostly from small towns; and small shopkeepers "who had 'fouled up' in business." These "nonpolitical" prisoners were leavened with about twenty "politicals," mostly young, and about a dozen who were artists, writers, or workers, who, as Rabinowitsch put it, "were on a level that one could talk with them after the work was done." The political prisoners generally felt nothing but contempt for the nonpoliticals; ironically, class and cultural prejudices colored their judgments: "petty bourgeois who for the most part were without any interest in anything at all besides eating and sleeping" was Rabinowitsch's dismissal of the nonpoliticals.[163]

Each barrack at Dachau was divided into six dormitories. The politicals of Block 6 banded together into Dorm 3. The men of Dorm 3 were, as one of them wrote to Irmgard Litten, "the elite." Among them were such prominent figures as Ernst Heilmann, the leader of the Social Democratic caucus in the Prussian Parliament before 1933, and Heinz Eschen, whose leadership qualities (and fame, within a small circle) had emerged only in the twilight world of the camps. Then there was a small group of young men with whom Litten would become especially close; apart from Eschen himself, the dominant figure of this circle, there was Alfred Dreifuss, who had worked in theater in Berlin; Alfred Grünebaum, a ship's boy who had made the mistake of returning to Germany to see his mother and was sent to Dachau; Oscar Winter (born Oskar Winterberger); and Fritz Rabinowitsch (Alfred Laurence was a member of this circle but was released just as Litten arrived).[164]

Eschen and the other politicals did their best to ease Litten's arrival at Dachau. That first evening, as the prisoners sat around the barrack chatting in small groups, Eschen asked for the guitar. "So, after everyone had gone to sleep and the lights had been turned out, we began to sing songs: songs, like we had sung earlier hiking: mercenary songs, songs from the time of the Peasants' War—soldiers' songs. Hans Litten sat down by us right away, and sang along. After two hours we stopped. Every one of us had the impression that Hans belonged in our community."[165]

Heinz Eschen's senior prisoner position reflected both the degree of self-government the Nazis allowed their prisoners and the cunningly malevolent tactics of camp administration. Alfred Grünebaum remembered that the SS usually picked "the most brutal, asocial elements"— generally habitual criminals—to be senior prisoners in order to undermine the prisoners' solidarity. Eschen was one of the very few politicals to become a senior prisoner. Twenty-seven years old in 1937, he had been a prisoner at Dachau since the summer of 1933. Fellow prisoners described him as short and "almost ugly," but athletic and powerfully built. Upon his arrival at Dachau he had been singled out for special abuse as both a Jew and a Communist. He endured beatings and tortures with a stoicism that earned him the respect of prisoners and guards alike. He also organized discussions, an emergency cash fund, and newspaper readings, smuggled medicine to the sick, got prisoners released from dangerous work, and "always intervened when someone was in grave danger." He managed this with a combination of courage and savvy. "He had connections everywhere—to all offices in the camp, to all SS posts, even to the commandant's office," said one former prisoner. He mastered the thick Bavarian dialect spoken by the SS guard or "block leader" for Block 6, Vincenz Schöttl, so that he could sometimes talk Schöttl out of violence. On one occasion he astonished the commander of the prisoners' camp, the especially sadistic *SS Standartenführer* (Colonel) Hermann Baranowski, by volunteering to take twenty-five lashes for another prisoner. This earned Eschen a good deal of credit with Baranowski, at least for a time, so that he could sometimes get Baranowski to discipline SS men who had been especially brutal to prisoners.[166]

Inevitably Eschen made enemies as well as friends and admirers. To be effective he had to convince the SS that he was really their man. That was why he beat and yelled at other prisoners, especially new arrivals, while also softly reassuring them. A. E. Laurence wrote perceptively of the compromises Eschen made to protect "his" prisoners. Eschen adopted "the shiny jackboots, the tone of voice, the sneering cynical remarks, the despising of any kind of sentimentality and softness." Laurence recognized the "theatricality" of Eschen's beatings of prisoners and the logic of the "lesser evil." Not all prisoners were so sympathetic. Ludwig Bendix was so enraged by Eschen's abuse of the Communist lawyer Werner Scholem that he threatened to bring charges against Eschen in the Communist Party's internal court. More dangerously, Eschen's influence with Baranowski stirred up hatred among some of the SS block leaders. As Alfred Grünebaum wrote, Eschen was a man who knew too many secrets: "It was clear to us that Heinz would never be released alive."[167]

Eschen and Litten, sharing experiences and interests in the youth movement and radical politics, soon became close friends. Unlike Litten's other close friendships, such as with Max Fürst or Hans Cieslack, with Eschen Litten was not the dominant party. He looked up to Eschen, "a daredevil, life-affirming" man, with admiration and envy.[168]

Alfred Grünebaum said that Litten now saw "no possibility" of his own release. But still partly crippled from his 1934 injuries and bearing the psychological as well as physical scars of all the beatings and torture, the suicide attempt, the poor food, the hard labor, the boredom, and years of uncertainty and fear, he was also increasingly unable to bear imprisonment. "Here began for me the period in which Hans made his decision to end his own life," said Fritz Rabinowitsch. Eschen organized the prisoners of Dorm 3 to take turns keeping watch over Litten at night. Litten seems to have attempted suicide early in his time at Dachau, on a night when Rabinowitsch was taking his turn at the watch. "When I saw Hans coming I awakened Heinz immediately. Heinz took him by the hand and led him back to bed. I heard them talking for a long time afterwards. I can still hear how Hans declared: 'Five years I've been in; I just won't do a sixth year under these conditions.'"[169]

Contributing to Litten's growing despair was the hard labor demanded especially of Jewish prisoners. Litten told Alfred Dreifuss that his biggest fear was that the SS would assign him work outside the camp that he would not be able to do. "We all suffered watching Litten work and being unable to help him," said Rabinowitsch; the work—it was "outdoor work: hoeing, digging, pushing wheelbarrows"—was too hard for him. "Everyone could see what an effort it cost him to be able to walk at all." Litten's inability to bear the same burdens as the other prisoners upset him. Eschen used his influence to get him indoor work chopping wood. Even this was too much. One day Litten collapsed and was taken to the infirmary. The prisoners there kept him as long as they could. When he was released from the infirmary he was given "light duties."

"And so," wrote Rabinowitsch, "approximately six weeks passed."[170]

Isolation

In late November Irmgard Litten finally secured the permission to visit Hans that she had sought since the summer, and journeyed to Dachau along with his brother Heinz. She found Hans's manner and appearance frightening. The high table between them kept her from seeing anything of him below the chest, but she noted that he was tanned, "indicating outdoor work." Although she could detect no signs of physical abuse, he spoke, she remembered, with a "strangely soft and soundless voice." He seemed "like another person." She asked after his health, and he replied, tonelessly, that it was "excellent," but he gestured toward his heart several times. From his failure to respond to questions about his reading, Irmgard inferred that the authorities either did not permit the prisoners to have reading material or did not allow them any time. She noticed that Hans wore a "yellow patch," a new development for Jewish prisoners.[171]

Irmgard told him stories about the Fürst children, with the implied message "Don't give up." But when she told him that she had once again secured permission to visit him every three months, he gave her a look that seemed to say "We will not see each other again." When the time was up, Hans said good-bye to his mother "with an infinitely sweet and sad smile." "He knew," she wrote, "that it was his farewell."[172]

Irmgard would at least have been cheered to know that, as all of his fellow prisoners reported, Litten came back from the visit in significantly better spirits. What Irmgard did not know at her visit, but soon learned, was that the SS had just subjected Hans and the other prisoners of Block 6 to a special new regime.[173]

In the autumn of 1937, reports had appeared in newspapers in Czechoslovakia, the Netherlands, France, Sweden, and Great Britain charging Dachau authorities with the deaths of several Jewish prisoners. Heinz Eschen, with his connections, was responsible for at least some of these stories getting to the outside world. In a memo to the Foreign Office, the Gestapo wrote the reports off as "the usual agitation and atrocity propaganda" of the "Marxist" and especially "emigrant" press. But toward the prisoners the regime's reaction was not so dismissive.[174]

On the evening of November 24, when the prisoners of Block 6 returned from their workday, Standartenführer Baranowski appeared with two other SS officers and ordered the "Jew Block" to turn out. When the prisoners were assembled, Baranowski spoke, his voice shaking with rage. "Lies" were being reported in the "Jewish criminal press abroad" about "our fine camp." Therefore the Jewish prisoners would "remain in complete isolation until further notice." Irmgard reproduced Rabinowitsch's account of what isolation was like:

The windows were screwed fast and whitewashed, the doors locked. . . . I do not know if it is possible to convey the atmosphere of an "isolation" to an outsider. The air is nauseating.

The strawbags lie so close on the floor that there is no room to move about.... Thefts of bread began. One had to spend the whole day doing nothing on the strawbags (three men to every two bags), without a book, without a newspaper, without a pencil. Quarrels were constantly occurring on the slightest pretext, and in the overcharged atmosphere they soon degenerated into fights.[175]

The isolation of Block 6 was a kind of blackmail, an attempt to intimidate the exile press into remaining silent about the crimes of the Nazi regime. This ham-handed reaction to bad foreign press was made even more ludicrous by what came next. The Jewish prisoners were all ordered to write letters to friends and relatives in Germany and abroad.

Irmgard duly received her letter from Hans, dated November 27, listing a number of German-language publications in Austria, Czechoslovakia, and France that had been spreading "atrocity lies" about the concentration camps. "The Jews in Dachau," the letter continued, "stand once again under suspicion of having smuggled lying reports out of the camp." The Jewish prisoners would remain in isolation until the "culprits" were found, and therefore recipients of the letters were asked "to influence the emigrant Jews ... to abstain in the future from such idiotic lies about the concentration camps, since the Jews in Dachau as racial comrades will be held responsible for them."[176]

One former prisoner recalled that the prisoners were very glad to write the letters, as they believed the clumsiness of the Nazi measures could only bring more focused international attention to their plight. To remove the slightest doubt that camp authorities had dictated this text to the prisoners, Litten signed his letter to his mother "Hans Litten." Two weeks later Irmgard received a postcard from Hans in which he wrote that the "so-called" German People's News of Prague had printed another article containing "shameless lies" about the Dachau concentration camp. "Because of this article, the isolation imposed on us has been extended by a week. We have been informed that every new lying report extends the isolation imposed on us by one week." This card was also signed "Hans Litten."[177]

Irmgard responded to this latest crisis with skill. She drafted a letter to the various foreign papers, reporting what was happening in

Dachau. The letter explained that her son had recently assured her that he was very well. But through her use of the special German subjunctive form, which distances the writer from a quote, she suggested that his assurances were a lie. Irmgard obtained the Gestapo's approval of her letter, the subjunctive of their mother tongue having apparently escaped their notice. She made sure to send carbon copies to all the papers so the editors would understand that it was a mass mailing. The message got through: a Prague newspaper printed a facsimile of her note under the headline "Himmler's Blackmail Letter."[178]

In many ways the isolation was a relief for the political prisoners, illustrating how poorly the SS grasped the nature and quality of their opponents. "The politicals among us used the fact that the march to labor was cancelled to carry out discussions and courses in the isolated block," said one prisoner. "The themes ranged from history and foreign languages to philosophy and psychology—and the lecturers! The sum of intellect and knowledge that was concentrated in Block 6 alone outweighed a thousand-fold what the semi-illiterates of the SS had to offer." The division of labor was characteristic. Eschen, the hard-boiled young Communist, delivered lectures on political subjects—a choice with fateful consequences. Litten, the wide-ranging intellectual, focused on literature and other cultural subjects.[179]

In this tense atmosphere Litten's erudition and photographic memory came to the rescue. Day after day he kept the prisoners entertained, reciting Rilke and other favorite writers from memory. The other prisoners gently teased him in return: on a "cabaret evening," one of the younger prisoners, dressed in two sheets, hopped around the barrack as the ghost of Rilke, demanding that Litten recite his *unpublished* poems as well. To vary the program Litten also discussed history and recounted anecdotes from his trials. He even set up practice as a Freudian analyst and interpreted the prisoners' dreams. "There was nothing," Alfred Dreifuss recalled, "absolutely nothing intellectual that he had not profoundly mastered." Litten talked about all of these learned things "in such a simple and decent way," said another prisoner, "that it was impossible—in spite of differences of opinion—not to like him."

Litten's new role seemed to revive his spirits. Before the isolation, the circle of politicals had sought to help him at every opportunity, protecting him as much as possible from hard labor and looking out for his safety. But now, said Rabinowitsch, Litten "came to life" and became the center of the community: "The feeling of a tight-knit community strengthened him." Certainly the prisoners harbored no illusions about the state of Litten's health. "One evening he suddenly collapsed and was unconscious for a long time," remembered Rabinowitsch. "But despite our pleas, he would not spare himself." To be able to be useful to the other prisoners, "to give us something," was "the greatest satisfaction for him." Many of the prisoners had shared Litten's experiences in the youth movement, and when at night they sang songs from those days, "one felt directly how the memories of his youth came back to him." Dreifuss wrote that for Litten the isolation was "the happiest time of his imprisonment." The rest and the sense that for a little while he was safe in the dry and warm barrack "released an inner cheerfulness and merriness in him, such as we had not seen in him for a long time."[180]

Lord Allen

By 1935, as we have seen, Irmgard Litten had realized that her chances of getting Nazi leaders to release Hans were slim. With good contacts in Great Britain, however, she began to hope that pressure from abroad could do what internal pressure could not. From the autumn of 1935 Litten's fate became caught up in the intricacies of Anglo-German diplomacy in the age of appeasement, especially through the agency of one highly principled British politician.

Clifford Allen was born in 1889 into a family that in many ways was a British equivalent to the Littens. His father was a prosperous businessman, his mother a devout evangelical. After reading history at Cambridge he was offered a job by the social reformers Sidney and Beatrice Webb, and became involved with Britain's fledgling Labour Party. During the First World War he served two years in prison as a conscientious objector (he refused to do the war-related civilian work that would have kept him free), which left his health seriously and permanently weakened. He could not face the rigors of a parliamentary career, but he became an important figure in Labour circles, and in 1932 his friend Prime Minister Ramsay MacDonald raised him to the peerage. Clifford Allen took the title Baron Allen of Hurtwood.[181]

By the 1930s many on the British left had come to believe that if the Great War had been an act of collective madness, it made no sense to hold the German state exclusively responsible for its outbreak. Allen shared this belief and hoped that revision of the Treaty of Versailles could create "a bond of confidence between Britain and Germany." The problem was that when the British government got around to implementing this eminently reasonable policy, the democratic Germany of the postwar years was gone, and in its place was the Germany of Hitler and Göring and Goebbels. Nonetheless Allen's reputation as a man sympathetic to Germany's demands, with the ear of the prime minister, afforded him access to many of the leaders of Hitler's new Reich. Thus a terrible irony arose. Allen was far from blind to the barbarities of Hitler's regime, but he found himself not only hobnobbing with Hitler's ambassador to Great Britain (and later foreign minister), the fanatical Nazi Joachim von Ribbentrop, and, on two occasions, Hitler himself, but also working with politicians on the British right who saw Nazi Germany as a useful bulwark against the greater threat of Communism. Allen's defense was that those who simply denounced the Nazi regime at every turn and refused practical efforts to help individual political prisoners did nothing more than indulge their "conspicuous morality." At the same time, officials like the British ambassador to Germany Sir Nevile Henderson often reproached Allen, arguing that public campaigns on behalf of political prisoners hurt the individuals themselves, while also seriously damaging the chance of peace between Britain and Germany. Allen was fully alive to the moral dilemmas inherent in his work. After he had become involved in lobbying for Litten, he wrote to a friend of his "sadness" that he had "perhaps slightly diminished" his influence with German leaders through his work for Litten. "I had a feeling," he said, "that I was being a little useful in the general work of reconciliation until this case occurred."[182]

In 1935, however, Lord Allen appeared to the Littens as Hans's best and perhaps only hope. And so the fate of this gentle and idealistic embodiment of the Edwardian British conscience became ever more closely tied to that of the uncompromising German lawyer.

Irmgard Litten and the Fürsts, working through a network of Quakers, had made Litten's circumstances well known to anyone in Britain interested in what was happening in Germany. Since the summer of 1934 Litten's case had been a frequent subject of discussion on the letters page of the London *Times*. In December 1934, in response to a fiery anti-Communist speech by Göring, the *Times* commented that there were still "prominent persons" who were not Communist functionaries and yet remained in custody, among them "Dr. [*sic*] Hans Litten, the lawyer whose sufferings are well known." The German Foreign Office was acutely aware of this bad publicity. The ambassador to Great Britain, Leopold von Hoesch, wrote in a memo appraising these articles that cases like Litten's were especially important in shaping British opinion of the new Germany. The ambassador delicately suggested that the German Reich's image would greatly improve if political opponents were handled by the regular courts according to the rule of law rather than being incarcerated in concentration camps. In June 1935 Hoesch asked the Foreign Office to consider a reexamination of Litten's case, "the importance of which for public opinion is not to be underestimated." Hoesch thought Litten's release would have a "pronounced favorable effect" on British attitudes toward Germany.[183]

In January 1935 Lord Allen traveled to Germany and there met not only with Interior Minister Wilhelm Frick but also with Hitler himself. It is possible, though not recorded, that Allen raised Litten's case with Hitler at this meeting. Frick agreed that Allen could write to him about some of the political prisoners in whom Allen had taken an interest. This was, of course, a dance of mutual manipulation. Before Allen's visit, an official at the German Foreign Office had recorded the importance of letting Allen meet Hitler. "I regard this as a chance to influence the attitude of [Labour] circles, which have so far been openly hostile," read the memo, adding that Allen was a "personal friend" of Prime Minister MacDonald.[184]

Allen duly wrote to Frick, listing nine persons "whose cases are much talked of in our country" and suggesting that Frick consider releasing them to live in Britain. The last of the names was "Dr." Hans Litten. Allen's description of Litten's case included what seems to be a delicate reference to Litten's encounter with Hitler in the Eden Dance Palace trial: "I know there are special difficulties about this man," he wrote, "but his case arouses very strong feelings among certain people in my country." That Allen would refer, even so indirectly, to the Eden Dance Palace case and the "special difficulties" it created is a hint of Hitler's determination to keep Litten imprisoned. His careful phrasing suggests that Frick or another official had told him about those "special difficulties."[185]

Appeals from abroad on behalf of political prisoners in Germany were far from rare in the 1930s, but petitioners and German Foreign Official personnel (who were often sympathetic to the appeals, if only for pragmatic reasons) often ran up against the brick wall of the Nazis' domestic leadership. Wilhelm Frick replied to Allen with a long letter attempting to justify the continued custody of the prisoners Allen had mentioned. He wrote that Litten was "a fanatical Communist" who had become known for the "disreputable" manner in which he had provoked the courts and "abetted" the "Communist terrorists" for whom he acted. Litten's actions, said Frick, were nothing but "Communist propaganda and agitation" under "the cover of the legal profession." It would not only pose a danger to the state, Frick added, but would be "iniquitous" to let the "leaders" go while the followers, who had been led into political activity by the agitation of people like Litten, languished in prison. Litten's release could "therefore not be considered at this time."[186]

If more proof of Hitler's vindictive hatred was needed, it was on the way. At the end of October 1935 Allen addressed a petition to Hitler, signed by more than a hundred distinguished British barristers and public servants. The text of the petition expressed the signatories' concern with upholding "the great principle of law, recognized in all constitutional and civilized countries, that lawyers should always preserve the duty of secrecy which they owe to their clients." Noting that German authorities had never brought criminal charges against Litten, the petition closed with an appeal to "Mr. Chancellor" Hitler "to render the prestige of your Reich and of the legal system thereof, the great service of directing that Rechtsanwalt [Advocate] Hans Litten should be released." Allen himself was careful to preface the petition with the insistence, "I have, from the very day on which the Treaty of Versailles was signed, fought publicly in my country . . . for justice and equality for Germany," and even "When a country passes through a revolution, it is compelled to take severe measures against some of its citizens." But he concluded by telling the chancellor that the British people had become troubled by cases like Litten's, and noted that the list of signatories attached to the petition was remarkable for its breadth and depth. Following Irmgard's approach, Allen suggested that Litten be allowed to go to Britain in return for a promise that he would never take part in politics again.[187]

Allen's petition gave Hitler his most direct and public test on Litten's fate, and it is the one instance for which we have inside information on Hitler's response. In the surviving documents of Hitler's Reich Chancellery there is a copy of the petition, with a note dated November 7, 1935, recording that the petition asking for the freeing of "the lawyer Litten, who has been in custody since March 1933," came from Lord Allen, "who a few months ago was received by the Führer."[188]

On November 13, Hans-Heinrich Lammers, the state secretary in Hitler's Reich Chancellery, sent Allen's petition to Joachim von Ribbentrop. In 1935 Ribbentrop, later famous as Hitler's foreign minister, was "ambassador extraordinary and plenipotentiary on special mission" to Great Britain and head of the Ribbentrop Agency, a foreign policy think tank founded to give Hitler advice more congenial to his temperament than what he got from the Foreign Office. "On the orders of the Führer and Reich Chancellor," wrote Lammers, "I am most respectfully sending you enclosed a letter to the Führer from Lord Allen of Hurtwood. The Führer asks you to report to him as to a reply to this letter. I request that a copy of any response sent as a result be forwarded to me."[189]

The memo is revealing. Hitler was obviously unsure of how to respond; whichever way the decision went, he wanted to be distanced from it, as he always did from difficult or potentially unpopular decisions. The decision, when it came, would have to *appear* to come from Ribbentrop. Most important, here we have confirmation that an appeal for Litten's release reached Hitler.[190]

That Hitler would himself decide the fate of a prisoner was not just an administrative fiction. From the available documentation it is clear that this happened frequently, at least in the early years of the Third Reich. Two months before the Chancellery received Lord Allen's petition, Göring had asked Hitler for his opinion on a petition for the release of a Communist activist, Beppo Römer. Lammers responded that "the Führer and Reich Chancellor has been unable to declare himself in agreement with the release of Dr. Römer from protective custody." In July 1938 the Gestapo in Vienna complained that its office had been asked to report on such an overwhelming number of petitions sent to Hitler that "soon it will no longer be possible to maintain an orderly conduct of business."[191]

Other circumstantial evidence tells us something about the manner in which Hitler and Ribbentrop must have decided Litten's fate. Erich Kordt, an assistant to Ribbentrop from 1934 to 1940, reported that Ribbentrop "endeavored to anticipate Hitler's opinions and, if anything, to be in advance of Hitler along the path he might follow." Ribbentrop would loiter in the antechambers of the Chancellery to "learn from the hangers-on what Hitler was thinking" so that he could support the policy as if it were his own. We can be sure, therefore, that the formal response to Lord Allen's petition, though written by Ribbentrop, was very much Hitler's own.[192]

The *Attack*, along with many other German papers, printed Ribbentrop's response in mid-December under the defiant headline "Litten Is Staying Where He Is." Instructions to newspapers from Goebbels's Propaganda Ministry betrayed the official anxiety about the public relations damage Litten's case could cause. The papers were not to print Lord Allen's original letter or refer "in text, headlines or any commentary" to the coverage of Allen's appeal in the London *Times*. Ribbentrop's letter was to be printed in full, along with an introductory paragraph supplied by the Propaganda Ministry. A special courier delivered Ribbentrop's letter to Allen. Ribbentrop regretted that "after careful examination" he could not support letting Litten go. Litten had been "one of the intellectual leaders" of German Communism, involved in "activities directed against the state," and "the attitude which he has all along adopted does not allow his release in these circumstances." Allen's "English legal friends," Ribbentrop continued, did not understand how the Weimar justice system had failed to "keep up with the problems of our time," or how, "contrary to the natural feelings of the German people," it had "condemn[ed] the freedom fighter Adolf Hitler through the same paragraphs as the Communist Hans Litten" and driven "a great people to the edge of the abyss." Ribbentrop went so far as to predict that impartial historians would one day consider the National Socialist struggle for power a "model revolution, such as can only be carried through by a nation with the highest level of culture."[193]

There was one final reason for the refusal to release Litten, and that was the "bad example of Dimitrov." Dimitrov was a Bulgarian Communist who had been tried and acquitted in connection with the burning of the Reichstag. He and several of his fellow prisoners were released partly, said Ribbentrop, as a result of pressure from the West. The results had been unfortunate. Dimitrov remained "an incorrigible enemy of humanity," who, after being sent to the USSR, had become the general secretary of the Moscow-run Communist International, or Comintern. The 7th Comintern Congress in Moscow had, among other things, named Hitler as the greatest obstacle to world revolution; once National Socialist Germany was defeated, the way would be clear for the destruction of "British imperialism" as well. This, said Ribbentrop, was the result of "the liberal British world view, and German good humor and generosity." What was more, "the entire public opinion and press of England" had failed to take the slightest notice of Dimitrov's release, despite their earlier "terrible excitement" about the case.[194]

Allen nonetheless kept up his campaign, though the only real result was that Frick's Interior Ministry got serious about trying to damage Allen's credibility. Frick wrote to the German Embassy in London in January 1936 to "instruct" its staff that Allen had recently attended an international peace conference in Moscow, raising the suspicion that he was merely working for "Soviet-friendly circles" in Britain. The letter drew an indignant response from the embassy, arguing that Allen's desire for peace with Russia was an example of the same outlook that caused him to work for German-English understanding.[195]

Hitler's uncertainty about the response to Lord Allen's petition suggests that the appeal may have been Litten's last real chance. As the 1930s wore on, rising international tensions rendered any efforts to free one political prisoner much more complicated. Allen had been planning a trip to Germany to lobby for Litten in March 1936 when Hitler sent troops into Germany's Rhineland, defying the prohibition in the

Treaty of Versailles against the stationing of any military forces there. The weak international response to the Rhineland occupation may have convinced Hitler and Ribbentrop that they had no incentive to curry favor abroad through the release of high-profile political prisoners. Ribbentrop's and Hitler's growing dislike for Great Britain also played a role. As a defendant at Nuremberg Ribbentrop wrote in his memoirs, "From the years 1935–1936 [Hitler] viewed everything that came from England with slowly but steadily growing mistrust." Unrepentant and spectacularly mendacious as Ribbentrop's memoirs are, his evidence on this point is plausible.[196]

Allen nonetheless secured an invitation from Ribbentrop to attend the 1936 summer Olympics in Berlin and an invitation from Hitler to the Nazi Party Rally in Nuremberg. At Nuremberg Ribbentrop promised Allen "further action" on the Litten case, and a man close to Himmler promised to take the matter up with the Reichsführer SS as well. But in December Allen wrote regretfully, "Things are not going as I should have wished with regard to Hans Litten's case." In just the kind of bid for British opinion Allen hoped would tempt Nazi leaders to release Litten, they had let Carl von Ossietzky go in 1936. At the end of the year Ossietzky won the Nobel Peace Prize. Allen complained bitterly about this "foolish decision": "If only our good peace friends had been willing for these individual notable cases to be quietly released without political agitation, then we could have opened the prison doors I think to most of the others." Ossietzky, who had been released to a hospital, never regained his health and died in May 1938.[197]

Litten's British friends knew of his moves to Buchenwald and Dachau in the fall of 1937, and they knew that the conditions of his imprisonment were deteriorating. The prospects for successful lobbying from Britain were also worsening as the Nazi regime radicalized and grew bolder. In April 1936 Ambassador to Britain Leopold von Hoesch died suddenly of an apparent heart attack. There were rumors in the German expatriate press that his death was a suicide, as he knew that the regime would soon replace him. Hoesch's replacement was in fact none other than Ribbentrop. By 1937 the German Foreign Office was growing increasingly fed up with the stream of appeals from abroad on behalf of prisoners. A stern memo to the embassy in London warned that such inquiries should be answered only in "exceptional" cases.[198]

Allen tried to recruit a more influential British politician with ties to Germany for Litten's case. Lord Londonderry, the center of a major pro-appeasement circle, turned Allen down with the explanation, "In my relationship with the Germans, I have to consider everything I do and everything I say from the point of view of strengthening and not weakening the little influence I may have." Lord Lothian begged off with the excuse that he knew about Litten only from hearsay. He recommended a public campaign on Litten's behalf through the press, rather than one from behind the scenes.[199]

Allen tried Ribbentrop one more time. On January 13, 1938, he sent a blunt letter to the ambassador, expressing his "distress" that he had not received a reply to or even an acknowledgment of his most recent letter. Allen repeated his offer of an assurance that Litten would refrain from any political activity in Britain, and continued, "I certainly should feel it my duty to make a statement to the *Times* newspaper paying a warm tribute to the German Government" if Litten were finally released. Ribbentrop's reply, however, was equally blunt. An embassy official wrote Allen on January 28 that the circumstances of the case were such that "nothing could be done at this time."[200]

In the fall of 1937 Allen had asked Kurt Hahn, a German émigré and former secretary to Prince Max of Baden, to prepare a letter for publication in the *Times*, launching a public campaign for Litten's freedom. Allen had held back while he hoped that Ribbentrop might still be influenced; then, in January 1938, rumors circulated in Britain that the Nazi regime would soon declare another amnesty for political prisoners. But at the end of January no amnesty was in sight, and in the wake of the embassy's response of January 28, Litten's English friends decided to go ahead with the public campaign.[201]

Passion

The isolation of Dachau's Block 6 was finally lifted on December 27. Hans sent a postcard on New Year's Day to inform Irmgard. He had little else to say. The card contained only five lines of writing, although camp regulations permitted ten. He hoped that the family had passed a pleasant Christmas. The signature, "Hans," was another disturbing sign. Irmgard inferred that Hans expected to die soon.[202]

Litten was assigned to a work commando whose task was to clear away the snow. Alfred Dreifuss was assigned to the same commando and recalled how the men sheltered the frail Litten: "Hans did not have to shovel. We put him in the wagon, one comrade on the left, me on the right, so he would not be noticed." Hans told them about his translations of medieval poetry, Dreifuss remembered. But he had given up much hope of a future. "One day," said Dreifuss, "he said to me suddenly: 'Look, I gave myself a five-year limit. If I don't get out I will give up all hope and make an end of it.'"[203]

On January 8 Litten wrote Irmgard asking her to buy a recently published book on the baroque churches of Swabia and Old Bavaria for his friend Paul. Irmgard did as he wished and replied that the book demonstrated how "the Wesobrunner school achieved world-wide fame. . . . The Asam brothers [church builders whom Litten especially admired] also came from the area." This was her way of hinting about the possibility of freedom in Britain. In a letter written five days later she made the point stronger. She had noticed a small advertisement in the book for a "special book about the Asam brothers" that was in preparation. "Naturally," she continued, "quite a while can pass from the appearance of such a notice to publication, but I am very curious about it." She inferred from the impending book that "interest in the Asam brothers, who earlier were certainly not so well known, has greatly increased, as it has for the whole south German school." She would soon be able to write him with more precise information on the matter. "I am collecting just that material (which in connection with this era is not very easy) and will work on it thoroughly." Hans's brother Heinz had "incidentally stumbled onto the same territory in his Anglo-Saxon studies, since he has discovered that various highly placed persons there were Benedictines."[204]

There can be little doubt about what Irmgard was saying here. The book that would soon appear, though she did not know when; the interest that had increased, not just in the Asam brothers but in the whole "south German school" (all the prisoners of Dachau); the talk about collecting the material; and that Heinz with his "Anglo-Saxon studies" was by chance working in the same field—this was a message about Lord Allen's impending campaign. It is impossible to know how much of this Litten grasped, but if he understood what Irmgard was saying, his letter of January 30 is striking. Irmgard's "report on the book about the Baroque churches of Swabia and Old Bavaria was very interesting," he said. "From your letter I fear that you gave it [the book] too early," it continued, "because Paul's birthday is not until February 26, and you know that I am very much against early birthday presents. Then I would also really like to know how people liked my Christmas presents." This was a question in family code about Allen's progress and a warning against premature hopes of success. Hans asked Irmgard to "greet everyone" for him. Once again the letter was signed only "Hans." It was the last Irmgard would receive from him.[205]

Meanwhile, a series of alarming developments affected the lives of the prisoners of Block 6. Surviving prisoners told the story in different ways and with different emphases, but they overlap and supplement rather than refute each other. At the heart of all the prisoners' recollections is the fact that after nearly five years in Dachau, Heinz Eschen had made too many enemies.

One of those enemies was a prisoner named Waldemar Millner, a businessman from Riga. One prisoner said Eschen and Millner had gotten into a fight, which the SS had broken up and then sent Millner for one of the most infamous of tortures, "tree-hanging," in which the prisoner was hanged by his wrists from a 2.5-meter-high pole for hours. Another prisoner recalled that Millner refused to contribute to a "welfare fund" that Eschen maintained for the less well-off prisoners. Two prisoners said that Millner had reported to the SS on political meetings organized by Eschen. Fritz Rabinowitsch, who probably knew best, said that Eschen ordered him to find evidence to use against prisoners dealing in black-market cigarettes, of whom Millner was one. Rabinowitsch found the evidence and Eschen wrote a detailed report. The report sparked a fight between Eschen and Litten. "On the basis of his experience" Litten warned Eschen against submitting the report; Eschen grew angry, called Litten a "coward," and submitted the report anyway.[206]

Now, said Rabinowitsch, "the other side went to work." The "other side" consisted of the whole "prisoner boss-ocracy" which "lived from

Jewish bribes," SS guards who were furious at the special position Eschen held in the commandant's eyes, and prisoners like Millner who held grudges against Eschen. An additional allegation surfaced: that Eschen had been involved in a homosexual relationship with a sixteen-year-old prisoner. This claim seems to have been true and features in the accounts of Rabinowitsch and Ludwig Bendix. It gave "the other side" additional ammunition. Camp authorities interrogated the boy, and as these things tend to go, the boy "confessed" not only to the affair with Eschen but to others as well.[207]

On what must have been the evening of January 29, Baranowski came into Block 6 and announced, "Filthy outrages have been reported to me from the Jew Block: ass-fucking. If the guilty parties do not report themselves voluntarily, we will find them and punish them." His announcement aroused suspicions among the prisoners. It could hardly be news to Baranowski that such things went on in the camp, as they would where men were confined for long periods of time. Baranowski had to have another motive.[208]

On January 30 the guards took Eschen to the *Jourhaus*, the cells in the camp's central administrative block. Oscar Winter remembered seeing the door swing behind Eschen: "That was the last that any of us saw of [him]." That afternoon Eschen was "tree-hanged" for nine hours. He betrayed no fellow prisoners. After this he was put in a cell next to Heinz Feldheim, a prisoner who was being held in the Jourhaus in pretrial custody. Later Feldheim overheard the SS *Scharführer* (Company Leader) Johann Kantschuster come by with his *Kalfactor* (servant prisoner). The Kalfactor went in the cell and called out, "Oh, he is dead!" The SS announced Eschen's death to the prisoners the next day. Another version of Eschen's death is nearly consistent with this story. A prisoner named Sepp Eberl worked at the time in the SS canteen. During one of their banquets he heard drunken SS men arguing over who should "bump Eschen off." Since they could not agree they drew lots. The winner was Kantschuster, who came back a half hour later saying, "It's been taken care of." Kantschuster, who had been at Dachau since 1933, had carried out a number of other such murders of prisoners in the past.[209]

Given how close he was to Eschen, Litten could not avoid being drawn into the widening investigations. Some prisoners thought Litten was taken in for questioning because he stood "under suspicion of being involved in Heinz's political actions." Some said Litten was questioned about a "revolutionary" song one of the prisoners had written. Litten may have been questioned about homosexual activities in Block 6, although no surviving prisoner thought he was involved in them. In any event, there is no doubt that Litten was interrogated and that it was Baranowski who conducted the interrogations. Litten returned to Block 6 after two days, unharmed; Rabinowitsch even recalled that when Litten returned to Block 6 after his interrogation "he was rather cheerful" and told his friends that he had gotten Baranowski into a discussion of German art. Max Fürst would have had no trouble interpreting this as the Scheherazade strategy: storytelling as self-defense. Baranowski gave Irmgard Litten a very similar account of this conversation. But Baranowski also seems to have threatened Litten. Again accounts differ. One prisoner said that Litten was sentenced to twenty-five lashes for his involvement with Eschen. Others said (in an echo of Spandau in 1933) that Litten had refused to reveal secrets about his fellow prisoners and that Baranowski had warned him that the next interrogation would "not be carried out only with words."[210]

While Litten was away Dreifuss changed the linen on his mattress, and under the pillow found "a rope, which had been neatly tied into a noose." He showed it to some of Litten's friends. They told him that it was not the first one they had found.[211]

Eschen had died while Litten was being interrogated, and the other prisoners faced the task of breaking the news to Hans. "[Litten] froze, looked straight ahead and said very softly, 'Well then, tonight I will be together with Heinz,' " Rabinowitsch recalled. "My friend Alfred said to me, 'Fritz, Hans will probably commit suicide tonight.' " Dreifuss wrote that when Litten found that his noose was missing he became agitated. "I've lost something," he told his friends. "I have to speak to Heinz Eschen right away," he added, and left the barrack. About twenty minutes later Litten came back and went to bed. He was clearly seriously disturbed. Dreifuss said he did not dare to start up a conversation with him. Hans could be heard muttering, over and over, "I *must*, I *must* without fail speak to Heinz Eschen."[212]

Dreifuss recalled that after a while Litten fell asleep. Sometime in the night—it had to have been before midnight—Dreifuss heard someone get up and move around in the barrack. "I was too drunk with sleep ... to pay much attention," he wrote, and in any case it was hardly unusual for prisoners to go to the latrines in the small hours. A prisoner named August Cohn had a similar recollection. He said that a few minutes before midnight Litten got up very quietly and went out. After ten minutes, he had not returned.[213]

It was Cohn who found him. Litten was hanging in the latrine, his face to the wall, dressed only in a shirt. Cohn summoned a doctor from among the prisoners, but it was too late. Hans Litten's five-year martyrdom was over. "In the early morning hours," Dreifuss remembered, "August, Walter, and quite a few other friends went out to say farewell to him." Hans had left behind a brief note, which contained "a few words of farewell, and the assurance that he had made his own decision to seek death."[214]

News

A police officer brought the news to Fritz Litten in Berlin later that day, February 5. The old patriarch could not bring himself to tell his wife and called Heinz to come home and deliver the news instead. But Irmgard overheard the conversation and "saw immediately from my husband's condition what kind of news he had received." The police offered to deliver the body to the family. Irmgard insisted on traveling to Bavaria herself. A doctor friend accompanied her. Fritz did not.[215]

At Dachau, Irmgard was met by a "short, fat man in SS uniform with a collection of medals on his chest." This was Baranowski, who wanted to convince Irmgard that he was not responsible for Litten's death. Litten had seemed calm when he had asked him about a couple of prisoners "who had done stupid things during the isolation." Baranowski insisted that Hans had told other prisoners he planned to take his own life at the five-year mark. He was clearly eager that Irmgard not see her son's death as murder.[216]

Irmgard was convinced otherwise. Everything Baranowski told her only fed her suspicions. He said that Hans had hanged himself ten minutes before midnight. Irmgard wanted to know how the commandant could be so precise about the timing. The SS refused to let her see Hans's last note, and in any case she did not see why Hans should leave a note making clear that his death was a suicide. No one would have suspected his fellow prisoners. When she was taken to see the body she found that it did not look like that of a hanged man. As a child she had once seen a man hanging in the woods. Hans had no bulging eyes or outstretched tongue. And she could see only his head; a sheet covered the body. Irmgard wanted to throw herself at it and tear off the sheet, but Baranowski was holding her arms. This, too, fed her suspicions.[217]

His face, Irmgard wrote, was severe and gaunt, "drained of its spirit, but with a certain expression of relief." St. Francis must have looked like this, she thought. She was allowed to stay by the body as long as she wanted. "I knew that I stood by my son's body with my son's murderers," she wrote.

> I began to talk to him, very softly and carefully; I was afraid that he would not understand me if I was silent. My friend feared that I would be careless and gestured to the commandant that he should interrupt. He did not move. The conversation with my son was, like all of my exchanges with him in the last five years, disguised, and apparently so well disguised, that the others did not understand it. As I began to reel slightly, we went outside.[218]

Hans Litten was cremated in Munich and his ashes sent back to Berlin and buried in the Wilmersdorf Cemetery (later moved to the Cemetery Pankow III in the former East Berlin). Irmgard was the only member of the Litten family present for the funeral. She had chosen the simplest possible arrangements for the cremation: "It seemed to me a mockery to bury my son with any kind of splendor after this life." She refused to have any cleric, for fear she would "fall into the hands of a [Nazi] German-Christian," and she had ensured that no camp or Gestapo personnel would "profane" the ceremony by their presence. Her one request was musical: she wanted the organist to play the section from Bach's *St. Matthew Passion* that follows the Evangelist's recitative "Then all the disciples forsook Him and fled."[219]

Coming so soon after the death of Heinz Eschen, Litten's death deeply affected the prisoners of Dachau. Dreifuss remembered that the seniors of the other blocks came to Block 6 "to express their sympathy and to discuss what was to be done." Litten's block mates were given ten days of punishment: every evening between 8 and 10 they had to stand at the assembly square, under rain or snow, watched over by searchlights. For the authorities, Litten's death was something of an embarrassment. Rabinowitsch reported that Baranowski "interrogated many of us regarding the motive" and reproached Rabinowitsch for not bringing to his attention that Hans was "perhaps 'agitated.' He would have kept him a few more days in 'isolation,' that is, in the bunker." Two prominent prisoners were ordered to the Jourhaus to write obituaries for Litten to be published in the foreign press. According to Dreifuss, these statements were to say that Litten's suicide could not be attributed to mistreatment in the camp.[220]

Official embarrassment can also be detected between the lines in the judicial file on Litten's death. On February 9, the chief prosecutor at Munich's Superior Court II wrote to his superior at the Court of Appeal to say that the proceedings regarding the "death of the Jewish protective custody prisoner Hans Litten, lawyer from Berlin, in the Dachau Concentration Camp" had been stayed. The letter went on: Litten had been found hanged at ten minutes past midnight in the latrines. He had "hanged himself" by means of a rope tied around a floorboard that had been placed over the latrine. The judicial inspection and autopsy "have confirmed these facts." The letter concluded, "It is with certainty a case of suicide. No signs of violence by third persons can be found."[221]

Curiously, however, the record also contains a ministerial note, written nearly two years after Litten's death, that a special report about "Cases of Death among Prisoners in Concentration Camps" had been presented to Ministerial Director Wilhelm Crohne. The note went on to say that pursuant to a regulation of October 1939, all SS and concentration camp personnel were no longer subject to the jurisdiction of the regular courts. The presence of this note in the file on Litten's death is a hint that someone in the Reich Justice Ministry thought that there was something about Litten's death for which an SS man might *need* protection from the regular courts.[222]

The file also contains clippings from the exile press—obituaries for Litten that left no doubt that he had died a victim of Nazi barbarism, and stressed in particular that Nazi hatred for him stemmed from the cross-examination of Hitler. These clippings are marked with bold red stamps reading "Confidential" and "Forbidden." As a last official tribute, the Nazis sent these documents—like the earlier file about the abuse of Litten at Esterwegen—to the archives for preservation on the grounds that they were "historically valuable."[223]

Little by little the news spread around the world, especially to Paris, Prague, London, New York, and Shanghai, where German expatriates had settled. Max Fürst wrote an obituary for one of the exile papers: "How often had we already received the news [of his death]," he wrote resignedly; "it seemed he had so many lives, and every single one had to end with torment. We feared so often that the end had been reached, because how could a man suffer all this without losing his reason.— Now the news is confirmed; a few newspapers carry obituaries, and it is over." Fürst, like most, assumed that the reason for Litten's martyrdom was the "clash with Hitler," in which Litten so "pinned down" the future dictator that the latter "could only save himself with perjury and a hysterical fit." Rudolf Olden wrote in the *New Diary,* "Hans Litten's crime consisted solely of having once... cross-examined the Führer himself." In 1940, reviewing the English edition of Irmgard's memoir, the London *Times* noted that Litten had "given [Hitler] a very uncomfortable hour" in the witness box, and concluded, "There would seem to be not the smallest doubt that Litten, against whom no charge was preferred, was slowly done to death out of implacable revengefulness."[224]

A month after Litten's death, Lord Allen and several colleagues wrote to the *Times* to voice the fear that "what is happening in Germany's concentration camps" could become a "new and formidable obstacle" to Anglo-German understanding. They had so far kept to private advocacy, and they were still reluctant to "specify by name" some of the political prisoners "who we know without a shadow of doubt are at this moment being broken in body—thought not in spirit—by terrible suffering in the German camps." But, they continued, "the news which has just reached us through the press of the death of Dr. [*sic*] Hans Litten in Dachau Camp impels us to publish the facts of this man's tragic story as given to us. We had hoped to send you such a letter as an appeal on behalf of a man still living. That is now too late. But we feel it incumbent upon us to say that such a case as this must fatally prejudice Anglo-German goodwill."[225]

After Irmgard Litten's memoir was published in 1940, the story of the Littens' struggle against the Nazis reached as far as Eleanor Roosevelt. In September of that year, as the Battle of Britain was raging and FDR was running for an unprecedented third presidential term, she wrote in her "My Day" column, "One cannot help but be proud for the whole human race that such people as Hans Litten and his mother have lived in the world and kept faith to the end." But, she added, "When one sees what an able fight was put up to preserve justice and respect for the law and freedom under the law, one must tremble for what may happen to the rest of the world if such a regime as Hans Litten fought gains mastery permanently over a great area."[226]

Epilogue: "Only Where There Are Graves Are There Resurrections"

Ten days after Hans's death, Irmgard Litten fled Germany with Heinz. She claimed in a 1939 letter that a Gestapo officer warned her Heinz was about to be arrested to ensure her public silence. She stayed briefly in Switzerland and in France, and then moved on to Britain, where she spent the war. Fritz Litten remained in Germany until it was almost too late, refusing to move until he could be accommodated in a manner consistent with his dignity. Irmgard's letters from her first years in exile bear abundant testimony to the strains the long, dark years of Hans's imprisonment had put on her marriage. She complained incessantly about Fritz's passivity and his demands on her time. When he died, in Northern Ireland early in 1940, his obituary in the London *Times* said very little about him, focusing instead on the career of his eldest son.[1]

In the early years of the war Irmgard appeared regularly in a BBC series called *For the German Woman*. She also lectured widely on such themes as "The Danger of Fascism for the Entire World" and "The Heroism and Suffering of the German Resistance Fighters"—naturally enough, a favorite topic. She was determined to promote the awareness that "Hitler's first victims were Germans," and perhaps for this reason her broadcasts for the BBC fell off after the first years of the war. Her ideas about effective propaganda were, she said, "too different" from those of the BBC. By the end of the war she had taken up a new task: giving lectures to German prisoners of war in Britain in an effort to inculcate "anti-fascist thinking" and a "progressive and peace-loving world view." She promised the soldiers that she would remain in

Britain until the last of them had been set free, and she kept her word. She did not return to Germany until the end of the decade.[2]

At first she went to live in Bavaria, in democratic West Germany. Here she confronted the resentments that many Germans felt after the war toward those who had gone abroad, especially those who had in some way worked for the Allies—the same kind of attitude that led to demonstrations against Marlene Dietrich when the singer returned to perform in West Berlin in 1960. To many Germans, Irmgard was simply a traitor. Officials refused her the survivor benefits from her husband's university pension. Frustrated and disillusioned, and "fed up with begging," as she told Max Fürst, she moved to Communist East Berlin, where the state accorded her the status of a recognized "victim of fascism" and paid her a pension. Only now, Max wrote, could she afford to become old. She became ill almost immediately and died in East Berlin on June 30, 1953.[3]

Heinz Litten had also found refuge in Great Britain—and served in the British army. After the war he returned to East Berlin, where he worked for a time as intendant of the "People's Stage" and later ran a theater school. Heinz had always suffered from depression, and for all his early promise never achieved great success. The death of his mother seemed to rob him of "his last hold," as Max wrote. He took his own life in 1955.[4]

Rainer Litten had left Germany in 1934 for what he described as a "restless life of wandering." He worked as an actor at the German Theater in Prague, then in the Municipal Theater in Lucerne, and later at the Municipal Theater in Bern. He worked in France for a time and tried unsuccessfully to emigrate to the United States before returning to Switzerland, where he would spend the rest of his life.

The war made permanent the breakup of the Litten family. Irmgard wrote in 1942 that her letters to Rainer "as a rule do not arrive," and she got only occasional news by telegram of such major events as Rainer's marriage. Even the end of the war did not change things. The funerals of his mother and brother could not lure Rainer Litten back to a postwar Germany where former Nazis lived in comfort and even, like Kurt-Georg Kiesinger, West German chancellor in the 1960s, reached the highest positions. "I sometimes have the feeling," his daughter Patricia says, "he was very jealous of Heinz, because Heinz had accompanied Mimi [Irmgard] in her fight for Hans and into the emigration.... In some way he had a bad conscience his whole life that he had left Mimi in the lurch, and actually hated Heinz because he hadn't done so." Rainer died on Good Friday 1972.[5]

O nly where there are graves are there resurrections," wrote Nietzsche in *Thus Spake Zarathustra*. Litten, who so loved to cite Nietzsche, quoted these words in one of his articles from Comrades days. This was apt: for from his own grave, he has been resurrected many times in many different guises.[6]

As we have seen, Irmgard Litten shaped her memoir of Hans in order to have an effect on readers in Britain and the United States, and especially on German conservatives who might be pried lose from the Nazis. This was why the Hans Litten she described was deeply Christian, not Jewish, and why religious faith rather than political conviction was his driving motive. Max wrote in the 1970s, "Mother Litten brought in the Christianity business for opportunistic reasons." But her book, as one of the very few in-depth accounts of Hans Litten's life, has had an enduring influence and is the founding text of one of three "Littens" that exist in the public consciousness today: "the Martyred Christian."[7]

To be persuasive as a martyr, Litten needed to have been a victim of murder rather than suicide. Irmgard claimed to be convinced that the SS had murdered Litten in the same way they murdered Erich Mühsam and Heinz Eschen. To make this case, however, her memoir embroidered what Litten said in his letters in the fall of 1937 to play up his fears of being murdered, and neglected the evidence of Litten's suicide she had received from his fellow prisoners. It was clear, Irmgard wrote, that Litten had been told he had to "make an end of it within three months," and he tried to warn her that help from Lord Allen might come too late. But the references to Lord Allen she quotes from Hans do not appear in any of the surviving 1937 letters, although the collection of letters in the Federal Archives in Berlin appears to be complete for that year.[8]

She knew, certainly, that Hans's fellow prisoners believed he had committed suicide and indeed felt responsible for it. The accounts of Hans's last days from Dachau survivors like Rabinowitsch and Grünebaum came in letters to Irmgard, which she quoted very selectively in her memoirs. Much of what these former prisoners said came in response to her questions about whether Hans had understood the possibility of rescue from Britain (the fact that she asked such questions underscores that she had had no such confirmation from Hans's letters or from their conversation at Dachau). "For me it is certain that Hans hanged himself," was Rabinowitsch's conclusion.[9]

One can easily imagine how little Irmgard wanted to hear this message. She had spent five exhausting, heartbreaking years fighting for Hans's release; the thought that he had killed himself must have been extraordinarily painful. If in fact she did embroider or willfully misinterpret the evidence, one can hardly blame her. Her motives are not only understandable; they were, given the nature of her enemy and of her struggle against that enemy, perfectly legitimate. Indeed, in what was perhaps something of a hint, she wrote, "[Although] all my life I have told the truth," when dealing with the Nazis "I was compelled to lie. And I found that I was able to lie most beautifully. I never felt the slightest conscientious scruples. I was acting in self-defense against criminals, and it was a positive satisfaction to see them swallow my lies."[10]

And on a moral level, there *is* no distinction between saying SS men murdered Hans Litten and saying that the SS drove Litten to suicide through five years of brutal treatment with little hope of release or improvement; the second still amounts morally to murder. And in the end, certainly from 1935 on, it was Hitler himself who bore the responsibility for Litten's fate, so that his death was nothing but revenge for the cross-examination of 1931. Rabinowitsch was speaking of this kind of murder when he wrote, his rage as eloquent as Irmgard's, "Should it be attempted, by the Nazis or anyone else at all, to put even the slightest blemish on Heinz Eschen or Hans Litten, I would see it as my duty to...be the prosecutors of the camp command as the real murderers of the noblest men I have ever met."[11]

In 1950 Max and Margot Fürst, who felt that they did not belong in Israel, returned to Germany and settled in Stuttgart, where they would remain for the rest of their lives. Max reestablished himself as a furniture maker, while Margot worked as an assistant for the artist HAP Grieshaber (her daughter, Birute, said many years later that Grieshaber took the place of Hans Litten as the man to whose work and ideals she could devote herself completely). Max died of a heart attack in 1978. Margot, vital and determined to the end, lived until 2003.

Through all of these years the Fürsts carried Litten with them. "They always thought he was part of our family, always," said Birute. "If he is still alive," she added, "it is because of them." Max and Margot played crucial roles in transmitting Litten's memory from the bitter postwar years to a time more ready to hear of him.[12]

In the early 1970s, recovering from his first heart attack, Max started writing a memoir. Published in 1973 as *Gefilte Fish: A Youth in Königsberg*, the book covers his childhood, his apprenticeship as a carpenter, his involvement in the youth movement, and his friendship with Hans Litten. "The book," Max wrote, "seemingly appeared just in the nick of time to catch the generation which is already dying off." He received a flood of letters from many old friends he had presumed dead, and by 1974 he could write proudly, "The book has become a bit of a hit." No less a literary figure than Nobel Prize–winner Heinrich Böll wrote an enthusiastic review ("A book from which one can learn, without being taught"), and Böll and Fürst also carried on a friendly correspondence. Thus encouraged, Max wrote a second volume, published three years later, *Talisman Scheherezade: The Difficult 'Twenties*, which took the Fürsts' story up through their emigration to Palestine in 1935.[13]

Litten is a central figure in both books, and it was his good fortune to have had a Boswell of Max's caliber, for these two volumes are singularly wise, eloquent, and powerful books. The Litten who emerges from them—and Max saw his books as a corrective to what had been written before about Litten, by which he had to mean Irmgard's memoir—is a man who wanted to be "completely Jewish." Politically, Max and Litten had gotten their bearings from "Stefan George, Karl Marx and Lenin," while Rosa Luxemburg was "one of our heroes." Fürst became the advocate of the second "Litten" of public memory: "The Political Litten."[14]

The Political Litten was much more acceptable to the East than the West. The German Democratic Republic (East Germany), as Max wrote, had a "very strong emotional relationship" to Litten, in large part because of the gratitude of former clients and fellow prisoners, as well as colleagues from the Berlin bar who had moved into positions of power there. In 1951 the Berlin Magistrat—the government of the eastern sector of the city—renamed New Frederick Street, on which stood East Berlin's main courthouse, Hans Litten Street. A plaque reading "Hans Litten/Undaunted fighter for humanity and peace/ Advocate and defender of the oppressed/Murdered in Dachau Concentration Camp" was mounted next to the court's main entrance and a bust of Litten installed inside the building. An article on the renaming ceremony characterized Litten as "the ideal of the proletarian advocate for proletarian defendants." One of the speakers paying tribute to Litten was Hilde Benjamin, a former colleague of Litten's. In 1951 Benjamin was a senior judge in the GDR; two years later she would become its justice minister, and in this capacity would oversee the prosecutions of protestors—workers—from the uprising of June 17, 1953.[15]

The street and the plaque were not the only signs of honor that the GDR bestowed on Litten. In the 1950s law students received their initial training at the Hans Litten School. Irmgard Litten spoke at the school's inauguration on March 28, 1950 (and gave lectures there on several later occasions). Its first director was Kurt Neheimer, who in the 1980s would carry out an immense amount of research toward a biography of Litten that he would not live to complete.[16]

Litten was not around to run afoul of those GDR leaders keen to claim the dead hero's mantle. The record of his conflict with the Red Aid and the Communist Party before 1933, however, offers a clue as to how he would have fared in the GDR; his attitude to the Soviet brand of Communism offers another. As Max wrote, "What Hans had for religious faith would probably have been damned by every church as heresy, just as his political convictions would have been by the GDR." The truth of this can be demonstrated by comparing editions of Irmgard's book published in the GDR with those published elsewhere. Extensive passages from the 1940 edition dealing with Litten's politics, especially his dislike of the Communist Party and his friendship with nonconformist leftist intellectuals such as Kurt Hiller, were silently excised from the East German reprint.[17]

In 1975 the only book about Litten not written by a close friend or family member appeared in the GDR: *A Man Who Pushed Hitler to the Wall* by Carlheinz von Brück. Brück, a survivor of the Theresienstadt concentration camp, was a member of the GDR's version of postwar

Germany's liberal party, the LDPD. His book appears on first reading to be a standard example of heavy-handed Eastern Bloc propaganda. Litten, said Brück, was the kind of enlightened bourgeois who "set himself bravely on the side of the revolutionary working class." In doing so he became an ideological founder of the GDR: "That democratic justice in the service of the people for which Hans Litten strove has become a reality in the German Democratic Republic."[18]

But beneath such orthodoxy there are some surprising moments in Brück's text. Litten's bourgeois origins prevented him from fully grasping Communist ideology, wrote Brück; this is why Litten called himself a "revolutionary Marxist" who was "far left" of the Communist Party. Indeed, Litten never found what Brück called "complete political clarity." Brück believed the reason lay in Litten's social background, his general "humanistic" outlook, and, still more, his religious faith. "Fundamental Christian ethical principles" had been the essence of Irmgard Litten's lessons for her sons and contributed to Litten's rejection of dialectical materialism.[19]

This emphasis ensured Brück a cool reception among many of Litten's surviving clients and associates in the GDR. Max's judgment was more nuanced. He thought that Brück had performed a valuable service and hinted at the influences that the regime had "slipped in" to the book. After the collapse of the GDR, Margot wrote that the "misunderstanding, or the half truth," of insisting on Litten's religious motivation had begun with Brück. But she also understood the delicate political situation in which he had to work. He could hardly have emphasized Litten's distance from the Communists. Brück had therefore to dismiss this distance as the "craziness of a bourgeois"; attributing Hans Litten's motivation to religious faith could make this "craziness" credible.[20]

Max and Margot had much to do with the production of Brück's book. They supplied him with information, as well as most of the book's photographs. They therefore contributed greatly to the preservation of Litten's memory in the East as well as the West.[21]

By the late 1970s a movement was under way among a small group of West German lawyers that would add more dimensions to the memory of Hans Litten in his native land. For the Federal Republic of

Germany (West Germany), the 1970s were darkened by terrorism from groups like the Red Army Faction, the bitter residue of the broader student movements of the 1960s. Faced with self-defined "urban guerrillas" who hijacked airliners and kidnapped and in some cases murdered prominent politicians and business leaders, the West German state cracked down with sometimes highly repressive legislation and murky police tactics (Red Army Faction prisoners had a striking tendency to commit suicide in prison). Lawyers such as Heinrich Hannover and Otto Schily (later Germany's interior minister) made names for themselves as courtroom defenders of accused terrorists—at the price of often bitter public controversy. Schily spoke of the "social ostracism" and the "outsider role" that lawyers for accused terrorists had to face. In a number of these cases, lawyers who, in the eyes of the court, were too aggressive about protecting their clients' interests were expelled from the trials. In the clash between an increasingly authoritarian state and increasingly lawless radicals, many West Germans, on the right as well as the left, saw alarming parallels to the late Weimar years. Heinrich Böll (who himself, with his novel *The Lost Honor of Katarina Blum*, waded into the terrorism controversies) drew parallels between the 1930s and the 1970s in his review of Max Fürst's second book. "It began," he said, "with the destruction of the law, the destruction of literature came only later; and it began with the threatening of lawyers."[22]

German lawyers broadly agree that amid this political and legal turbulence, there took place a "renaissance of criminal defense," a renewed willingness of lawyers to exploit all of the defendant's substantive and procedural rights. The Nazis had destroyed the aggressive bar that had developed by the end of Weimar. Most of the leading Weimar defense lawyers were both left-leaning and of Jewish origin, and in any case criminal defense conceived as a vindication of the rights of the individual vis-à-vis the state was a profoundly anti-Nazi concept. With so many of the leaders of the Weimar bar dead or in exile, it took several decades for the German legal profession to recover. Looking back, one lawyer spoke of the "pre-democratic understanding" typical of the West German bar's official organization, the German Lawyers' Association, as late as the 1970s.[23]

A rebirth of historical consciousness among German lawyers was central to the renaissance of criminal defense. In the 1980s and 1990s a small circle of German lawyers began to concern themselves seriously with their profession's past, especially the Weimar years, and their efforts yielded a growing number of publications. Gerhard Jungfer spearheaded the formation of the Forum for Lawyers' History, which now carries on annual conferences and maintains a web page with information about the history of the German bar. As these lawyers reached back for precedents for engaged and passionate defense, especially in political cases, inevitably they came upon Hans Litten. Starting in the 1980s, articles on Litten began to appear in legal and professional journals and reference books. These texts give us a third Hans Litten: "the Lawyers' Litten."[24]

The Lawyers' Litten is very different from the Political Litten but has close affinities to the Martyred Christian. The roots of the Lawyers' Litten lie in Rudolf Olden's preface to Irmgard Litten's book. "Hans Litten," said Olden, "had nothing to do with the Communist Party or any other, with politics in the narrower sense." To Olden, Litten amounted to a kind of latter-day St. Thomas More, a "hero and martyr" of the German bar, who "preferred to give up his life [rather] than the secrets entrusted to him in his office."[25]

This is the Litten—brushed up and sanitized, his rough, revolutionary edges smoothed over—who has haunted the pages of legal professional journals and certain kinds of legal ceremonies in Germany since the 1980s. In 1988, two German organizations, the Association of Democratic Lawyers and the Republican Lawyers' Association, since joined by the European Association of Lawyers for Democracy and World Human Rights, began awarding a biennial Hans Litten Prize to lawyers who distinguish themselves through work for human rights. The awarding of the prize is often the occasion for evocations of the Lawyers' Litten. The 1994 winner, for example, was Dr. Helmut Kramer, a judge on the Court of Appeal in Braunschweig. "The name Hans Litten," he said in his acceptance speech, "stands for a courageous defense of democracy and law"—this of a man who was, in the words of Max Fürst, against democracy, who thought no useful politics could be conducted by voting, and who voiced nothing but contempt for the Weimar Republic. On the occasion of Litten's one hundredth birthday, Annette Wilmes wrote, "Hans Litten died for his convictions, for his convictions as a lawyer. He was no Communist, even if he defended many workers, Communists and Socialists. . . . Hans Litten was an advocate of the law."[26]

As the Lawyers' Litten was in gestation, Litten also came to the attention of many in West Germany by a separate route. Countess Marion Dönhoff was one of the most influential journalists in the Federal Republic, for many years editor and later publisher of the weekly *Die Zeit* (*Time*) of Hamburg. Like the Littens, she was from East Prussia. Her brothers had studied with and admired Fritz Litten. An early anti-Nazi, she had been on the fringes of the aristocratic-military resistance group that sent Count Claus von Stauffenberg to kill Adolf Hitler in July 1944. In 1986 Countess Dönhoff came upon an old copy of Irmgard Litten's *A Mother Fights Hitler*. The book had a powerful effect on her, and she devoted a long article in December to, as her title put it, "The Forgotten Sacrifice" of Hans Litten. The countess's Litten was, like Irmgard's, the Martyred Christian. She concluded with the thought that perhaps Litten was "one of those righteous men for whose sake the Lord did not allow the city—the country, the nation—to be entirely ruined." Here the countess was consciously echoing Henning von Tresckow, one of the men of the July 1944 plot, who shortly before his death told a friend, "If God promised Abraham that He would not destroy Sodom if only ten righteous men could be found there, then I hope for our sakes God will not destroy Germany."[27]

Countess Dönhoff's stature, and the way she evoked the inherent drama of Litten's last years, combined to give his story a considerable impact in West Germany. Three weeks later the *Time* printed a selection of letters in response to the countess's article. She herself wrote an introduction, acknowledging that there had been "no current occasion" inspiring her to write about Hans Litten. "I only wrote the article to leave a small memorial for one, as I thought, forgotten victim of barbarism." But, she continued, "Hans Litten is not forgotten." Among the letters was one from Margot Fürst, thanking the countess for the article.[28]

I n November 1989, the failing GDR opened the Berlin Wall. By October of the following year, West Germany had absorbed the former East.

On October 2, 1990, the day before the official reunification, the Berlin lawyer Stefan König, who a few years before had published an important book on defense lawyers in the Third Reich, remembered that there was a Hans Litten Street in East Berlin and a courthouse in which Litten's bust was on display. "I feared," he wrote, "that in the course of the dissolution of the court [the bust] would fall victim to the drive for the elimination of all traces and symbols of the vanquished, lost social system and its state." Many people, König thought, might identify Litten with the corrupt justice system of East Germany. He wrote to the senator for justice in the government of Berlin, Jutta Limbach, who assured him that the bust would remain where it was.[29]

Another issue with Hans Litten's memory was about to emerge. In the newly reunified Berlin of 1991 and 1992, the local government, by then dominated by the conservative Christian Democratic Union (CDU), literally took to the streets of East Berlin with a vengeance— removing street names that the GDR had bestowed in honor of its leading figures. The new administration sought to return these streets to the names they had borne before 1949, or even before 1933. In some cases the government reached for new names.

On February 12, 1992, *Tagesspiegel* (the *Daily Mirror*) reported that the Berlin CDU caucus had recently decided on a raft of new street names. Among them, Karl-Liebknecht Street was to be renamed Europa Avenue (Liebknecht, also a successful lawyer, had been one of the founders of the Communist Party before being murdered in January 1919), and Hans Litten Street was to become On the Cloisters.[30]

The keepers of Litten's legacy responded swiftly. Margot Fürst wrote in burning indignation the very next day to Jutta Limbach: "I am disgusted and appalled that it should be possible in the Federal Republic to dispute the honoring of a man who fought against Hitler and his gang even before 1933, who therefore was dragged through the concentration camps and repeatedly tortured from the night of the Reichstag Fire until the end in Dachau on February 5, 1938." Gerhard Jungfer lobbied the Berlin Lawyers' Chamber to get involved, and supplied a *Daily Mirror* reporter named Rüdiger Scheidges with information about Litten. Scheidges published an article very much as Jungfer wished on February 21. Noting that GDR authorities had cut passages of Irmgard's memoir stressing Litten's distance from the Communists, he argued, "In fact the 1951 renaming of the former New Frederick Street as Litten Street was based on a historical misrepresentation, a political confiscation of a man who proved himself to be a resolute lawyer and not a political agitator." Johannes Blum found that arguments about Litten's historic merits made no impact on a municipal official, but Countess Dönhoff's article did. Litten Street remained on the map.[31]

If the issue of renaming Hans Litten Street had been about the relationship of reunified Germany to the Stalinist past of its eastern regions, another controversy of the year 2000 involved the awkward relationship between the Lawyers' Litten and the Political Litten. Plans were afoot to name the new headquarters of the Federal Lawyers' Chamber (*Bundesrechtsanwaltskammer*, or BRAK, the professional association for all of Germany's lawyers), which was being built on Hans Litten Street in Berlin, the Hans Litten House. This time, Gerhard Jungfer and Tilmann Krach (another lawyer-historian involved with the Forum for Lawyers' History) opposed using Litten's name. In an open letter to the president and members of the presidium of the BRAK, Jungfer and Krach reached back to Erich Eyck's 1932 article on Litten's expulsion from Felseneck, quoting Eyck's words: "Certainly we do not approve of everything that Advocate Litten has done." "Without doubt: Litten was a great personality, an engaged lawyer, an original thinker, a great fighter, brave and stubborn," Jungfer and Krach continued, but "he was by no means generally accepted or even respected within the profession. And as someone who practiced purely criminal defense, he was by no means representative of the broader profession." There were other lawyers of the Weimar era who were more suitable for being honored with the name of the legal profession's home, all the more so given that Litten had already been honored with a street, a plaque, and a bust in the courthouse.[32]

This letter drew a blistering response from Heinrich Hannover, himself a historian of the justice system of the Weimar era as well as one of the engaged, left-leaning lawyers who had led the "renaissance" of criminal defense in the 1970s. The alternative names Krach and Jungfer had proposed for the naming of the headquarters, establishment figures and civil rather than criminal lawyers, "amount to a de-politicization." Hannover found it "astonishing" that with a quote from the "conservative" historian Erich Eyck, Krach and Jungfer would "awaken doubts in Litten's integrity."[33]

The BRAK stayed with the name Hans Litten House. Anton Braun, the business manager of the BRAK, explained why in an article later in 2001. The BRAK sought a name that could serve to unify West and East Germans, he said; furthermore, "today everyone talks about marketing." Litten's name, already linked with the street, was well known and thus too convenient not to be used. So Litten, the independent revolutionary, was to serve as a symbol of reconciliation between former Communists and middle-class liberals and conservatives; Litten the radical professional outsider was to lend his name to the "marketing" of the main institutions of that profession. Perhaps Litten would have appreciated the multiple ironies.[34]

A century after his birth Litten has reached a kind of apotheosis. The opening of Hans Litten House on February 15, 2001, represented the triumph of the Lawyers' Litten. One can read on the BRAK's web page "The address of the BRAK is inseparably connected to the name Hans Litten"; when the building's cornerstone was laid in 1999, the president of the chamber noted that Litten was an "engaged lawyer and a tireless fighter for freedom and justice."[35]

Hans Litten is now a well-known name in the Federal Republic of Germany. But he has been shorn of much of his complexity. Margot Fürst made this point in an eloquent and poignant letter at the moment it became clear that Hans Litten Street would not be renamed. Writing again to Jutta Limbach, Margot noted that her satisfaction at the outcome was mixed with "uneasiness." "One reads everywhere now how Hans Litten's name was abused by the GDR, that he was never a Communist," she wrote. Although it was certainly true that Hans never belonged to the Communist Party, she continued, were he to be classified politically it would be to the "left of the Party." Litten was "a religious man," but his "political convictions" were "strictly rational." She attributed the Christian martyr myth to Brück. Full honesty would have compelled her to lay it at Irmgard Litten's door, but this was a step that Margot, like Max, did not wish to take. Brück had written as he had because of the political pressures in the GDR. "Why must we commit historical misrepresentations from the other side today?" she wondered. "Can we still not bear to accept a great man, obsessed with duty to the point of self-surrender . . . as he was?"[36]

The Political Litten, the Lawyers' Litten, and the Martyred Christian all contain elements of Litten's complex and contradictory character. But none of them defines the whole person. The Fürsts, who knew Litten as well as anyone, downplayed the religious element, and especially the Christian religious element, in Litten's character and motivation. And yet, as we have seen, Litten's own words show clearly how important his faith was to him and how little he was concerned with allegiance to specific "approaches" to God, to historical forms of Judaism or Christianity. The Lawyers' Litten is an honorable construct developed for honorable reasons by lawyers who have fought an often bruising battle for civil liberties in Germany. But as much as Litten undoubtedly cared about the rule of law, he cared about revolutionary politics at least as much. Once again, Max best expressed the challenge of confronting Hans Litten: "I must remind myself that Hans did not belong to me."[37]

Writing his preface in 1939 for Irmgard Litten's memoir, Rudolf Olden noted, "The law is always the cause of the weak; the strong need no law, and since they already have the power, they are all too easily inclined to get along without it." Olden had his eye firmly fixed on the strong of that moment, the ones who had driven him from his homeland and who would soon kill him by torpedoing his ship on the North Atlantic: that complex of aristocratic, business, and military power, married to the chaotic force of Hitler's movement, which had first crushed those Germans who believed in a freer and more peaceful future, and then made of the land of poets and thinkers the scourge of the civilized world. Still, Olden closed his preface with a note of hope: "If [this book] will stimulate disgust and horror at Nazi Germany, so may it also serve to keep the admiration for a people that can bring forth such a mother and such a son from completely vanishing. For me, if I may say so, the reading of this book has strengthened my faith that Germany is not yet lost."[38]

Olden's point could be expanded. Nothing that Hitler and the National Socialists did is unique, or particularly German. Other regimes have violated the norms of domestic and international law, and still do; other regimes have stripped minorities of their rights, and still do; other regimes have brandished their patriotism as an excuse for every crime, and still do; other regimes have built gulags or concentration camps and held prisoners indefinitely, and still do; other regimes have tortured their opponents, and still do; other regimes have lied to launch wars of aggression, and still do; other regimes have committed genocide, and still do. The strong, like the poor, will always be with us, and if Olden was right, the strong will never feel the need of law. In the early twenty-first century, a senior legal official in the administration of U.S. president George W. Bush could write memos dismissing international law as "a tool of the weak."[39]

Hans Litten's niece Patricia bears a striking resemblance to her grandmother Irmgard and embodies much of the Litten family idealism. On a lovely June evening in 2006 in Nuremberg, where the Nazis held their rallies, she remembered ruefully how a lawyer once asked her why, exactly, she expected the world to be a just place.

"It is important to deal with history," she said. "But the one thing that I would really like to say is that we must be alert and ask questions. We have to ask what we would do if we were in that situation. And not one of us should be so arrogant as to be certain that we would not fall into exactly the same trap."[40]

Appendix:
Hans Litten's
Cross-Examination of
Adolf Hitler, May 8, 1931

*G*erman trials are not, and have never been, officially stenographically recorded in the manner of trials in the United States. Thus for the substance of this cross-examination we must depend on the various stenographic reports published in the newspapers.

Needless to say, the various reports differ one from another, in places considerably. The following transcript necessarily represents a synthesis of the best available sources. Professor Dr. Constantin Goschler performed a similar operation some years ago for the comprehensive edition of Hitler's "Speeches, Writings and Orders" published by the Institute for Contemporary History in Munich. Professor Goschler's transcription of the examination follows very closely that published in the Berliner Tageblatt, *which was certainly the most comprehensive and probably overall the most accurate. My version also largely follows the* Tageblatt, *but has more of the* Vossische Zeitung *and the 8 Uhr Abendblatt than Goschler's. I have included language from these other papers where it seems likely to contain accurate information absent from the* Tageblatt *or where the language seems clearer and more plausible. As the reader will see, the indications of the passage of time suggest that even the extensive* Tageblatt *transcription does not contain all of what was said in court that morning. I have included a few words from the account in* Angriff, *on the derivation of the term "roll commando," where it seems that this otherwise dubious source is likely to contain a correct rendering of what Hitler said.*

Legal experts may object that this was not, technically, a cross-examination; Litten was questioning a witness he himself had summoned. But in tone and content the questions are akin to what would happen in a cross-examination in an adversarial trial.

The first questions asked by Superior Court Director Ohnesorge were, in substance, the questions submitted by Hans Litten.

Superior Court Director Kurt Ohnesorge: The claim has been made by counsel for the private prosecutors that Storm 33, to which the four defendants belong, is a "roll commando." He claims this roll commando was deliberately organized with the goal of carrying out planned and premeditated killings, and that this plan was known to the Party leadership and approved by it. Do you know Storm 33? Do you know its leaders?

Adolf Hitler: No, it is absolutely impossible that any Storm in Berlin could have believed that it had been entrusted with such a mission, that would have been ruled out by the basic principles of the Party.

The Party utterly rejects violent methods. The SA groups were not formed to take action with bombs and hand grenades. The SA was formed for the mission of protecting the Party against the terror from the left and to carry out propaganda functions. I am of the view that the formation of roll commandos would be impossible just because such a fact would immediately be betrayed.

Now the claim is made that I myself have admitted to the formation of roll commandos in an article in the *Nationalist Observer* that I wrote on the occasion of the dismissal of Captain Stennes from office. I have already explained that the National Socialists are fundamentally legal. That is not just my heart's desire, it is a reality. I consider the present constitution to be terrible. But I can see that any attempt to come to power against the constitution would mean unnecessary bloodshed. If I were to badger my followers into this misfortune, I would betray the blind trust that has been granted to me as leader.

[Hitler turns now to Stennes and takes issue with Stennes's efforts at terror.]

If anyone at all suggests that Stennes formed roll commandos on the orders of the Party, that's laughable. As long as Stennes had a position in the Party he commanded 20,000 men. How can any one call such a mass a roll commando?

I am taking the legal path on the basis of my deep convictions. Now some within Party circles have accused me of being a coward, a conformist [*verspießt*], a party boss, a bourgeois. Naturally I have defended myself against this and I have pointed to my success, which is seen in the building up of a gigantic organization of millions. Before he entered the Party Captain Stennes had two hundred men.

Ohnesorge: Do you mean by your critics the organization that Herr Stennes formed?

Hitler: I do not want to characterize Stennes' activity within the Party. In the party he had, as I said, 20,000 men to command. But he did not accomplish anything more than a few miserable small organizations.

Ohnesorge: Do you mean that Stennes formed roll commandos before he joined the Party?

Hitler: The concept "roll commando" has taken on an absolutely ridiculous meaning here. What were the roll commandos earlier? The term emerged in the field [this means at the front during the war] when smaller units of 8 to 30 men that were given the mission of heroically rolling up an enemy trench, heedless of the losses, were designated as roll commandos. The term was then taken over for smaller units, and obviously in and of itself has nothing to do with the elimination of people. The SA is forbidden to commit violence or provoke it. But in a case of self-defense it is hard to say where the line is between self-defense and attack. When an SA man is pursued for months by red murderers . . .

Ohnesorge: I ask that you refrain from using this expression.

Hitler: When an SA man is pursued for months, I can imagine that in an emergency he would fail to recognize the moment of self-defense. But if an SA man really oversteps the boundary of self-defense, you can't hold a person responsible for that. Not once has the leadership of the Party given out the slogan: "Beat the opponent to death! Beat the Communists to death! Beat the SPD to death!" Those kinds of expression have only been used by the other side.

Ohnesorge: So you say you are not conscious of using the term "roll commando" in the manner in which you have been interpreted by the private prosecutors, and most especially not to refer to Storm 33?

Hitler: I do not know Storm 33.

Ohnesorge: In what sense did you use the term "roll commando" in your article? The private prosecutors base themselves on your article. Did you mean that these roll commandos had orders to kill people? Now I do not mean the entire SA, but rather a few selected units.

Hitler: I have already insisted that in my article I did not mean to indicate the activity of Captain Stennes in the Party, but rather his activity before he entered the Party. But even in this context I did not use the word roll commando in the sense that is imputed to me here.

Ohnesorge: I find the expression at least prejudicial.

Hitler: Naturally I did not know that one day I would be nailed by a lawyer for this expression.

Ohnesorge: You are also unaware whether any kind of plan, as is claimed by the private prosecutors, existed among the members of Storm 33?

Hitler: That I consider to be absolutely impossible.

Advocate Hans Litten: You have nonetheless raised the accusation that Captain Stennes did not accomplish anything more than the formation of a few miserable roll commandos. Anyone would have to take this to mean that Captain Stennes had set up roll commandos within the National Socialist movement. [Litten demonstratively holds in his hands Hitler's six-column article in the *Nationalist Observer*.]

Hitler: I did not mean to make any such accusation against Stennes. I did not mean to say that he worked illegally within the Party. I only meant to explain that if I wanted to refute the criticism that was made of me by Stennes and the other radical leaders, I would have to leave the legal path, and I will not do that under any circumstances. I will, as long as I have the honor to be the leader of the National Socialist Party, not allow myself to be driven away from the path of legality. [Striking himself on the chest.] The legality of the Party would only be placed in question if I were to approve roll commandos.

Litten: According to your testimony, you were afraid of Stennes.

Hitler: Not of his forming roll commandos, but of the hopes and wishes that were in Stennes' newspaper, which you can read there.

Litten: So you were afraid of Stennes' illegal ideas?

Hitler: I am not in a position to judge them.

Litten: So you can give no precise testimony over Stennes' activity in the National Socialist movement. Do you mean that Stennes' intentions and wishes, if they were fulfilled, would amount to illegality?

Hitler: If I were to identify myself with the ideas that Stennes bandies about in the paper, I would only be taking myself far away from my path.

Litten: Are you not aware from the terminology of the Free Corps, that the expression "roll commando" has taken on the meaning: a commando for the elimination of disliked opponents under all circumstances?

Hitler: Among us National Socialists the concept of a roll commando is a laughable one. Already seven years ago I wrote that our goals could not be reached with bombs, hand grenades, and pistols, but rather through setting masses in motion.

Litten: But you know that the expression roll commando is used in this way? Are you aware that in SA circles a particular "roll get-up" is spoken of?

Hitler: I have heard nothing of a "roll get-up." Our honorable uniform that has been taken from us. Now one wears a fantasy uniform.

Litten: You said that no violent actions are carried out by the National Socialist Party. But didn't Goebbels come up with the slogan "The enemy must be beaten to a pulp"?

Hitler: That is not to be taken literally! It means that one must defeat and destroy the opponent organizations, not that one attacks and murders the opponent.

Litten: You say it is impossible for the leader of a great movement to watch over his movement down to the last detail. If the subaltern leaders had formed roll commandos, would the Party leadership have found out about it?

Hitler: Not only the Party leadership, but also the local authorities, in whose district such a commando was formed, would find out about it. In Germany it is absolutely impossible that a storm of 200 men, a roll commando with such goals as are alleged here, could be formed and that such a roll commando could be kept secret. We know that in all our organizations there are informers. Let there be! But I can imagine that such a well-paid subject could creep into the party and form organizations that seriously incriminate the party. As leader I can do nothing more than give strict orders, and I insist once again that I consider it absolutely impossible that Storm 33 had any tasks besides those prescribed by the party. In Germany I have storms or squads who up to now have never had to survive a battle, because they are not threatened by an opponent or attacked. In other parts of Germany, for instance in the Ruhr region, there are storms that never get out of battle, all of whose members are wounded. But if there were any Storm that broke into a tavern today and abused harmless people, that would become known to the Party leadership, and we would send an investigating commission and the SA-inspection right away, and we would stop at nothing to dispense with these, our people.

Litten: Did you not accuse Captain Stennes of appointing an SA leader in Danzig, who formed roll commandos and even broke up your own Party meetings?

Hitler: But that has nothing to do with this case. This man had already been expelled from the Party. He had even broken up our own Party's Christmas celebration. Just from that you can see his incompetence.

[Later in his testimony Hitler declared that in Danzig the SA had received weapons with permits, and if the question of bearing weapons was going to be brought up here, he could only testify after the exclusion of the public, because it touched on the question of national defense.]

Supporting Judge: You have characterized the expression "roll commando" as blurry and fantastically misunderstood. Now I don't understand how you can *reproach* Captain Stennes with the formation of roll commandos.

Hitler: I used this expression in an article that I wrote in protecting the interests of the movement. Had I known the expression "roll commando" would be interpreted as it has been in this trial and used against me, I would not have used it.

Litten: For now I do not want to cast doubt on the honesty of your oath in Leipzig, but I am asking, does your struggle for power involve only the struggle against the state as it now exists, or does it also involve the struggle against the organizations of the working class that are opposed to you?

Hitler: What does the struggle for power consist of? It consists of defeating parties opposed to us. And of the struggle for the great masses. So if we use legal methods in the struggle against the state, we will use them in the struggle against the opposition workers' organizations also.

[...Questions asked by Curt Becker, counsel for the defendant storm troopers...]

[Advocate Litten now asks that the large package that is lying in front of the court table be opened and that Hitler be shown the weapons that were found at the scene of the attack. But it does not come to this; instead, Hitler makes further vague statements to the effect that probably sometimes a wrench or something similar can be found on an SA man. He declares, "I can understand it as a human being, when a man who is continually threatened by death gets himself a weapon, because I know what the fear of death is."

Now, since the examination of Hitler has already lasted for two hours, the presiding judge invites the defendants to sit down. The defendants, who have been standing in the dock since 9 a.m., reject the presiding judge's offer. Then Advocate Litten gives Hitler another opportunity for a rhetorical demonstration, by asking him if he would permit fighting with illegal means against the working class. Hitler raises his voice and insists, "It can pain no one more than me, that today there is still a battle of German workers against German workers. That is what the National Socialist movement is for, to render this battle impossible."

Advocate Litten has now formulated three questions that he wants to pose to the witness Hitler.

> Question 1: Whether Hitler considers what the defendants are charged with to be self-defense?
>
> Question 2: When Hitler made Goebbels Reich Propaganda Director, was he aware of the passage in Goebbels's book in which Goebbels declares that we must not shrink from revolution, the Parliament should be broken up and the government chased to the devil, and where the word "revolution" is printed in boldface type?
>
> Question 3: Did Hitler promise Reich Chancellor Brüning he would dissolve in the SA in the event that the National Socialist Workers' Party participated in the government?

After the defense lawyers, the representative of the private prosecutors, and the prosecution speak on the admissibility of the questions, the court retires for deliberations, which last approximately three-quarters of an hour, and then announces that question 1 is disallowed as unsuitable; questions 2 and 3 are permitted.]

Ohnesorge: Herr Hitler, you heard the question about appointing Herr Goebbels as Reich Propaganda Director. What do you have to say about that?

Hitler: I cannot say under oath whether I knew Goebbels' book at that time. The thesis in Goebbels' book is entirely without value for the Party, since the pamphlet does not bear the Party emblem and is also not officially sanctioned by the Party. Only what is officially sanctioned has validity. Goebbels was appointed because of his extraordinary ability for propaganda, and must stay within the guidelines which I, as Party leader, give him.

Litten: Is it correct that Goebbels had already been made Party boss [*Gauleiter*] of Berlin in 1926?

Hitler: I cannot confirm the date.

Litten: Must it not be so, that something that a man like Goebbels says outside of his official Party position exerts an extraordinary influence on the members of the Party who read his pamphlet?

Hitler: Our movement is a continuous melting pot, to which people come from all camps, from the Communists to the German Nationals. Might I refer to the fact that no party can be measured by the statements of an individual member, but only by the official party guidelines. We must be judged by the principle that we stand absolutely granite-hard on the basis of legality, from the conviction that there is no other way. The National Socialist Workers' Party will not shy away even from hard struggles, and it is ready to discipline and expel from its ranks anyone who takes another position.

Litten: You didn't discipline or expel Goebbels, but instead made him Reich Propaganda Director. Mustn't Goebbels' example rouse the idea in the Party that the program of legality hasn't gotten very far?

Hitler: The whole Party stands on the basis of legality, and Goebbels stands likewise on this basis. He is in Berlin and can be called here at any time.

Litten: Has Herr Goebbels been forbidden to disseminate his text?

Hitler: I don't know.

Litten: And are you aware that numerous SA men and Party members, especially in north Germany, hold to Goebbels' program of illegality?

Hitler: If that were the case, these people would have left me a month ago. Because a month ago they were all asked if they were in agreement with the course of one hundred percent legality. The result was overwhelming. May I request that the court summon the director of the investigation committee, the director of the SA and all the Gauleiter, so that they can confirm this, my standpoint.

Ohnesorge: We come now to the third question. Did you promise Reich Chancellor Brüning to dissolve the SA in the event of your joining the administration? The third question is supposed to show that you yourself saw the SA as something illegal.

Hitler (extraordinarily excited): I insist that Brüning has not offered me any participation in his government, nor have we asked for any participation on the basis of any sort of concession. Dissolving the SA would mean for me the end of the Party. The SA men are the first men of the Party. To ask me to dissolve the SA in order to join a government amounts to asking me to commit suicide or asking my Party to commit suicide....

[... Questions from Curt Becker...]

Hitler: The reorganization of the SA is a permanent condition, because this organization, which at first consisted of just a few thousand men, now numbers tens of thousands. And so it must always be made clear to new members that the SA man is not to follow the spirit of the Free Corps, but that he is a political soldier, must feel one hundred percent a member of the Party.

Litten: In your opinion, what is the spirit of the Free Corps?

Hitler: The Free Corps spirit lived in those who believed that a change in the fate of the German nation could be brought about through placing physical strength at the disposal of a particular government. The National Socialist, on the other hand, knows that the fate of the nation depends on a complete spiritual transformation of the German people.

Litten: Do you also include the notorious crimes and killings that were committed by the Free Corps as part of this spirit?

Hitler (in an outraged tone): I refuse to acknowledge that that kind of thing happened. The Free Corps committed no killings. They defended Germany.

Litten: Herr witness, is it correct that on the occasion of the so-called SA revolt last year you were accompanied on your tour of Berlin restaurants by armed SS men?

Hitler (who is once again outraged): That is complete lunacy! In all the taverns I was greeted with stormy enthusiasm. [Laughter and merriment in the spectators' gallery, which is censured by the presiding judge.]

[. . . There follows a break in the proceedings, and then the questioning of Walter Stennes and Ernst Wetzel . . .]

Litten (to Hitler): Do you still maintain what you said in the morning session: that if you had followed Stennes' course you would have had to leave the path of legality?

Hitler: I said the following. I am a dutiful guardian of my Party's interests. The view that Captain Stennes puts forward in his paper would lead me to leave the path that I have taken. But I have to insist that it must be left to Captain Stennes to refer to his goals as legal. That is a matter of opinion.

Litten: Is it correct that Goebbels' revolutionary text "The Commitment to Illegality" [Litten means Goebbels's pamphlet *The Nazi-Sozi*] has now been taken over by the Party publisher and has reached a printing of 120,000 copies?

[Advocate Kamecke, Hitler's counsel, objects to this question.]

Litten: I have just learned that this pamphlet is sanctioned by the Party, that it is sold at all Goebbels' meetings, and that it is available in all Party bookstores, contrary to Hitler's declarations about legality.

Ohnesorge: Herr Hitler, you in fact testified in the morning session that Goebbels' text was not an official Party publication.

Hitler: Nor is it. A text becomes official if it bears the printed seal of the Party. In any case it is the Propaganda Chief who must be heard on these things, and above all—[Hitler yells with a bright red face] Herr Advocate, how can you say that that is a call to illegality? That is a statement that can be proven by nothing!

Litten: How is it possible that the Party publisher took over this text, which stands in clear contradiction to the Party line?

Ohnesorge: That has nothing to do with this trial.

Litten: I can only say that the court now...

Ohnesorge: I ask that you not criticize the court.

Litten (on the question of swearing in the witness Hitler): What does the abbreviation SA mean? In the Schweidnitzer trial Advocate [Fritz] Löwenthal raised the accusation against Hitler that he had committed perjury on earlier occasions, because in contrast to the then-Senior Storm Section Leader Pfeffer von Salomon he defined the term SA as "Sport Section."

Hitler: I have already explained the development of the term on earlier occasions. We spoke earlier of a "Hall Guard Section," then of a "Sport Section," and since the great hall battle in Munich in 1921, of a "Storm Section."

Litten: Then why haven't you brought a libel case against Advocate Löwenthal?

Hitler (irritably): I have been slandered and insulted for five years. I have no time and no desire to pursue all of these trials.

[After a brief deliberation Hitler is given the oath and the proceedings adjourn.]

Sources: "Hitler als Zeuge," *Berliner Tageblatt*, May 8, 1931 (evening edition), and "Zu viel Legalität," *Berliner Tageblatt*, May 9, 1931 (morning edition); "Hitler's Zeugen-Aussage in Moabit," *Vossische Zeitung*, May 9, 1931; "Hitler schwört alles ab!," *8 Uhr Abendblatt*, May 8, 1931; "Legalität und Roll-kommandos," *Berliner Morgenpost*, May 9, 1931; "Hitler als Zeuge in Moabit," *BZ am Mittag*, May 8, 1931; "Unser Führer in Moabit," *Angriff*, May 8, 1931; Document 115, "Strafverfahren gegen vier NSDAP-Angehörige, Zeugenaussage vor dem Schwurgericht III Berlin-Moabit," in Constantin Goschler, ed., *Hitler: Reden, Schriften, Anordnungen. Februar 1925 bis Januar 1933*, Band IV: *Von der Reichstagswahl bis zur Reichspräsidentenwahl Oktober 1930—März 1932*, Teil 1: Oktober 1930–Juni 1931 (Munich: K. G. Saur, 1994), 360.

A Note on Sources

This book has been written almost entirely from printed and archival primary sources. The reader seeking detailed source information should, of course, refer to the notes. Here I give a brief summary of the kinds of sources that are available on Hans Litten and his world.

The English-language reader looking for more information on Hans Litten will find one book: Irmgard Litten's 1940 memoir, published in Great Britain as *A Mother Fights Hitler* (London: Allen & Unwin, 1940) and in the United States as *Beyond Tears* (New York: Alliance, 1940). Although the German version of this book has been reprinted several times in East Germany—with conspicuous cuts to the sections dealing with Litten's politics (see Irmgard Litten, *Eine Mutter kämpft gegen Hitler* [Frankfurt/Main: Röderberg-Verlag, 1984])—the English version has been out of print since the 1940s. Readers can find it in many libraries and on the secondhand market. In addition, Arthur Marwick's biography, *Clifford Allen: The Open Conspirator* (Edinburgh: Oliver & Boyd, 1964), contains a chapter on Allen's campaign for Litten, and Martin Gilbert's *Plough My Own Furrow: The Story of Lord Allen of Hurtwood as Told through His Writings and Correspondence* (London: Longmans, Green, 1965), reprints the relevant documents from the Allen papers. Stefanie Schüler-Springorum's article "Hans Litten 1903–2003: The Public Use of a Biography" is in the *Leo Baeck Institute Yearbook*, 2003, 205–19.

The English-language reader is in a much better position when it comes to finding more information on the political and social context in which Litten lived and worked. The literature on politics in Weimar and the rise of the Nazis is, of course, vast. Two comparatively recent and particularly thought-provoking studies are Henry Ashby Turner's *Hitler's Thirty Days to Power: January 1933*, (Reading, Mass.: Addison-Wesley, 1996), and Peter Fritzsche's *Germans into Nazis* (Cambridge, Mass.: Harvard University Press, 1998); a fine, more comprehensive account of the rise of the Nazis is Richard J. Evans's *The Coming of the Third Reich* (New York: Penguin, 2004). Two books deal directly with the kind of political violence that gave rise to Litten's trials: Eve Rosenhaft, *Beating the Fascists? The German Communists and Political Violence 1929–1933* (Cambridge, UK: Cambridge University Press, 1983), and Pamela Swett, *Neighbors and Enemies: The Culture of Radicalism in Berlin, 1929–1933* (Cambridge, UK: Cambridge University Press, 2004).

The German-language reader is naturally in a better position. Max Fürst's wonderful memoirs were recently reprinted as a one-volume paperback: Max Fürst, *Gefilte Fisch und wie es weiterging* (Munich: DTV, 2004). In addition there is Carlheinz von Brück's *Ein Mann, der Hitler in die Enge trieb. Hans Littens Kampf gegen den Faschismus. Ein Dokumentarbericht* (East Berlin: Union Verlag, 1975), which is marred by the propagandistic constraints of the GDR but still contains useful information. Knut Bergbauer and Stefanie Schüler-Springorum have done extensive research on the Black Mob for *"Wir sind jung, die Welt ist offen." Eine jüdische Jugendgruppe im 20. Jahrhundert* (Berlin: Gedenk- und Bildungsstätte, Haus der Wannsee Konferenz, 2002), and Schüler-Springorum is also the author of a fine study of the Königsberg Jewish community: *Die Jüdische Minderheit in Königsberg, 1871–1945* (Göttingen: Vandenhoeck & Ruprecht, 1996). Bergbauer, Schüler-Springorum, and Sabine Fröhlich are now the authors of a biography of Hans Litten published in German early in 2008, after my own book had gone into production; unfortunately I have not been able to take account of it here.

As a historical source, Rudolf Diels's memoir, *Lucifer ante Portas. Zwischen Severing und Heydrich* (Zürich: Interverlag A.G., 1949), raises all the usual problems of mendacity and apologetics but possesses the unusual benefits of stylistic brilliance and, in places, penetrating insight. Given Diels's central importance to Hans Litten's story, the memoir is a vital source, though it should certainly be read alongside the work of critical historians on the early Gestapo, such as Christoph

Graf's fine *Politische Polizei zwischen Demokratie und Diktatur. Die Entwicklung der preußischen Politischen Polizei vom Staatsschutzorgan der Weimarer Republik zum Geheimen Staatspolizeiamt des Dritten Reiches* (Berlin: Colloquium Verlag, 1983). Essential information on the legal profession as Litten knew it, with some discussion of his work, comes in two books: Stefan König, *Vom Dienst am Recht. Rechtsanwälte als Strafverteidiger im Nationalsozialismus* (Berlin: Walter de Gruyter, 1987), and Tilmann Krach, *Jüdische Rechtsanwälte in Preußen. Über die Bedeutung der freien Advokatur und ihre Zerstörung durch den Nationalsozialismus* (Munich: C. H. Beck, 1991).

Of course, to a great extent the story of Litten's legal career is contained, in many installments, in the daily press of the late 1920s and early 1930s. The challenge here for the researcher is that, given the nature of Litten's cases, it was generally the papers at the extreme ends of the spectrum—the Communist *Rote Fahne* (*Red Flag*) and *Welt am Abend* (*World in the Evening*), the Nazi *Angriff* (*Attack*)—that paid the closest attention, with inevitable propagandistic distortions. The coverage in the great liberal papers *Berliner Tageblatt* (*Berlin Daily News*) and *Vossische Zeitung* (*Voss's News*) was more sporadic, though unfailingly of higher quality.

Documents of importance for Hans Litten's story are scattered among a wide range of archives. The most important depositories include the following:

- Bibliothek Germanica Judaica, Köln: This is one of the few libraries with holdings of the various publications of the Comrades youth group.
- Bundesarchiv Berlin-Lichterfelde (BA-BL): This holds Hans Litten's personal papers (NY 4011); his Prussian Justice Ministry file (R. 22/66804), along with the files of other important people in this story, such as Ludwig Barbasch (R. 22/50743) and Otto Conrady (R. 22/53692); the documents from the arrest of Max and Margot Fürst (NJ 9782); the documents concerning Hitler's response to Lord Allen's petition (R. 43/II, Nr. 1541); the documents on the abuse of Litten at Sonnenburg and Esterwegen (NJ 14220, Bd. 2, and R. 3001/III w 282–284/38g); and the official documents on Litten's death (R.3001/III g 10 b 121/38).

Much important information is in the documents of the Reichssicherheitshauptamt (R 58).

- Deutsches Literatur Archiv, Marbach: This holds the papers of Max and Margot Fürst (although many important items, such as Margot's prison letters, remain in the private collection of Mrs. Birute Stern).
- Geheimes Staatsarchiv Preußischer Kulturbesitz, Berlin-Dahlem (GStA): The extremely rich collections of the Prussian Justice Ministry, Rep. 84a, are essential for any research on the justice system in Weimar. Of special importance for Hans Litten's story are the records of the Nazi expulsion of prosecutors, judges, and lawyers from the courts in 1933 (84a/20361–63); the records of the investigation of Hitler for perjury in 1931 (Rep 84a/53873); the records of the case against Ernst Friedrich (Rep 84a/53292); and the records of the Röntgen Street case (84a/51724). Rep. 90 Annex P holds important Gestapo records, some touching on Litten, including the "Schutzhaft" volumes, 64–66, and see also volumes 110, 137, and 138. Finally, the Prussian Interior Ministry records in Rep. 77 offer much important context; see especially R.77 Tit. 4043 Nr. 20, "Ausnahmegerichte," Rep. 77 Tit. 4043 Nr. 386, "Rote Hilfe," Rep. 77 Tit. 4043 Nr. 121, "Politische Ausschreitungen und Zusammenstöße."
- Institut für die Geschichte der deutschen Juden, Hamburg: This holds the research materials of Kurt Neheimer, an East German researcher who in the 1980s did exhaustive work on a biography of Hans Litten which he did not live to complete.
- Institut für Zeitgeschichte, Munich (IfZ): The IfZ has a file of newspaper clippings on Hans Litten (IfZ ZA Litten, Hans), along with a rich collection of documents on all aspects of National Socialist Germany, including records from the Nuremberg Trials and records from the Prussian and Reich Interior Ministries that supply important context for much of Litten's story.
- Landesarchiv Berlin (LAB): The main depository of documents on Hans Litten's trials is found in the collection A Rep. 358, the records of the Berlin prosecutors' office. Among them are Felseneck (Nr. 37) and several dealing with fallout from Felseneck (Nr. 1510, Nr. 1710, Nr. 2049, and Nr. 1285); the Eden Dance Palace

(Nr. 98); the Hitler perjury case (Nr. 515); libel of Litten in the *Attack* (Nr. 1175); one of the cases against Ernst Friedrich (Nr. 2093); and Richard Street (Nr. 8051–74). The Landesarchiv also has records of the Berlin police, including some dealing with the May Day 1929 shootings and Litten's role in the aftermath (A Pr. Br. Rep. 030 Nr. 21731-2); records from the Spandau prison, including some dealing with Litten's 1933 suicide attempt (A Rep. 362 Nr. 88); and documents from the municipal administration of postwar East Berlin dealing with the applications by Irmgard Litten and Margot Litten (Hans's sister-in-law) for compensation as "victims of fascism" (C Rep 118-01 Nr. A 22987 and C Rep 118-01 Nr. A 13644).

- Leo Baeck Institute, New York (LBI): In the "Hans Litten Collection," there are copies of Irmgard Litten's correspondence with Nazi authorities (AR 5112), in large part from the Wiener Library (see below). The LBI's excellent memoir collection includes the unpublished memoirs of Ludwig Bendix, Kurt Sabatzky, and A. E. Laurence (ME 40, ME 870, and ME 541).

- National Archives and Record Administration, College Park, Maryland (NARA): The "Captured German Documents" collection is an invaluable resource for researchers on this side of the Atlantic. Of particular relevance for Hans Litten are the SA and SS personal files, which include files for Storm 33's Fritz "Red" Hahn (RG 242 BDC SA Collections, P-Akten, Roll Number A 3341-SA-D098); Esterwegen commander Heinrich Remmert (RG 242 BDC SS Officers Roll A 3343 SSO-023B); Dachau commander Hans Loritz (RG 242 BDC SS Officers Roll Number A 3343 SSO-278 A); Dachau prisoners' camp commander Hermann Baranowski (RG 242 BDC SS Officers Roll Number A 3343 SSO-032); Lichtenburg commander Otto Reich (RG 242 BDC SS Officers Roll Number A 3343 SSO 016B); and Gestapo chief Rudolf Diels (RG 242 BDC SS Officers Roll Number A 3343 SSO 149).

- Niedersächsisches Landesarchiv, Hauptstaatsarchiv Hannover (NHH): This holds the personal papers of Rudolf Diels (VVP 46) as well as documents pertaining to Diels's time as local governor in Hannover (NHH NDS 100 [01] Acc. 134/97).

- Politisches Archiv des Auswärtigen Amts (PA): The Foreign Office "Referat Deutschland" collection contains important documents about efforts from Great Britain to free Hans Litten and revealing what German authorities, such as Ambassador Hoesch, Interior Minister Frick, and Justice Minister Gürtner, thought of Litten's imprisonment and the campaign for his release. See especially R. 99480–82 volumes 3–5, and R. 99574.
- Stiftung Neue Synagogue Berlin/Centrum Judaicum: This holds the most extensive collection of documents pertaining to the "Comrades" and the "Black Mob." See especially CJA 1 75C Wa 1 Nr. 1 and CJA 1 75C Wa 1 Nr. 10.
- Wiener Library/Institute of Contemporary History, London (WL): The collection WL Archive 572, "Hans Litten: Correspondence, 1933–1938," contains much of Irmgard Litten's correspondence from the 1930s, both private and with Nazi authorities.

Throughout this book, all translations from German sources are my own unless otherwise noted.

Acknowledgments

Hans Litten's trail has led me to a lot of places tourists in Germany do not usually bother with, and some locals must have wondered why the strange man with the camera was loitering outside of Zola Steet 1a (the former Koblank Street 1a, the Litten-Fürst apartment), or on Hebbel Street, where Storm 33 had its tavern. Röntgen Street looks very much as it did in the 1930s, as, in its way, does Felseneck; there is a garden colony there still, under a different name, but on a street now named in honor of the murdered Fritz Klemke. From there, it is only a short walk to Hans's grave in the Pankow III Municipal Cemetery. A long drive with a defective map brought me to Prettin and what used to be the Lichtenburg concentration camp; again, many people in small Brandenburg and Saxon towns were extraordinarily patient and helpful when the lost American stopped to ask for directions and found, once again, he was heading diametrically in the wrong direction. There is nothing left now of the building in which Litten & Barbasch had their offices. Instead, there is a Dunkin' Donuts, with an Internet café on the second floor. While you surf the Web and commune with Hans's ghost, you can look out the large windows to the south and see into Hans Litten Street, toward the superior court and the Hans Litten House. It might make you want to write a book.

Hans Litten's trail has also led me to a very large number of archives and libraries. I would like to thank the following institutions and individuals: Archiv und Bibliothek der KZ-Gedenkstätte Dachau (Herr Albert Knoll); Bibliothek Germanica Judaica, Köln (Frau Dr. Annette Haller); Brandenburgisches Landeshauptstaatsarchiv, Bornim;

Bundesarchiv Berlin-Lichterfelde (Herr Andreas Grunwald and Herr Torsten Zarwel); Deutsches Literatur Archiv, Marbach (Herr Dr. Jochen Meyer); Geheimes Staatsarchiv Preußischer Kulturbesitz, Berlin-Dahlem (Herr Thomas Binder); Institut für die Geschichte der deutschen Juden, Hamburg (Frau Dr. Stefanie Schüler-Springorum); Institut für Zeitgeschichte, Munich; Landesarchiv Berlin (Frau Bianca Welzing); Leo Baeck Institute, New York; National Archives and Record Administration, College Park, Maryland; the New York Public Library; Niedersächsisches Landesarchiv Hauptstaatsarchiv Hannover (Frau Dr. Claudia Kauertz); Politisches Archiv des Auswärtigen Amts (Herr Dr. Gerhard Keiper); Staatsbibliothek zu Berlin; Stiftung Neue Synagogue Berlin/Centrum Judaicum; Wiener Library/Institute of Contemporary History, London. At my home base, Mr. Norman Clarius, who handles interlibrary loans for the Hunter College Library, performed some miraculous feats of source location.

Frau Dr. Stefanie Schüler-Springorum, the director of the Institut für die Geschichte der deutschen Juden in Hamburg, was especially generous in giving me access to the Neheimer papers. A talented former student, Ms. Rachel Barbour, got the Litten materials at the Wiener Library in London for me. Two German lawyers who have also made names for themselves as writers of history, Dr. Tilmann Krach and Dr. Stefan König, generously made time to talk to me and to point me in the direction of critical sources.

I am very grateful for financial assistance for this research from the PSC-CUNY program and from the German Academic Exchange Service.

One of the great pleasures of working on Hans Litten has been the chance to meet people who in various ways have been a part of his story. Mrs. Birute Stern, the daughter of Max and Margot Fürst, graciously gave me hours of her time for an interview while she was in the last stages of clearing out her parents' Stuttgart apartment and moving everything to Jerusalem. Mrs. Stern was also most generous in supplying me with Max and Margot's prison letters and remarkable recordings of her parents reading Max's two volumes of memoirs. Frau Patricia Litten, daughter of Rainer and niece of Hans, agreed to speak to me on an evening in which she had been up for several days traveling, and she too supplied me with a rich stock of family papers and photographs. Herr Gerhard Jungfer, one of the leading figures in the revival of the German bar's historical knowledge, not only lent me his own collection of papers on Hans Litten, but also arranged for me to talk about Litten at one of his "Evenings in the Library" in Berlin in 2006.

Audiences and conference participants at Gerhard's "Evening," at the 2005 conference on "Modern Histories of Crime and Punishment" at the Baldy Center at the University of Buffalo Law School, and at the University of Saskatchewan, where I had the privilege of giving the 2007 Bilson Lecture on Hans Litten, at the CUNY Graduate Center, and the History Department of Hunter College have allowed me to try out ideas and given much needed feedback. Thanks are due to Markus Dubber, Lindsay Farmer, Chris Kent, and my old friend Dean McNeill. My colleagues at Hunter College and students in several of my classes on twentieth-century Germany and the Third Reich have listened with admirable patience to my tales of Hans Litten, and often enough contributed their own penetrating questions.

Another old friend, Robert Girvan, turned his deep learning and probing lawyer's mind to a critique of the initial manuscript, from which the book emerged drastically improved. I am grateful as well for the sensitive comments of Oxford University Press's two readers.

Huge thanks are due to my agent, Scott Mendel, and my editor at Oxford University Press, Tim Bent. Scott believed in the project from the beginning and stuck with it through thick and thin. Tim's superb, creative editing has sharpened the book and helped me find what I was really trying to say about Litten.

Needless to say, after so much support and generosity, the errors and shortcomings that remain in this book can only be my fault.

Over the past few years my wife, Corinna, has occasionally referred to Hans Litten as "the third person in our marriage." I could only respond that, after the Fürsts and the Reuters, this would make us at least the third couple of which this was true. With the book now completed, I hope the dedication offers some recompense for her love and patience.

New York, January 2008

Notes

PROLOGUE

1. Hans Litten, *Beweisantrag*, April 17, 1931, in LAB A Rep 358-02 Nr. 98, *Stief und Genossen*, Bd. 4, Bl. 41.

2. Hans Litten to his parents, May 7, 1931, in BA-BL NY 4011, *Nachlaß Hans Litten*, Bd. 4, Bl. 3.

3. Adolf Hitler, *Mein Kampf*, trans. Ralph Manheim (Boston: Houghton Mifflin, 1999), 215–16.

4. Max Fürst, *Gefilte Fisch und wie es weiterging* (Munich: DTV, 2004), 261–62, 650; Marion Gräfin Dönhoff, "Der vergessene Opfergang: Eine Mutter kämpfte gegen Hitler," *Die Zeit*, December 5, 1986; Kurt Hiller, in the *Sozialistische Warte*, July 15, 1938, in BA-BL NY 4011, *Nachlaß Hans Litten*, Bd. 8 *Artikel über Hans Litten 1937–1951*, Bl. 40; A. E. Laurence (Alfred Lomnitz) to Oscar Winter, February 21, 1979, in DA 1066, *Jüdische Häftlinge; Winterberger, Oscar, Berichte, Verschiedene*.

5. Fürst, *Gefilte Fisch*, 486; Birute Stern, interview with the author, Stuttgart, March 24, 2005; Rudolf Olden, "Hans Litten," in Irmgard Litten, *Eine Mutter kämpft gegen Hitler* (Frankfurt/Main: Röderberg-Verlag, 1984), 5, 6.

6. Max Fürst to Irmgard Litten, n.d. (Spring/Summer 1939), in Institut für die Geschichte der deutschen Juden, *Nachlaß Neheimer*, Band I, *Quellen*; Fürst, *Gefilte Fisch*, 218–19, 288.

7. Fürst, *Gefilte Fisch*, 387; Eva Eichelbaum to Rüdiger Scheidges, March 1992, private collection of Gerhard Jungfer.

8. Patricia Litten, interview with the author, Nuremberg, June 26, 2006.

1. Irmgard Litten, *Beyond Tears* (New York: Alliance, 1940), 3–4; Richard Wetzell, *Inventing the Criminal: A History of German Criminology 1880–1945* (Chapel Hill: University of North Carolina Press, 2000).
2. Hans Litten to Irmgard Litten, September 18, 1935, in BA-BL NY 4011, *Nachlaß Hans Litten, Bd. 3 Korrespondenz—Ausgehende*, Bl. 79.
3. I. Litten, *Beyond Tears*, 3; "Litten: Familiäre Daten," in Institut für die Geschichte der deutschen Juden, *Nachlaß Neheimer*, Band I, *Quellen*.
4. Max Fürst, *Gefilte Fisch und wie es weiterging* (Munich: DTV, 2004), 608; Amos Elon, *The Pity of It All: A History of Jews in Germany, 1743–1933* (New York: Metropolitan Books, 2002), 2; Professoren und Gelehrte an der Martin-Luther-Universität Halle, http://www.catalogus-professorum-halensis.de/littenfritz.html, last visited February 14, 2005; "Litten: Familiäre Daten," in Institut für die Geschichte der deutschen Juden, *Nachlaß Neheimer*, Band I, *Quellen*.
5. I. Litten, *Beyond Tears*, 4, 7, 9.
6. Fritz Litten to Adolf Hitler, July 24, 1935, in LBI AR 5112, *Hans Litten Collection*, 1/2, 147; Irmgard Litten to Hindenburg, March 5, 1934, in LBI AR 5112, *Hans Litten Collection*, 1/2, 37–38; Max Fürst, *Gefilte Fisch*, 262–64, 608; I. Litten, *Beyond Tears*, 10; Kurt Sabatzky, *Meine Erinnerungen an den Nationalsozialismus*, unpublished memoir, LBI Memoir Collection, ME 541, 11.
7. Max Fürst, *Gefilte Fisch*, 264–65.
8. I. Litten, *Beyond Tears*, 5; "Litten: Familiäre Daten," in Institut für die Geschichte der deutschen Juden, *Nachlaß Neheimer*, Band I, *Quellen*; Kurt Neheimer, *Hans Litten. Anwalt und Kläger*, unpublished manuscript, in Institut für die Geschichte der deutschen Juden, *Nachlaß Neheimer*, 42, 59.
9. Fragebogen, April 7, 1951, in LAB C Rep 118-01, Nr. A 22987, *Irmgard Litten: Antrag als Annerkennung als Opfer des Faschismus*, Bl. 1–3; Max Fürst, *Gefilte Fisch*, 263.
10. I. Litten, *Beyond Tears*, 4–5; Patricia Litten, interview with the author, Nuremberg, June 26, 2006; poems in the private collection of Patricia Litten; Neheimer, *Hans Litten*, 53, 76, 85; Hans Litten to Irmgard Litten, June 22, 1937, in BA-BL NY 4011, *Nachlaß Hans Litten, Bd. 3 Korrespondenz—Ausgehende*, Bl. 145.
11. I. Litten, *Beyond Tears*, 4–5; Irmgard Litten, "Mothers and Children," *United Nations News* 1, no. 1 (1946): 21–22, in BA-BL NY 4011, *Nachlaß Hans Litten*, Bd. 8, *Artikel über Hans Litten 1937–1951*, Bl. 54.
12. Fritz Stern, *Five Germanys I Have Known* (New York: Farrar, Straus and Giroux, 2006), 17; Max Fürst, *Gefilte Fisch*, 263.
13. Irmgard Litten to Paul von Hindenburg, March 5, 1934, in LBI AR 5112, *Hans Litten Collection*, Folder 1/2, 38; I. Litten, *Beyond Tears*, 5, 6.

14. Rudolf Olden, "Hans Litten," in Irmgard Litten, *Eine Mutter kämpft gegen Hitler* (Frankfurt/Main: Röderberg-Verlag, 1984), 15; Max Fürst, *Gefilte Fisch*, 609; Christopher Clark, *Iron Kingdom: The Rise and Downfall of Prussia, 1600–1947* (Cambridge, Mass.: Harvard University Press, 2006); Dietrich Orlow, *Weimar Prussia 1918–1925: The Unlikely Rock of Democracy* (Pittsburgh: University of Pittsburgh Press, 1986); Joachim Fest, *Begegnungen. Über nahe und ferne Freunde* (Reinbek bei Hamburg: Rowohlt Taschenbuch Verlag, 2006), 180.

15. I. Litten, *Beyond Tears*, 6; BA-BL NY 4011, *Nachlaß Hans Litten*, Bd. 1, *Gedichte von Hans Litten (aus seiner Kinderzeit)*.

16. Max Fürst, *Gefilte Fisch*, 266; I. Litten, *Eine Mutter kämpft*, 27–28.

17. Institut für die Geschichte der deutschen Juden, *Nachlaß Neheimer*, Band I, *Quellen*; Irmgard Litten to Hans Litten, February 19, 1934, in WL Archive 572, *Hans Litten: Correspondence, 1933–1938*, Reel MF Doc 54/28; photograph from the private collection of Patricia Litten; Fritz Litten to Adolf Hitler, July 24, 1935, in LBI AR 5112, *Hans Litten Collection*, 1/2, 146; I. Litten, *Beyond Tears*, 6–7.

18. Stern, *Five Germanys*, 28; Stefan Zweig, *Die Welt von Gestern. Erinnerungen eines Europäers* (Frankfurt/Main: S. Fischer Verlag, 2000).

19. Neheimer, *Hans Litten*, 94; Hans Litten to Fritz Litten, June 17, 1931, BA-BL NY 4011, *Nachlaß Hans Litten*, Bd. 4, Bl. 4; Max Fürst, *Gefilte Fisch*, 270.

20. Max Fürst, *Gefilte Fisch*, 610, 265; Heinz Wolfgang Litten, *Die Änderung des Bühnenwerkes durch die Aufführung. Eine theaterrechtliche Studie* (Königsberg: Gräfe & Unzer, 1927); Patricia Litten, interview with the author, Nuremberg, June 26, 2006.

21. Stern, *Five Germanys*, 24; I. Litten, *Beyond Tears*, 7; Max Fürst, *Gefilte Fisch*, 264, 611; "Referendarzeit," in BA-BL R. 22/66804, *Reichsjustizministerium Personalakten*, Hans-Joachim Litten, Bl. 2; Gerhard Jungfer, "Hans Litten zum 100. Geburtstag," in *BRAK Mitteilungen*, 4/2003, 161ff., 161–162.

22. Irmgard Litten to Joachim von Ribbentrop, January 2, 1936, in WL Archive 572, *Hans Litten: Correspondence, 1933–1938*, Reel MF Doc 54/29; Max Fürst, *Gefilte Fisch*, 611.

23. Gisela Konopka, *Courage and Love* (Edina, Minn.: Burgess, 1988), 40–41; Wolfgang Roth, *Haengt alles von der Beleuchtung ab. (Eine erzaehlte wahre Geschichte)*, unpublished memoir, LBI Memoir Collection, ME 315, film MM 65, 8.

24. Elon, *The Pity of It All*, 242; Erwin Lichtenstein, *Bericht an meine Familie. Ein Leben zwischen Danzig und Israel* (Darmstadt: Hermann Luchterhand Verlag, 1985), 26–28.

25. Max Fürst, *Gefilte Fisch*, 202–3; Lichtenstein, *Bericht*, 31.

26. Max Fürst, *Gefilte Fisch*, 203, 285–86; Stefanie Schüler-Springorum, "Hans Litten 1903–2003: The Public Use of a Biography," *Leo Baeck Institute Yearbook*, 2003, 205–19, 217.

27. Max Fürst, "Aus Königsberg," *Deutsch-Jüdischer Wanderbund Kameraden Gau Nordost*, Nr. 2, November 1923; Max Fürst, *Gefilte Fisch*, 276.

28. Max Fürst, *Gefilte Fisch*, 280–82; Knut Bergbauer and Stefanie Schüler-Springorum, *"Wir sind jung, die Welt ist offen." Eine jüdische Jugendgruppe im 20. Jahrhundert* (Berlin: Gedenk- und Bildungsstätte, Haus der Wannsee Konferenz, 2002), 24.

29. Max Fürst, *Gefilte Fisch*, 282, 364, 387; Bergbauer and Schüler-Springorum, *"Wir sind jung,"* 21, 23–24.

30. "Vom Schwarzen Haufen," February 1, 1926, *Kameraden, 17. Mitteilungsblatt* III 1926, in Institut für die Geschichte der deutschen Juden, *Nachlaß Neheimer*, Band IV: *Schriften, Aufsätze, Aufzeichnungen, Briefe*.

31. Protokoll der Führertagung vom 12. Juni 1927, in CJA 1 75C Wa 1 Nr. 1 Bl. 67–68, Bl. 75.

32. Bericht über den Bundestag des Schwarzen Haufens in Harzgerode, 31.7–2.8.1927, S. 12; in Sächsisches Staatsarchiv Leipzig, Polizeipräsidium, PP-V 4315, unpag., quoted in Bergbauer and Schüler-Springorum, *"Wir sind jung,"* 40; Max Fürst, *Gefilte Fisch*, 515.

33. Max Fürst to Irmgard Litten, n.d. (Spring/Summer 1939), in Institut für die Geschichte der deutschen Juden, *Nachlaß Neheimer*, Band I, Quellen.

34. Max Fürst, *Gefilte Fisch*, 438, 509. I am very grateful to Professor Joy Calico for information on the gifted but underappreciated Edmund Meisel.

35. Konopka, *Courage and Love*, 54; Margot Fürst to Max Fürst, January 16, 1934, private collection of Mrs. Birute Stern; Max Fürst, *Gefilte Fisch*, 464–65, 659.

36. Margot Fürst to Max Fürst, August 8, 1934, private collection of Mrs. Birute Stern.

37. Konopka, *Courage and Love*, 54; Alfons Rosenberg, quoted in Max Fürst, *Gefilte Fisch*, 462; Max Fürst, *Gefilte Fisch*, 468, 464.

38. Margot Fürst, interview with Kurt Neheimer, Stuttgart, February 12, 1985, in Institut für die Geschichte der deutschen Juden, *Nachlaß Neheimer*, Bd. III, *KZ-Haft/Erinnerungen*; Max Fürst, *Gefilte Fisch*, 470–71.

39. Max Fürst, *Gefilte Fisch*, 573–79, 471, 476–77; Hans Litten to Irmgard Litten, May 14, 1934, in BA-BL NY 4011, *Nachlaß Hans Litten, Bd. 3 Korrespondenz—Ausgehende*, Bl. 20.

40. Hans Litten to Margot Fürst, August 13, 1933, in BA-BL NY 4011, *Nachlaß Hans Litten, Bd. 3 Korrespondenz—Ausgehende*, Bl. 177.

41. Max Fürst, *Gefilte Fisch*, 542–43, 579; Hans Litten, letter of August 3, 1931, in BA-BL NY 4011, *Nachlaß Hans Litten, Bd. 4, Korrespondenz—Ausgehende. Briefe von Hans Litten an seine Eltern vor seiner Haftzeit 1931*, Bl. 2; I. Litten, *Beyond Tears*, 10; Max Fürst, "Hans Litten," in BA-BL NY 4011, *Nachlaß Hans Litten*, Bd. 8 *Artikel über Hans Litten 1937–1951*, Bl. 17–18.

42. Margot Fürst, interview with Kurt Neheimer.

43. I. Litten, *Beyond Tears*, 10; Max Fürst, *Gefilte Fisch*, 637; Margot Fürst, interview with Kurt Neheimer; Hans Litten to Irmgard Litten, December 20, 1936, in BA-BL NY 4011, *Nachlaß Hans Litten, Bd. 3 Korrespondenz— Ausgehende*, Bl. 127.

44. Max Fürst, *Gefilte Fisch*, 639–40.

45. Ibid., 476, 613–14, 651, 591–92.

46. Margot Fürst, interview with Kurt Neheimer; Max Fürst, *Gefilte Fisch*, 613, 12; Konopka, *Courage and Love*, 51, 54.

47. Neue Gesellschaft für Bildende Kunst e.V., *Walter Reuter. Berlin, Madrid, Mexiko. 60 Jahre Fotografie und Film 1930–1990* (Berlin: Argon Verlag, 1990), 25; Max Fürst, *Gefilte Fisch*, 641.

48. Margot Fürst, interview with Kurt Neheimer; Max Fürst, *Gefilte Fisch*, 642; Neue Gesellschaft, *Walter Reuter*, 26–27; "Aus der Geschichte des Mordsturms 33," *Arbeiter Illustrierte Zeitung*, Nr. 44 (1931).

49. Hans Litten to Irmgard Litten, January 23, 1934, in BA-BL NY 4011, *Nachlaß Hans Litten, Bd. 3 Korrespondenz—Ausgehende*, Bl. 10; Hans Litten to Sulamith Reuter, June 1935, in BA-BL NY 4011, *Nachlaß Hans Litten, Bd. 3 Korrespondenz—Ausgehende*, Bl. 10.

50. Rainer Maria Rilke, "Torso of an Archaic Apollo," in *Rilke: Selected Poems*, trans. C. F. MacIntyre (Berkeley: University of California Press, 1958), 93.

51. Hans Litten, "Jugend und moderne Kunst," reprinted in *Kameraden, Deutsch-Jüdischer Wanderbund, Bundesblatt*, Neue Folge: Drittes Heft, "Unser Bundestag 1925," 34; Lichtenstein, *Bericht*, 45.

52. I. Litten, *Beyond Tears*, 109–10, 35; Kurt Hiller, in *Sozialistische Warte*, July 15, 1938, in BA-BL NY 4011, *Nachlaß Hans Litten, Bd. 8 Artikel über Hans Litten 1937–1951*, Bl. 40; Alfred Dreifuss, "Wie Hans Litten starb," *Sonntag*, September 12, 1948, in BA-BL NY 4011, *Nachlaß Hans Litten, Bd. 8 Artikel über Hans Litten 1937–1951*, Bl. 23; Hans Litten to Sula-mith Reuter, October 23, 1936, in BA-BL NY 4011, *Nachlaß Hans Litten, Bd. 3 Korrespondenz—Ausgehende*, Bl. 233; Hans Litten to Irmgard Lit-ten, 29 November 1936, in BA-BL NY 4011, *Nachlaß Hans Litten, Bd. 3 Korrespondenz—Ausgehende*, Bl. 124.

53. "Hans Litten: Lebenschronik;" in Institut für die Geschichte der deut-schen Juden, *Nachlaß Neheimer, Bd. I, Quellen*; Max Fürst, *Gefilte Fisch*, 253; Sabatzky, *Erinnerungen*, 12.

54. Sabatzky, *Erinnerungen*, 12; Irmgard Litten, *Lebenslauf*, March 16, 1951, in LAB C Rep 118-01 Nr. A 22987, *Irmgard Litten: Antrag als Annerkennung als Opfer des Faschismus*, Bl. 5.

55. Max Fürst, *Gefilte Fisch*, 605; Hans Litten, "Was bedeutet uns der Tal-mud?" *Deutsch-jüdischer Wanderbund Kameraden, Gau-Nordost*, Nr. 4 (1924), quoted in Bergbauer and Schüler-Springorum, *"Wir sind jung,"* 19.

56. Max Fürst to Irmgard Litten, n.d. (Spring/Summer 1939), in Institut für die Geschichte der deutschen Juden, *Nachlaß Neheimer, Bd. I, Quellen*.

57. Max Fürst, *Gefilte Fisch*, 387; Eva Eichelbaum to Rüdiger Scheidges, March, 1992, private collection of Herr Gerhard Jungfer.

58. Max Fürst, *Gefilte Fisch*, 605; Max Fürst, obituary for Hans Litten, *Sozialistische Warte*, August 12, 1938, in BA-BL NY 4011, *Nachlaß Hans Litten*, Bd. 8 *Artikel über Hans Litten 1937–1951*, Bl. 17–18.

59. Hans Litten, "Zweite Jugendkulturtagung Östern 1924 in Hildesheim," *Kameraden Bundesblatt Neue Folge*, Heft 2 (September 1924): 51; Hans Litten, "Jugendbewegung und Politik," *Kameraden Bundesblatt Neue Folge*, Heft 3 (1925): 41; Hans Litten, "Gesetz," *Kameraden Gau Nordost*, Nr. 2 (November 1923).

60. Patricia Litten, interview with the author, Nuremberg, June 26, 2006; Neheimer, *Hans Litten*, 69; Johannes Blum, interview with the author, Nuremberg, June 26, 2006.

61. Der Schwarze Haufen, "Die Alten gegen die Jungen," *Schwarze Fahne*, Jahrgang 4, Nr. 39 (1928).

62. Hans Litten, "Neue Offensive gegen die Jugend. Das Schandurteil gegen Manasse Friedländer," *Schwarze Fahne*, Jahrgang 5, Nr. 21 (1929); Der Schwarze Haufen, "Die Alten gegen die Jungen;" Protokoll der Führertagung vom 12. Juni 1927, in CJA 1 75C Wa 1 Nr. 1, Bl. 62.

63. Hans Litten, "Einheitsfront der Alten," *Schwarze Fahne*, Jahrgang 5, Nr. 3 (1929).

64. Hans Litten, "Vaterland," *Kameraden Bundesblatt Neue Folge*, Heft 1 (June 1924): 9; Hans Litten to Julius Freund, May 5, 1927, in CJA 1 75C Wa 1 Nr. 10, Bl. 1061; Hans Litten, "Wie das Geschmeiß gegen Lampel 'kämpft,'" *Schwarze Fahne*, Jahrgang 5, Nr. 7 (1929).

65. Max Fürst, *Gefilte Fisch*, 498–99; Margot Fürst, interview with Kurt Neheimer.

66. Hans Litten to Sulamith Reuter, October 23, 1936, in BA-BL NY 4011, *Nachlaß Hans Litten, Bd. 3 Korrespondenz—Ausgehende*, Bl. 233; Margot Fürst, interview with Kurt Neheimer; Max Fürst, *Gefilte Fisch*, 611–12, 541.

67. Max Fürst, *Gefilte Fisch*, 289, 568; Margot Fürst, interview with Kurt Neheimer.

68. Margot Fürst, interview with Kurt Neheimer; Margot Fürst, interview broadcast on "Ich hänge tot an meinen Träumen," SFB, October 28, 1991, transcript from the private collection of Herr Gerhard Jungfer; Max Fürst, *Gefilte Fisch*, 309, 471, 566.

69. Margot Fürst told the book anecdote at a special law school course on the Felseneck trial organized by the Berlin lawyer and historian Stefan König in the late 1980s. Herr König relayed the story to me in a conversation in his office in Berlin, July 12, 2007. "Rigor" is from Margot Fürst, interview with Kurt Neheimer.

70. Hans Litten, "Jugendbewegung und Politik," 43; Protokoll der Führertagung vom 12. Juni 1927, in CJA 1 75C Wa 1 Nr. 1 Bl. 67.

71. I. Litten, *Eine Mutter Kämpft*, 34; Ludwig Barbasch to W. Arnold-Forster, September 7, 1937, in BA-BL NY 4011, *Nachlaß Hans Litten*, Bd. 8, *Artikel über Hans Litten 1937–1951*, Bl. 60; Rudolf Olden, obituary for Hans Litten, *Das Neue Tagebuch*, February 26, 1938, in BA-BL NY 4011, *Nachlaß Hans Litten*, Bd. 8, *Artikel über Hans Litten 1937–1951*, Bl. 35; Max Fürst, *Gefilte Fisch*, 505; Margot Fürst, quoted in "Ich hänge tot an meinen Träumen," transcript of broadcast on SFB, October 28, 1991, private collection of Herr Gerhard Jungfer; Margot Fürst, interview with Kurt Neheimer; "Betrifft: Versammlung der Deutschen Landsgruppe der I.J.V," September 14, 1932, in BA-BL R. 58/3305, Reichssicherheitshauptamt, Bl. 115–17.

72. Hans Litten, "Wie das Geschmeiß gegen Lampel 'kämpft.'"

73. Hans Litten, "Vom Berliner Führertreffen," *Kameraden Gau Nordost*, Nr. 5 (March 1924); Hans Litten, "Giftgas über Berlin. 1: Das Stück," *Schwarze Fahne*, Jahrgang 5, Nr. 12 (1929); Max Fürst, *Gefilte Fisch*, 657; Margot Fürst quoted in SFB, "Ich hänge tot an meinen Träumen."

74. Hans Litten, "Jugendbewegung und Politik," *Kameraden Bundesblatt Neue Folge*, Drittes Heft, "Unser Bundestag 1925," 41–42; Hans Litten, "Jugend und moderne Kunst," 33; Max Fürst, *Gefilte Fisch*, 612.

75. Hans Litten, "Kunst," in DA 993, *Jüdische Häftlinge. Litten, Hans. Dokumente*; Ludwig Barbasch to W. Arnold-Forster, September 7, 1937, in BA-BL NY 4011, *Nachlaß Hans Litten*, Bd. 8, *Artikel über Hans Litten 1937–1951*, Bl. 59; Hans Litten, "Zweite Jugendkulturtagung Östern 1924 in Hildesheim," 50–51; Hans Litten, "Jugend und moderne Kunst," 33–34.

76. Ernest R. Kunney to Paula (sic) Fürst, January 22, 1993, in Deutsches Literatur Archiv Marbach, *Nachlaß Fürst*; Konopka, *Courage and Love*, 51–52.

77. Report on Referendariat, in BA-BL R. 22/66804, *Reichsjustizministerium Personalakten, Hans-Joachim Litten*, Bl. 2.

78. Götz Berger, interview with Kurt Neheimer, February 4, 1986, in Institut für die Geschichte der deutschen Juden, *Nachlaß Neheimer*, Band III, *KZ-Haft/Erinnerungen*.

79. Max Fürst, *Gefilte Fisch*, 472–73, 611; Margot Fürst, interview with Kurt Neheimer; Hans Litten, "Wie das Geschmeiß gegen Lampel 'kämpft.'"

80. Max Fürst, *Gefilte Fisch*, 474; Report on Referendariat, in BA-BL R. 22/66804, *Reichsjustizministerium Personalakten, Hans-Joachim Litten*, Bl. 2.

81. I. Litten, *Beyond Tears*, 8; recollection of Clara Kückert, Hans Litten: Lebenskronik, in Institut für die Geschichte der deutschen Juden, *Nachlaß Neheimer*, Bd. I, *Quellen*; Ludwig Barbasch to W. Arnold-Forster, September 7, 1937, in BA-BL NY 4011, *Nachlaß Hans Litten*, Bd. 8, *Artikel über Hans Litten 1937–1951*, Bl. 59.

82. Note on Barbasch, in Institut für die Geschichte der deutschen Juden, *Nachlaß Neheimer*, Band III, *KZ-Haft/Erinnerungen*; Report of

Kammergericht President, April 22, 1919, in BA-BL R. 22/50743, *Reichsjustizministerium Personalakten: Dr. Ludwig Barbasch*, Bl. 4; Barbasch, *Antrag*, April 10, 1933, in BA-BL R. 22/50743, *Reichsjustizministerium Personalakten: Dr. Ludwig Barbasch*, Bl. 27–28; Max Fürst, *Gefilte Fisch*, 563–64.

83. Report of Kammergericht President, April 22, 1919, in BA-BL R. 22/50743, *Reichsjustizministerium Personalakten: Dr. Ludwig Barbasch*, Bl. 4–5; Barbasch to JM, December 23, 1921, in BA-BL R. 22/50743, *Reichsjustizministerium Personalakten: Dr. Ludwig Barbasch*, Bl. 22; Max Fürst, *Gefilte Fisch*, 564.

84. Ludwig Barbasch to W. Arnold-Forster, September 7, 1937, in BA-BL NY 4011, *Nachlaß Hans Litten*, Bd. 8, *Artikel über Hans Litten 1937–1951*, Bl. 59.

85. Ibid.; Max Fürst, *Gefilte Fisch*, 564.

86. Max Fürst, *Gefilte Fisch*, 564–66.

87. Ibid., 591, 632–33.

88. Margot Fürst, interview with Kurt Neheimer; Max Fürst, *Gefilte Fisch*, 649–50; Hans Litten to Fritz Litten, June 17, 1931, in BA-BL NY 4011, *Nachlaß Hans Litten*, Bd. 4, *Korrespondenz—Ausgehende. Briefe von Hans Litten an seine Eltern vor seiner Haftzeit 1931*, Bl. 5; I. Litten, *Beyond Tears*, 75.

89. Litten to his parents, April 19, 1931, in BA-BL NY 4011, *Nachlaß Hans Litten*, Bd. 4, *Korrespondenz—Ausgehende. Briefe von Hans Litten an seine Eltern vor seiner Haftzeit 1931*, Bl. 2; Litten to the Jury Court LG III, February 4, 1932, in LAB A Rep. 358-02 Nr. 98, *Stief und Genossen*, Bd. 5, Bl. 175; Litten, Letter of August 3, 1931, in BA-BL NY 4011, *Nachlaß Hans Litten*, Bd. 4, *Korrespondenz—Ausgehende. Briefe von Hans Litten an seine Eltern vor seiner Haftzeit 1931*, Bl. 6.

90. Heinz-Jürgen Schneider, Erika Schwarz, and Josef Schwarz, *Die Rechtsanwälte der Roten Hilfe Deutschlands. Politische Strafverteidiger in der Weimarer Republik. Geschichte und Biografien* (Bonn: Pahl-Rugenstein Verlag Nachfolger, 2002), 16.

91. Ibid.; Nachrichtensamelstelle, Reichsministerium des Innern, December 31, 1931, in BA-BL R. 58/507, *Rote Hilfe, Unterstützung durch Rechtsanwälte 1931–1935*, Bl. 2; "What Was the Exchange Rate Then?" http://eh.net/hmit/exchangerates/, last visited November 20, 2006; "Auszug aus einer Liste von für die Rote Hilfe tätigen Rechtsanwälten", in BA-BL R. 22/66804, *Reichsjustizministerium Personalakten, Hans-Joachim Litten*, Bl. 90; "Auszug aus einer Liste von für die Rote Hilfe tätigen Rechtsanwälten," in GStA Rep. 84a/20363, *Durchführung des Berufsbeamtengesetzes bezgl. Rechtsanwälte und Notare 1933*, Bl. 30–32; also in BA-BL R. 22/50743, *Reichsjustizministerium Personalakten: Dr. Ludwig Barbasch*, Bl. 30, and in "Geleistete Zahlungen und eingegangene Rechnungen der Rechtsanwälte im Jahre 1931," in GStA Rep.77 Tit. 4043 Nr. 386, "Rote Hilfe," Bl. 89–90.

92. Bernhard Behnke, interview with Kurt Neheimer, Potsdam, summer 1984 and December 31, 1985, in Institut für die Geschichte der deutschen Juden, *Nachlaß Neheimer*, Band III, KZ-Haft/Erinnerungen.

93. Max Fürst, *Gefilte Fisch*, 628–29; Kurt Neheimer, "Hans Litten. Lebenschronik," in Institut für die Geschichte der deutschen Juden, *Nachlaß Neheimer*, Bd. I, *Quellen*; *Schwarze Fahne*, Bd. 4 1928, Nr. 27; "Noske von einem deutschen Gericht beschimpft!" *Schwarze Fahne*, Bd. 4 1928, Nr. 29; GStA Rep. 84a/53292, *Strafsache gegen Friedrich (Beleidigung des Oberpräsidenten Noske)*, Bl. 2.

94. Litten to the Court, February 18, 1929, in GStA Rep. 84a/53292, *Strafsache gegen Friedrich (Beleidigung des Oberpräsidenten Noske)*, Bl. 10, Bl. 13. Bl. 14, Bl. 16.

95. Erich Frey, *Ich beantrage Freispruch* (Hamburg: Blüchert Verlag, 1959), 352; Olden, "Hans Litten," 6.

96. Olden, "Hans Litten," 6–7, 15.

97. "Wahrheitsbeweis gegen Noske Verboten," *Die Rote Fahne*, March 15, 1929; "Prozess Bericht," *Schwarze Fahne*, Bd. 5 1929 Nr. 14; *Vorstrafen*, Ernst Friedrich, in LAB A Rep. 358-01 Nr. 2093, *Strafsache gegen Friedrich wegen Beleidigung*, Bl. 97; Judgment, March 14, 1929, in GStA Rep. 84a/53292, *Strafsache gegen Friedrich (Beleidigung des Oberpräsidenten Noske)*, Bl. 22–24.

98. GSA KG to JM, April 17, 1929, in GStA Rep. 84a/53292, *Strafsache gegen Friedrich (Beleidigung des Oberpräsidenten Noske)*, Bl. 19–20; GSA KG to JM, July 12, 1929, in GStA Rep. 84a/53292, *Strafsache gegen Friedrich (Beleidigung des Oberpräsidenten Noske)*, Bl. 25; Vermerk, March 26, 1929, in GStA Rep. 84a/53292, *Strafsache gegen Friedrich (Beleidigung des Oberpräsidenten Noske)*, Bl. 17; GSA KG to EG der Anwaltskammer, February 23, 1932, in BA-BL R. 22/66804, *Reichsjustizministerium Personalakten, Hans-Joachim Litten*, Bl. 14.

99. Ruth Glatzer, *Berlin zur Weimarer Zeit. Panorama einer Metropole* (Berlin: Siedler Verlag, 2000), 375.

100. Reich Commissar for Public Order to RIM, April 23, 1929, in LAB A. Pr. Br. Rep. 030 Nr. 21732, *Rundschreiben, Richtlinien und Aufrufe des ZK der KPD... und des Maikommittees in Berlin zum 1. Mai 1929*, Bl. 218; Lagebericht Stuttgart Nr. W.8 v. 17.4.29, in LAB A. Pr. Br. Rep. 030 Nr. 21732, *Rundschreiben, Richtlinien und Aufrufe des ZK der KPD... und des Maikommittees in Berlin zum 1. Mai 1929*, Bl. 219.

101. KPD Memo of March 30, 1929, in LAB A. Pr. Br. Rep. 030 Nr. 21732, *Rundschreiben, Richtlinien und Aufrufe des ZK der KPD... und des Maikommittees in Berlin zum 1. Mai 1929*, Bl. 11–12; Reichskommissar für Überwachung der öffentlichen Ordnung an die Nachrichtenstellen der Länder, April 10, 1929, in LAB A. Pr. Br. Rep. 030 Nr. 21732, *Rundschreiben, Richtlinien und Aufrufe des ZK der KPD... und des Maikommittees in Berlin zum 1. Mai 1929*, Bl. 179.

102. *Berlin am Morgen*, March 24, 1929; *Berlin am Morgen*, April 21, 1929; Paul Fröhlich, *Der Berliner Blut-Mai* (Berlin: Junius-Verlag, 1929), 4; Karl Zörgiebel to the Amtsgericht (Schöffengericht) Köpenick, February 1930, in LAB A Pr. Br. Rep. 030 Nr. 21731, *Überwachung des Ausschusses zur Untersuchung der blutigen Maiereignisse*, Bl. 236.

103. Leopold Schwarzschild in *Tagebuch*, quoted in Glatzer, *Berlin zur Weimarer Zeit*, 375–77; "Merkblatt über die Strafverfahren aus Anlass der Berliner Mai-Unruhen 1929 (Stand d. Verfahren: Ende November 1929)," in GStA Rep 84a/51191, *Straf- und Ermittlungsverfahren im Zusammenhang mit den Maidemonstrationen 1929 in Berlin*, Bl. 1–2; Carl von Ossietzky, "Zörgiebel ist Schuld!" *Weltbühne*, May 7, 1929, reprinted in Ossietzky, *Rechenschaft. Publizistik aus den Jahren 1913–1933* (Frankfurt/Main: Fischer Taschenbuch Verlag, 1972), 100, 102–3; *Berliner Volkszeitung*, May 2, 1929, quoted in Fröhlich, *Berliner Blut-Mai*, 8.

104. Regierungsdirektor Department I A, May 2, 1929, in LAB A. Pr. Br. Rep. 030 Nr. 21732, *Rundschreiben, Richtlinien und Aufrufe des ZK der KPD . . . und des Maikommittees in Berlin zum 1. Mai 1929*, Bl. 78; Reports, May 2, 1929; in LAB A. Pr. Br. Rep. 030 Nr. 21732, *Rundschreiben, Richtlinien und Aufrufe des ZK der KPD . . . und des Maikommittees in Berlin zum 1. Mai 1929*, Bl. 82, Bl. 83, Bl. 95.

105. Max Fürst, *Gefilte Fisch*, 567–68; Hans Litten, Application, July 12, 1929, in LAB A Pr. Br. Rep. 030 Nr. 21731, *Überwachung des Ausschusses zur Untersuchung der blutigen Maiereignisse*, Bl. 232.

106. "Merkblatt über die Strafverfahren aus Anlass der Berliner Mai-Unruhen 1929 (Stand d. Verfahren: Ende November 1929)," in GStA Rep. 84a/51191, *Straf- und Ermittlungsverfahren im Zusammenhang mit den Maidemonstrationen 1929 in Berlin*, Bl. 1–2.

107. Max Fürst, *Gefilte Fisch*, 569; Memo, Abteilung I A, May 10, 1929, in LAB A Pr. Br. Rep. 030 Nr. 21731, *Überwachung des Ausschusses zur Untersuchung der blutigen Maiereignisse*, Bl. 28; Report on the Meeting of the Committee for the Public Investigation of the Mayday Events, May 15, 1929, in LAB A Pr. Br. Rep. 030 Nr. 21731, *Überwachung des Ausschusses zur Untersuchung der blutigen Maiereignisse*, Bl. 34.

108. Report on the Meeting of the Committee for the Public Investigation of the Mayday Events, May 15, 1929, in LAB A Pr. Br. Rep. 030 Nr. 21731, *Überwachung des Ausschusses zur Untersuchung der blutigen Maiereignisse*, Bl. 36.

109. Ibid., Bl. 36–37.

110. Ibid.

111. Report on the public demonstration of the May Committee for the public investigation of the Mayday events on Friday, July 5, 1929, in Seitz's Festsälen, Spandau, signed Commissar Meyer, in LAB A Pr. Br. Rep. 030 Nr. 21731, *Überwachung des Ausschusses zur Untersuchung der blutigen Maiereignisse*, Bl. 158.

112. Hans Litten, Application, July 12, 1929, in LAB A Pr. Br. Rep. 030 Nr. 21731, *Überwachung des Ausschusses zur Untersuchung der blutigen Maiereignisse*, Bl. 228.

113. Ibid., Bl. 227.

114. Ibid., Bl. 228–29.

115. Ibid., Bl. 229–32.

116. Beschluß, 3. Strafsenat des Kammergerichts, October 14, 1929, in LAB A Pr. Br. Rep. 030 Nr. 21731, *Überwachung des Ausschusses zur Untersuchung der blutigen Maiereignisse*, Bl. 233–4.

117. "Heidrichs Urteil," *Welt am Abend*, November 27, 1931; Decision of the Strafkammer, LG I, November 26, 1931, in LAB A Rep 358-01 Nr. 2544, MFNr B 300, *Strafsache gegen Heidrich*, Bd. 2, Bl. 127ff., Bl. 133–5.

PART II

1. Joseph Goebbels, diary entry, May 9, 1931, in Goebbels, *Tagebücher 1924–1945*, ed. Ralf Georg Reuth, Bd. 2, 1930–1934 (Munich: Piper Verlag, 1992), 592; Joseph Goebbels, diary entry, May 8, 1931, in *Tagebücher. Sämtliche Fragmente*, ed. Elke Fröhlich, Teil I: Aufzeichnungen 1924–1942, Band 2, 1.1.1931–31.12.1936 (Munich: K.G. Saur, 1987), 61; "Legalität und Rollkommandos," *Berliner Morgenpost*, May 9, 1931; "Hitler schwört alles ab!" *8-Uhr-Abendblatt*, May 8, 1931; "Rund um das Kriminalgericht," *8-Uhr-Abendblatt*, May 8, 1931.

2. "Hitlers Zeugen-Aussage in Moabit," *Vossische Zeitung*, May 9, 1931; "Hitler wird als Zeuge in Moabit vernommen," *Völkischer Beobachter*, May 10–11, 1931; "Wie sie lügen," *Welt am Abend*, May 7, 1931; "Hitler als Zeuge," *Berliner Tageblatt*, May 8, 1931, A.

3. OSTA LG III to PJM, May 5, 1931, in LAB A Rep. 358-02 Nr. 98, *Stief und Genossen*, Bd. 6, Bl. 57.

4. Ibid.; "Hitler als Zeuge," *Berliner Tageblatt*, May 8, 1931, A; "Hitler Zeugt in Moabit," *Welt am Abend*, May 8, 1931. For the layout of the court buildings, see Benjamin Carter Hett, *Death in the Tiergarten: Murder and Criminal Justice in the Kaiser's Berlin* (Cambridge, Mass.: Harvard University Press, 2004), 15–18.

5. "Hitler wird als Zeuge in Moabit vernommen," *Völkischer Beobachter*, May 10–11, 1931; "Hitlers Zeugen-Aussage in Moabit," *Vossische Zeitung*, May 9, 1931; "Unser Führer in Moabit," *Angriff*, May 8, 1931.

6. "Hitler als Zeuge in Moabit," *BZ am Mittag*, May 8, 1931.

7. Max Fürst, *Gefilte Fisch und wie es weiterging* (Munich: DTV, 2004), 647; Margot Fürst, interview with Kurt Neheimer, Stuttgart, February 12, 1985, Institut für die Geschichte der deutschen Juden, *Nachlaß Neheimer*, Bd. III, *KZ-Haft/Erinnerungen*.

8. "Hitlers Zeugen-Aussage in Moabit," *Vossische Zeitung*, May 9, 1931.

9. Richard J. Evans, *The Coming of the Third Reich* (New York: Penguin, 2004), 170, 173; Adolf Hitler, *Mein Kampf*, trans. Ralph Manheim (Boston: Houghton Mifflin, 1999), 215–16; Joachim Fest, *Hitler. Eine Biographie* (Berlin: Ullstein Taschenbuch, 2005), 117; Ian Kershaw, *Hitler 1889–1936: Hubris* (New York: Norton, 1999), 126–65, 170–219.

10. "Deutschland: Wahl zum 4. Reichstag 1928," Wahlen in der Weimarer Republik, http://www.gonschior.de/weimar/Deutschland/RT4.html, last visited November 17, 2006; Jürgen W. Falter, *Hitlers Wähler* (Munich: C. H. Beck, 1991), 25, 29–38.

11. Ralf Georg Reuth, *Goebbels. Eine Biographie* (Munich: Piper Verlag, 2005), 136; Peter Fritzsche, *Germans into Nazis* (Cambridge, Mass.: Harvard University Press, 1998), 137–214; Kershaw, *Hitler 1889–1936*, 333.

12. Peter Longerich, *Geschichte der SA* (Munich: Verlag C. H. Beck, 2003), 111.

13. Rudolf Diels, *Lucifer ante Portas. Zwischen Severing und Heydrich* (Zürich: Interverlag, 1949), 153.

14. Detlev Peukert, *The Weimar Republic: The Crisis of Classical Modernity* (New York: Hill and Wang, 1993), 94–95; Joseph Goebbels, *Kampf um Berlin*, quoted in Reuth, *Goebbels*, 112.

15. Eve Rosenhaft, *Beating the Fascists? The German Communists and Political Violence 1929–1933* (Cambridge, UK: Cambridge University Press, 1983); Pamela Swett, *Neighbors and Enemies: The Culture of Radicalism in Berlin, 1929–1933* (Cambridge, UK: Cambridge University Press, 2004); Reuth, *Goebbels*, 112–20; Dirk Blasius, *Weimars Ende. Bürgerkrieg und Politik 1930–1933* (Göttingen: Vandenhoeck und Ruprecht, 2005).

16. Rosenhaft, *Beating the Fascists?* 19; *Storm 33. Hans Maikowski Geschrieben von Kameraden des Toten*, 1st Auflage (Berlin-Schöneberg: NS Druck und Verlag, 1933), 2.

17. Walter Stennes, *Lebenslauf*, July 11, 1928, in IfZ MA 747, *Personalien des Polizeipräsidiums Berlin*; Constantin Goschler, ed., *Hitler: Reden, Schriften, Anordnungen. Februar 1925 bis Januar 1933*, Band IV: *Von der Reichstagswahl bis zur Reichspräsidentenwahl Oktober 1930—März 1932*, Teil 1: Oktober 1930–Juni 1931 (Munich: K. G. Saur, 1994), 248 n. 1.

18. Reuth, *Goebbels*, 141; Kershaw, *Hitler 1889–1936*, 172–73, 346–47.

19. Adolf Hitler, "Zeugenaussage vor dem IV. Strafsenat des Reichsgerichts in Leipzig," September 25, 1930, in Christian Hartmann, ed., *Hitler: Reden, Schriften, Anordnungen. Februar 1925 bis Januar 1933*, Band III: *Zwischen den Reichstagswahlen Juli 1928–September 1930*, Teil 3: Januar 1930–September 1930 (Munich: K. G. Saur, 1995), 434–51, 434 and 434 n. 1, 438, 441.

20. Goschler, *Reden, Schriften, Anordnungen*, 183, 200, 229–30.

21. "Die Stennes Revolte. Aus den Mitteilungen des Landeskriminalamt-Polizeiamts (IA) Berlin, May 1, 1931, Nr. 9," in IfZ MA 747, *Personalien des Polizeipräsidiums Berlin*.

22. Ibid.; Goschler, *Reden, Schriften, Anordnungen*, 248 n. 2; Kershaw, *Hitler 1889–1936*, 172–73, 349.

23. Diels, *Lucifer*, 83.

24. Joseph Goebbels, diary entries, March 29, March 31, February 23, March 16, and April 28, 1931, in Goebbels, *Tagebücher*, ed. Reuth, Bd. 2, 1930–1934, 573–74, 563, 566, 588; Reuth, *Goebbels*, 191.

25. "Die Stennes Revolte. Aus den Mitteilungen des Landeskriminalamt-Polizeiamts (IA) Berlin, May 1, 1931, Nr. 9," in IfZ MA 747, *Personalien des Polizeipräsidiums Berlin*; Diels, *Lucifer*, 185, 107; Reuth, *Goebbels*, 191.

26. Goschler, *Reden, Schriften, Anordnungen*, 251, 255, 257.

27. Kershaw, *Hitler 1889–1936*, 350.

28. Election data from Landeswahlleiter des Landes Berlin, http://www.berlin.de/wahlen, last visited November 12, 2006; Heinrich August Winkler, *Weimar, 1918–1933: Die Geschichte der ersten Deutschen Demokratie* (Munich: Verlag C. H. Beck, 1998), 595.

29. Rosenhaft, *Beating the Fascists?* 19–20; Richard Bessel, "Violence as Propaganda: The Role of the Storm Troopers in the Rise of National Socialism," in Thomas Childers, ed., *The Formation of the Nazi Constituency 1919–1933* (London: Croom Helm, 1986), 131–46, 142; Christoph Graf, *Politische Polizei zwischen Demokratie und Diktatur. Die Entwicklung der preußischen Politischen Polizei vom Staatsschutzorgan der Weimarer Republik zum Geheimen Staatspolizeiamt des Dritten Reiches* (Berlin: Colloquium Verlag, 1983), 47; "Der 'Mördersturm' im Kampf gegen Mord und Lüge," *Angriff*, December 18, 1931.

30. "Die Kasernen des braunen Mords," *Welt am Abend*, September 3, 1931; "Widersprechende Zeugenaussagen im Edenpalast-Prozeß," *Angriff*, April 21, 1931; *Anklageschrift*, February 25, 1931, in LAB A Rep. 358-02 Nr. 98, *Stief und Genossen*, Bd. 3, 4 (page number of Schrift, not file).

31. Max Liebscher, Protocol of Examination, December 6, 1930, in LAB A Rep. 358-02 Nr. 98, *Stief und Genossen*, Bd. 7, Bl. 1; Konrad Stief, Protocol of Examination, December 6, 1930, in LAB A Rep. 358-02 Nr. 98, *Stief und Genossen*, Bd. 7, Bl. 3; Albert Berlich, Protocol of Examination, December 6, 1930, in LAB A Rep. 358-02 Nr. 98, *Stief und Genossen*, Bd. 7, Bl. 6; Rudolf Wesemann, Protocol of Examination, December 6, 1930, in LAB A Rep. 358-02 Nr. 98, *Stief und Genossen*, Bd. 7, Bl. 1, 3, 6, 4; *Anklageschrift*, February 25, 1931, in LAB A Rep. 358-02 Nr. 98, *Stief und Genossen*, Bd. 3, 1–5 (page number of Schrift, not file).

32. Joachim Tiburtius, Protocol of Examination, January 31, 1931, Max Liebscher, Protocol of Examination, December 6, 1930, in LAB A Rep 358-02 Nr. 98, *Stief und Genossen*, Bd. 7, Bl. 35–6, Bl. 1; Judgment, June 2, 1931, in LAB A Rep. 358-02 Nr. 98, *Stief und Genossen*, Bd. 4, Bl. 156.

33. Willi Köhler, Protocol of Examination, January 14, 1931, in LAB A Rep. 358-02 Nr. 98, *Stief und Genossen*, Bd. 7, Bl. 20; *Anklageschrift*, February

25, 1931, in LAB A Rep. 358-02 Nr. 98, *Stief und Genossen*, Bd. 3, 5–11 (page number of Schrift, not file).

34. *Anklageschrift*, February 25, 1931, in LAB A Rep. 358-02 Nr. 98, *Stief und Genossen*, Bd. 3, 11–12 (page number of Schrift, not file); Judgment, June 2, 1931, in LAB A Rep. 358-02 Nr. 98, *Stief und Genossen*, Bd. 4, 151.

35. *Anklageschrift*, February 25, 1931, in LAB A Rep. 358-02 Nr. 98, *Stief und Genossen*, Bd. 3, 12–19 (page number of Schrift, not file); Judgment, June 2, 1931, in LAB A Rep. 358-02 Nr. 98, *Stief und Genossen*, Bd. 4, 158–159.

36. Michael Kohlhaas, "Der 'Rote Hahn' kommt vors Gericht," *Welt am Abend*, August 11, 1931; "Aus der Geschichte des Mordsturms 33," *Arbeiter Illustrierte Zeitung*, Nr. 44, 1931.

37. Vernehmungsniederschrift, May 19, 1937, in NARA RG 242, BDC SA Collections, P-Akten, Roll Number A 3341-SA-D098, 344; Kohlhaas, "Der 'Rote Hahn' kommt vors Gericht"; Anklageschrift, July 11, 1931, in NARA RG 242, BDC SA Collections, P-Akten, Roll Number A 3341-SA-D098, 730–34; Fritz Hahn to Herrn Direktor Stutzbach, Commerz- und Privatbank A.G., April 2, 1931, in NARA RG 242, BDC SA Collections, P-Akten, Roll Number A 3341-SA-D098, 698; "Nazi-Sturm 33 auf der Anklagebank," *Welt am Abend*, August 13, 1931; *Das Strafgesetzbuch für das Deutsche Reich vom 15. Mai 1871. Mit den Entscheidungen des Reichsgerichts*, von Dr. P. Daude, 17. Auflage, bearbeitet und herausgegeben von Dr. E. Daude (Munich: Verlag von H.W. Müller, 1930), 126–27.

38. The other defendants were Martin Froschauer, Fritz Domming, Konrad Domming, and Paul Foyer. A seventh defendant, Karl Kliemt, had fled. "Durch Messerstiche getötet," *Berliner Morgenpost*, April 1, 1931; "Heute Prozeß wegen der Vorfälle in der Hebbelstraße," *Angriff*, March 31, 1931; "Neue Beweisaufnahme im Hebbelstraße-Prozeß," *Angriff*, April 3, 1931; Hans Litten to his parents, April 19, 1931, in BA-BL NY 4011, *Nachlaß Hans Litten*, Bd. 4, Bl. 1; "Unerhörte Gefängnisstrafen für unsere S.A.-Leute," *Angriff*, April 10, 1931.

39. Hans Litten to his parents, April 19, 1931, in BA-BL NY 4011, *Nachlaß Hans Litten*, Bd. 4, Bl. 1; "Interview mit Rechtsanwalt Litten," *Rote Fahne*, August 17, 1932; Paul Stenig, *Äußerung*, July 13, 1933, in GStA Rep. 84a/ 20361, *Gesetz zur Wiederherstellung des Berufsbeamtentums betr. Staatsanwälte*, Bl. 101.

40. Carlheinz von Brück, *Ein Mann, der Hitler in die Enge trieb. Hans Littens Kampf gegen den Faschismus. Ein Dokumentarbericht* (East Berlin: Union Verlag, 1975), 14; *Welt am Abend*, August 24, 1931; "Interview mit Rechtsanwalt Litten," *Rote Fahne*, August 17, 1932; Report, GSA KG to JM, July 20, 1933, in GStA Rep. 84a/20361, *Gesetz zur Wiederherstellung des Berufsbeamtentums betr. Staatsanwälte*, Bl. 91–2; "Neue 'Köpfe' in Moabit," *Berliner Börsen-Zeitung*, March 29, 1931, in GStA Rep. 84a/ 20250–20251, *Zeitungs-Auschnitte über wirkliche oder vermeintliche*

Mißstände bei Gerichten des Kammergerichtsbezirks, 1930–34, Bl. 120; Reinhard Neubert to GSA KG, July 2, 1933, NSDAP Gauleitung Groß-Berlin, August 15, 1933, in GStA Rep. 84a/20361, *Gesetz zur Wiederherstellung des Berufsbeamtentums betr. Staatsanwälte*, Bl. 89, Bl. 94.

41. Litten to the court, April 30, 1931, in LAB A Rep 358-02 Nr. 98, *Stief und Genossen*, Bd. 4, Bl. 90–1; "Mordführer Hahn läuft noch frei herum," *Rote Fahne*, May 1, 1931.

42. Max Fürst, *Gefilte Fisch*, 647.

43. "Zwischenfall im Edenpalast-Prozeß," *Angriff*, April 23, 1931; "Zahlreiche Entlastungen im Edenpalast-Prozeß," *Angriff*, May 1, 1931; Judgment, June 2, 1931, in LAB A Rep. 358-02 Nr. 98, *Stief und Genossen*, Bd. 4, Bl. 165; Gerhard Jungfer, interview with the author, Berlin, July 15, 2006; Max Fürst, *Gefilte Fisch*, 650.

44. Rudolf Olden, "Hans Litten," in Irmgard Litten, *Eine Mutter kämpft gegen Hitler* (Frankfurt/Main: Röderberg-Verlag, 1984), 11–12; "Stennes beugt sich vor Hitler," *Welt am Abend*, May 9, 1931.

45. Joseph Goebbels, diary entry for May 7, 1931, diary entry for May 8, 1931, in *Tagebücher*, ed. Fröhlich, Teil I, Band 2, 61.

46. Erich Frey, *Ich beantrage Freispruch. Aus den Erinnerungen des Strafverteidigers Prof. Dr. Dr. Erich Frey* (Hamburg: Blüchert Verlag, 1959), 405–62; Joseph Goebbels, diary entry for April 30, 1931, diary entry for May 21, 1932, in *Tagebücher*, ed. Fröhlich, Teil I, Band 2, 58, 68; *Berliner Morgenpost*, April 3, 1931; *Berliner Morgenpost*, April 22, 1931; Siegfried Kracauer, *From Caligari to Hitler: A Psychological History of the German Film* (Princeton: Princeton University Press, 1947), 219; "'M'—Fritz Langs erster Tonfilm," *Berliner Morgenpost*, May 13, 1931; "Legalität und Rollkommandos," *Berliner Morgenpost*, May 9, 1931.

47. Winkler, *Weimar*, 362–63; Henry Ashby Turner Jr., *Hitler's Thirty Days to Power: January 1933* (Reading, Mass.: Addison-Wesley, 1996), 6–7, 19–21; Gordon A. Craig, *The Politics of the Prussian Army, 1640–1945* (London: Oxford University Press, 1964), 436–37.

48. Goschler, *Reden, Schriften, Anordnungen*, 360–61; "Hitlers Zeugen-Aussage in Moabit," *Vossische Zeitung*, May 9, 1931.

49. LAB Rep. 358/690, *Strafsache gegen Marschner*; Sling (Paul Schlesinger), *Richter und Gerichtete. Neu eingeleitet und kommentiert von Robert M.W. Kempner* (Munich: Rogner & Bernhard, 1969), 302–3; Thomas Vormbaum, *Die Lex Emminger vom 4. Januar 1924. Vorgeschichte, Inhalt und Auswirkungen: Ein Beitrag zur deutschen Strafrechtsgeschichte des 20. Jahrhunderts* (Berlin: Duncker & Humblot, 1988).

50. Goschler, *Reden, Schriften, Anordnungen*, 361; "Hitlers Zeugen-Aussage in Moabit," *Vossische Zeitung*, May 9, 1931.

51. Goschler, *Reden, Schriften, Anordnungen*, 361; "Hitlers Zeugen-Aussage in Moabit," *Vossische Zeitung*, May 9, 1931.

52. "Hitlers Abrechnung mit den Rebellen," *Völkischer Beobachter*, April 4, 1931, in Goschler, *Reden, Schriften, Anordnungen*, 257; Hitlers Zeugen-Aussage in Moabit," *Vossische Zeitung*, May 9, 1931.

53. Goschler, *Reden, Schriften, Anordnungen*, 361; "Unser Führer in Moabit," *Angriff*, May 8, 1931; "Hitlers Zeugen-Aussage in Moabit," *Vossische Zeitung*, May 9, 1931.

54. "Hitlers Zeugen-Aussage in Moabit," *Vossische Zeitung*, May 9, 1931; "Unser Führer in Moabit," *Angriff*, May 8, 1931; Goschler, *Reden, Schriften, Anordnungen*, 361.

55. Rosenhaft, *Beating the Fascists?*; Goschler, *Reden, Schriften, Anordnungen*, 361–62; "Hitlers Zeugen-Aussage in Moabit," *Vossische Zeitung*, May 9, 1931.

56. Goschler, *Reden, Schriften, Anordnungen*, 362.

57. Götz Berger, interview with Kurt Neheimer, February 4, 1986, in Institut für die Geschichte der deutschen Juden, *Nachlaß Neheimer*, Bd. III, *KZ-Haft/Erinnerungen*; Hilde Benjamin, interview with Kurt Neheimer, July 18, 1984, in Institut für die Geschichte der deutschen Juden, *Nachlaß Neheimer*, Bd. III, *KZ-Haft/Erinnerungen*; Olden, "Hans Litten," 6.

58. "Hitler schwört alles ab!" *8-Uhr-Abendblatt*, May 8, 1931.

59. Ibid.; Goschler, *Reden, Schriften, Anordnungen*, 362.

60. Goschler, *Reden, Schriften, Anordnungen*, 362.

61. Ibid., 362, 364; Adolf Hitler, "Wohin die Tätigkeit des Hauptmann Stennes führt," *Völkischer Beobachter*, April 5/6/7, 1931.

62. Goschler, *Reden, Schriften, Anordnungen*, 364.

63. Ibid.

64. Ibid.

65. *Angriff*, January 23, 1930; Goschler, *Reden, Schriften, Anordnungen*, 363.

66. Goschler, *Reden, Schriften, Anordnungen*, 363; "Hitler schwört alles ab!" *8-Uhr-Abendblatt*, 8 May 1931.

67. "Hitler schwört alles ab!" *8-Uhr-Abendblatt*, May 8, 1931.

68. Goschler, *Reden, Schriften, Anordnungen*, 365–66.

69. "Hitlers Zeugen-Aussage in Moabit," *Vossische Zeitung*, May 9, 1931; Goschler, *Reden, Schriften, Anordnungen*, 364–65; "Hitler schwört alles ab!" *8-Uhr-Abendblatt*, May 8, 1931.

70. Goschler, *Reden, Schriften, Anordnungen*, 366; "Adolf Hitler rechnet ab," *Angriff*, May 9, 1931.

71. Litten to the court, May 5, 1931, in LAB A Rep. 358-02 Nr. 98, *Stief und Genossen*, Bd. 4, Bl. 116.

72. Ibid., Bl. 116–117; Goschler, *Reden, Schriften, Anordnungen*, 366; Goebbels quote from Fest, *Hitler*, 374.

73. Goschler, *Reden, Schriften, Anordnungen*, 366–67.

74. Ibid., 367.

75. "Hitlers Zeugen-Aussage in Moabit," *Vossische Zeitung*, May 9, 1931; Goschler, *Reden, Schriften, Anordnungen*, 367.

76. Goschler, *Reden, Schriften, Anordnungen*, 367; "Hitler schwört alles ab!" *8-Uhr-Abendblatt*, May 8, 1931.

77. Goschler, *Reden, Schriften, Anordnungen*, 368.

78. Heinrich Brüning, *Memoiren 1918–1934* (Stuttgart: Deutsche Verlags-Anstalt, 1970), 191–96.

79. Goschler, *Reden, Schriften, Anordnungen*, 368.

80. Ibid., 368–69.

81. Ibid., 369; "Unser Führer in Moabit," *Angriff*, May 8, 1931.

82. Goschler, *Reden, Schriften, Anordnungen*, 369.

83. "Zu viel Legalität," *Berliner Tageblatt*, May 9, 1931, M; "Hitlers Zeugen-Aussage in Moabit," *Vossische Zeitung*, May 9, 1931; "Hitler schwört alles ab!" *8-Uhr-Abendblatt*, May 8, 1931.

84. "Zu viel Legalität," *Berliner Tageblatt*, May 9, 1931, M; "Adolf Legalité," *Vossische Zeitung*, May 9, 1931; "Adolf Hitlers Zeugenaussagen in Moabit," *Völkischer Beobachter*, May 10–11, 1931.

85. "Adolf Legalité," *Vossische Zeitung*, May 9, 1931; "Zu viel Legalität," *Berliner Tageblatt*, May 9, 1931, M; "Stennes als Zeuge," *Vossische Zeitung*, May 9, 1931.

86. "Zu viel Legalität," *Berliner Tageblatt*, May 9, 1931, M; Trial Protocol, May 8, 1931, in LAB A Rep 358-02 Nr. 98, *Stief und Genossen*, Bd. 4, Bl. 120–21.

87. "Zu viel Legalität," *Berliner Tageblatt*, May 9, 1931, M; Goschler, *Reden, Schriften, Anordnungen*, 369.

88. Goschler, *Reden, Schriften, Anordnungen*, 369–70.

89. Kershaw, *Hitler 1889–1936*, 126; Max Fürst, *Gefilte Fisch*, 648; Goschler, *Reden, Schriften, Anordnungen*, 370.

90. Goschler, *Reden, Schriften, Anordnungen*, 370.

91. "Zu viel Legalität," *Berliner Tageblatt*, May 9, 1931, M; "Stennes als Zeuge," *Vossische Zeitung*, May 9, 1931; Trial Protocol, May 8, 1931, in LAB A Rep 358-02 Nr. 98, *Stief und Genossen*, Bd. 4; Goschler, *Reden, Schriften, Anordnungen*, 370.

92. Goschler, *Reden, Schriften, Anordnungen*, 370; Trial Protocol, May 8, 1931, in LAB A Rep 358-02 Nr. 98, *Stief und Genossen*, Bd. 4, Bl. 121, 124.

93. Joseph Goebbels, diary entry May 9, 1931, in *Tagebücher*, ed. Fröhlich, Teil I, Band 2/I, 402–403.

94. Goebbels to the court, May 9, 1931, in LAB A Rep 358–02 Nr. 98, *Stief und Genossen*, Bd. 4, Bl. 126; "Halbjude Litten und der 'Nazi-Sozi,'" *Angriff*, May 10, 1931.

95. "Unser Führer in Moabit," *Angriff*, May 8, 1931; "Adolf Hitler rechnet ab," *Angriff*, May 9, 1931; Goebbels, *Tagebücher*, ed. Fröhlich, Teil I, Band 2, 62; Goebbels, *Tagebücher*, ed. Reuth, Teil I, Band 2/I, 402–3.

96. "Der legale Faschismus," *Welt am Abend*, May 9, 1931; "Legalität und Rollkommandos," *Berliner Morgenpost*, May 9, 1931; "Adolf Legalité," *Vossische Zeitung*, May 9, 1931.

97. "Zu viel Legalität," *Berliner Tageblatt*, May 9, 1931, M.
98. "Ungeheuerliche Strafanträge des Staatsanwalts," *Angriff*, May 12, 1931; "Hetze gegen die vier Angeklagten," *Angriff*, May 13, 1931.
99. "Hetze gegen die vier Angeklagten," *Angriff*, May 13, 1931.
100. "Die Angeschuldigten sind unschuldig!" *Angriff*, May 16, 1931.
101. Judgment, June 2, 1931, in LAB A Rep. 358-02 Nr. 98, Bd. 4, Bl. 188.
102. Ibid., Bl. 164.
103. Ibid., Bl. 164–65.
104. Ibid., Bl. 165–67.
105. Ibid., Bl. 184–85, Bl. 189.
106. Ibid., Bl. 193–95.
107. Hans Litten, *Revisionsschrift*, July 16, 1931, in LAB A Rep. 358-02 Nr. 98, *Stief und Genossen*, Bd. 6, Bl. 125.
108. Ibid., Bl. 132.
109. Decision of the *Reichsgericht*, November 19, 1931, in LAB A Rep. 358-02 Nr. 98, *Stief und Genossen*, Bd. 6, Bl. 157–60.
110. Hans Litten, "Jugendbewegung und Politik," *Kameraden Bundesblatt Neue Folge*, Heft 3, 1925, 41.
111. Prussian Minister for Science, Art, and Public Education to PJM, November 12, 1931, private collection of Frau Patricia Litten; "Professor Litten und das Finanzamt," *Ostpreußische Rundschau*, Beilage zu Nr. 22, 1st week of November, 1931, private collection of Frau Patricia Litten.
112. "An den Disziplinarhof für nichtrichterliche Beamte in Berlin," October 24, 1931; private collection of Frau Patricia Litten.
113. *Ostpreußische Rundschau*, Beilage zu Nr. 22, 1st week of November, 1931, private collection of Frau Patricia Litten.
114. Ibid.
115. Hans Litten to Fritz Litten, June 17, 1931, in BA-BL NY 4011, *Nachlaß Hans Litten*, Bd. 4, *Korrespondenz—Ausgehende. Briefe von Hans Litten an seine Eltern vor seiner Haftzeit 1931*, Bl. 5.
116. Fritz Litten to Adolf Hitler, July 24, 1935, in LBI AR 5112, *Hans Litten Collection*, 1/2, 146–47; Irmgard Litten to Paul von Hindenburg, March 5, 1934, in LBI AR 5112, *Hans Litten Collection*, 1/2, 38.
117. Prussian Minister for Science, Art, and Public Education to PJM, 12 November 1931, private collection of Frau Patricia Litten.
118. Patricia Litten, interview with the author, Nuremberg, June 26, 2006.
119. Paul Stenig to OSA, July 26, 1931, in LAB A Rep. 358-02 Nr. 98, *Stief und Genossen*, Bd. 6, Bl. 74.
120. "Adolf Hitler rechnet ab," *Angriff*, May 9, 1931.
121. Joseph Goebbels, diary entry, May 10, 1931, in Goebbels, *Tagebücher*, ed. Fröhlich, Teil I, Band 2, 62.
122. Note dated October 29, 1931, in IfZ MA 734, NSDAP Hauptarchiv.
123. Helmut Klotz to Staatsanwaltschaft I Berlin, May 12, 1931, in LAB A Rep. 358 nr. 515, Bd. I, *Strafsache gegen Hitler wegen Meineides*, Bl. 1; Staat-

sanwaltschaftsrat Paul Stenig, "Dienstliche Äusserung, June 29, 1931," in LAB A Rep. 358 nr. 515, Bd. I, *Strafsache gegen Hitler wegen Meineides*, Bl. 26; Adolf Hitler to *Untersuchungsrichter* LGR Kemmer, August 6, 1931, in LAB A Rep. 358 nr. 515, Bd. I, *Strafsache gegen Hitler wegen Meineides*, Bl. 32–39.

124. Adolf Hitler to *Untersuchungsrichter* LGR Kemmer, August 6, 1931, in LAB A Rep. 358 nr. 515, Bd. I, *Strafsache gegen Hitler wegen Meineides*, Bl. 32–39; Polizeipräsident in Berlin Abteilung IA to GSA LG I, September 9, 1931, in LAB A Rep. 358 nr. 515, Bd. I, *Strafsache gegen Hitler wegen Meineides*, Bl. 42; Köhler to Klotz, October 5, 1931, in LAB A Rep. 358 nr. 515, Bd. I, *Strafsache gegen Hitler wegen Meineides*, Bl. 46–47; Wilde to PJM, August 22, 1931, in Hartmann, *Hitler*, Band IV: *Von der Reichstagswahl bis zur Rechspräsidentenwahl, October 1930–März 1932*, Teil 2: Juli 1931–Dezember 1931, 51, 53.

125. Kershaw, *Hitler 1889–1936*, 218, 223–24; Rudolf Olden, "Zu viel Legalität," *Berliner Tageblatt*, May 9, 1931, M.

126. Diels, *Lucifer*, 75.

127. Winkler, *Weimar*, 422–24.

128. Ibid.; "Dr. Litten verhaftet," *Welt am Abend*, August 10, 1931.

129. Max Fürst, *Gefilte Fisch*, 643–44.

130. "Dr. Litten verhaftet," *Welt am Abend*, August 10, 1931; Max Fürst, *Gefilte Fisch*, 644.

131. Hans Litten to the Police Presidium, May 27, 1931, in BA-BL R. 22/66804, *Reichsjustizministerium Personalakten, Hans-Joachim Litten*, Bl. 14–15; Hans Litten to PIM, September 16, 1931, in BA-BL R. 22/66804, *Reichsjustizministerium Personalakten, Hans-Joachim Litten*, Bl. 22–25.

132. Hans Litten to the Police Presidium, May 27, 1931, in BA-BL R. 22/66804, *Reichsjustizministerium Personalakten, Hans-Joachim Litten*, Bl. 14–15; Hans Litten to PIM, September 16, 1931, in BA-BL R. 22/66804, *Reichsjustizministerium Personalakten, Hans-Joachim Litten*, Bl. 22–25; Police President to Hans Litten, June 15, 1931, in BA-BL R. 22/66804, *Reichsjustizministerium Personalakten, Hans-Joachim Litten*, Bl. 15–16; Hans Litten to Police President, July 17, 1931, in BA-BL R. 22/66804, *Reichsjustizministerium Personalakten, Hans-Joachim Litten*, Bl. 17–19.

133. Hans Litten to Police President, August 1, 1931, in BA-BL R. 22/66804, *Reichsjustizministerium Personalakten, Hans-Joachim Litten*, Bl. 19–21; Governing President Berlin-Brandenburg to Hans Litten, August 8, 1931, in BA-BL R. 22/66804, *Reichsjustizministerium Personalakten, Hans-Joachim Litten*, Bl. 21–2; Hans Litten to PIM, 16 September 16, 1931, in BA-BL R. 22/66804, *Reichsjustizministerium Personalakten, Hans-Joachim Litten*, Bl. 22–25.

134. IM to JM November 30, 1931, in BA-BL R. 22/66804, *Reichsjustizministerium Personalakten, Hans-Joachim Litten*, Bl. 6; GSA to JM, February 1, 1932, in BA-BL R. 22/66804, *Reichsjustizministerium Personalakten,*

Hans-Joachim Litten, Bl. 9; Ehrengericht Eröffnungsbeschluß, March 5, 1932, in BA-BL R. 22/66804, *Reichsjustizministerium Personalakten, Hans-Joachim Litten*, Bl. 44; Vermerk, September 1932, in BA-BL R. 22/66804, *Reichsjustizministerium Personalakten, Hans-Joachim Litten*, Bl. 46; GSA KG to JM, September 14, 1932, in BA-BL R. 22/66804, *Reichsjustizministerium Personalakten, Hans-Joachim Litten*, Bl. 49; Judgment, Jury Court of Superior Court I, October 13, 1931, quoted in Anschuldigungsschrift, September 29, 1932, in BA-BL R. 22/66804, *Reichsjustizministerium Personalakten, Hans-Joachim Litten*, Bl. 56–67; Anschuldigungsschrift, September 29, 1932, in BA-BL R. 22/66804, *Reichsjustizministerium Personalakten, Hans-Joachim Litten*, Bl. 51–78; Beschluß, EG of the AK, October 4, 1932 (adding the Rückert case to the weapon permit case), in BA-BL R. 22/66804, *Reichsjustizministerium Personalakten, Hans-Joachim Litten*, Bl. 80.

135. BLHA Rep. 12B/11–13, *Staatsanwaltschaft beim Landgericht Berlin: Strafsache gegen Hoffman-Burges wegen Anstiftung zum Meineid*; "Neuer Prozeß gegen Sturm 33," *Angriff*, September 4, 1931; "Anarchist Litten phantasiert," *Angriff*, September 16, 1931; "Strafanträge gegen Sturm 33," *Welt am Abend*, September 28, 1931; "Unerhörte Anträge im Sturm 33-Prozeß," *Angriff*, September 28, 1931.

136. "Strafanträge gegen Sturm 33," *Welt am Abend*, September 28, 1931; "Unerhörte Anträge im Sturm 33 Prozeß," *Angriff*, September 28, 1931; Michael Kohlhaas, "Verzweiflung einer Mutter," *Welt am Abend*, October 1, 1931; Kube quoted in *Völkischer Beobachter*, October 10, 1931, in GStA Rep. 84a/20250, *Zeitungs-Auschnitte über wirkliche oder vermeintliche Mißstände bei Gerichten des Kammergerichtsbezirks, 1930–34*, Bl. 167; "Der Prozeß gegen den Sturm 33," *Angriff*, August 13, 1931.

137. Meldung, October 16, 1931, in LAB A Rep 358-01 Bde. 8051–8074, *Beyer und Gen, Hagemann und Gen (früher Deig und Genossen), Richardstraße Prozess*, Bd. 8051, Bl. 12; Judgment, Jury Court, Landgericht II, April 30, 1932, in LAB A Rep 358-01 Nr. 8072, *Urteil in Strafsache gegen Deig und Genossen*, Bl. 15, Bl. 22–27, Bl. 30; Hans Litten to the court, March 17, 1932, in LAB A Rep 358-01 Bde. 8051–8074, *Beyer und Gen, Hagemann und Gen (früher Deig und Genossen), Richardstraße Prozess*, Bd. 8057, Bl. 114; "15 Jahre Zuchthaus, 34 Jahre Gefängnis gegen Neuköllner Antifaschisten beantragt," *Rote Fahne*, April 24, 1932; Winkler, *Weimar*, 450, 473.

138. Litten to the court, March 14, 1932, in LAB A Rep 358-01 Bde. 8051–8074, *Beyer und Gen, Hagemann und Gen (früher Deig und Genossen), Richardstraße Prozess*, Bd. 8057, Bl. 97–98; Hans Litten to the court, November 20, 1931, in LAB A Rep 358-01 Bde. 8051–8074, *Beyer und Gen, Hagemann und Gen (früher Deig und Genossen), Richardstraße Prozess*, Bd. 8052, Bl. 175–77; Hans Litten to the Examining Magistrate, December 19, 1931, in LAB A Rep 358-01 Bde. 8051–8074, *Beyer und Gen, Hagemann und Gen (früher Deig und Genossen), Richardstraße Prozess*, Bd. 8054, Bl.

164–65; "Der Terror der Richardstraße-Nazis," *Rote Fahne*, April 14, 1932; "Die Rolle der Polizei im Richardstr.-Prozeß," *Rote Fahne*, April 19, 1932; Judgment, Jury Court, Landgericht II, April 30, 1932, in LAB A Rep 358–01 Bde. 8051–8074, *Beyer und Gen, Hagemann und Gen (früher Deig und Genossen), Richardstraße Prozess*, Bd. 8072, Bl. 46–48, Bl. 53, Bl. 66; "Groener und Prozeß Richardstraße," *Rote Fahne*, April 23, 1932; Kriminal-Assistant Marowsky, "Vermerk," October 22, 1932, in LAB A Rep 358–01 Nr. 37, *Adam und Genossen (Felseneck)*, Handakten Bd. II, Microfilm Roll 422.

139. Hans Litten to the court, March 31, 1932, in LAB A Rep 358-01 Bde. 8051–8074, *Beyer und Gen, Hagemann und Gen (früher Deig und Genossen), Richardstraße Prozess*, Bd. 8056, n.p.; "Groener und Prozeß Richardstraße," *Rote Fahne*, April 22, 1932; "SA Leute bedrohten Frauen mit Revolver," *Welt am Abend*, April 22, 1932; "Theater im Gerichtssaal," *Angriff*, 23 April 1932; Vermerk, in LAB A Rep 358-01 Nr. 1510, *Strafsache gegen Litten wegen Begünstigung*, Bl. 3; Heinz Schüler, Statement, October 1, 1932, in LAB A Rep 358-01 Bde. 8051–8074, *Beyer und Gen, Hagemann und Gen (früher Deig und Genossen), Richardstraße Prozess*, Bd. 8060, Bl. 32–33.

140. Judgment, Jury Court, Landgericht II, April 30, 1932, in LAB A Rep 358–01 Nr. 8072, *Urteil in Strafsache gegen Deig und Genossen*, Bl. 44–45, 51–52, 110–11, 115, 117–20; "Hohe Gefängnisstrafen im Prozess um die Richardstraße," *Welt am Abend*, April 30, 1932.

141. Heinrich Hannover and Elisabeth Hannover-Drück, *Politische Justiz 1918–1933* (Frankfurt/Main: Fischer, 1966; revised ed., Bornheim-Merten: Lamuv, 1987); Theo Rasehorn, *Justizkritik in der Weimarer Republik. Das Beispiel der Zeitschrift "Die Justiz"* (Frankfurt/Main: Campus Verlag, 1985); Ralph Angermund, *Deutsche Richterschaft 1919–1945. Krisenerfahrung, Illusion, politische Rechtsprechung* (Frankfurt/Main: Fischer, 1990); Emil Julius Gumbel, *Vier Jahre politischer Mord* (Berlin: Verlag der neuen Gesellschaft, 1922); Wolfgang Schild, "Berühmte Berliner Kriminalprozesse der Zwanziger Jahre," in Friedrich Ebel and Albrecht Randelzhofer, eds., *Rechtsentwicklungen in Berlin. Acht Vorträge gehalten anläßlich der 750-Jahrfeier Berlins* (Berlin: de Gruyter, 1988), 125; Robert Kuhn, *Die Vertrauenskrise der Justiz (1926–1928). Der Kampf um die Republikanisierung der Rechtspflege in der Weimarer Republik* (Cologne: Bundesanzeiger, 1983).

142. Marginal notes on a review from *Tempo*, November 24, 1931, in GStA Rep. 84a/20250, *Zeitungs-Auschnitte über wirkliche oder vermeintliche Mißstände bei Gerichten des Kammergerichtsbezirks, 1930–34*, Bl. 170; *Vossische Zeitung*, December 24, 1931, in GStA Rep. 84a/20250, *Zeitungs-Auschnitte über wirkliche oder vermeintliche Mißstände bei Gerichten des Kammergerichtsbezirks, 1930–34*, Bl. 173; Gottfried Zarnow, *Gefesselte Justiz. Politische Bilder aus deutscher Gegenwart* (Munich: Lehmann,

1931), Band I; Gottfried Zarnow, *Gefesselte Justiz. Politische Bilder aus deutscher Gegenwart* (Munich: Lehmann, 1932), Band 2, 2. Auflage.

143. Winkler, *Weimar*, 401–2.

144. "Statistik der in den Monaten Januar bis Dezember 1931 in Berlin vorgekommenen politischen Gewalttaten," January 14, 1932, in GStA Rep. 77 Tit 4043 Nr. 121, *Politische Ausschreitungen und Zusammenstöße*, Bd. 2 1931–1932, Bl. 125–26; "Statistik der in den Monaten Januar bis März 1932 in Berlin vorgekommenen politischen Gewalttaten," April 23, 1932, in GStA Rep. 77 Tit 4043 Nr. 121, *Politische Ausschreitungen und Zusammenstöße*, Bd. 2 1931–1932, Bl. 375–76; PIM to Police Presidents, May 12, 1932, in GStA Rep. 77 Tit 4043 Nr. 121, *Politische Ausschreitungen und Zusammenstöße*, Bd. 2 1931–1932, Bl. 313. The numbers of culprits were of course higher than the numbers of victims as multiple persons tended to be involved in the attacks. Although the figures also show the numbers of culprits and victims who belonged to other political organizations, they make clear that the battles were overwhelmingly between Nazis and Communists. For Graf, see Graf, *Politische Polizei*, 46.

145. LGP II to KGP, February 22, 1928, GStA Rep. 84a/20304, *Vorwürfe gegen die Justizverwaltung*, 271–75; Sling, *Richter und Gerichtete*; Sling, *Der Fassadenkletterer vom "Kaiserhof"* (East Berlin: Verlag Das Neue Berlin, 1989); Frey, *Freispruch*, 352–53.

146. "Staatsanwälte, die nicht nach Berlin wollen," *Berliner Morgenpost*, February 17, 1930, in GStA Rep. 84a/20250, *Zeitungs-Auschnitte über wirkliche oder vermeintliche Mißstände bei Gerichten des Kammergerichtsbezirks, 1930–34*, Bl. 23; LGP III to KGP, December 28, 1928, in GStA Rep 84a/20307, *Vorwürfe gegen die Justizverwaltung, 1928–29*, Bl. 144; Pr. Richterverein to PJM, July, 1929, in GStA Rep. 84a/2944, *Richter und Staatsanwälte, 1927–30*, Bl. 237–38; LGD Steinhaus to AGP, February 17, 1933, in GStA Rep. 84a/20313, *Vorwürfe gegen die Justizverwaltung, 1932–3*, Bl. 57–58.

147. "Merkblatt" in GStA Rep. 84a/20307, *Vorwürfe gegen die Justizverwaltung, 1928–29*, 132, listing the names of the judges criticized in a *Tagebuch* article; LGP II to KGP, February 22, 1928, in GStA Rep. 84a/20307, *Vorwürfe gegen die Justizverwaltung, 1928–29*, Bl. 271–75; Frey, *Freispruch*, 342–43; *Börsenzeitung*, May 24, 1928, in GStA Rep. 84a/20304, *Vorwürfe gegen die Justizverwaltung*, 285; Otto Braun, *Von Weimar zu Hitler*, Zweite Auflage (New York: Europa Verlag, 1940), 240.

148. "Rechtsanwälte in Wahlkampf," *Montag Morgen*, n.d. (no. 249, probably 1928), in GStA Rep. 84a/20154, *Anwaltskammer in Berlin, 1912–28*, Bl. 280; David Clay Large, *Berlin* (New York: Basic Books, 2000), 138; Birger Schulz, *Der republikanische Richterbund* (Frankfurt/Main: Peter Lang, 1982).

149. Hett, *Death in the Tiergarten*; Alfred Apfel, "Alsberg," *Die Weltbühne*, 1932, 2. Halbjahr, 759; Professor Dr. Siegert, "Das Judentum im Straf-

verfahrensrecht," in *Das Judentum in der Rechtswissenschaft. Ansprachen, Vorträge und Ergebnisse der Tagung der Reichsgruppe Hochschullehrer des NSRB am 3. und 4. Oktober 1936* (Berlin: Deutscher Rechts-Verlag, 1936), 19; Thomas Blanke et al., eds., *Streitbare Juristen. Eine Andere Tradition* (Baden-Baden: Nomos, 1988); Helmut Heinrichs et al., eds., *Deutsche Juristen jüdischer Herkunft* (Munich: C. H. Beck, 1993); Douglas G. Morris, *Justice Imperiled: The Anti-Nazi Lawyer Max Hirschberg in Weimar Germany* (Ann Arbor: University of Michigan Press, 2005).

150. Otto Kamecke to Commerz und Privatbank, April 22, 1931, in NARA RG 242, BDC SA Collections, P-Akten, Roll Number A 3341-SA-D098, 860; "Moabiter Stellenbesetzung. Was macht den Strafrichter bei der Justizbehörde beliebt?" *Deutsche Zeitung*, September 18, 1929, in GStA Rep 84a/20308, *Vorwürfe gegen die Justizverwaltung, 1929–30*, Bl. 77.

151. Robert A. Dahl, "Decision-Making in a Democracy: The Supreme Court as National Policy Maker," *Journal of Public Law* 6 (1957): 279–95.

152. Ruth Glatzer, ed., *Berlin zur Weimarer Zeit. Panorama einer Metropole* (Berlin: Siedler Verlag, 2000), 399, 395–96, 393; Carl Zuckmayer, *Als wär's ein Stück von mir. Horen der Freundschaft* (Frankfurt/Main: Fischer, 1997), 525.

153. Karl-Heinz Minuth, ed., *Das Kabinett von Papen. 1. Juni is 3. Dezember 1932, Band 1: Juni bis September 1932* (Boppard am Rhein: Harald Boldt Verlag, 1989), 82–83; Blasius, *Weimars Ende*, 65–67, 82–83, 55.

154. Blasius, *Weimars Ende*, 42.

155. Blasius, *Weimars Ende*, 87–88; "Urteile gegen Mordschützen," *Angriff*, September 1, 1932.

156. Rudolf Olden, "Sondergerichte," *Weltbühne*, Bd. 33, August 16, 1932, 223.

157. "Kampfkongress gegen Sondergerichte," *Welt am Abend*, October 10, 1931; "Rote Hilfe mobilisiert gegen Sonderjustiz" and "Litten spricht," *Rote Fahne*, September 5, 1932; Brück, *Ein Mann*, 77; "Todesstrafe droht 4 Arbeitern Charlottenburgs" and "Kampfkongress der Roten Hilfe," *Welt am Abend*, September 16, 1932; "Todesurteile gegen Arbeiter?" *Welt am Abend*, September 12, 1932; "Erstes Sondergericht in Berlin," *Welt am Abend*, August 24, 1932.

158. 1st Abteilung des Sondergerichts beim Landgericht I Berlin, Judgment, October 6, 1932, in GStA Rep 84a/51724, *Strafverfahren gegen den kaufmännischen Angestellten Werner Calm u.a. wegen bewaffneten Zusammenstoßes mit Faschisten am 29.8.1932 in Charlottenburg, Sept 1932–Nov 1932 (Röntgenstrasse)*, 4–5.

159. Michael Kohlhaas, "Das Sondergericht gegen die acht Arbeiter," *Welt am Abend*, September 21, 1932; 1st Abteilung des Sondergerichts beim Landgericht I Berlin, Judgment, October 6, 1932, in GStA Rep 84a/51724, *Strafverfahren gegen den kaufmanischen Angestellten Werner Calm u.a. wegen bewaffneten Zusammenstoßes mit Faschisten am 29.8.1932 in Charlottenburg, Sept 1932–Nov 1932 (Röntgenstrasse)*, 10–11, 15, 17, 26–30;

"Der Führer gibt dem SA-Mann Gatschke das letzte Geleit," *Angriff*, September 5, 1932.

160. Anklage, September 9, 1932, in GStA Rep 84a/51724, *Strafverfahren gegen den kaufmanischen Angestellten Werner Calm u.a. wegen bewaffneten Zusammenstoßes mit Faschisten am 29.8.1932 in Charlottenburg, Sept 1932– Nov 1932 (Röntgenstrasse)*, Bl. 2–19; "Die Sache ist recht duster," *Welt am Abend*, September 23, 1932; "Todesstrafe droht in Moabit," *Welt am Abend*, September 20, 1932.

161. "Dr. Litten wird verhört," *Welt am Abend*, October 1, 1932; "Nazi-Anwälte gegen Litten," *Welt am Abend*, September 27, 1932; "Rechtsanwalt Litten als Zeuge geladen. Nazi Vorstoss im Sondergericht. Nazi-Verteidiger drohen mit Strafanträgen gegen die linke Presse," *Berlin am Morgen*, September 28, 1932; "Die Zeugenfabrik soll geschlossen werden," *Angriff*, September 28, 1932; "Litten's meineidiger 'Deutschnationaler,' " *Angriff*, September 27, 1932.

162. "Wer schoß in der Röntgenstraße?" *Welt am Abend*, September 21, 1932; "Die Blutnacht von Charlottenburg," *Angriff*, September 1, 1932; Michael Kohlhaas, "Nazizeugen im Röntgenstraßen-Prozeß," *Welt am Abend*, September 22, 1932; Michael Kohlhaas, "Die Sache ist recht duster," *Welt am Abend*, September 23, 1932; "Die Mordschützen wollen 'ganze Arbeit' leisten!" *Angriff*, September 23, 1932.

163. 1st Abteilung des Sondergerichts beim Landgericht I Berlin, Judgment, October 6, 1932, in GStA Rep 84a/51724, *Strafverfahren gegen den kaufmanischen Angestellten Werner Calm u.a. wegen bewaffneten Zusammenstoßes mit Faschisten am 29.8.1932 in Charlottenburg, Sept 1932–Nov 1932 (Röntgenstrasse)*, 82; "Sensation im Röntgenstraßen-Prozeß. Haftentlassung oder 24 Jahre Zuchthaus," *Welt am Abend*, October 5, 1932; "Umschwung im Calm-Prozeß," *Vossische Zeitung*, October 5, 1932, A; "Wer schoß in der Röntgenstraße?" *Welt am Abend*, September 21, 1932.

164. "Sensation im Röntgenstraßen-Prozeß. Haftentlassung oder 24 Jahre Zuchthaus," *Welt am Abend*, October 5, 1932; "Die Mörder des SA-Mannes Gatschke aus der Haft entlassen!" *Angriff*, October 6, 1932; "Umschwung im Calm-Prozeß," *Vossische Zeitung*, October 5, 1932, A.

165. "Die neun Charlottenburger Arbeiter freigelassen," *Berlin am Morgen*, October 6, 1932; Michael Kohlhaas, "Wie die neun Arbeiter freigelassen wurden. Begeisterte Begrüßung vor den Toren des Gefängnisses," *Welt am Abend*, October 6, 1932; "Die Mörder des SA-Mannes Gatschke aus der Haft entlassen!" *Angriff*, October 6, 1932; "Heute nachmittag Urteil im Calm-Prozeß," *Vossische Zeitung*, October 6, 1932, A.

166. "Die Begründung des Freispruchs," *Welt am Abend*, October 7, 1932; "Unverständlicher Freispruch im Röntgenstraße-Prozeß," *Angriff*, October 7, 1932; 1st Abteilung des Sondergerichts beim Landgericht I Berlin, Judgment, October 6, 1932, in GStA Rep 84a/51724, *Strafverfahren gegen den kaufmanischen Angestellten Werner Calm u.a. wegen bewaffneten*

Zusammenstoßes mit Faschisten am 29.8.1932 in Charlottenburg, Sept 1932–Nov 1932 (Röntgenstrasse), 37, 39, 71–72, 82.

167. "Alle Angeklagte freigesprochen," *Vossische Zeitung*, October 7, 1932, M; "Solidarität siegt!" *Berlin am Morgen*, October 7, 1932; "Der Verteidiger im Röntgenstraßen-Prozeß über die kämpfende Arbeiter-Presse," *Berlin am Morgen*, October 7, 1932; Hans Litten, "Der Bankrott der Sonder-gerichts-Justiz," *Berlin am Morgen*, October 9, 1932; Rote Hilfe Deutschlands, "Massenverteidigung. Der wirksamste Kampf gegen die Klassenjustiz," October 30, 1932, in GSTA Rep. 77 Tit. 4043 Nr. 386, "Rote Hilfe," Bl. 397–99.

168. Police President to PIM, September 30, 1932, in GStA Rep 84a/51163, *Verbot der Protestversammlungen der "Roten Hilfe" gegen die Sonderge-richte 1932*, Bl. 1–3; Vermerk, September 19, 1932. in GStA Rep 84a/51724, *Strafverfahren gegen den kaufmanischen Angestellten Werner Calm u.a. wegen bewaffneten Zusammenstoßes mit Faschisten am 29.8.1932 in Char-lottenburg, Sept 1932–Nov 1932 (Röntgenstrasse)*, n.p.; Vermerk, October 8, 1932, in GStA Rep 84a/51724, *Strafverfahren gegen den kaufmanischen Angestellten Werner Calm u.a. wegen bewaffneten Zusammenstoßes mit Faschisten am 29.8.1932 in Charlottenburg, Sept 1932–Nov 1932 (Röntgen-strasse)*, Bl. 27.

169. "Schützenkette und Sperrfeuer der Nazis," *Welt am Abend*, September 23, 1932; Vermerk: Betrifft Besprechung, October [n.d.] 1932, in GStA R.77 Tit. 4043 Nr. 20, "Ausnahmegerichte" 1932–33, Bl. 12.

170. Winkler, *Weimar*, 512–14; Kohlhaas, "Wie die neun Arbeiter freigelassen wurden."

171. Judgment, Jury Court, LG III, December 22, 1932, in BA-BL R. 22/66804, *Reichsjustizministerium Personalakten, Hans-Joachim Litten*, Bl. 84; Brück, *Ein Mann*, 86–107.

172. "Rote Laubenkolonien in Berlin," *Rote Fahne*, January 29, 1932; "Bei den Siedlern des Pflanzervereins Felseneck," *Welt am Abend*, January 20, 1932; Statement of Kurt Hohmann, no date, in LB A Rep 358-01 Nr. 37, *Adam und Genossen (Felseneck)*, Bd. 5, Bl. 16 Microfilm Roll 420; Judg-ment, Jury Court, LG III, December 22, 1932, in BA-BL R. 22/66804, *Reichsjustizministerium Personalakten, Hans-Joachim Litten*, Bl. 84, 23–24; Hans Litten, "Zu grunde gerichtet! 4 Monate Felsenecke-Prozess," *Arbeiter Illustrierte Zeitung*, Nr. 37, September 9, 1932.

173. Alfred Andree, Statement, February 2, 1932, in LAB A Rep 358-01 Nr. 37, *Adam und Genossen (Felseneck)*, Bd. 5, Bl. 113–15, Microfilm Roll 419; Judgment, Jury Court, LG III, December 22, 1932, in BA-BL R. 22/66804, *Reichsjustizministerium Personalakten, Hans-Joachim Litten*, Bl. 84, 58–60; Paul Klepka, Statement, February 2, 1932, in LAB A Rep 358-01 Nr. 37, *Adam und Genossen (Felseneck)*, Bd. 5, Bl. 99, Microfilm Roll 419.

174. "Wieder drei Todesopfer der roten Mordpest," *Der Angriff*, January 19, 1932; *Bericht*, Polizei-Major Lennarts, January 19, 1932, in LAB A Rep

358-01 Nr. 37, *Adam und Genossen (Felseneck)*, Bd. 1; "Wie die SA-Führer die Mordaktion organisierten," *Welt am Abend*, January 20, 1932; Hans Litten, Beschwerde, October 16, 1932, in LAB A Rep 358-01 Nr. 37, *Adam und Genossen (Felseneck)*, Bd. 12 Bl. 136; Hans Litten, "Zugrunde gerichtet! 4 Monate Felseneck-Prozess," *A.J.Z.*, September 11, 1932, in LAB A Rep 358-01 Nr. 37, *Adam und Genossen (Felseneck)*, Bd. 11 Bl. 234.

175. "Öffentliche Verhandlung des Untersuchungsausschusses über Hakenkreuzterror," *Welt am Abend*, January 26, 1932; "Nazi-Leute überfällt Felseneck-Versammlung," *Welt am Abend*, January 27, 1932; "Grzesinski verbietet Felseneck-Kundgebung," *Welt am Abend*, February 2, 1932.

176. "Der Felsenecke-Prozesse in Moabit," *Welt am Abend*, April 19, 1932; "24 überfallene Kolonisten angeklagte!" *Rote Fahne*, April 21, 1932; "Die Ueberfallenen der Kolonie Felseneck als Angeklagte vor dem Schwurgericht," *Welt am Abend*, April 20, 1932.

177. "SA-Leute bedrohten Frauen mit Revolver. Berichte über Richardstrasse, Felsenecke, Beamtenbank," *Welt am Abend*, April 22, 1932; "24 überfallene Kolonisten angeklagte!" *Rote Fahne*, April 21, 1932; Heinrich Villwock, Statement, February 3, 1932, in LAB A Rep 358-01 Nr. 37, *Adam und Genossen (Felseneck)*, Handakten Bd. IV, Microfilm Roll 422; "Einer von Klemke's Mördern," *Welt am Abend*, April 27, 1932; "Kommune Umlegen," *Welt am Abend*, April 28, 1932.

178. "Einer von Klemke's Mördern," *Welt am Abend*, April 27, 1932; "Kommune Umlegen," *Welt am Abend*, April 28, 1932; " 'Kommune umlegen und dann weg,' " *Rote Fahne*, April 28, 1932.

179. "Eheaffäre im Felseneck-Prozess," *Welt am Abend*, June 15, 1932; Report, STA III, June 16, 1932, in LAB A Rep 358-01 Nr. 1710, *Strafsache gegen Grewen*, Bl. 15–17.

180. "Polizeizeugen im Felseneck-Prozeß," *Rote Fahne*, May 24, 1932; "Sensation im Felseneck-Prozeß. Klemkes Mörder Entüllt," *Welt am Abend*, May 26, 1932; Wilhelm Grewen, Examination, May 31, 1932, in LAB A Rep. 358-01 Nr. 1710, *Strafsache gegen Grewen*, Blattsammlung, Bl. 16–18; "Der Nazi mit der Schupo-Kanone," *Welt am Abend*, June 3, 1932; "Gen. Klemke mit einem Polizeirevolver ermordet?" *Rote Fahne*, June 3, 1932; "Sportwart Grewen Sturmbann 4," *Welt am Abend*, June 7, 1932; Report, STA III, June 16, 1932, in LAB A Rep. 358-01 Nr. 1710, *Strafsache gegen Grewen*, Bl. 19; "Felseneck-Prozeß unter Polizeibedeckung," *Rote Fahne*, June 7, 1932; "Selbstmordversuch des Meineid-Schupos?" *Welt am Abend*, June 8, 1932; "Justizskandal um Wachtmeister Oldenstedt," *Welt am Abend*, June 9, 1932; "Wo ist der Polizeibeamte Oldenstedt geblieben?" *Rote Fahne*, June 9, 1932; "Sensation im Felseneck-Prozeß. Klemkes Mörder Entüllt," *Welt am Abend*, 26 May 1932.

181. "Sensation im Felseneck-Prozeß. Klemkes Mörder Entüllt," *Welt am Abend*, May 26, 1932; Wilhelm Grewen, Examination, May 31, 1932, in LAB A Rep 358-01 Nr. 1710, *Strafsache gegen Grewen*, Blattsammlung, Bl.

18; Report, STA III, June 16, 1932, in LAB A Rep. 358-01 Nr. 1710, *Strafsache gegen Grewen*, Bl. 17–19; Note, May 27, 1932, in LAB A Rep. 358–01 Nr. 1710, *Strafsache gegen Grewen*, Bl. 2; Hans Litten to the STA III, June 6, 1932, in LAB A Rep. 358-01 Nr. 1710, *Strafsache gegen Grewen*, Blattsammlung, Bl. 38–43; OSA Sethe to Litten, June 10, 1932, in LAB A Rep. 358-01 Nr. 1710, *Strafsache gegen Grewen*, Blattsammlung, Bl. 45; Report, STA III, June 16, 1932, in LAB A Rep. 358-01 Nr. 1710, *Strafsache gegen Grewen*, Bl. 21.

182. OSA Sethe to Litten, February 28, 1933, in LAB A Rep. 358-01 Nr. 1710, *Strafsache gegen Grewen*, Blattsammlung, Bl. 51.

183. Typed excerpts from protocol, LAB A Rep 358-01 Nr. 37, *Adam und Genossen (Felseneck)*, Handakten Bd. II, Microfilm Roll 422; "Felseneck Kolonisten entlarven Mordnazis," *Rote Fahne*, July 2, 1932; "Zwei Nazi Lockspitzel im Norkus-Prozeß enlarvt. Hochflut von Prozessen gegen Antifaschisten in Moabit," *Rote Fahne*, July 6, 1932.

184. Hans Litten to the Court, July 21, 1932, in LAB A Rep 358-01 Nr. 37, *Adam und Genossen (Felseneck)*, Handakten Bd. I, Microfilm Roll 422; GSA Wilde, LG I, to PJM, July 29, 1932, in LAB A Rep 358-01 Nr. 2049, *Strafsache gegen Litten wegen Beleidigung des Reichspräsidenten*, Bl. 5–6.

185. OSA Sethe to GSA KG, July 28, 1932, in LAB A Rep 358-01 Nr. 37, *Adam und Genossen (Felseneck)*, Handakten Bd. II, Bl. 1–16, Microfilm Roll 422.

186. Ibid.

187. Statement of LGD Bombe, JM to KGP, March 1926, KGP to JM, March 27, 1926, Braun to JM, October 15, 1926, in GStA Rep. 84a/20315-16, *Angriffe gegen die Justizverwaltung aus Anlaß der Fememordprozesse 1926–7*, Bl. 1/5-11, Bl. 1/13, Bl. 1/21-2, Bl. 1/42-3; "Felseneck-Prozeß—und kein Ende. Hinter den Kulissen des Gerichts—Unwürdige Zustände—Ist das noch Rechtssprechung?" *Germania*, August 11, 1932.

188. Ruling of the Jury Court, August 15, 1932, in LAB A Rep 358-01 Nr. 37, *Adam und Genossen (Felseneck)*, Handakten Bd. II, Bl. 21–32.

189. "Wie Lange darf Litten noch provozieren? Legt dem Anarchisten endlich das unsaubere Handwerk!" *Angriff*, June 3, 1932; *Berliner Zeitung*, quoted in "Interview mit Rechtsanwalt Litten," *Rote Fahne*, August 17, 1932.

190. Erich Cohn-Bendit, "Plädoyer für Litten," *Weltbühne*, August 30, 1932, 314–17.

191. "Interview mit Rechtsanwalt Litten," *Rote Fahne*, August 17, 1932.

192. "Heute wieder Sondergericht und Felseneck," *Rote Fahne*, August 25, 1932; Bode and Kuhlo to the jury court, September 2, 1932, in LAB A Rep 358-01 Nr. 37, *Adam und Genossen (Felseneck)*, Bd. 11 Bl. 125; "Felsenecke-Verhandlung ohne Verteidiger," *Welt am Abend*, August 25, 1932.

193. Bode and Kuhlo to the jury court, September 2, 1932, in LAB A Rep 358-01 Nr. 37, *Adam und Genossen (Felseneck)*, Bd. 11, Bl. 125–26, 129, *Tempo* quoted in "Heraus mit Felsenecke-Kolonisten!" *Rote Fahne*, September 6, 1932.

194. STA Stenig to Vors. des Schwurgerichts III, October 11, 1932, in LAB A Rep 358-01 Nr. 37, *Adam und Genossen (Felseneck)*, Bd. 11, Bl. 222; Protocol of Schwarz's evidence, October 10, 1932; in LAB A Rep 358-01 Nr. 37, *Adam und Genossen (Felseneck)*, Bd. 11 Bl. 223; "Neue Sensation im Felsenecke-Prozess," *Welt am Abend*, October 13, 1932.

195. Erich Cohn-Bendit, Protocol, October 13, 1932, in LAB A Rep 358-01 Nr. 37, *Adam und Genossen (Felseneck)*, Handakten Bd. II, Bl. 225–27; Karl Böttcher, Protocol, October 13, 1932, in LAB A Rep 358-01 Nr. 37, *Adam und Genossen (Felseneck)*, Handakten Bd. II, Bl. 228–30; Hans Litten, Protocol, October 13, 1932, in LAB A Rep 358-01 Nr. 37, *Adam und Genossen (Felseneck)*, Handakten Bd. II, Bl. 230.

196. *Vossische Zeitung*, October 15, 1932 A; Ruling of the Jury Court, October 15, 1932, in LAB A Rep 358-01 Nr. 37, *Adam und Genossen (Felseneck)*, Bd. 11 Bl. 235–36.

197. Ruling of the Jury Court, October 15, 1932, in LAB A Rep 358-01 Nr. 37, *Adam und Genossen (Felseneck)*, Bd. 11 Bl. 235–39, 241–42.

198. "Warum Rechtsanwalt Litten nicht verteidigen darf," *Vossische Zeitung*, October 16, 1932, M; Erich Eyck, "Der verdächtige Verteidiger," *Vossische Zeitung*, October 21, 1932, M.

199. Quoted in "Felseneck-Kolonisten verweigern Aussage," *Rote Fahne*, October 19, 1932; "Litten soll nicht mehr verteidigen dürfen!" *Rote Fahne*, October 16, 1932.

200. Hett, *Death in the Tiergarten*, 220–26; Margaret Lavinia Anderson, *Practicing Democracy: Elections and Political Culture in Imperial Germany* (Princeton: Princeton University Press, 2000).

201. Hans Litten, Complaint, October 16, 1932, in LAB A Rep 358-01 Nr. 37, *Adam und Genossen (Felseneck)*, Bd. 12, Bl. 126–27, 129–33; "Felseneck-Prozeß—und kein Ende," *Germania*, August 11, 1932; "Betrifft: Versammlung der Deutschen Landesgruppe der I.J.V. Internationalen Juristischen Vereinigung," September 14, 1932, in BA-BL R58/3305, Reichssicherheitshauptamt, Bl. 115–17; "Litten bleibt ausgeschlossen," *Welt am Abend*, October 18, 1932.

202. OSA LG III to GSA KG, October 20, 1932, in LAB A Rep 358-01 Nr. 37, *Adam und Genossen (Felseneck)*, Bd. 12 Bl. 160–61.

203. Kammergericht Beschluß of October 28, 1932, in LAB A Rep 358-01 Nr. 37, *Adam und Genossen (Felseneck)*, Bd. 13, Bl. 205ff., Bl. 207–11.

204. Hans Litten, "Notverordnung des Kammergerichts," *Weltbühne*, November 22, 1932, 757–60.

205. Rudolf Olden, "Der Geist der Bevormundung," *Berliner Tageblatt*, November 29, 1932, M; Anwaltskammer Berlin, Beschlüsse v. 21 November 1932; *Juristische Wochenschrift*, 1932, 3744; "Freiheit der Verteidigung. Beschlüsse der Berliner Anwaltskammer," *Vossische Zeitung*, November 22, 1932, A.

206. Tigges to Wolff, November 30, 1932, in *Berliner Anwaltsblatt*, 1933, 11 (I am grateful to the Rechtsanwälte Gerhard Jungfer and Tillmann Krach for this source); President of the 2nd Criminal Senate to KGP, November 29, 1932, in *Berliner Anwaltsblatt*, 1933, 13; Wolff to Tigges, December 13, 1932, in *Berliner Anwaltsblatt*, 1933, 15; Olden, "Der Geist der Bevormundung."

207. "Litten als Zeuge," *Welt am Abend*, December 1, 1932; "Felseneck-Prozeß wieder aufgeflogen," *Angriff*, October 18, 1932; "Wiederbeginn mit Hindernissen," *Vossische Zeitung*, October 18, 1932, M; "Zusammenstöße im Felsenecke-Prozeße," *Welt am Abend*, October 20, 1932; "Ein unzurechnungsfähiger Kronzeuge," *Angriff*, December 9, 1932; "Die Strafanträge im Felseneck-Prozess," *Vossische Zeitung*, December 15, 1932, A; "Sturmszenen im Felsenecke-Prozeß," *Welt am Abend*, December 16, 1932; "Kommunistische Angeklagte und Zuhörer klatschen dem Staatsanwalt Stenig Beifall," *Angriff*, December 13, 1932.

208. Judgment, Jury Court, LG III, December 22, 1932, in BA-BL R. 22/66804, *Reichsjustizministerium Personalakten, Hans-Joachim Litten*, Bl. 84, 87; "Sondergerichte beseitigt," *Berliner Tageblatt*, December 21, 1932, A; "Ossietzky freigelassen," *Berliner Tageblatt*, December 23, 1932, M.

209. Judgment, Jury Court, LG III, December 22, 1932, in BA-BL R. 22/66804, *Reichsjustizministerium Personalakten, Hans-Joachim Litten*, Bl. 84, 5, 7, 10–11, 14–15, 20–22, 28.

210. Ibid., 76–79.

211. Ibid., 36.

212. Ibid., 44; Dieter Gosewinkel, *Adolf Arndt. Die Wiederbegründung des Rechtsstaats aus dem Geist der Sozialdemokratie (1945–1961)* (Bonn: Verlag J. H. W. Dietz Nachf., 1991), 15, 21.

213. Judgment, Jury Court, LG III, December 22, 1932, in BA-BL R. 22/66804, *Reichsjustizministerium Personalakten, Hans-Joachim Litten*, Bl. 82–96.

214. "Freisprüche im Felsenecke-Prozess. Einstellung des Verfahrens auf Grund der Amnestie," *Vossische Zeitung*, December 23, 1932 M; "Das 'Felseneck' Urteil," *Berliner Tageblatt*, December 23, 1932, M.

215. Blasius, *Weimars Ende*, 82–83.

216. Hans Litten to Sulamith Reuter, n.d. (presumably 1935), in BA-BL NY 4011, *Nachlaß Hans Litten, Bd. 3 Korrespondenz—Ausgehende*, Bl. 225; Hans Litten to Irmgard Litten, August 14, 1936, in BA-BL NY 4011, *Nachlaß Hans Litten, Bd. 3 Korrespondenz—Ausgehende*, Bl. 113; Hans Litten to Irmgard Litten, November 3, 1935, in BA-BL NY 4011, *Nachlaß Hans Litten, Bd. 3 Korrespondenz—Ausgehende*, Bl. 83; Irmgard Litten to Dr. Grunow, March 19, 1934, in LBI AR 5112, *Hans Litten Collection*, 1/2, 15–16.

217. Max Fürst, *Gefilte Fisch*, 650.

218. OSA LG II to OSA LG III, December 20, 1932, in LAB A Rep 358-01 Nr. 1510, *Strafsache gegen Litten wegen Begünstigung*, Bl. 1; Heinz Schüler,

Examination, October 1, 1932, in LAB A Rep 358-01 Nr. 1510, *Strafsache gegen Litten wegen Begünstigung*, Bl. 2; Vermerk, in LAB A Rep 358-01 Nr. 1510, *Strafsache gegen Litten wegen Begünstigung*, Bl. 3; STA Volk, Äußerung, in LAB A Rep 358-01 Nr. 1510, *Strafsache gegen Litten wegen Begünstigung*, Bl. 3; Verfügung: Einstellung, in LAB A Rep 358-01 Nr. 1510, *Strafsache gegen Litten wegen Begünstigung*, Bl. 5.

219. Irmgard Litten, *Beyond Tears* (New York: Alliance, 1940), 29; Litten, *Eine Mutter kämpft*, 17; Max Fürst, obituary for Hans Litten, *Sozialistische Warte*, August 12, 1938, in BA-BL NY 4011, *Nachlaß Hans Litten*, Bd. 8 *Artikel über Hans Litten 1937–1951*, Bl. 17.

220. Rudolf Diels, *Lebenslauf*, September 2, 1935, in NARA BDC Microfilm, Roll Number A 3343 SSO-149, 1255–56; Affidavit of Alfred Martin, October 6, 1954, in NHH VVP 46 *Nachlaß Rudolf Diels*, Bd. 15; Rudolf Diels to PJM, July 2, 1932, in BA-BL R. 22/66804, *Reichsjustizministerium Personalakten*, Hans-Joachim Litten, Bl. 36; Statement of Rudolf Diels, November, 1945, IfZ Bestand OMGUS-Akten, 3/71–3/4 PROP-PLEA, 3; Robert M. W. Kempner, *Ankläger einer Epoche. Lebenserinnerungen* (Frankfurt/Main: Verlag Ullstein, 1983), 110–11; Jürgen Schmädeke, Alexander Bahar, und Wilfried Kugel, "Der Reichstagsbrand in neuem Licht," in *Historische Zeitschrift*, Band 269, Heft 3 (Dezember 1999), 635–36; Diels, *Lucifer*, 151; Alexander Bahar and Wilfried Kugel, *Der Reichstagsbrand. Wie Geschichte gemacht wird* (Berlin: Quintessenz-Verlag, 2001), 170–71; Hans Otto Meissner and Harry Wilde, *Die Machtergreifung. Ein Bericht über die Technik des Nationalsozialistischen Staatsstreichs* (Stuttgart: J. G. Cotta'sche Buchhandlung Nachf., 1958), n. 58, 301.

PART III

1. Irmgard Litten, *Eine Mutter kämpft gegen Hitler* (Frankfurt/Main: Röderberg-Verlag, 1984), 17.

2. Henry Ashby Turner Jr., *Hitler's Thirty Days to Power: January 1933* (Reading, Mass.: Addison-Wesley, 1996), 1–2; *Arbeiter Illustrierte Zeitung*, January 1, 1933; Joseph Goebbels, diary entry, December 24, 1932, in Goebbels, *Tagebücher 1924–1945*, ed. Ralf Georg Reuth, Bd. 2, 1930–1934 (Munich: Piper Verlag, 1992), 740; Carl Zuckmayer, *Als wär's ein Stück von mir. Horen der Freundschaft* (Frankfurt/Main: Fischer Taschenbuch Verlag, 1997), 522.

3. Schleicher to H. Foersch, quoted in Joachim Fest, *Hitler. Eine Biographie* (Berlin: Ullstein Taschenbuch, 2005), 506; Gordon A. Craig, *The Politics of the Prussian Army, 1640–1945* (London: Oxford University Press, 1964), 460–61.

4. Turner, *Hitler's Thirty Days to Power*, 31–52, 135–61; Heinrich August Winkler, *Weimar, 1918–1933: Die Geschichte der ersten Deutschen Demokratie* (Munich: Verlag C. H. Beck, 1998), 567–94.

5. Max Fürst, *Gefilte Fisch und wie es weiterging* (Munich: DTV, 2004), 658–59.

6. Ibid., 661–62.

7. Ibid.

8. Rudolf Diels, *Lucifer ante Portas. Zwischen Severing und Heydrich* (Zürich: Interverlag, 1949), 169.

9. Ibid., 143–44; translation from J. Noakes and G. Pribram, eds., *Nazism 1919–1945, A Documentary Reader, Volume 1: The Rise to Power 1919–1934* (Exeter, U.K.: University of Exeter Press, 1998), 139–41.

10. Diels, *Lucifer*, 146, 144.

11. Max Fürst, *Gefilte Fisch*, 662.

12. I. Litten, *Eine Mutter kämpft*, 17–18; Max Fürst, *Gefilte Fisch*, 662–63.

13. *Braunbuch über Reichstagsbrand und Hitlerterror. Faksimile Nachdruck der Originalausgabe von 1933* (Frankfurt/Main: Röderberg-Verlag, 1978), 363–64.

14. Simone Ladwig-Winters, *Anwalt ohne Recht. Das Schicksal jüdischer Rechtsanwälte in Berlin nach 1933* (Berlin: be.bra Verlag, 1998), 28–36; Egon Erwin Kisch, *Mein Leben für die Zeitung. 1926–1947: Journalistische Texte 2* (East Berlin: Aufbau Verlag, 1983), 322.

15. Text in Ernst Rudolf Huber, ed., *Dokumente zur Deutschen Verfassungsgeschichte*, 3rd ed., Bd. 4 (Stuttgart: Verlag W. Kohlhammer GmbH, 1991), 663–64; translation of the Decree from Noakes and Pribram, *Nazism*, 142.

16. I. Litten, *Eine Mutter kämpft*, 18.

17. Ernst Wolff to Prussian Interior Ministry, March 3, 1933; in GStA Rep. 84a/20155, Bl. 89, 91 (I am grateful to Rechtsanwalt Dr. Tilmann Krach for drawing this source to my attention); Tilmann Krach, *Jüdische Rechtsanwälte in Preußen. Über die Bedeutung der freien Advokatur und ihre Zerstörung durch den Nationalsozialismus* (Munich: C. H. Beck, 1991), 89; PJM to Anwaltskammer, March 28, 1933, in BA-BL R. 22/66804, *Reichsjustizministerium Personalakten*, Hans-Joachim Litten, Bl. 82a; PJM to PIM, March 6, 1933, in BA-BL R. 22/66804, *Reichsjustizministerium Personalakten*, Hans-Joachim Litten, Bl. 82.

18. Diels, *Lucifer*, 196.

19. Arbeitskreis Ehemaliges KZ Sonnenburg, *Sonnenburg—Slonsk. Materialien Nr. 1. Geschichte und Funktion des KZ Sonnenburg* (Berlin: Neue Wege, 1987), 5; I. Litten, *Eine Mutter kämpft*, 20.

20. Kreszentia Mühsam, *Der Leidensweg Erich Mühsams* (Berlin: Harald-Kater-Verlag, 1994; originally published Zürich: Mopr Verlag, 1935), 20–24, 29; I. Litten, *Eine Mutter kämpft*, 21, 35; *Braunbuch*, 285–86.

21. "Bericht über Sonnenburg," n.d., in BA-BL NJ 14220, Bd. 2, Bl. 304.

22. I. Litten, *Eine Mutter kämpft*, 22; Max Fürst, *Gefilte Fisch*, 664.

23. I. Litten, *Eine Mutter kämpft*, 20.

24. Ibid., 26.

25. Diels, *Lucifer*, 163; LAB A Rep. 358/1175, *Krause wegen Beleidigung RAs Litten im "Angriff,"* Microfilm Roll A 730; I. Litten, *Eine Mutter kämpft*, 24–25.

26. "Bericht über Sonnenburg," n.d., in BA-BL NJ 14220, Bd. 2, Bl. 304; "Ausschnitte aus einem Bericht des Schutzhaftdezernenten Mittelbach an Oberregierungsrat Diels (ohne Datum) betr. Besichtigung des Polizeigefängnisses Sonnenburg vom 10.4.1933," reprinted in Christoph Graf, *Politische Polizei zwischen Demokratie und Diktatur. Die Entwicklung der preußischen Politischen Polizei vom Staatsschutzorgan der Weimarer Republik zum Geheimen Staatspolizeiamt des Dritten Reiches* (Berlin: Colloquium Verlag, 1983), 431–32; Diels, *Lucifer* 197; I. Litten, *Eine Mutter kämpft*, 27.

27. Wilhelm Hoegner, *Der Schwierige Aussenseiter*, translation from Noakes and Pribram, *Nazism*, 159; Max Domarus, *Hitler: Speeches and Proclamations 1932–1945*, vol. 1 1932–1934 (Wauconda, Ill.: Bolchazy-Carducci, 1990), 289.

28. Lothar Gruchmann, *Justiz im Dritten Reich 1933–1940. Anpassung und Unterwerfung in der Ära Gürtner* (Munich: R. Oldenbourg Verlag, 2001), 87–88; "Jüdische Strafrichter verschwinden," *Deutsche Zeitung*, March 20, 1933, "Umbesetzung bei Berliner Gerichten. Strafkammer-Vorsitzende übernehmen Zivilkammern," *Berliner Montagspost*, March 20, 1933, "Berliner Strafgerichte judenrein. Jüdische Staatsanwälte als Sitzungsvertreter nicht mehr zugelassen," *Völkischer Beobachter*, March 21, 1933, *Deutsche Zeitung*, March 31, 1933, *Frankfürter Zeitung*, April 1, 1933, *Berliner Lokal-Anzeiger*, April 1, 1933, *Tägliche Rundschau*, April 2, 1933, in GStA Rep. 84a/20251, *Zeitungs-Ausschnitte über wirkliche oder vermeintliche Mißstände bei Gerichten des Kammergerichtsbezirks*, Bl. 77–78, Bl. 82, Bl. 90, 97–98, 109.

29. "Erste Verordnung zur Durchführung des Gesetzes zur Wiederherstellung des Berufsbeamtentums vom 11. April 1933," *Reichsgesetzblatt* 1933 I, 195.

30. "Gesetz zur Wiederherstellung des Berufsbeamtentums vom 7. April 1933," *Reichsgesetzblatt* 1933 I, 175, April 7, 1933 (emphasis added); "Gesetz über die Zulassung zur Rechtsanwaltschaft vom 7. April 1933," *Reichsgesetzblatt* 1933 I, 188; "Die Reform der Justiz. Interview mit Ministerialdirektor Freisler," *Berliner Tageblatt*, April 12, 1933, in IfZ MA-108, *Reichsjustizministerium Rechtsgestaltung und Rechtspolitik—Allgemeine vom 1. April 1933 bis September 1934*, Bd. 1, Bl. 5.

31. Ewarth, letter of March 3, 1933 (probably April 3), in GStA Rep. 84a/20361, *Gesetz zur Wiederherstellung des Berufsbeamtentums betr. Staatsanwälte*, Bl. 27–8; OSA Amtsgericht Berlin Mitte to GSA KG, June 3, 1933, in GStA Rep. 84a/20361, *Gesetz zur Wiederherstellung des Berufsbeamtentums betr. Staatsanwälte*, Bl. 30; JM to Ewarth and GSA KG, August 7, 1933, in GStA Rep. 84a/20361, *Gesetz zur Wiederherstellung des*

Berufsbeamtentums betr. Staatsanwälte, Bl. 35–36; Gertrud Köhler to JM, September 1, 1933, Geheimes Staatspolizeiamt to JM, September 4, 1933, Benno Köhler's statement, August 31, 1933, in GStA Rep. 84a/20361, *Gesetz zur Wiederherstellung des Berufsbeamtentums betr. Staatsanwälte*, Bl. 83–87; *Völkischer Beobachter*, September 10, 1933, in GStA Rep. 84a/20251, *Zeitungs-Ausschnitte über wirkliche oder vermeintliche Mißstände bei Gerichten des Kammergerichtsbezirks*, Bl. 158.

32. Ralf Georg Reuth, *Goebbels. Eine Biographie* (Munich: Piper Verlag, 2005), 200; Paul Stenig, *Äußerung* July 13, 1933, in GStA Rep. 84a/20361, *Gesetz zur Wiederherstellung des Berufsbeamtentums betr. Staatsanwälte*, Bl. 101; Reinhard Neubert to GSA KG, July 2, 1933, in GStA Rep. 84a/20361, *Gesetz zur Wiederherstellung des Berufsbeamtentums betr. Staatsanwälte*, Bl. 89; Otto Kamecke to GSA KG, July 15, 1933, in GStA Rep. 84a/20361, *Gesetz zur Wiederherstellung des Berufsbeamtentums betr. Staatsanwälte*, Bl. 90; Report of the GSA KG to JM, July 20, 1933, in GStA Rep. 84a/20361, *Gesetz zur Wiederherstellung des Berufsbeamtentums betr. Staatsanwälte*, Bl. 93–95, 99; NSDAP Gau Groß-Berlin to JM, August 15, 1933, Notice, September 8, 1933, in GStA Rep. 84a/20361, *Gesetz zur Wiederherstellung des Berufsbeamtentums betr. Staatsanwälte*, Bl. 113–15.

33. *BZ am Mittag*, April 21, 1933, in GStA Rep. 84a/20251, *Zeitungs-Ausschnitte über wirkliche oder vermeintliche Mißstände bei Gerichten des Kammergerichtsbezirks*, Bl. 111; *Börsenzeitung*, April 20, 1933, in GStA Rep. 84a/20251, *Zeitungs-Ausschnitte über wirkliche oder vermeintliche Mißstände bei Gerichten des Kammergerichtsbezirks*, Bl. 113; "Schwurgerichtstagung in Potsdam feierlich eröffnet," *Berliner Lokal-Anzeiger*, August 21, 1933, in GStA Rep. 84a/20251, *Zeitungs-Ausschnitte über wirkliche oder vermeintliche Mißstände bei Gerichten des Kammergerichtsbezirks*, Bl. 147; *Der Montag*, March 20, 1933, in GStA Rep. 84a/20251, *Zeitungs-Ausschnitte über wirkliche oder vermeintliche Mißstände bei Gerichten des Kammergerichtsbezirks*, Bl. 81.

34. Ian Kershaw, *Hitler 1936–1945: Nemesis* (London: Penguin, 2000), 508–9; H. W. Koch, *In the Name of the Volk: Political Justice in Hitler's Germany* (London: I. B. Tauris, 1989), 32; *Deutsche Zeitung*, March 20, 1933, in GStA Rep. 84a/20251, *Zeitungs-Ausschnitte über wirkliche oder vermeintliche Mißstände bei Gerichten des Kammergerichtsbezirks*, Bl. 78; letter of February 15, 1933, printed in *Deutsche Zeitung*, March 2, 1933, in GStA Rep. 84a/2945, *Richter und Staatsanwälte, 1931–35*, 199.

35. *Tempo*, April 1, 1933, in GStA Rep. 84a/20251, *Zeitungs-Ausschnitte über wirkliche oder vermeintliche Mißstände bei Gerichten des Kammergerichtsbezirks*, Bl. 102; Krach, *Jüdische Rechtsanwälte*, 210; Leo Plaut to PJM, April 7, 1933, in BA-BL R. 22/70917, *Reichsjustizministerium Personalakten Dr. Leo Plaut*, Bl. 11–15.

36. Krach, *Jüdische Rechtsanwälte*, 210; BLHA Rep. 4a/7118, *Kammergerichtsbezirk Personalia Curt Becker*; BA-BL R. 22/62504, *Reichsjustizministerium*

Personalakten Otto Kamecke; BA-BL R. 22/70930, *Reichsjustizministerium Personalakten Dr. Ernst Plettenberg*; BA-BL R. 22/73293, *Reichsjustizministerium Personalakten Dr. Alfons Sack*; Walther Kiaulehn, *Berlin. Schicksal einer Weltstadt* (Munich: Verlag C. H. Beck, 1997), 510; BLHA Rep. 4a/9951, *Kammergerichtsbezirk Personalia Reinhard Neubert.*

37. GSA KG to Kommissar des Reiches, April 10, 1933, in BA-BL R. 22/66804, *Reichsjustizministerium Personalakten, Hans-Joachim Litten*, Bl. 92; Prussian Justice Ministry to Hans Litten, May 6, 1933, in BA-BL R. 22/66804, *Reichsjustizministerium Personalakten, Hans-Joachim Litten*, Bl. 88–89.

38. Notice to KPG, PJM to PIM, June 2, 1933, in BA-BL R. 22/66804, *Reichsjustizministerium Personalakten, Hans-Joachim Litten*, Bl. 91, Bl. 86.

39. Kisch, *Mein Leben für die Zeitung*, 327; Hans-Rainer Sandvoß, *Widerstand in Spandau. Heft 3 der Schriftenreihe über den Widerstand in Berlin von 1933 bis 1945* (Berlin: Gedenkstätte Deutscher Widerstand, 1988), 31.

40. Ludwig Bendix ("Reversus"), *Konzentrationslager Deutschland und andere Schutzhafterinnerungen 1933 bis 1937*, unpublished memoir, LBI Memoir Collection, ME 40, Films MM 6 and MM 7, Bk. I, 5, 8–9.

41. Hans Litten to Irmgard Litten, May 17, 1933, in BA-BL NY 4011, *Nachlaß Hans Litten, Bd. 3 Korrespondenz—Ausgehende*, Bl. 1; Bendix, *Konzentrationslager Deutschland*, Bk. I, 11–12; LAB A Rep 362 Nr. 516, Bl. 483, 486, 497, 499, 573, 627.

42. I. Litten, *Eine Mutter kämpft*, 32–33; Max Fürst, *Gefilte Fisch*, 665.

43. I. Litten, *Eine Mutter kämpft*, 30–31; Hans Litten to Irmgard Litten, June 3, 1933, in BA-BL NY 4011, *Nachlaß Hans Litten, Bd. 3 Korrespondenz—Ausgehende*, Bl. 2.

44. I. Litten, *Eine Mutter kämpft*, 30–31, 35; Max Fürst, *Gefilte Fisch*, 665.

45. I. Litten, *Eine Mutter kämpft*, 63–65.

46. Ibid., 65–66.

47. Ibid., 63–65; Ministerialrat S. Kunisch to Gestapo, August 21, 1934, in BA-BL R. 22/66804, *Reichsjustizministerium Personalakten, Hans-Joachim Litten*, Bl. 97; Gruchmann, *Justiz im Dritten Reich*, 64, 244, 246; Helmut Ortner, *Der Hinrichter. Roland Freisler—Mörder im Dienste Hitlers* (Göttingen: Steidl Verlag, 1995), 124; Diels, *Lucifer*, 215.

48. Diels, *Lucifer*, 185; Hildegard Stennes, *Entschädigungsantrag*, July 3, 1957, in NHH VVP 46, *Nachlaß Rudolf Diels*, Bd. 20.

49. Diels, *Lucifer*, 222–23; Alexander Bahar and Wilfried Kugel, *Der Reichstagsbrand. Wie Geschichte gemacht wird* (Berlin: Quintessenz-Verlag, 2001), 722.

50. Graf, *Politische Polizei*, 318–19; 323, 328; Statement of Rudolf Diels, November 1945, IfZ Bestand OMGUS-Akten, 3/71–3/4 PROP-PLEA, 1–2; Robert M. W. Kempner, *Ankläger einer Epoche. Lebenserinnerungen* (Frankfurt/Main: Verlag Ullstein, 1983), 112–13; Hans Bernd Gisevius, *Bis*

zum bitteren Ende. Vom Reichstagsbrand bis zum 20. Juli 1944 (Hamburg: Rütten & Loenig Verlag, 1960), 99–100.

51. Vermerk, September 27, 1954, in NHH NDS 100 (01) Acc. 134/97 Nr. 64, *Diels, Rudolf, Regierungspräsident Band 2 1954*, Bl. 18; Diels to Ernst Müller-Meiningen, n.d. (1954), in NHH VVP 46, *Nachlaß Rudolf Diels*, Bd. 15; Rudolf Diels, *Der Fall Otto John. Hintergründe und Lehren* (Göttingen: Göttinger Verlagsanstalt, 1954), 15; Diels to Heinrich Himmler, October 10, 1933, in NARA BDC Microfilm, Roll Number A 3343 SSO-149, 1294; Kempner, *Ankläger*, 116–18.

52. Hildegard Diels, Statement, n.d., in NHH VVP 46 *Nachlaß Rudolf Diels*, Bd. 27; Diels, *John*, 19; Gisevius, *Ende*, 100; Carl Severing, *Mein Lebensweg*, Bd. II: *Im Auf und Ab der Republik* (Cologne: Greven Verlag, 1950), 341–42; Wilhelm Abegg to Carl Severing, August 4, 1932, in IfZ F 48, *Dokumente aus den Akten des Staatsministers Severing*, Bl. 7–8; Bahar and Kugel, *Reichstagsbrand*, 38–39.

53. Rudolf Diels, *Lebenslauf*, September 2, 1935, in NARA BDC Microfilm, Roll Number A 3343 SSO-149, 1255–56; Affidavit of Alfred Martin, October 6, 1954, in NHH VVP 46 *Nachlaß Rudolf Diels*, Bd. 15.

54. Rudolf Diels to PJM, July 2, 1932, in BA-BL R. 22/66804, *Reichsjustizministerium Personalakten, Hans-Joachim Litten*, Bl. 36; Police President to PIM, September 30, 1932, in GStA Rep 84a/51163, *Verbot der Protestversammlungen der "Roten Hilfe" gegen die Sondergerichte 1932*, Bl. 1–3.

55. Statement of Rudolf Diels, November 1945, IfZ Bestand OMGUS-Akten, 3/71–3/4 PROP-PLEA, 3.

56. "Nachweisung über Schutzhäftlinge, die länger als ein Jahr in Schutzhaft einsitzen und für die Amnestie nicht in Vorschlag gebracht waren," in GStA Rep. 90, *Staatsministerium*, Annex P, *Geheime Staatspolizei*, Nr. 110, Bl. 62.

57. Rudolf Diels, Memo to Robert Kempner, June 20, 1946, in NHH VVP 46 *Nachlaß Rudolf Diels*, Bd. 21; Rudolf Diels, "Pol. Pol. 33 Anfange und Übergang," n.d. (1946), in NHH VVP 46, *Nachlaß Rudolf Diels*, Bd. 22; Diels, *Lucifer*, 151.

58. Kempner, *Ankläger*, 110–11; Grauert to Göring, November 2, 1933, in BA-BL R. 3003/204, Bl. 255; Jürgen Schmädeke, Alexander Bahar, and Wilfried Kugel, "Der Reichstagsbrand in neuem Licht," *Historische Zeitschrift*, Band 269, Heft 3 (Dezember 1999), 603–51, 635–36; Police President to PIM, September 30, 1932, in GStA Rep 84a/51163, *Verbot der Protestversammlungen der "Roten Hilfe" gegen die Sondergerichte 1932*, Bl. 1–3.

59. Kempner, *Ankläger*, 110–11; Hans Otto Meissner and Harry Wilde, *Die Machtergreifung. Ein Bericht über die Technik des Nationalsozialistischen Staatsstreichs* (Stuttgart: J. G. Cotta'sche Buchhandlung Nachf., 1958), 301 n.58; "Peter Brandes" (Curt Riess), "Feuer über Deutschland," *Stern*, November 9, 1957, December 7, 1957.

60. Joseph Goebbels, "Kommunismus ohne Maske," Speech at the 1935 Nuremberg Nazi Party Rally, in PA Auswärtiges Amt, *Referat Deutschland*, R. 98688 "Kommunismus ohne Maske."

61. *Angriff*, June 12, 1933; *Angriff*, June 13, 1933; *Sozialdemokrat*, December 20, 1933, in DA 2858, *Presseberichte über das Lager Dachau. Ausland. Sozialdemokrat (Prag)*.

62. Diels, *Lucifer*, 216; Ministerialrat S. Kunisch to Gestapo, August 21, 1934, in BA-BL R. 22/66804, *Reichsjustizministerium Personalakten, Hans-Joachim Litten*, Bl. 97; Irmgard Litten to Hans Litten, February 3, 1934, in WL Archive 572, *Hans Litten: Correspondence, 1933–1938*, Reel MF Doc 54/28.

63. Undated typescript, BA-BL NY 4011, *Nachlaß Hans Litten*, Bd. 8 *Artikel über Hans Litten 1937–1951*, Bl. 63–64; H. Bernhard und D. Elazar (Chefredakteur), *Der Reichstagsbrandprozeß und Georgi Dimitroff. Dokumente*, Bd. 2 (East Berlin: Dietz Verlag, 1989), 115–24; Bendix, *Konzentrationslager Deutschland*, Bk. I, 5–6.

64. I. Litten, *Eine Mutter kämpft*, 36.

65. Undated typescript (Autumn 1933), in BA-BL NY 4011 *Nachlaß Hans Litten*, Bd. 8 "Artikel über Hans Litten 1937–1951," Bl. 63–68; GSA LG Berlin, August 18, 1933, in LAB A Rep 358–01 Nr. 37, *Adam und Genossen (Felseneck)*, Handakten Bd. II Bl. 71–74, Microfilm Roll 422.

66. "Rechtsanwalt Litten als Mitwisser entlarvt," *Angriff*, August 12, 1933, "Felsenecke-Bluttat geklärt," *Berliner Tageblatt*, August 12, 1933, "Kommunist gesteht Mord an S.A. Mann Schwarz! Rotfront-Litten der Begünstigung überführt und ebenfalls geständig," *Völkischer Beobachter*, August 13–14, 1933, in LAB A Rep 358-01 Nr. 37, *Adam und Genossen (Felseneck)*, Handakten Bd. III, Bl. 70, Film 422.

67. Hans Litten to Margot Fürst, August 13, 1933, in BA-BL NY 4011, *Nachlaß Hans Litten, Bd. 3 Korrespondenz—Ausgehende*, Bl. 177–78.

68. Hans Litten to Inspector Hohwedel, August 15, 1933, in LAB A Rep. 362 Nr. 88, *Spezialakten der Strafanstalt zu Spandau Betreffend Todesfälle*, Bl. 164; I. Litten, *Eine Mutter kämpft*, 39.

69. Hans Litten to Inspector Hohwedel, postscript, August 16, 1933, in LAB A Rep. 362 Nr. 88, *Spezialakten der Strafanstalt zu Spandau Betreffend Todesfälle*, Bl. 164.

70. Report to the President of the Prison Office, August 16, 1933, in LAB A Rep. 362 Nr. 88, *Spezialakten der Strafanstalt zu Spandau Betreffend Todesfälle*, Bl. 162.

71. Irmgard Litten, *Beyond Tears* (New York: Alliance, 1940), 42; I. Litten, *Eine Mutter kämpft*, 38, 42–43; typed notes of a prisoner's account, n.d., in BA-BL NY 4011, *Nachlaß Hans Litten*, Bd. 7, Bl. 43.

72. I. Litten, *Eine Mutter kämpft*, 74–75; BA-BL R. 22/53692, *Reichsjustizministerium Personalakten Dr. Otto Conrady*.

73. I. Litten, *Beyond Tears*, 51; I. Litten, *Eine Mutter kämpft*, 46.

74. GSA Hamm to Ministerialdirektor Lentz, Januar 29, 1943, in BA-BL R. 22/53692, *Reichsjustizministerium Personalakten Dr. Otto Conrady*, Bl. 58; Information on Conrady's death supplied by the Deutsche Dienststelle für Nachrichten, April 7, 2005.

75. Hans Litten to Irmgard Litten, September 7, 1933, in BA-BL NY 4011, *Nachlaß Hans Litten, Bd. 3 Korrespondenz—Ausgehende*, Bl. 5; Hans Litten to Irmgard Litten, January 23, 1934, in BA-BL NY 4011, *Nachlaß Hans Litten, Bd. 3 Korrespondenz—Ausgehende*, Bl. 10; Hans Litten to Irmgard Litten, September 16, 1933, in BA-BL NY 4011, *Nachlaß Hans Litten, Bd. 3 Korrespondenz—Ausgehende*, Bl. 6.

76. GSA LG to JM through GSA KG, September 25, 1933, in LAB A Rep 358-01 Nr. 37, *Adam und Genossen (Felseneck)*, Felseneck Handakten Bd. II Bl. 78–82, Microfilm Roll 422.

77. GSA LG to PJM through GSA KG, November 15, 1933, GSA LG to PJM through GSA KG, November 24, 1933, in LAB A Rep 358-01 Nr. 37, *Adam und Genossen (Felseneck)*, Handakten Bd. II, Bl. 84, Microfilm Roll 422.

78. I. Litten, *Eine Mutter kämpft*, 69–72.

79. Ibid., 72; I. Litten, *Beyond Tears*, 107–9.

80. I. Litten, *Eine Mutter kämpft*, 72; Kurt Hiller, *Rote Ritter: Erlebnisse mit deutschen Kommunisten* (Berlin: A. W. Mytze, 1980), 54–55; I. Litten, *Beyond Tears*, 106.

81. Hiller quoted in I. Litten, *Beyond Tears*, 109–10 (in the edition of Irmgard Litten's book published in the GDR, all references to Kurt Hiller, and much of this material associated with him, was cut); I. Litten, *Beyond Tears*, 106; Max Fürst, *Gefilte Fisch*, 702.

82. I. Litten, *Eine Mutter kämpft*, 74–86; Irmgard Litten to Rudolf Diels, in BA-BL NY 4011, *Nachlaß Hans Litten*, Bd. 6, *Briefwechsel der Mutter Hans Littens 1937–1940*, Bl. 84; Direktor, staatl. Konzentrationslager Brandenburg, to Irmgard Litten, November 7, 1933, in BA-BL NY 4011, *Nachlaß Hans Litten*, Bd. 6, *Briefwechsel der Mutter Hans Littens 1937–1940*, Bl. 83; I. Litten, *Beyond Tears*, 110; reference to Hiller in I. Litten, *Beyond Tears*, 110–11.

83. Hans Litten to Margot Fürst, August 13, 1933, in BA-BL NY 4011, *Nachlaß Hans Litten, Bd. 3 Korrespondenz—Ausgehende*, Bl. 178.

84. Margot Fürst to Max Fürst, May 2, 1934, private collection of Mrs. Birute Stern; I. Litten, *Eine Mutter kämpft*, 68–69, 93.

85. Margot Fürst, interviewed for "Ich hänge tot an meinen Träumen," broadcast on SFB, October 28, 1991, transcript in the private collection of Herr Gerhard Jungfer; Max Fürst, *Gefilte Fisch*, 681–82; *Braunbuch*, 68.

86. Joseph Goebbels to Prince Carl of Sweden, summer 1933 (August?), in AA-PA R. 98460, *Referat Deutschland, Konzentrationslager*.

87. Margot Fürst, interviewed for "Ich hänge tot an meinen Träumen," broadcast on SFB, October 28, 1991, transcript in the private collection of Herr Gerhard Jungfer; I. Litten, *Beyond Tears*, 113–14.

88. Max Fürst, *Gefilte Fisch*, 683; GSA beim Landgericht to ORA Leipzig, February 26, 1934, in BA-BL NJ 9782, Bl. 1–2; I. Litten, *Beyond Tears*, 114.

89. I. Litten, *Beyond Tears*, 113; Max Fürst, *Gefilte Fisch*, 692.

90. Max Fürst, *Gefilte Fisch*, 684; Birute Stern, interview with the author, February 16, 2005; Margot Fürst to Max Fürst, March 27, 1934, private collection of Mrs. Birute Stern.

91. Max Fürst, *Gefilte Fisch*, 684–85, 687; GSA beim Landgericht to ORA Leipzig, February 26, 1934, in BA-BL NJ 9782, Bl. 1–2.

92. Margot Fürst to Bernhard Hartkorn, December 18, 1933, Frau Meisel to Max Fürst, December 20, 1933, Margot Fürst to the Meisels, December 21, 1933, private collection of Mrs. Birute Stern; Max Fürst, *Gefilte Fisch*, 687–88, 697, 711.

93. Max Fürst, *Gefilte Fisch*, 688–89.

94. Namensverzeichnis Lex 1 Pol a 1934, in LB A Rep 358-02 Bde. 110–124, Film Nr. 3867, and Bde. 125–143, Film Nr. 3868; GSA beim Landgericht to ORA Leipzig, February 26, 1934, in BA-BL NJ 9782, Bl. 1, Bl. 4; ORA Leipzig to GSTA beim Landgericht, March 3, 1934, in BA-BL NJ 9782, Bl. 6.

95. Max Fürst, *Gefilte Fisch*, 692–93, 694–95, 701; Max Fürst to Frau Meisel, April 16, 1934, Margot Fürst to Max Fürst, May 16, 1934, Margot Fürst to Max Fürst, June 21, 1934, private collection of Mrs. Birute Stern.

96. I. Litten, *Beyond Tears*, 119; Birute Stern, interview with the author, Stuttgart, March 24, 2005.

97. Margot Fürst to Max Fürst, December 28, 1933; Margot Fürst to Max Fürst, January 16, 1934; Max Fürst to Margot Fürst, January 18, 1934, private collection of Mrs. Birute Stern.

98. Max Fürst to Margot Fürst, March 27, 1934; Margot Fürst to Max Fürst, April 3, 1934; Max Fürst to Margot Fürst, June 4, 1934; Max Fürst to Margot Fürst, August 14, 1934, private collection of Mrs. Birute Stern.

99. I. Litten, *Beyond Tears*, 120.

100. "Gesetz über die Gewährung von Straffreiheit vom 7. August 1934," *Reichsgesetzblatt* 1934 Teil 1 Bl 769–70; Margot Fürst to Max Fürst, August 14, 1934, private collection of Mrs. Birute Stern; Max Fürst, *Gefilte Fisch*, 710, 724.

101. Max Fürst, *Gefilte Fisch*, 726–27; 733–34, 751.

102. Irmgard Litten to Commandant of KZ Brandenburg, December 17, 1933, in LBI AR 5112, *Hans Litten Collection*, Folder 1/2, 60; Commandant of the Lagerwache, KZ Brandenburg, to Irmgard Litten, December 22, 1933, in LBI AR 5112, *Hans Litten Collection*, Folder 1/2, 61; Irmgard Litten to Otto Conrady, n.d., in LBI AR 5112, *Hans Litten Collection*, Folder 1/2, 62; Irmgard Litten to Otto Conrady, January 23, 1934, in LBI AR 5112, *Hans Litten Collection*, Folder 1/2, 52; Irmgard Litten to Hans Litten, January 10, 1934, in WL Archive 572, *Hans Litten: Correspondence, 1933–1938*, Reel MF Doc 54/28; Irmgard Litten to Hans Litten, January 16, 1934, in WL Archive 572, *Hans Litten: Correspondence, 1933–1938*, Reel MF Doc 54/28;

Irmgard Litten to Hans Litten, February 19, 1934, in WL Archive 572, *Hans Litten: Correspondence, 1933–1938*, Reel MF Doc 54/28.

103. Max Fürst, *Gefilte Fisch*, 692; GSTA beim Landgericht to ORA Leipzig, February 26, 1934, in BA-BL NJ 9782, Bl. 1–3.

104. I. Litten, *Beyond Tears*, 121–23, 132; Max Fürst, *Gefilte Fisch*, 692; Kurt G. W. Ludecke, *I Knew Hitler: The Story of a Nazi Who Escaped the Blood Purge* (New York: Charles Scribner's Sons, 1937), 717–18, 721.

105. Hans Litten, n.d., in BA-BL NY 4011, *Nachlaß Hans Litten, Bd. 3 Korrespondenz—Ausgehende*, Bl. 231.

106. Hans Litten to Irmgard Litten, November 29, 1936, in BA-BL NY 4011, *Nachlaß Hans Litten, Bd. 3 Korrespondenz—Ausgehende*, Bl. 124; Margot Fürst to Max Fürst, March 20, 1934, private collection of Mrs. Birute Stern; Max Fürst, *Gefilte Fisch*, 711.

107. Bendix, *Konzentrationslager Deutschland*.

108. Richard J. Evans, *The Third Reich in Power 1933–1939* (New York: Penguin Press, 2005), 13–14, 22, 39–40; first Röhm quote and translation from Noakes and Pribram, *Nazism*, 167–69; second Röhm quote from Hermann Rauschning, *Gespräche mit Hitler* (Zurich: Europa Verlag, 1940), 143; SA quote and translation from Noakes and Pribram, *Nazism*, 187.

109. Evans, *The Third Reich in Power*, 26, 81.

110. Statement of Rudolf Diels, November 1945, in IfZ Bestand OMGUS-Akten, 3/71–3/4 PROP-PLEA, 14; Diels, *Lucifer*, 300; Diels, undated typescript on the Gestapo in 1933, NHH VVP 46, *Nachlass Rudolf Diels*, Bd. 21.

111. Prussian Minister President to PJM, April 28, 1934, in BA-BL R. 22/53692, *Reichsjustizministerium Personalakten Dr. Otto Conrady*, Bl. 30; H. Himmler to PJM, May 31, 1934, in BA-BL R. 22/53692, *Reichsjustizministerium Personalakten Dr. Otto Conrady*, Bl. 40; Prussian Minister President to PJM, October 10, 1934, in BA-BL R. 22/53692, *Reichsjustizministerium Personalakten Dr. Otto Conrady*, Bl. 43; Min. Rat. Dorffler, note to file, November 16, 1937, in BA-BL R. 22/53692, *Reichsjustizministerium Personalakten Dr. Otto Conrady*, Bl. 48; I. Litten, *Eine Mutter kämpft*, 114; Mühsam, *Leidensweg*, 36.

112. Hans Litten to Irmgard Litten, January 22, 1934, in BA-BL NY 4011, *Nachlaß Hans Litten, Bd. 3 Korrespondenz—Ausgehende*, Bl. 9; Hans Litten to Irmgard Litten, January 30, 1934, in BA-BL NY 4011, *Nachlaß Hans Litten, Bd. 3 Korrespondenz—Ausgehende*, Bl. 11.

113. Personal-Bericht/Beurteilung, Hans Loritz, July 31, 1935, in NARA RG 242 BDC SS Officers Roll Number A 3343 SSO-278 A, Loritz, 172–73; Nikolaus Wachsmann, *Hitler's Prisons: Legal Terror in Nazi Germany* (New Haven: Yale University Press, 2004), 102–3, 106–7.

114. Hans Litten to Irmgard Litten, February 11, 1934, in BA-BL NY 4011, *Nachlaß Hans Litten, Bd. 3 Korrespondenz—Ausgehende*, Bl. 13.

115. Commandant KZ Papenburg to Irmgard Litten, February 20, 1934, in LBI AR 5112, *Hans Litten Collection*, 1/2, 50; Irmgard Litten to Commander KZ Papenburg, February 22, 1934, in LBI AR 5112, *Hans Litten Collection*, 1/2, 49; Irmgard Litten to Verwaltung des Städtischen Krankenhauses Papenburg, March 1, 1934, in LBI AR 5112, *Hans Litten Collection*, 1/2, 44; I. Litten, *Eine Mutter kämpft*, 106–7; Hans Litten to Irmgard Litten, March 2, 1934, in BA-BL NY 4011, *Nachlaß Hans Litten, Bd. 3 Korrespondenz— Ausgehende*, Bl. 16.

116. Irmgard Litten to Gestapo Dezernat II b Berlin, April 3, 1934, in LBI AR 5112, *Hans Litten Collection*, 1/2, 26; Hans Litten to Irmgard Litten, May 1, 1934, in BA-BL NY 4011, *Nachlaß Hans Litten, Bd. 3 Korrespondenz— Ausgehende*, Bl. 19; Hans Litten to Irmgard Litten, June 2, 1934, in BA-BL NY 4011, *Nachlaß Hans Litten, Bd. 3 Korrespondenz—Ausgehende*, Bl. 21.

117. Hans Litten, application for release, February 11, 1934, in BA-BL NY 4011, *Nachlaß Hans Litten, Bd. 3 Korrespondenz—Ausgehende*, Bl. 235–37.

118. Ibid., Bl. 237–38.

119. Hans Dittrich to Irmgard Litten, March 24, 1934, in LBI AR 5112, *Hans Litten Collection*, 1/2, 17; I. Litten, *Eine Mutter kämpft*, 113–14; Werner Best, Memo of October 2, 1935, quoted in Stefan König, *Vom Dienst am Recht. Rechtsanwälte als Strafverteidiger im Nationalsozialismus* (Berlin: Walter de Gruyter, 1987), 103.

120. Irmgard Litten to Hans Litten, June 17, 1934, in WL Archive 572, *Hans Litten: Correspondence, 1933–1938*, Reel MF Doc 54/28.

121. I. Litten, *Eine Mutter kämpft*, 144.

122. "Litten: Familiäre Daten," in Institut für die Geschichte der deutschen Juden, *Nachlaß Neheimer*, Band I, Quellen; I. Litten, *Beyond Tears*, 153; Irmgard Litten to Hans Litten, April 20, 1934, in WL Archive 572, *Hans Litten: Correspondence, 1933–1938*, Reel MF Doc 54/28; Hans Litten to Irmgard Litten, July 19, 1937, in BA-BL NY 4011, *Nachlaß Hans Litten, Bd. 3 Korrespondenz—Ausgehende*, Bl. 150; Irmgard Litten to Hans Litten, November 7, 1934, in WL Archive 572, *Hans Litten: Correspondence, 1933– 1938*, Reel MF Doc 54/28.

123. Irmgard Litten to President Hindenburg, March 5, 1934, in LBI AR 5112, *Hans Litten Collection*, 1/2, 38–41; I. Litten, *Eine Mutter kämpft*, 147; Diels, *Lucifer*, 77.

124. Irmgard Litten to Adolf Hitler, April 18, 1934, in LBI AR 5112, *Hans Litten Collection*, 1/2, 29.

125. Führer und Reichskanzler to the RIM, the Reichstatthaltern, the State Governments and for Prussia the Minister President, August 7, 1934, in GStA Rep. 90, *Staatsministerium, Annex P. Geheime Staatspolizei*, Nr. 137, Bl. 2.

126. Irmgard Litten to Adolf Hitler, August 12, 1934, in LBI AR 5112, *Hans Litten Collection*, 1/2, 91–93.

127. "Nachweisung über Schutzhäftlinge, die länger als ein Jahr in Schutzhaft einsitzen und für die Amnestie nicht in Vorschlag gebracht waren," in GStA Rep. 90, *Staatsministerium, Annex P. Geheime Staatspolizei*, Nr. 110, Bl. 57, Bl. 63; "Häftlingsübersichten. Aug.–Nov 1934," in GStA Rep. 90, *Staatsministerium, Annex P. Geheime Staatspolizei*, Nr. 137, Bl. 99.

128. "Nachweisung über Schutzhäftlinge, die länger als ein Jahr in Schutzhaft einsitzen und für die Amnestie nicht in Vorschlag gebracht waren," in GStA Rep. 90, *Staatsministerium, Annex P. Geheime Staatspolizei*, Nr. 110, Bl. 62.

129. Diels, *Lucifer*, 251; Hermann Göring, *Anweisung*, September 7, 1934, in GStA Rep. 90, *Staatsministerium, Annex P. Geheime Staatspolizei*, Nr. 137, Bl. 88; BA-BL, *Gestapo Kartei*, Hans Litten.

130. Irmgard Litten to the Führer's Adjutant, September 16, 1934, in LBI AR 5112, *Hans Litten Collection*, 1/2, 10; Irmgard Litten to Adolf Hitler, December 17, 1934, in LBI AR 5112, *Hans Litten Collection*, 1/2, 11; State Secretary Lammers to Irmgard Litten, December 19, 1934, in LBI AR 5112, *Hans Litten Collection*, 1/2, 119; Gestapo to Irmgard Litten, no date, in LBI AR 5112, *Hans Litten Collection*, 1/2, 120; Ministerdirigent Dr. Doehle to Irmgard Litten, March 5, 1935, in LBI AR 5112, *Hans Litten Collection*, 1/2, 137.

131. I. Litten, *Beyond Tears*, 154.

132. Fritz Litten to Adolf Hitler, July 24, 1935, in LBI AR 5112, *Hans Litten Collection*, 1/2, 146–48.

133. I. Litten, *Eine Mutter kämpft*, 58–60; RJM to Auswärtiges Amt, August 3, 1935, in AA-PA R. 99481, *Referat Deutschland, Lügenmeldungen über Misshandlungen und Inhaftierungen politischer Gegner*, Band 4.

134. I. Litten, *Eine Mutter kämpft*, 124, 127, 131, 148; Irmgard Litten to Hans-Heinrich Frodien, November 24, 1934, in LBI AR 5112, *Hans Litten Collection*, 1/2, 114; Hans-Heinrich Frodien to Irmgard Litten, November 26, 1934, in LBI AR 5112, *Hans Litten Collection*, 1/2, 115; Irmgard Litten to Hans-Heinrich Frodien, June 11, 1935, in LBI AR 5112, *Hans Litten Collection*, 1/2, 142; Werner Best to Auswärtiges Amt, August 3, 1935, in AA-PA R. 99481, *Referat Deutschland, Lügenmeldungen über Misshandlungen und Inhaftierungen politischer Gegner*, Band 4.

135. I. Litten, *Eine Mutter kämpft*, 148–50; Irmgard Litten to Emmy Sonnemann, December 22, 1933, in LBI AR 5112, *Hans Litten Collection*, 1/2, 74–75; Diels, *Lucifer*, 183, 247, 251; Irmgard Litten to Hermann Göring, August 12, 1934, in LBI AR 5112, *Hans Litten Collection*, 1/2, 6–8.

136. Diels, *Lucifer*, 253.

137. Hans Litten to Irmgard Litten, June 26, 1934, in BA-BL NY 4011, *Nachlaß Hans Litten, Bd. 3 Korrespondenz—Ausgehende*, Bl. 25–6; Hans Litten to Irmgard Litten, July 22, 1934, in BA-BL NY 4011, *Nachlaß Hans Litten, Bd. 3 Korrespondenz—Ausgehende*, Bl. 28; Irmgard Litten to Hans Litten,

November 24, 1934, in WL Archive 572, *Hans Litten: Correspondence, 1933–1938*, Reel MF Doc 54/28; Kurt Neheimer to Margot Fürst, December 2, 1985, in Institut für die Geschichte der deutschen Juden, *Nachlaß Neheimer*, Correspondence Volume.

138. Hans Litten to Irmgard Litten, June 7, 1934, in BA-BL NY 4011, *Nachlaß Hans Litten, Bd. 3 Korrespondenz—Ausgehende*, Bl. 22; Hans Litten to Irmgard Litten, June 14, 1934, in BA-BL NY 4011, *Nachlaß Hans Litten, Bd. 3 Korrespondenz—Ausgehende*, Bl. 23; I. Litten, *Eine Mutter kämpft*, 138–39, 119; Bendix, *Konzentrationslager Deutschland*, Bk. IV, 70.

139. Hans Litten to Irmgard Litten, October 21, 1934, in BA-BL NY 4011, *Nachlaß Hans Litten, Bd. 3 Korrespondenz—Ausgehende*, Bl. 37.

140. Ibid.

141. Hans Litten to Irmgard Litten, November 18, 1934, in BA-BL NY 4011, *Nachlaß Hans Litten, Bd. 3 Korrespondenz—Ausgehende*, Bl. 41–2; Hans Litten to Irmgard Litten, December 4, 1934, in BA-BL NY 4011, *Nachlaß Hans Litten, Bd. 3 Korrespondenz—Ausgehende*, Bl. 46; Irmgard Litten to Hans Litten, January 25, 1935, in WL Archive 572, *Hans Litten: Correspondence, 1933–1938*, Reel MF Doc 54/28; I. Litten, *Eine Mutter kämpft*, 135–36; Hans Litten to Sulamith Reuter, June, 1935, in BA-BL NY 4011, *Nachlaß Hans Litten, Bd. 3 Korrespondenz—Ausgehende*, Bl. 224–25; Hans Litten to Sulamith Reuter, March 26, 1935, in BA-BL NY 4011, *Nachlaß Hans Litten, Bd. 3 Korrespondenz—Ausgehende*, Bl. 218.

142. I. Litten, *Eine Mutter kämpft*, 132.

143. Hans Litten to Irmgard Litten, August 4, 1935, in BA-BL NY 4011, *Nachlaß Hans Litten, Bd. 3 Korrespondenz—Ausgehende*, Bl. 75; BA-BL NY 4011, *Nachlaß Hans Litten*, Bd. 5 *Briefe und Karte an Hans Litten 1934–1938*.

144. Hans Litten to Sulamith Reuter, July 5, 1936, in BA-BL NY 4011, *Nachlaß Hans Litten, Bd. 3 Korrespondenz—Ausgehende*, Bl. 231; Hans Litten to Sulamith Reuter, October 23, 1936, in BA-BL NY 4011, *Nachlaß Hans Litten, Bd. 3 Korrespondenz—Ausgehende*, Bl. 233; Hans Litten to Irmgard Litten, March 21, 1937, in BA-BL NY 4011, *Nachlaß Hans Litten, Bd. 3 Korrespondenz—Ausgehende*, Bl. 135.

145. Hans Litten to Sulamith Reuter, March 26, 1935, in BA-BL NY 4011, *Nachlaß Hans Litten, Bd. 3 Korrespondenz—Ausgehende*, Bl. 218; Sulamith Reuter quoted in Hans Litten to Irmgard Litten, May 16, 1935, in BA-BL NY 4011, *Nachlaß Hans Litten, Bd. 3 Korrespondenz—Ausgehende*, Bl. 67–68.

146. Hans Litten to Irmgard Litten, May 16, 1935, in BA-BL NY 4011, *Nachlaß Hans Litten, Bd. 3 Korrespondenz—Ausgehende*, Bl. 67–68; Hans Litten to Sulamith Reuter, June 1935, in BA-BL NY 4011, *Nachlaß Hans Litten, Bd. 3 Korrespondenz—Ausgehende*, Bl. 225; Hans Litten to Irmgard Litten, February 10, 1935, in BA-BL NY 4011, *Nachlaß Hans Litten, Bd. 3 Korrespondenz—Ausgehende*, Bl. 54; Hans Litten to Irmgard Litten, February 27, 1935, in BA-BL NY 4011, *Nachlaß Hans Litten, Bd. 3 Korrespondenz—*

Ausgehende, Bl. 56; Hans Litten to Irmgard Litten, November 29, 1936, in BA-BL NY 4011, *Nachlaß Hans Litten, Bd. 3 Korrespondenz—Ausgehende*, Bl. 125.

147. Hans Litten to Irmgard Litten, November 29, 1936, in BA-BL NY 4011, *Nachlaß Hans Litten, Bd. 3 Korrespondenz—Ausgehende*, Bl. 124–25; Irmgard Litten to Hans Litten, December 15, 1936, in WL Archive 572, *Hans Litten: Correspondence, 1933–1938*, Reel MF Doc 54/28; Hans Litten to Irmgard Litten, January 17, 1937, in BA-BL NY 4011, *Nachlaß Hans Litten, Bd. 3 Korrespondenz—Ausgehende*, Bl. 130.

148. Hans Litten to Sulamith Reuter, February 16, 1937, in BA-BL NY 4011, *Nachlaß Hans Litten, Bd. 3 Korrespondenz—Ausgehende*, Bl. 220–21; Irmgard Litten to Hans Litten, February 23, 1937, in WL Archive 572, *Hans Litten: Correspondence, 1933–1938*, Reel MF Doc 54/28; Hans Litten to Irmgard Litten, March 21, 1937, in BA-BL NY 4011, *Nachlaß Hans Litten, Bd. 3 Korrespondenz—Ausgehende*, Bl. 135; Hans Litten to Irmgard Litten, July 19, 1937, in BA-BL NY 4011, *Nachlaß Hans Litten, Bd. 3 Korrespondenz—Ausgehende*, Bl. 150.

149. Max Fürst, *Gefilte Fisch*, 618.

150. I. Litten, *Eine Mutter kämpft*, 136–38; Hans Litten to Irmgard Litten, September 18, 1935, in BA-BL NY 4011, *Nachlaß Hans Litten, Bd. 3 Korrespondenz—Ausgehende*, Bl. 78; Bendix, *Konzentrationslager Deutschland*, Bk. IV, 70–71.

151. Bendix, *Konzentrationslager Deutschland*, Bk. IV, 70–71.

152. The date April 1934 is probably a mistake, since Hans Litten's letters show that he was not in the Esterwegen camp in April, but there is certainly no reason to disbelieve the account. It probably occurred in May 1934.

153. BA-BL R. 3001 / III w 282–284 / 38g, *Esterwegen*; Heinrich Remmert, Lebenslauf, NARA BDC RG 242 SS Officers Microfilm Roll A 3343 SSO-023B, Heinrich Remmert, 760; OSA Osnabrück to PJM—Zentralstaatsanwaltschaft Berlin, September 11, 1934, in BA-BL R. 3001 / III w 282–284 / 38g, *Esterwegen*, Bl. 1; Haftbefehl, August 2, 1934, in NARA BDC Microfilm Roll A 3343 SSO-023B, Heinrich Remmert, 664; PJM to OSA Osnabrück, September 21, 1934, in BA-BL R. 3001 / III w 282–284 / 38g, *Esterwegen*, Bl. 2; OSA Osnabrück to PJM—Zentralstaatsanwaltschaft Berlin, November 9, 1934, in BA-BL R. 3001/III w 282–284/38g, *Esterwegen*, Bl. 3.

154. PJM/RJM to OSA Osnabrück, November 30, 1934, in BA-BL R. 3001/III w 282–284/38g, *Esterwegen*, Bl. 4; Heinrich Remmert, Lebenslauf, NARA RG 242 BDC SS Officers Microfilm Roll A 3343 SSO-023B, Heinrich Remmert, 760.

155. Translation from I. Litten, *Beyond Tears*, 179; James Brophy, *Popular Culture and the Public Sphere in the Rhineland, 1800–1850* (Cambridge, U.K.: Cambridge University Press, 2007), 78.

156. I. Litten, *Eine Mutter kämpft*, 184.

157. Hans Litten to Irmgard Litten, July 16, 1937, in BA-BL NY 4011, *Nachlaß Hans Litten, Bd. 3 Korrespondenz—Ausgehende*, Bl. 149; Hans Litten to Irmgard Litten, July 19, 1937, in BA-BL NY 4011, *Nachlaß Hans Litten, Bd. 3 Korrespondenz—Ausgehende*, Bl. 150–151; Irmgard Litten to Hans Litten, August 12, 1937, in WL Archive 572, *Hans Litten: Correspondence, 1933–1938*, Reel MF Doc 54/28; I. Litten, *Eine Mutter kämpft*, 186.

158. Hans Litten to Irmgard Litten, August 15, 1937, in BA-BL NY 4011, *Nachlaß Hans Litten, Bd. 3 Korrespondenz—Ausgehende*, Bl. 154; Hans Litten to Irmgard Litten, August 29, 1937, in BA-BL NY 4011, *Nachlaß Hans Litten, Bd. 3 Korrespondenz—Ausgehende*, Bl. 157–8; Hans Litten to Irmgard Litten, September 12, 1937, in BA-BL NY 4011, *Nachlaß Hans Litten, Bd. 3 Korrespondenz—Ausgehende*, Bl. 159.

159. Evans, *The Third Reich in Power*, 64–65, 87–88.

160. Hans Litten to Irmgard Litten, September 26, 1937, in BA-BL NY 4011, *Nachlaß Hans Litten, Bd. 3 Korrespondenz—Ausgehende*, Bl. 162–3; I. Litten, *Eine Mutter kämpft*, 190; Einstellungsverfügung, February 9, 1938, in BA-BL R.3001/III g 10 b 121/38, *Tod des RAs Hans Litten*, Bl. 2; Hans Litten to Irmgard Litten, October 24, 1937, in BA-BL NY 4011, *Nachlaß Hans Litten, Bd. 3 Korrespondenz—Ausgehende*, Bl. 165.

161. Bendix, *Konzentrationslager Deutschland*, Bk. V, 4, 21; A. E. Laurence, *Out of the Night*, unpublished memoir, LBI Memoir Collection, ME 870, film MM II 11, 355–56.

162. Alfred Dreifuss, "Wie Hans Litten starb," *Sonntag*, September 12, 1948, in BA-BL NY 4011, *Nachlaß Hans Litten*, Bd. 8 *Artikel über Hans Litten 1937–1951*, Bl. 22; Fritz Rabinowitsch to Dr. Nathan, n.d. (1939), in BA-BL NY 4011, *Nachlaß Hans Litten*, Bd. 6, *Briefwechsel der Mutter Hans Littens 1937–1940*, Bl. 38–39.

163. Fritz Rabinowitsch to Dr. Nathan, n.d. (1939), in BA-BL NY 4011, *Nachlaß Hans Litten*, Bd. 6, *Briefwechsel der Mutter Hans Littens 1937–1940*, Bl. 38.

164. Emil ? to Irmgard Litten, n.d., in BA-BL NY 4011, *Nachlaß Hans Litten*, Bd. 6, *Briefwechsel der Mutter Hans Littens 1937–1940*, Bl. 31; Fred M. Roberts (Fritz Rabinowitsch) to Dr. Nathan, June 4, 1939, in BA-BL NY 4011, *Nachlaß Hans Litten*, Bd. 6, *Briefwechsel der Mutter Hans Littens 1937–1940*, Bl. 3.

165. Fritz Rabinowitsch to Dr. Nathan, n.d. (1939), in BA-BL NY 4011, *Nachlaß Hans Litten*, Bd. 6, *Briefwechsel der Mutter Hans Littens 1937–1940*, Bl. 39; Bendix, *Konzentrationslager Deutschland*, Bk. V, 68–69.

166. Fritz Rabinowitsch to Dr. Nathan, n.d. (1939), in BA-BL NY 4011, *Nachlaß Hans Litten*, Bd. 6, *Briefwechsel der Mutter Hans Littens 1937–1940*, Bl. 38; Alfred Grünebaum to Irmgard Litten, n.d. (1939), in BA-BL NY 4011, *Nachlaß Hans Litten*, Bd. 6, *Briefwechsel der Mutter Hans Littens 1937–1940*, Bl. 10; Alfred Eduard Lomnitz (A. E. Laurence), "Heinz Eschen zum Gedächtnis," July 3, 1939, in DA 951, *Jüdische Häftlinge. Eschen,*

Heinz. Berichte; Laurence, *Out of the Night*, 358, 380; Karl Heinz Jahnke, "Heinz Eschen—Kapo des Judenblocks im Konzentrationslager Dachau bis 1938," *Dachauer Hefte 7, Solidarität und Widerstand*, 24–26.

167. Lomnitz, "Heinz Eschen zum Gedächtnis"; Laurence, *Out of the Night*, 358; Bendix, *Konzentrationslager Deutschland*, Bk. V, 6; Emil ? to Irmgard Litten, n.d., in BA-BL NY 4011, *Nachlaß Hans Litten*, Bd. 6, *Briefwechsel der Mutter Hans Littens 1937–1940*, Bl. 31; "Heinz Eschen," by a prisoner, in DA 951, *Jüdische Häftlinge. Eschen, Heinz. Berichte*; Alfred Grünebaum to Irmgard Litten, n.d. (1939), in BA-BL NY 4011, *Nachlaß Hans Litten*, Bd. 6, *Briefwechsel der Mutter Hans Littens 1937–1940*, Bl. 12.

168. Fritz Rabinowitsch to Dr. Nathan, n.d. (1939), in BA-BL NY 4011, *Nachlaß Hans Litten*, Bd. 6, *Briefwechsel der Mutter Hans Littens 1937–1940*, Bl. 40.

169. Fred M. Roberts (Fritz Rabinowitsch) to Dr. Nathan, June 4, 1939, in BA-BL NY 4011, *Nachlaß Hans Litten*, Bd. 6, *Briefwechsel der Mutter Hans Littens 1937–1940*, Bl. 3; Fritz Rabinowitsch to Dr. Nathan, n.d. (1939), in BA-BL NY 4011, *Nachlaß Hans Litten*, Bd. 6, *Briefwechsel der Mutter Hans Littens 1937–1940*, Bl. 39–40.

170. Dreifuss, "Wie Hans Litten starb"; Fritz Rabinowitsch to Dr. Nathan, n.d. (1939), in BA-BL NY 4011, *Nachlaß Hans Litten*, Bd. 6, *Briefwechsel der Mutter Hans Littens 1937–1940*, Bl. 40.

171. I. Litten, *Eine Mutter kämpft*, 207–12; Irmgard Litten to the Commandant at Dachau, November 30, 1937, in WL Archive 572, *Hans Litten: Correspondence, 1933–1938*, Reel MF Doc 54/28.

172. Irmgard Litten to Kommandatur Dachau, November 30, 1937, in WL Archive 572, *Hans Litten: Correspondence, 1933–1938*, Reel MF Doc 54/29; I. Litten, *Eine Mutter kämpft*, 211–13.

173. Fritz Rabinowitsch to Irmgard Litten, August 30, 1939, in BA-BL NY 4011, *Nachlaß Hans Litten*, Bd. 6, *Briefwechsel der Mutter Hans Littens 1937–1940*, Bl. 3; Alfred Grünebaum to Irmgard Litten, n.d. (1939), in BA-BL NY 4011, *Nachlaß Hans Litten*, Bd. 6, *Briefwechsel der Mutter Hans Littens 1937–1940*, Bl. 10, 15; Fritz Rabinowitsch to Dr. Nathan, n.d. (1939), in BA-BL NY 4011, *Nachlaß Hans Litten*, Bd. 6, *Briefwechsel der Mutter Hans Littens 1937–1940*, Bl. 38–49.

174. Oscar Winter, "Riesenfeld," in DA 1066, *Jüdische Häftlinge. Winterberger. Oscar. Berichte, Verschiedener*; Gestapo to AA, November 24, 1937, in AA-PA R. 99482, *Referat Deutschland, Lügenmeldungen über Misshandlungen und Inhaftierungen politischer Gegner*, Band 5.

175. Oscar Winter, "Riesenfeld," in DA 1066, *Jüdische Häftlinge. Winterberger. Oscar. Berichte*, Verschiedener; I. Litten, *Beyond Tears*, 289.

176. Hans Litten to Irmgard Litten, November 27, 1937, in BA-BL NY 4011, *Nachlaß Hans Litten, Bd. 3 Korrespondenz—Ausgehende*, Bl. 169.

177. "Bericht eines inzwischen Freigelassenen, der mit Hans Litten in Dachau war," n.d., in BA-BL NY 4011, *Nachlaß Hans Litten*, Bd. 6, *Briefwechsel*

der Mutter Hans Littens 1937–1940, Bl. 35; Hans Litten to Irmgard Litten, November 27, 1937, in BA-BL NY 4011, *Nachlaß Hans Litten, Bd. 3 Korrespondenz—Ausgehende*, Bl. 169; Hans Litten to Irmgard Litten, December 10, 1937, in BA-BL NY 4011, *Nachlaß Hans Litten, Bd. 3 Korrespondenz—Ausgehende*, Bl. 170.

178. Irmgard wrote, "Mein Sohn hat mir versichert, daß es ihm sehr gut gehe." Irmgard Litten, "An die Redaktion," December 4, 1937, in WL Archive 572, *Hans Litten: Correspondence, 1933–1938*, Reel MF Doc 54/29; I. Litten, *Eine Mutter kämpft*, 220, 222.

179. "Heinz Eschen," by a prisoner, in DA 951, *Jüdische Häftlinge. Eschen, Heinz. Berichte*; Bericht eines inzwischen Freigelassenen, der mit Hans Litten in Dachau war," n.d., in BA-BL NY 4011, *Nachlaß Hans Litten, Bd. 6, Briefwechsel der Mutter Hans Littens 1937–1940*, Bl. 35.

180. Dreifuss, "Wie Hans Litten starb," Bl. 22–23; Fritz Rabinowitsch to Dr. Nathan, n.d. (1939), in BA-BL NY 4011, *Nachlaß Hans Litten, Bd. 6, Briefwechsel der Mutter Hans Littens 1937–1940*, Bl. 40, 46–47.

181. Arthur Marwick, *Clifford Allen: The Open Conspirator* (Edinburgh: Oliver & Boyd, 1964), 4; Martin Gilbert, ed., *Plough My Own Furrow: The Story of Lord Allen of Hurtwood as Told through His Writings and Correspondence* (London: Longmans, Green, 1965), xi.

182. Gilbert, *Plough My Own Furrow*, xi, 332–33; Henderson to Halifax, March 10, 1938, quoted in Marwick, *The Open Conspirator*, 173; Allen to Price Holmes, April 27, 1937, quoted in Marwick, *The Open Conspirator*, 166.

183. "German Concentration Camps," (London) *Times*, August 16, 1934; "The Case of Hans Litten," (London) *Times*, August 25, 1934; "The Case of Hans Litten," (London) *Times*, September 3, 1934; Marwick, *The Open Conspirator*, 170; "General Göring's Apologia," (London) *Times*, December 13, 1934; Gilbert, *Plough My Own Furrow*, 356–58; Ambassador von Hoesch to Auswärtiges Amt, January 26, 1935, in AA-PA R. 99574, *Referat Deutschland, Organisation der Konzentrationslager*; Ambassador Hoesch to Auswärtiges Amt, June 26, 1935, in AA-PA R. 99481, *Referat Deutschland, Lügenmeldungen über Misshandlungen und Inhaftierungen politischer Gegner*, Band 4.

184. Marwick, *The Open Conspirator*, 170; "General Göring's Apologia," (London) *Times*, December 13, 1934; Gilbert, *Plough My Own Furrow*, 356–58.

185. Allen to Frick, April 17, 1935, in AA-PA R. 99480, *Referat Deutschland, Lügenmeldungen über Misshandlungen und Inhaftierungen politischer Gegner*, Band 3.

186. Christopher Browning, *The Final Solution and the German Foreign Office: A Study of Referat D III of Abteilung Deutschland 1940–1943* (New York: Holmes & Maier, 1978), 12; Hans-Jürgen Döscher, *Das Auswärtige Amt im Dritten Reich. Diplomatie im Schatten der "Endlösung"* (Berlin: Siedler Verlag, 1987), 120; RIM Frick to Ambassador Hoesch, August 27, 1935, in

AA-PA R. 99480, *Referat Deutschland, Lügenmeldungen über Misshandlungen und Inhaftierungen politischer Gegner*, Band 3.

187. "Petition: To the Chancellor and Leader of the German Reich," Allen to Hitler, October 31, 1935, in AA-PA R. 99480, *Referat Deutschland, Lügenmeldungen über Misshandlungen und Inhaftierungen politischer Gegner*, Band 3.

188. Vermerk, November 7, 1933, in BA-BL R. 43/II, *Reichskanzlei*, Nr. 1541, "Freilassung des Rechtsanwalts Litten," Bl. 31.

189. Lammers to Ribbentrop, November 13, 1935, in BA-BL R. 43/II, *Reichskanzlei*, Nr. 1541, "Freilassung des Rechtsanwalts Litten," Bl. 33.

190. Kershaw, *Hitler 1889–1936*.

191. Göring to Lammers, August 21, 1935, in GStA Rep. 90, *Staatsministerium, Annex P. Geheime Staatspolizei*, Nr. 66, Schutzhaft Bd. 4, Bl. 135; Lammers to Göring, September 6, 1935, in GStA Rep. 90, *Staatsministerium, Annex P. Geheime Staatspolizei*, Nr. 66, Schutzhaft Bd. 4, Bl. 137; Geheimes Staatspolizeistelle Wien to Geheimes Staatspolizeiamt Berlin, July 28, 1938, in IfZ Fa 183/1, *Himmler, Heinrich, Stellv. Chef d. Preuß. Gest.*, Bd. 1, Bl. 1.

192. Quote in Michael Block, *Ribbentrop* (London: Bantam Press, 1992), 82.

193. "Litten bleibt, wo er ist. Botschafter Ribbentrop beantwortet eine englische Eingabe," *Angriff*, December 18, 1935, in BA-BL NY 4011, *Nachlaß Hans Litten*, Bd. 6, *Briefwechsel der Mutter Hans Littens 1937–1940*, Bl. 89; BA-BL R. 901/58602, "Offener Brief Ribbentrop an Lord Allen of Hurtwood (13. Dezember 35), Bl. 22, 25; Marwick, *The Open Conspirator*, 169; Ribbentrop to Allen, December 8, 1935, in Gilbert, *Plough My Own Furrow*, 370–71.

194. "Litten bleibt, wo er ist. Botschafter Ribbentrop beantwortet eine englische Eingabe," *Angriff*, December 18, 1935, in BA-BL NY 4011, *Nachlaß Hans Litten*, Bd. 6, *Briefwechsel der Mutter Hans Littens 1937–1940*, Bl. 89.

195. Allen to Ribbentrop, January 6, 1936, in Gilbert, *Plough My Own Furrow*, 371–72; MdI to German Embassy in London, January 3, 1936, Embassy to AA, n.d. (January 1936), in AA-PA R. 9480, *Referat Deutschland, Lügenmeldungen über Misshandlungen und Inhaftierungen politischer Gegner*, Band 3.

196. Allen to Ribbentrop, July 15, 1936, in Gilbert, *Plough My Own Furrow*, 375; Joachim von Ribbentrop, *Zwischen London und Moskau. Erinnerungen und letzte Aufzeichnungen. Aus den Nachlaß herausgegeben von Annelies von Ribbentrop* (Leoni am Starnberger See: Drüffel-Verlag, 1953), 72–73.

197. Marwick, *The Open Conspirator*, 170–71; Allen to Dorothy Buxton, September 8, 1936, in Gilbert, *Plough My Own Furrow*, 379–80; Evans, *The Third Reich in Power*, 153.

198. *New Statesman and Nation*, November 13, 1937, in AA-PA R. 99482, *Referat Deutschland, Lügenmeldungen über Misshandlungen und Inhaftierungen politischer Gegner*, Band 5; *Daily Telegraph*, April 11, 1936,

Pariser Tageblatt, April 11, 1936, in BA R. 901/58916, *Zum Tode des Botschafters v. Hoesch (10.IV.36)—Kombinationen der Auslandspresse*, Bl. 2, Bl. 5; AA to German Embassy in London, August 21, 1937, in AA-PA R. 99534, *Referat Deutschland, Proteste fremder Organisationen*, Band 5.

199. Dorothy Buxton to Allen, November 11, 1937, in Gilbert, *Plough My Own Furrow*, 386; Londenderry to Allen, February 8, 1937, in Gilbert, *Plough My Own Furrow*, 380; Lothian to Kurt Hahn, October 27, 1937, in Gilbert, *Plough My Own Furrow*, 384–86.

200. Allen to Ribbentrop, January 13, 1938, in Gilbert, *Plough My Own Furrow*, 388; Ernst Woermann to Allen, January 28, 1938, in Gilbert, *Plough My Own Furrow*, 388–89.

201. I. Litten, *Beyond Tears*, 291–92.

202. Hans Litten to Irmgard Litten, January 1, 1938, in BA-BL NY 4011, *Nachlaß Hans Litten, Bd. 3 Korrespondenz—Ausgehende*, Bl. 171; I. Litten, *Beyond Tears*, 291.

203. Fritz Rabinowitsch to Dr. Nathan, n.d. (1939), in BA-BL NY 4011, *Nachlaß Hans Litten, Bd. 6, Briefwechsel der Mutter Hans Littens 1937– 1940*, Bl. 41; Alfred Dreifuss, "Wie Hans Litten starb," Bl. 23.

204. Hans Litten to Irmgard Litten, January 8, 1938, in BA-BL NY 4011, *Nachlaß Hans Litten, Bd. 3 Korrespondenz—Ausgehende*, Bl. 173; Irmgard Litten to Hans Litten, January 22, 1938, in WL Archive 572, *Hans Litten: Correspondence, 1933–1938*, Reel MF Doc 54/28; Irmgard Litten to Hans Litten, January 27, 1938, in WL Archive 572, *Hans Litten: Correspondence, 1933–1938*, Reel MF Doc 54/28.

205. Hans Litten to Irmgard Litten, January 30, 1938, in BA-BL NY 4011, *Nachlaß Hans Litten, Bd. 3 Korrespondenz—Ausgehende*, Bl. 175–76.

206. "Bericht eines inzwischen Freigelassenen, der mit Hans Litten in Dachau war," n.d., in BA-BL NY 4011, *Nachlaß Hans Litten, Bd. 6, Briefwechsel der Mutter Hans Littens 1937–1940*, Bl. 35; Lomnitz, "Heinz Eschen zum Gedächtnis"; Laurence, *Out of the Night*, 443; "Heinz Eschen," by a prisoner, in DA 951, *Jüdische Häftlinge. Eschen, Heinz. Berichte*; Alfred Grünebaum to Irmgard Litten, n.d. (1939), in BA-BL NY 4011, *Nachlaß Hans Litten, Bd. 6, Briefwechsel der Mutter Hans Littens 1937–1940*, Bl. 12; Fritz Rabinowitsch to Dr. Nathan, n.d. (1939), in BA-BL NY 4011, *Nachlaß Hans Litten, Bd. 6, Briefwechsel der Mutter Hans Littens 1937– 1940*, Bl. 41; Fritz Rabinowitsch to Irmgard Litten, August 30, 1939, in BA-BL NY 4011, *Nachlaß Hans Litten, Bd. 6, Briefwechsel der Mutter Hans Littens 1937–1940*, Bl. 6.

207. Fritz Rabinowitsch to Dr. Nathan, n.d. (1939), in BA-BL NY 4011, *Nachlaß Hans Litten, Bd. 6, Briefwechsel der Mutter Hans Littens 1937– 1940*, Bl. 41; Alfred Grünebaum to Irmgard Litten, n.d. (1939), in BA-BL NY 4011, *Nachlaß Hans Litten, Bd. 6, Briefwechsel der Mutter Hans Littens 1937–1940*, Bl. 12; Lomnitz, "Heinz Eschen zum Gedächtnis"; Fritz Rabinowitsch to Irmgard Litten, August 30, 1939, in BA-BL NY 4011,

Nachlaß Hans Litten, Bd. 6, *Briefwechsel der Mutter Hans Littens 1937–1940*, Bl. 6; Bendix, *Konzentrationslager Deutschland*, Bk. V, 72.

208. Winter, "Riesenfeld."

209. Ibid.; Jahnke, "Heinz Eschen—Kapo des Judenblocks im Konzentrationslager Dachau bis 1938," 32–33; Adi Meislinger and Hans Kaltenbacher to Heinz Müller, August 8, 1975, in DA 951, *Jüdische Häftlinge. Eschen, Heinz. Berichte*; STA Landgericht München II, to the Generalstaatsanwalt Oberlandesgericht München, June 1, 1933, in NARA RG 238, War Crimes Records Collection, Prosecution Exhibits Submitted to the International Military Tribunal T 988 Roll 17: A 217 Item 450.

210. Alfred Grünebaum to Irmgard Litten, n.d. (1939), in BA-BL NY 4011, *Nachlaß Hans Litten*, Bd. 6, *Briefwechsel der Mutter Hans Littens 1937–1940*, Bl. 13; Emil ? to Irmgard Litten, n.d., in BA-BL NY 4011, *Nachlaß Hans Litten*, Bd. 6, *Briefwechsel der Mutter Hans Littens 1937–1940*, Bl. 31; Winter, "Riesenfeld"; Dreifuss, "Wie Hans Litten starb," Bl. 23; "Heinz Eschen," by a prisoner, in DA 951, *Jüdische Häftlinge. Eschen, Heinz. Berichte*; Laurence, *Out of the Night*, 377.

211. Dreifuss, "Wie Hans Litten starb," Bl. 23.

212. Fritz Rabinowitsch to Dr. Nathan, n.d. (1939), in BA-BL NY 4011, *Nachlaß Hans Litten*, Bd. 6, *Briefwechsel der Mutter Hans Littens 1937–1940*, Bl. 48; Dreifuss, "Wie Hans Litten starb," Bl. 23.

213. Dreifuss, "Wie Hans Litten starb," Bl. 23; Einstellungsverfügung, February 9, 1938, in BA-BL R.3001/III g 10 b 121/38, *Tod des RAs Hans Litten*, Bl. 2; Winter, "Riesenfeld."

214. Dreifuss, "Wie Hans Litten starb," Bl. 23; Winter, "Riesenfeld."

215. I. Litten, *Eine Mutter kämpft*, 229.

216. Ibid., 231.

217. Ibid., 233.

218. Ibid., 234.

219. Ibid., 238–39.

220. Dreifuss, "Wie Hans Litten starb," Bl. 23; Fritz Rabinowitsch to Irmgard Litten, August 30, 1939, in BA-BL NY 4011, *Nachlaß Hans Litten*, Bd. 6, *Briefwechsel der Mutter Hans Littens 1937–1940*, Bl. 6.

221. Einstellungsverfügung, February 9, 1938, in BA-BL R.3001/III g 10 b 121/38, *Tod des RAs Hans Litten*, Bl. 2.

222. Vermerk, November 3, 1939, in BA-BL R.3001/III g 10 b 121/38, *Tod des RAs Hans Litten*, Bl. 6.

223. "Hans Litten im Konzentrationslager gestorben," *Pariser Tageszeitung*, February 18, 1938; "Ein Nachruf auf Hans Litten von Maitre Moro-Giafferi," *Pariser Tageblatt*, February 20–21, 1938, in BA-BL R.3001/III g 10 b 121/38, *Tod des RAs Hans Litten*, Bl. 3, 4.

224. Max Fürst, obituary for Hans Litten, *Sozialistische Warte*, August 12, 1938, in BA-BL NY 4011, *Nachlaß Hans Litten*, Bd. 8, *Artikel über Hans Litten 1937–1951*, Bl. 17–18; Rudolf Olden, obituary for Hans Litten, *Das neue*

Tagebuch, February 26, 1938, in BA-BL NY 4011, *Nachlaß Hans Litten*, Bd. 8, *Artikel über Hans Litten 1937–1951*, Bl. 35; "Gestapo Victim," (London) *Times*, September 7, 1940.

225. Letter to the editor, (London) *Times*, March 9, 1938.

226. Eleanor Roosevelt, "My Day," September ? 1940, in BA-BL NY 4011, *Nachlaß Hans Litten*, Bd. 8, *Artikel über Hans Litten 1937–1951*, Bl. 88.

EPILOGUE

1. Irmgard Litten to Alfred Grünebaum, August 7, 1939, in BA-BL NY 4011, *Nachlaß Hans Litten*, Bd. 6, *Briefwechsel der Mutter Hans Littens 1937–1940*, Bl. 4; "Litten: Familiäre Daten," in Institut für die Geschichte der deutschen Juden, *Nachlaß Neheimer*, Band I, *Quellen*; Irmgard Litten's letters, private collection of Frau Patricia Litten; "Dr. F. J. Litten: Father and Son Victims of Nazi Terror," (London) *Times*, February 22, 1940; Max Fürst, *Gefilte Fisch und wie es weiterging* (Munich: DTV, 2004), 268.

2. Irmgard Litten to Baldur Olden, n.d. (1942), in Deutsches Literatur Archiv, Marbach, *Nachlaß Fürst*; "Germany and the Camps," (London) *Times*, May 4, 1945; Irmgard Litten, "Antrag als Annerkennung als Opfer des Faschismus," March 16, 1951, in LAB Berlin C Rep. 118-01 Nr. A 22987, Bl. 5–6.

3. Irmgard Litten, *Lebenslauf*, March 16, 1951, letter to the "Hauptausschuss, Opfer des Faschismus," March 10, 1951, Vermerk, July 4, 1953, in LAB C Rep 118-01 Nr. A 22987, *Irmgard Litten: Antrag als Annerkennung als Opfer des Faschismus*, Bl. 5–6, 9, 16; Margot Litten, *Lebenslauf*, in LAB C Rep. 118-01 Nr. A 13644, *Margot Litten: Antrag als Annerkennung als Opfer des Faschismus*, Bl. 2; Max Fürst, *Gefilte Fisch*, 270.

4. Margot Litten, *Lebenslauf*, in LAB C Rep. 118-01 Nr. A 13644, *Margot Litten: Antrag als Annerkennung als Opfer des Faschismus*, Bl. 2; Max Fürst to Dr. Hans Litten, February 13, 1974, in Deutsches Literatur Archiv, Marbach, *Nachlaß Fürst*; Patricia Litten and Johannes Blum, interview with the author, Nuremberg, June 26, 2006.

5. Irmgard Litten to Baldur Olden, n.d. (1942), in Deutsches Literatur Archiv, Marbach, *Nachlaß Fürst*; Rainer Litten, "Curriculum Vitae," May 6, 1962, private collection of Frau Patricia Litten; Patricia Litten and Johannes Blum, interview with the author, Nuremberg, June 26, 2006.

6. Hans Litten, "Unserer Eindrücke vom Bundestag," *Deutsch-Jüdischer Wanderbund Kameraden, Gau Nordost*, Nr. 1, Oktober 1923, 2.

7. Max Fürst to Irmgard Litten, n.d. (probably spring/summer 1939), in Institut für die Geschichte der deutschen Juden, *Nachlaß Neheimer*, Band I *Quellen*; Max Fürst to Dr. Hans Litten, n.d., Deutsches Literatur Archiv, Marbach, *Nachlaß Fürst*; Irmgard Litten, *Lebenslauf*, March 16, 1951, in LAB C Rep 118-01 Nr. A 22987, *Irmgard Litten: Antrag als Annerkennung als Opfer des Faschismus*, Bl. 5.

8. BA-BL NY 4011, *Nachlaß Hans Litten, Bd. 3 Korrespondenz—Ausgehende*; Irmgard Litten, *Eine Mutter kämpft gegen Hitler* (Frankfurt/Main: Röderberg-Verlag, 1984), 191, 210–11; WL Archive 572, *Hans Litten: Correspondence, 1933–1938*, Reel MF Doc 54/28.

9. Fritz Rabinowitsch to Irmgard Litten, August 30, 1939, in BA-BL NY 4011, *Nachlaß Hans Litten, Bd. 6, Briefwechsel der Mutter Hans Littens 1937–1940*, Bl. 3, 6.

10. Irmgard Litten, *Beyond Tears* (New York: Alliance, 1940), 261.

11. Fritz Rabinowitsch to Dr. Nathan, n.d. (1939), in BA-BL NY 4011, *Nachlaß Hans Litten, Bd. 6, Briefwechsel der Mutter Hans Littens 1937–1940*, Bl. 41.

12. Max and Margot Fürst, interview with Ingela Lundgren, n.d., "Anfang der 70er Jahren," in Deutsches Literatur Archiv, Marbach, *Nachlass Fürst*; Birute Stern, interview with the author, Stuttgart, March 24, 2005.

13. Max Fürst to Dr. Hans Litten, February 13, 1974, in Deutsches Literatur Archiv, Marbach, *Nachlaß Fürst*; Heinrich Böll, " 'Ich glaube, meine Erinnerung liebt mich,' " *Süddeutsche Zeitung*, December 6, 1973; Heinrich Böll, "Vergebliche Suche nach politischer Kultur. Max Fürsts Erinnerung an die schwierigen zwanziger Jahre," *Süddeutsche Zeitung*, November 20–21, 1976; Max Fürst to Heinrich Böll, October 11, 1976, in Deutsches Literatur Archiv, Marbach, *Nachlaß Fürst*.

14. Max Fürst, *Gefilte Fisch*, 604, 253, 249, 274.

15. Max Fürst to Dr. Hans Litten, November 12, 1975, Deutsches Literatur Archiv, Marbach, *Nachlass Fürst*; *Die Tat*, Nr. 27, July 7, 1951, in BA-BL NY 4011, *Nachlaß Hans Litten, Bd. 8*, "Artikel über Hans Litten 1937–1951," Bl. 50.

16. Kurt Neheimer to Margot Fürst, July 24, 1984, in Institut für die Geschichte der deutschen Juden, *Nachlaß Neheimer*, Correspondence Volume.

17. Max Fürst to Dr. Hans Litten, n.d., in Deutsches Literatur Archiv, Marbach, *Nachlaß Fürst*.

18. Max Fürst to Dr. Hans Litten, November 12, 1975, in Deutsches Literatur Archiv, Marbach, *Nachlaß Fürst*; Carlheinz von Brück, *Ein Mann, der Hitler in die Enge trieb. Hans Littens Kampf gegen den Faschismus. Ein Dokumentarbericht* (East Berlin: Union Verlag, 1975), 47–48, 139.

19. Brück, *Ein Mann*, 24–25, 46.

20. Götz Berger, interview with Kurt Neheimer, April 4, 1986, in Institut für die Geschichte der deutschen Juden, *Nachlaß Neheimer*, Band III *KZ-Haft/Erinnerungen*; Max Fürst to Dr. Hans Litten, January 2, 1976, in Deutsches Literatur Archiv, Marbach, *Nachaß Fürst*; Margot Fürst to Johann-Heinrich Lüth, February 22, 1987, in Institut für die Geschichte der deutschen Juden, *Nachlaß Neheimer*, Correspondence Volume; Margot Fürst to Jutta Limbach, February 26, 1992, private collection of Herr Rechtsanwalt Gerhard Jungfer; Max Fürst to Dr. Hans Litten, April 16, 1977, in Deutsches Literatur Archiv, Marbach, *Nachlaß Fürst*.

21. Max Fürst to Dr. Hans Litten, June, 1974, Max Fürst to Dr. Hans Litten, November 12, 1975, in Deutsches Literatur Archiv, Marbach, *Nachlaß Fürst*.

22. Gerhard Jungfer, "Strafverteidigung und Strafprozeß: Festgabe für Ludwig Koch, *Berliner Anwaltsblatt* 1990, 50; Joachim Fest, *Begegnungen. Über nahe und ferne Freunde* (Reinbek: Rowohlt Verlag, 2006), especially 21–54; Böll, "Vergebliche Suche nach politischer Kultur"; Max Fürst to Dr. Hans Litten, November 12 1975, and January 2, 1976, in Deutsches Literatur Archiv, Marbach, Nachlaß Fürst.

23. Benjamin Carter Hett, *Death in the Tiergarten: Murder and Criminal Justice in the Kaiser's Berlin* (Cambridge, Mass.: Harvard University Press, 2004), especially chapter 3; Rechtsanwalt Dr. Holtfort, quoted in Jungfer, "Strafverteidigung und Strafprozeß," 50.

24. See Forum Anwaltsgeschichte e.V., http://www.anwaltsgeschichte.de, last visited February 14, 2007; Thomas Blanke et al., eds., *Streitbare Juristen. Eine Andere Tradition* (Baden-Baden: Nomos, 1988).

25. Erich Eyck, "Der verdächtige Verteidiger," *Vossische Zeitung*, October 21, 1932, M; Rudolf Olden, "Hans Litten," in I. Litten, *Eine Mutter kämpft*, 5–16; Rudolf Olden, obituary for Hans Litten, *Das neue Tagebuch*, February 26, 1938, in BA-BL NY 4011, *Nachlaß Hans Litten*, Bd. 8 *Artikel über Hans Litten 1937–1951*, Bl. 35.

26. "Hans-Litten-Preis für zwei Rechtsanwältinnen," *Tagesspiegel*, January 7, 1988; Walter Gierlich, "Erinnerung an die 'andere Juristentradition,'" *Süddeutsche Zeitung*, February 8, 1988; Vereinigung Demokratischer Juristinnen und Juristen e.V., http://www.vdj.de/Litten/Kramer-Dan kesrede.html, copy in the private collection of Herr Gerhard Jungfer; Rechtsanwalt Dr. Gerhard Baatz, "Zum 100. Geburtstag von Hans Litten," *Neue Juristische Wochenschrift* 2003, Heft 25, 1784–1785; Annette Wilmes, "Anwalt für das Recht. Zum 100. Geburtstag von Hans Litten," *BRAK Magazin*, February 2003, 14.

27. Marion Gräfin Dönhoff, "Der vergessene Opfergang. Eine Mutter kämpfte gegen Hitler," *Die Zeit*, December 5, 1986; Henning von Tresckow quoted in Jeremy Noakes, ed., *Nazism 1919–1945: A Documentary Reader*, vol. 4, *The German Home Front in World War II* (Exeter, U.K.: University of Exeter Press, 1998), 618.

28. "'Ein Mann, der Hitler in die Enge trieb.' Hans Litten ist nicht vergessen," *Die Zeit*, December 26, 1986; Margot Fürst to Kurt Neheimer, February 22, 1987, in Institut für die Geschichte der deutschen Juden, *Nachlaß Neheimer*, Correspondence Volume.

29. Stefan König to Jutta Limbach, October 19, 1990, Jutta Limbach to Stefan König, December 28, 1990, private collection of Herr Gerhard Jungfer.

30. "Senat will nun doch nicht das Berliner Straßengesetz ändern," *Tagesspiegel*, February 12, 1992.

31. Margot Fürst to Jutta Limbach, February 13, 1992, private collection of Herr Gerhard Jungfer; Rüdiger Scheidges, "Anwalt des Rechts in einer Zeit wachsender Rechtslosigkeit," *Tagesspiegel*, February 21, 1992; Patricia Litten and Johannes Blum, interview with the author, Nuremberg, June 26, 2006; "Landowsky: CDU nicht gegen die Littenstraße," *Tagesspiegel*, February 22, 1992.

32. Tillmann Krach and Gerhard Jungfer to the President and Members of the Presidium of the BRAK, July 2000, private collection of Herr Gerhard Jungfer.

33. Hannover to Krach, December 30, 2000, private collection of Herr Gerhard Jungfer.

34. "Warum eigentlich 'Hans-Litten-Haus,'" *Berliner Anwaltsblatt* 4, 2001, 190.

35. "Einweihung der neuen Geschäftsräume der Bundesrechtsanwaltskammer in Berlin," Bundesrechtsanwaltskammer, http://www.brak.de/seiten/04_01_04.php, last visited February 19, 2007; Bundesrechtsanwaltskammer, http://www.brak.de/seiten/02_01_00.php, last visited February 17, 2007; "Grundsteinlegung für das 'Haus der Verbände' in Berlin. Regierender Bürgermeister Diepgen nimmt Zeremonie vor," September 8, 1999, Bundesrechtsanwaltskammer, http://www.brak.de/seiten/04_99_33.php, last visited February 17, 2007.

36. Margot Fürst to Jutta Limbach, February 26, 1992, private collection of Herr Gerhard Jungfer.

37. Max Fürst to Dr. Hans Litten, June 1974, in Deutsches Literatur Archiv, Marbach, *Nachlaß Fürst*.

38. Olden, "Hans Litten," 16.

39. David Cole, "The Man behind the Torture," *New York Review of Books*, December 6, 2007.

40. Patricia Litten, interview with the author, Nuremberg, June 26, 2006.

Index